THE
Art of Cookery
IN THE
Middle Ages

THE
Art of Cookery
IN THE
Middle Ages

Terence Scully

THE BOYDELL PRESS

First published 1995
The Boydell Press, Woodbridge
Reprinted in paperback, 1997, 2000, 2002, 2005

ISBN 978-0-85115-611-8 hardback
ISBN 978-0-85115-430-5 paperback

Transferred to digital printing

The Boydell Press is an imprint of Boydell & Brewer Ltd
PO Box 9, Woodbridge, Suffolk IP12 3DF, UK
and of Boydell & Brewer Inc.
668 Mt. Hope Avenue, Rochester NY 14620, USA
website: www.boydellandbrewer.com

A CIP catalogue record for this title is available
from the British Library

This book is printed on acid-free paper

CONTENTS

ONE

Introduction

Food Habits

What we eat is largely a matter of habit. Of course there are several other reasons that lie behind our choice of chicken over pork, or of sloppy joes over caviar and crackers. There are foodstuffs that we may or may not eat, and there are others that we can or cannot eat. But on the whole, within certain generally defined limits, what we bring into our kitchens, cook and serve to ourselves tends to be repeated, within certain limits, from week to week and from month to month. We know that we can handle these preparations without too much fuss and without unreasonable expense; above all we know from experience that we are not going to *dislike* the finished dish when we sit down to eat it. We know that when we set our fork into our food our hunger is going to be eased, and sometimes even that we shall have a certain degree of pleasure in satisfying our appetite.

In short, we have tried something before, we like it, we try it again . . . and again. Such and such a preparation, we find, is 'dependable'. We build up personal repertoires of foods and dishes that as individuals each of us can manage, economically in terms of time and money, and that we know we will find more or less satisfying. These basic repertoires – whose make-up is still subject to modification from time to time, along with additions and deletions – are broad enough to allow us sufficient variety from day to day, but comprehensive enough that most of the preparations in it can exist in our memory. These are foods and dishes that we feel comfortable with. They constitute our habitual diet.

People generally seem to need habits. They seem to need things they can count on or take for granted. It simplies life enormously not to have to worry about the unknown. And above all it makes living a lot safer. For these reasons alone the foods we eat have to belong firmly to a pattern of what is known – the tried and true, the tested and proven.

Food is intimatedly bound up with who we are – an observation that is now far from original. But more than any other human activity, eating has infinitely rich personal associations for the individual. For the baby, feeding

1

affords the very definition of the notion of comfort; for the adolescent, a quick experience; for the adult, satisfaction. Perhaps. Everyone is different. For the baby, adolescent or adult, to eat is more than simply to stave off hunger pangs. To eat usually means satisfying oneself in more ways than one, and satisfying oneself in these ways is fundamentally and richly egotistical. Eating is a self-centreed activity: you cannot eat for someone else; generally you eat by and for yourself alone.

Certainly what every human being experiences is hunger. Everyone *has* to eat; we simply have no choice there. However, as much as food is a necessity to continue living, it can also constitute a threat to life. Who among us has not come across something that 'didn't agree with his/her stomach'? We learn through painful experience that it is better to avoid this or that foodstuff, that such-and-such a food or dish is not for us. The child is very quick to identify 'bad' foods, foods that no amount of patient coaxing, perhaps with the odd threat, will ever persuade him or her to eat. A parent can lecture until utter exhaustion that something on the child's plate is 'good for you' – the child learns early on that while some foods are good (ice cream, peanut butter), others are downright dangerous (spinach, broccoli). For most of us a subconscious selection process continues through life to distinguish between foods that are good and foods that are bad. In many cases the distinction is not particularly rational; most often what is good and bad in our food is just a matter of habit. To put on airs, we call those habits 'personal taste'.

Of course, one man's meat may well be another man's poison. The human digestive system involves many complex physical and chemical processes that vary in capability from one person to the next. Bread, 'the staff of life', nuts, even mother's milk, can kill some individuals. While all of us have to eat, we have to be careful about what we eat. It is not just a matter of our eventual health, it could be an immediate matter of our life. The potentates of the past lived in constant fear of a deliberate poisoning of their food; even today we still have to be aware of the dangers of accidental food poisoning.

Again, we accept that in the matter of food it is normally safer to stick with what we know. We have our dull routines, our social customs and our food habits, but at least we can be fairly certain that the familiar usually does not harbour any unsuspected dangers. And so it is perhaps with our society as a whole. Some foreign customs and habits, including food habits, remain just that: foreign. All of which is understandable. Better safe than sorry.

One argument of this book is that what on the surface may look foreign may not be foreign in reality. Specifically, our proposition is that the food habits of Europe five and six hundred years ago should not be looked upon as historic curiosities, worth only a glance from an archeologist or a social historian. In fact, what people ate at the end of the Middle Ages was good and, despite the passage of a couple of hundred years (a mere dozen-and-a-half generations, a brief twenty generations at the most!), is still good. By the fourteenth and fifteenth centuries the French, English, Italians, Hispanics and Germans had developed certain habits in the area of foods and cooking with which they felt very comfortable, and from which they drew a great deal of pleasure. These habits had a lot in common right across Europe, and they had their own little peculiarities from country to country, relatively local customs having to do mostly with the availability of ingredients. What we hope the reader will realize is that, taken as a whole and despite what is really a short distance of time, the dishes prepared for the tables of this period retain much if not all of their gastronomic interest today.

Furthermore, these late-medieval dishes are not really 'foreign' in the sense that what they offer is archaic in any way. Yes, it is true that if a person looks long enough in the odd manuscript collection of the period he or she can indeed find recipes whose main ingredients are fish intestines or stag testicles. And the outline for preparing a boar's head may not be every twentieth-century cook's idea of practicality. But the point is that these dishes were not in every fourteenth-century cook's working repertoire either. What the professional cook dealt with from day to day in the thirteen and fourteen hundreds were menus consisting of well-rounded meals of sops, stews, pies, torts, flans, biscuits, roasts, sauces, jellies and 'desserts'. Some dishes could have come from 'Everyman''s kitchen – and actually did; on the other hand, some dishes were preparations that called for no less devoted work than do the preparations of the most celebrated restaurants today, and afforded not a whit less pleasure to the persons before whom they were eventually set.

Though documentary sources for an understanding of late-medieval food and cookery are many and varied, it is particularly upon the customary dishes of the period that we should like to base our survey of the field. They will illustrate the nature of foods and food preparations of the earlier day; they will demonstrate both the homogeneity and the diversity of that cookery; most particularly, they will prove our contention that those food habits should not be dismissed as foreign, as practices that no longer have anything of interest to offer us.[1]

---

[1] It is lamentable that even a decade ago writers who should have known much better were still perpetuating an unjustifiable disparagement of medieval cookery. 'On a essayé d'exécuter les recettes laissés par Taillevent ou par ses contemporains; le résultat en a toujours été déplorable. L'historien Alfred Franklin a voulu préparer un canard à la dodine rouge et une galimafrée selon les indications du maître queux de Charles V [Taillevent]. Ce fut une vraie catastrophe.' Henriette Parienté and Geneviève de Ternant, *La fabuleuse histoire de la cuisine française*, Paris (O.D.I.L.), 1981, p.118.

In 1987 Maguelonne Toussaint-Samat still repeated these denigrations of medieval taste, with, according to her, 'the outcome of grand banquets serving political ambition rather than gastronomy; today as yesterday.' *A History of Food* (translated from the French by Anthea Bell), Oxford (Blackwell), 1992, p.84.

The Europeans of the late Middle Ages knew how to eat well. It would be a shame, for us and for our taste buds, not to avail ourselves of their experiences.

The Late Middle Ages and Modern Sources

Just what is the period about which we are talking? When *were* the late Middle Ages? And how much do we really know about the food of that time?

Firstly, the time period. The outer dates of the Middle Ages, the maximum time span, as it were, for a study of anything qualified as medieval, must be determined by the Fall of Rome on the one hand and the so-called Renaissance on the other. To neither phenomenon can very precise dates be fixed, but if we were to take for the first the total dissolution of Roman administrative authority throughout its European empire, and for the second a firm conviction that one could repossess all of Roman (and Greek) culture and learning, in part because of the printing press, then we have the ten centuries between the sixth and the fifteenth, inclusive.

One thousand years of history are virtually impossible to grasp, let alone typify. Fortunately, for our purposes we may concentrate our attention upon only a very small part of the medieval millenium, and that is the two hundred years of the 'end' of the Middle Ages. Even this last qualification of the fourteenth and fifteenth centuries may disturb some historians, but for the food historian who depends primarily upon hand-written evidence the period with which he must be concerned is relatively short and fairly clearly delimited.

The earliest extant recipe manuscripts to afford us a glimpse into the foods that were being prepared and consumed in the late Middle Ages were written sometime toward the end of the 1200s, that is, in the late-thirteenth century. These early recipe manuscripts are quite rare. The practice of writing down recipes and collecting them into books seems to have caught on in the subsequent century, and by the fifteenth it was no longer unusual for such 'cookbook' manuscripts to be compiled and copied. By the time printers were casting around for likely material to typeset and sell to a broader audience than the odd wealthy bibliophile or dilettante, the recipe compendium was clearly a genre, and one that offered the enterprising printer very good prospects for general sales. With few exceptions these published cookery books from about 1500 were based ultimately upon earlier texts that had existed only in manuscript form up until then. Some had been lying around libraries, and perhaps even kitchens, in a more rudimentary form since the late 1200s.

Before the end of this present chapter we shall review the documentary evidence offered by these recipe collections.

If we may talk of a hey-day for medieval cookery, then, it would have to be during the fourteenth and fifteenth centuries, but this is only because of the incomparably greater availability of evidence that subsists from this relatively late period. There are, however, a couple of caveats that we must observe if we are going to rely, as we shall, upon late-medieval manuscripts in our efforts to understand the nature of the cookery then. Both have to do simply with the fact that the main source of our information about medieval food and cooking is in written form. The first area of caution is that these recipe manuscripts reflect aristocratic and upper-bourgeois practice; the second is that written recipes were in fact not really necessary to the professional medieval cook – or indeed to any cook at this time.

Only the most affluent members of medieval society could afford to buy a manuscript, or to have one either written or copied for them. In the earlier of our two main centuries a manuscript was generally made of carefully treated calfskin, vellum, a substance whose value can easily be imagined. Later, paper, though very much less respected because it was less durable, became broadly available and adopted for most day-to-day uses. Paper was certainly cheaper than vellum. But what remained just as costly was the actual writing out of every word, of every folio that composed a manuscript. The making of a single manuscript, whether illuminated or not, was what today we would call a 'labour intensive' project. It was, furthermore, necessarily slow work, and could be rushed only at the expense of accuracy. As a consequence, then, early recipe collections were written for and within a well-to-do, privileged milieu. It is significant that the most important of the books were compiled in distinctly noble milieux: the *Forme of Cury* reflects usage at the royal court of England; the *Viandier of Taillevent*, its counterpart in France; the German *Buch von guter Spise*, that of the Bishop of Würzburg; the *On Cookery*, that of the Ducal house of Savoy. The food these cookery books talk about was intended for those who could afford the services of both chef and scribe, and who indeed probably took a certain pride-of-class in committing to posterity a record of these the best of their dining privileges.

There was also at this time, as at most other times in the history of any society, a desire among the aristocracy to distinguish clearly between those who belonged and those who did not. The dining table was a fundamental means of demonstrating membership in the aristocracy.

> Those who served peacocks and other edible birds on platters did not seem to me to be squanderers since from them are made dishes which are more delicious than others and more suitable to the tables of kings and princes than the lowly and men of little property. The common people ... should beware of tasting such fare, much less eating it. These will be the dishes of distinguished people, and especially of those whom not virtue and hard work but fortune and the rashness of men have raised, by luck alone, from the depths, namely from cook ships, brothels and cheap eateries, not only to riches, which would have to be

tolerated, but even to the highest ranks of dignity. These are the ones thanks to whom peacocks and pheasants seem to be bred and captured. To them are owed expensive clothes, expensive furniture and whatever nature offers which is exceptional.[2]

It is perhaps unfortunate that we have to accept this limitation to our detailed understanding of what people ate in the past. We can of course guess, and quite accurately, what was usually placed on the tables of the peasantry and the lesser bourgeoisie. Their food was comparatively cheap and it did not call for much preparation. Generally speaking, roast meats were rare in the diet of the relatively poor – in part because any meat was not as common on a peasant's table as on that of an aristocrat, and in part because a roasting-fire is a very uneconomical use of cooking heat; the ubiquitous stew pot, filled primarily with cereal grains or vegetables, was the source of most cooked foods for the lower classes.

A record from 1493 details the food provided to the farm workers, both male and female (as well as to the cook), of a priory at Indersdorf, Upper Bavaria:

> From St George's Day [24 April] to Michaelmas [29 September] the servants and maids and all who work at the farm are given a water soup with pork fat, called a *Rabl*. Then at midday it might be a barley loaf, cabbage and some milk. If fruit, peas and millet are available it is for the steward to distribute them if the people have been good-tempered and hard-working. At night a milk soup, called *Gräman*, cabbage and milk as usual.
>
> ... Every week from Easter to Whitsun on three [meat] days – Sunday, Tuesday and Thursday – each day four pounds of pork cooked with the cabbage, making 12 pounds of meat in a week, which was not usual earlier, only on feastdays.[3]

---

[2] Book V, Chapter 1 of Bartolomeo Sacchi (1421–1481), known as Platina, *De honesta voluptate et valitudine ad amplissimum ac doctissimum D. B. Rouerellam, S. Clementi presbiterum cardinalem*, n.p., n.d. [c.1474]; Rome (Uldericus Gallus), 1475; Venice (Petro Mocenico), 1475; etc. The book was written – or rather adapted from several sources – about 1450 and is useful as a summary of mid-fifteenth-century Italian theory and practice in matters of food. A partial translation into modern English was published by Elizabeth B. Andrews, *On Honest Indulgence and Good Health*, St Louis (Mallinckrodt Chemical Works), 1967. A new critical edition and English translation of the large work is currently in preparation by Mary Ella Milham for the Renaissance Society of America.

It is sometimes difficult, as here, to know when Platina is giving way to his bent for sarcasm. Later, in Chapter 8 of the same Book V, we learn which fowl are appropriate for ordinary stomachs: 'Starlings, which we commonly say have the flesh of the devil, are completely rejected as food by upper-class people'.

[3] G. Wiegelmann, *Alltags- und Festspeisen. Wandel und gegenwärtige Stellung* (Atlas des deutschen Volkskunde N.F., Beiheft 1), Marburg, 1967; as reproduced in Edith Ennen, *The Medieval Woman*, Oxford (Blackwell), 1989, p.259.

For the same year 1493 at Erbach in the Odenwald the servants of the publican Erasmus were meted out the following victuals:

> ... All hired day-labourers and all bondsmen shall usually, like the servants and maids, be given meat twice daily and something with it and half a jug of wine, excepting on feast-days, when they shall have fish or other nutritious food. And all those who have worked during the week shall be generously treated on Sundays and feast-days after mass and the sermon. They shall have sufficient bread and meat and half a jug of wine. On high feast-days there will also be plentiful roasts. They shall be given a good loaf of bread to take home and as much meat as two can eat in one meal.[4]

The basis of the common meal was the cereal grains and the stew pot, in which were boiled leafy vegetables (in Germany particularly cabbage) and a variable amount of the locally available meat.

A manual composed in France, likewise toward the end of our period, the *Grant Kalendrier et compost des bergiers avecq leur astrologie, etc.*,[5] purports to summarize the activities and usages of those who live the pastoral life, with, *inter alia* the dishes eaten, if not favoured, by French shepherds or pseudo-bucolics of modest means. Not surprisingly these dishes echo some of the simplest preparations described in aristocratic cookery: fish stew, chicken or rabbit stew, pea or bean *cretonnée*, pork-and-peas (as popular a dish as pork-and-beans today), stewed leeks, brussels sprouts, mutton *haricoq* (another variety of stew), leg of mutton, veal pies, tripe stew, slices of fried, curdled milk, cheese tarts, and so forth. That this so-called peasant's food was not unique to them is not surprising: what we find in upper-class cookery is merely a refinement upon menus – with the notable addition of a variety of pasties and of roast and fried meats – that have a long-established base for the European population as a whole.

Most regretfully, there is not much documentation describing the food of the humbler classes. The written recipes of the wealthy, on the other hand, do let us see very clearly both the complexity of the professional cookery of the day and the extensive range of ingredients, some of which were quite exotic, with which this cookery normally worked. Nutritionists and social historians may be upset that the records of early alimentation are not equally explicit for all social levels, but we do at least possess quite adequate information to keep the modern gastronome extremely happy.

The other drawback that is attached to our reliance upon manuscript sources for our knowledge of food practices is, ironically, that a written recipe ought in actual fact to have been a superfluity as far as any professional cook in the Middle Ages was concerned. He had no need to

---

[4] Reproduced in Ennen, *Loc. cit.*
[5] Published with sixteenth-century woodcuts, Paris (Editions Siloe), 1881.

consult an outline of any dish he was preparing; there was, furthermore, no advantage to him personally to write such an outline down. Recipes, quantities, processes, final flavours and appearances, all existed in his head. Either they had been learned and indelibly fixed in his memory from the time he began his career as an young apprentice in the kitchen, or else a particular dish was an invention elaborated by a particular cook. In the former case he had attentively observed all of the work being done around him as he was initiated into his profession under the close supervision of a master; knowing ingredients, quantities and methods of preparation were the essence of the cook's craft. To suggest that he, a trained craftsman and perhaps a recognized member of the cook's guild, could prepare a meal only if a cookbook were propped open at his elbow would have impugned his very dignity.

A recipe collection was compiled in manuscript form not for the cook in a noble or bourgeois household but for the master or mistress of that household. It served to document certain standards of an elite class. Occasionally revised with additions, deletions and modifications, occasionally copied, with the approval of the master or mistress in order to please a flattering friend or relative, a manuscript collection of recipes reposed in the household library, not in its kitchen. With only the odd exception, these books are in good, clean condition – a tribute, if not to the intrinsic value of the data they contain, at least to the cost of the material and labour that went into their making. Normally very few copies, between one and four on average, of each text survive today; this number undoubtedly reflects a very low number of contemporary copies made.

Certain consequences stem from this function of the medieval recipe collection as pseudo-social document. In the first place written recipes are frequently concise, not to say laconic or elliptical. Regularly they omit any mention of the quantities to be used of any ingredient. Occasionally the absence of punctuation makes a recipe incomprehensible as such. In one extant copy of the so-called *Viandier of Taillevent*, a series of some two dozen recipes lacks *names* for the recipes; the same scribe nonchalantly transcribed another block of recipes (for various sorts of fish) into a single paragraph, with neither title, nor the name of the fish, nor any indication of the beginning or end of each of the original recipes. It was perhaps as well that that particular copy of the *Viandier* remained out of the kitchen and out of the hands of a neophyte.

Then again, not everything that was normally done in the kitchen was mentioned in these books. A great deal of the chef's activities – or if not *his* personally, certainly those of one of the many underlings, the kitchen help, for whom he was responsible – concerned routine preparations. Such petty things as the making of pea puree, a staple if ever there was one in the Middle Ages, is referred to in only one of these books. Similarly, pastry making is rarely worth written space, except perhaps to specify that it should be made with eggs (for special dishes) or not (for ordinary use). The making of bread, a commercial trade in itself, is simply not mentioned in these recipe collections. If we are reduced largely to guessing how the medieval pastry chef or professional baker went about making pie dough and bread, they themselves would merely have laughed. Pea puree, pastry or bread have no place among the significant recipes of a house,[6] to be passed down from generation to generation. The recipes may call for a particular spice mixture as an ingredient; they will not bother to instruct the reader on its composition.

This, then, is the food with which we are dealing: it is food prepared by professional cooks for social milieux in which their employers not only have quite a broad choice in what they will eat but are not at all shy about letting others of their class know how well they eat. Today we call this conspicuous consumption. Another generation or two after them, royalty will attempt to restrict such a demonstration of one-upmanship by imposing sumptuary laws. Our recipe collections present a food which properly belongs to the aristocracy and the upper bourgeoisie, and in a sense helps to define them, not only as distinct from the other classes, the peasantry and the clergy, but also helps to define them to themselves. It is, in the full sense of the term, noble food.

Documentary Evidence

Foods

Medieval cooks drew from the same foodstuff groups as do modern cooks. They used cereal grains, legumes (peas, beans), leafy vegetables and root vegetables, fruits from trees, shrubs and vines, nuts, meats, fish and poultry, eggs, milk and its products, oils and fats, and condiments (herbs and spices), all in quite a broad variety. There was not a category of foodstuff that was unused in the Middle Ages to produce food for the table. A modern dietician, or even a modern conservationist, could not fault the medieval cook for a narrowness in his choice of food sources. At least potentially, the medieval diet was neither restricted, unhealthy nor monotonous.

---

[6] Though Master Chiquart, in his *Du fait de cuisine*, does provide relatively terse directions for making *Puree de pois* as a preliminary to all of his lean dishes that will call for it as an ingredient. See Terence Scully, 'Du fait de cuisine par Maistre Chiquart 1420', *Vallesia*, 40 (1985), pp.101–231; Recipe 22. This work is translated into modern English by the same editor, as *Chiquart's 'On Cookery.' A Fifteenth-Century Savoyard Culinary Treatise*, New York, Berne and Frankfurt am Main (Lang), 1986, p.54. Chiquart was the chief cook of the first Duke of Savoy, Amadeus VIII, who became Pope as Felix V.

A number of sources afford us a good picture of the basic items available to even the ordinary housewife and cook. Writers of the day enumerate what plants and trees should be cultivated in a good kitchen garden. Other writers reproduce the street cries of specialized hawkers of foodstuffs as they passed through urban streets, or else chronicle the conditions of daily life that they saw about them. The account books and expense registers of institutions and private households survive and show the daily or monthly outlays for foodstuffs. Thanks to the scrupulous care with which records were kept in certain municipalities, we have historic documentation concerning the yield of slaughterhouses. Merchants compiled professional manuals to describe the qualities and costs of those items of quasi-exotic food they traded in. A little more colourfully, miniaturists, illuminating manuscript works of the time, afford on the one hand informative sketches of typical vegetable plots to be found on noble estates or in a bourgeois setting, and on the other hand detailed botanical sketches of individual vegetables, fruits and herbs.

An important documentary source of information about late-medieval cookery, specifically, is afforded by the many recipe manuscripts that survive. We shall survey these briefly a little later.

The first variety of source for our knowledge of normal foodstuffs in the late Middle Ages, the enumerations compiled by descriptive writers, didactic in intent, was often incorporated into a vocabulary list of one sort or another. Generally speaking, the intention that underlay such a catalogue might lead us to suspect that not all of the items found in it enjoyed everyday use, even in the wealthier kitchens of the time. The authors of these vocabularies sought to be comprehensive within the categories of terminology they were dealing with. Their compositions often amounted to the late-medieval equivalent of today's bilingual pictorial dictionary – though unfortunately without illustrations – where, for instance, the writer describes in two languages what someone would find as he or she passed through the street, the stable, the kitchen or the garden, of some ubiquitary existence.[7] So-called conversation manuals with parallel texts in two languages sometimes set out a list of the proper terms identifying articles of food, and give us an idea of the most common items bargained for on the marketplace

[7] The late-thirteenth-century *Treatise of Walter of Bibbesworth* (properly, in Anglo-Norman, *La Treytez ke moun sire Gauter de Bibelesworth fist*) represents a typical effort to survey the vocabulary associated with particular spheres of contemporary life or activity. Its author aims to instruct the presumably ignorant, but well disposed, English reader in the proper French terminology for what he or she is apt to see and do in moderately high society. In places Bibbesworth offers parallel texts in both Anglo-Norman and Middle English, along with some interlinear and marginal glosses of the French terms in English. See the edition by Richard Wright in *A Volume of Vocabularies. Illustrating the condition and manners of our forefathers, as well as the history of the forms of elementary education and of the languages spoken in this island from the tenth century to the fifteenth*, 2 vols.: Vol. I, [privately printed], 1857; Vol. II, [privately printed], 1873; repr. 1882; I, p.142.

and consumed at table.[8] But again, the intent of these writers is primarily lexicographical; the modern reader can only suppose that there is likely to be some close relation between the foods catalogued here and those that an actual traveller in the Lowlands, France or England would commonly hear referred to, and used, in everyday life.

When John of Garland drafted his *Dictionarius*[9] sometime before the year 1250, however, he provided his reader a detailed inventory of, in part, the contents of a good Parisian garden in his time. It is clear that some sort of domestic garden plot, with a fruit tree or two, was quite common even in the largest, most densely populated towns. John of Garland's list enumerates trees bearing cherries, pears, apples, plums, quince, medlars, peaches, chestnuts, walnuts, filberts, figs; grapevines; the potherbs sage, parsley, dittany, hyssop, celandine, fennel, pellitory, columbine, rose, lily, violet, nettle and holy thistle (as well as several medicinal herbs, *mercurialis*, mallow, agrimony, garden nightshade (belladonna) and sunflower); the 'vegetables' cabbage, borage, chard, leeks, garlic, mustard, chives, scallions, elecampane, burnet, pilosella, sanicle, bugloss, *lancea* – and, as John himself writes, loath to omit the mention of any possibility, whether fruit, herb or vegetable: etc.

That orchards were, if not commonplace in every backyard, certainly highly valued and subject to serious practical study, is evident in the chapters devoted to the care of fruit trees in treatises and handbooks current in the period. It is understandable that knowledge about the cultivation of fruit and fruit trees was almost entirely empiric. Physicians could, and did, speculate about the 'virtues' of various fruits, and their respective humoural temperaments; but the physicians stopped at the theoretical level, and were usually content merely to cite as authority the opinions of the most learned Greek and Arab doctors. For the thoroughly practical questions of site, espaliering, diseases, pruning and grafting, medieval scholars took their information more or less directly from farmers and distilled it into compendia on agriculture. The great Latin works of Palladius, *Opus agriculturæ*, Columella, *De re rustica*,[10] Cato, *De re rustica*, Varro, *De re rustica*,

---

[8] An example of this sort of composition might be the *Livre des mestiers de Bruges et ses dérivés: quatre anciens manuels de conversation*, edited by Jean Gessler, 6 vols., Bruges (Gruuthuse, Sainte-Catherine, Desclée-DeBrouwer), 1931. Various versions of this work juxtapose texts in the Flemish, French and English of the fourteenth and fifteenth centuries.

[9] This Latin work is edited also by Richard Wright in his *Volume of Vocabularies*; I, p.136. For an extensive study of other, particularly German, works on cultivated plants see Walter Janssen, 'Mittelalterliche Gartenkultur. Nahrung und Rekreation,' in Bernd Hermann (ed.), *Mensch und Umwelt im Mittelalter*, Stuttgart (Deutsche Verlags-Anstalt), 1986 and Stuttgart (Fischer Taschenbuch), 1990, pp.224–43.

[10] Ed. and transl. by E.S. Forster and Edward H. Hefner as *On Agriculture and Trees*, 3 vols., London (Heinemann) and Cambridge, Mass., (Harvard), 1955. Several early

and Petrus Crescentius, *Commodorum ruralium*[11] – this last summarizing much of what is contained in the others – were familiar manuals on very large estates. The respected information and advice they presented was sought by anyone who was seriously interested in the culture of various fruits. Such technical questions as grafting were dealt with in specialist monographs like the *Maniere de henter soutillement*;[12] the *Menagier de Paris* itself incorporates a paragraph on grafting (II,ii,§43), among the practical counsel its author lavishes upon his young wife for the maintenance and enrichment of his bourgeois household.

Accounts of the foodstuffs that were cried by street-peddlers are a solid source of information about early diet; they never pose any doubts as to the actual use of these foodstuffs in contemporary cookery. Foods hawked by itinerant merchants, or foods displayed in town shops, were without any doubt those foods that *were* handled in ordinary kitchens on a daily basis, and that turned up quite normally on the dining boards of what we might consider to be generally representative people of the time.[13] The medieval street was a particularly vital place – and necessarily a very noisy one. As well as the cries advertising an enormous variety of foods being offered for sale, there were *appeals for* food from beggars, from representatives of a variety of mendicant orders, and from enterprising fowlers offering small birds in exchange for bread. Criers of and for items of food were merely a part of the oral business in the street. Raucous shouts echoed on all sides along the narrow alleyways from a host of individuals: from buyers of old iron, old pots and pans, from candle sellers, from tradesmen offering their services, from bath-house keepers, from makers of baskets, wicker-work and matting, of soap, brooms, tannin, combs, glassware and wooden hoops, from dealers in firewood and coal, in thatching, in old clothes and shoes, as well as from official town criers making public announcements, and from individuals with a hand bell apprising the community of someone's death.

vernacular translations exist of Columella's work: in Italian (*De l'agricoltura*, Venetia, 1544), and in French (*Des choses rustiques*, Paris (Keruer), 1556).

[11] This work, one of the best known among late-medieval and Renaissance scholars, was also one of the first to be propagated by that new invention of the fifteenth century, the printing press: printed editions of it appear in Augsburg (Johannes Schussler) in 1471, in Louvain, in about 1474, and in Mayence in 1493. The popularity of Crescentius's work demanded vernacular translations, which were themselves in turn printed: in French (*Rustican*, [Dijon (Rabutot), 1373] and *Le livre des prouffitz champestres et ruraulx*, Paris (Jean Bon Homme), 1486, and again, 1529), in Italian (*D'agricoltura*, Venetia, 1542 and *Ruralia commoda*, Venetia (Capcasa), 1495), and in German (*Ruralia commoda*, Speier [Peter Drach], 1493).

[12] Ed. by Carole Lambert in *Le recueil de Riom et la Maniere de henter soutillement*, (*Le Moyen Français*, 20), Montréal (CERES), [1988].

[13] A major repository for French cries is the poem of Guillaume de la Villeneuve, *Les Crieries de Paris*, ed. Etienne Barbazan in *Fabliaux et contes des poètes françois des XIe, XIIe, XIIIe, XIVe, et XVe siècles*, 2 vols., Paris, 1808; repr. Genève (Slatkine), 1976; Vol. I, pp.276–286.

Cooks and their kitchen-boys kept crying, 'Hot pies, hot!
Good pork and geese! Let's go dine!'
Tavern-keepers told them a tale of the same sort,
'White wine of Alsace and wine of Gascony,
Of the Rhine and of LaRochelle, to wash the roast down with!'[14]

From morning to night, right across Europe virtually every foodstuff was cried in the street:

Mussels, lily-white mussels!
I have ripe strawberries, ripe strawberries!
Buy my dish of great smelts!
Fine oranges, fine lemons!

Anguille fresche! Anguille!   Italian: 'Fresh eels!']
Qui veut des lapins! [French: 'Rabbits for sale!']
Qui veut bon lait! [French: 'Milk for sale!']

A lot of the urban life of medieval Europe was necessarily related to the street.[15]

The list of the commonly used foods peddled through town streets – solid evidence of the raw materials of actual medieval cookery – is remarkably extensive: there are no fewer than 79 articles of raw foodstuffs and prepared food itemized in Les Crieries de Paris. The streets of medieval Paris, and hence any major European town, seem to have been filled with an endless cacophony of chants for local fruits and vegetables (garlic, onions, shallots, salad greens, fresh peas in their shells, fresh beans, turnips, watercress, leeks, lettuce, mushrooms (several varieties), melons, red apples, pears (several

---

[14]   Cokes [cooks] and here knaves · crieden, 'Hote pies, hote!
     Gode gris and gees · gowe dyne, gowe!'
     Taverners until hem · tolde the same,
     'White wyn of Oseye · and red wyn of Gascoigne,
     Of the Ryne and of the Rochel · the roste to defye.'
William Langland, The Vision of William concerning Piers the Plowman (1377 A.D.), ed. Walter W. Skeat, ('B' Text), E.E.T.S. Vol. 28, Pt. 2, London (Oxford University Press), 1869; Prologue, ll. 225-9, p.10.

[15] Because more was peddled in the streets than just foodstuffs, these old cries of tradesmen offering their services can let us glimpse quite a bit of the life of the time:
     Rats or mice to kill!
     Seignor, quar vous alez baingnier [bathe],
     et estuver [sweat in a hot-tub] sans delaier,
     li baing sont chaut, c'est sanz mentir!
The texts of a remarkable anonymous three-part motet from the fourteenth century, in a manuscript located today in the Biblioteca Capitolare at Ivrea in Italy, are composed mainly of street cries for a wide variety of articles. Most interestingly, the Tenor text seems to consist solely of the cry, 'Old shoes, old shoes! (Soulés viex, soulés viex!)' sung over and over. See Gordon K. Greene and Terence Scully, Polyphonic Music of the Fourteenth Century, Vol. 21, Virelais, Monaco (Oiseau Lyre), 1987, N° 31a.

varieties), medlars, peaches, cherries, plums, sorb-apples, service-berries, sloeberries, rose-hips, walnuts, hazelnuts), for 'imported' fruits and vegetables (figs from Malta, raisins from Damascus, gardencress from Orléans, white apples from the Auvergne, cooking pears from Burgundy, chestnuts from Lombardy), for milk, fresh butter, and several cheeses (from Champagne and Brie), for eggs, for fowl (small birds, doves), for salt meats and dressed meats, for fish (fresh herring, smoked herring, live minnows, bleak, eels), for flour milled from a variety of grains (oatmeal, coarse and fine wheat), for half a dozen different qualities of wines, for vinegars, verjuice, honey, walnut oil, for herbs and spices (chervil, purslane, pepper, aniseed), even for yeast-water[16] for bread – in short for virtually every foodstuff but fresh meats. As well as raw foods, criers hawked a number of 'ready-mixed' condiments or prepared dishes: garlic sauce, green sauce, prepared mustard, cooked peas, fried peas, cooked beans. In this last category – somewhat analogous to the offerings found in today's delicatessens – we can read in particular the cries for baked goods, for flans, wafers, cakes, simnel cakes, bean cakes, pies and rissoles.

The presence in town streets of sellers of milk raises an interesting observation. Animal milk, whether from ewes, goats or cows, was not refrigerated, of course. Carted, or borne in a donkey's paniers or on the seller's back, inevitably with a constant jouncing motion, under the warm sun and through a long itinerary of streets, this milk, even if relatively fresh at the beginning of a day, could not remain so for long. The *Vivendier*, along with other recipe collections, contains warnings that the cook should rely only upon milk that comes more or less directly from the cow.[17] The shortness of what we would call its shelf-life has always been a serious drawback for animal milk, even though universally otherwise one of the most useful of all human foodstuffs. Besides this rather serious shortcoming, a suspicion seems to have been common in the Middle Ages that sellers of milk adulterated their product by watering it: writers occasionally warn the ingenuous buyer to beware of diluted milk – maybe in the same spirit that canny shoppers today, at a butcher's counter, learn to suspect that under the visible, lean top of a tightly wrapped package of meat a lot of fat or heavy bone is apt to be hidden.

For most cooks in the Middle Ages the dubious quality of the animal milk that they were likely to be able to procure added to their reluctance to depend upon it at all in their cookery. Keeping milk on hand in the kitchen for any length of time was of course unthinkable – at least if you wanted eventually to be able to draw upon sweet milk. Most milk was therefore destined either to be put to immediate use in cooking or to be converted into

---

[16] This could be the dregs of still-fermenting beer, used as a leavening for bread.

[17] . . . *Puis ayez lait de vache nouvellement trait* . . . : ' . . . Then get newly drawn cow's milk . . . .' *Vivendier*, Recipe 30, folio 159r.

its longer-lasting products, butter or cheese. Even these latter substances almost invariably had salt added to them in order to prolong their life.

Rather than animal milks, what early cooks knew they *could* depend upon to function in much the same culinary way as animal milk was a nut milk, and particularly the milky liquid produced by the grinding of almonds or walnuts. This liquid, high in natural fats, could be prepared fresh whenever and in whatever quantity was needed for a recipe. Alternatively, almond milk could be prepared considerably ahead of time and set aside with no immediate danger of a loss of quality. Because of its fat content, almond milk also enjoyed an additional advantage in that, like animal milks, it could be churned into butter, almond butter – which, unlike animal-milk butter, did not need the admixture of salt to prolong its life.[18] A final drawback to animal milks and their products was that they could not be consumed on days that the Church had designated to be lean days; this restriction did not apply to other milks and butters. To make a success of their trade, the street-peddlers of animal milks must have had more than the usual amount of buyer resistance to overcome.

The diaries of individuals who observed the daily life of the people in their society occasionally touch usefully upon food, its availability, quality and even cost. For instance the thirteenth-century Lombard Bonvesin de la Riva wrote *On the Marvels of Milan* (*De magnalibus Mediolani*)[19] in which a thoroughly exhaustive catalogue of the agricultural products of the region simply glows with patriotic pride. This paean to the fertility of the local land and the abundance of its harvests gives us solid, and amazing, information about the wealth of foodstuffs available around Milan at this time. For French urban life one chronicle is particularly evocative, the *Parisian Journal*, in which an anonymous bourgeois describes the daily concerns and conditions with which his fellow citizens lived, more or less constantly under siege from bad weather, bad government and plundering soldiers representing several mortally hostile causes. The *Journal* is a highly detailed record of their joys, fears and sufferings from month to month during the first half of the fifteenth century. For instance for the year 1420, at the time of the entry into Paris of the Queen of France and the Queen of England and their respective suites, we read:

> Within a week of their arrival the price of corn [grain] and flour went up so that a *setier* of wheat by Paris measure in the Paris Halles cost

---

[18] A German recipe collection offers directions to make a variety of butter with much the same advantages as presented by nut butter but made from pea flour. Hans Wiswe, 'Ein mittelniederdeutsches Kochbuch des 15.Jahrhunderts', *Braunschweigisches Jahrbuch*, 37 (1956), pp.19–55; recipe 101. Nowdays hazelnuts and peanuts have all but supplanted almonds as sources of nut butters.

[19] The long list of herbs, vegetables and fruits may be read in Massimo Montanari, *Convivio. Storia e cultura dei piaceri della tavola dall'antichità al medioevo*, Bari (Laterza), 1989, §197, pp.368–71.

thirty francs of the money then current, good flour thirty-two francs, and other grain correspondingly according to its kind. There was no bread under 24 penny *parisis* a loaf, made with the bran, and the heaviest weighed no more than about twenty ounces. Poor people and poor priests did very badly in those days because they were paid only 2 sous *parisis* for a mass, and poor people ate no bread, nothing but cabbages and turnips and such dishes, without any bread or salt. Bread got so dear before Christmas came that a four-*blanc* loaf cost eight *blancs* and even then no one could buy any without going to the baker's before daybreak and standing pints and quarts to the bakers and their assistants (there was no wine then, either, at anything under 12 penny a quart), but still you were lucky if you could get it, since by eight o'clock there was such a crowd at the bakers' doors as one could never have believed without seeing it. Poor creatures! trying to get bread for their poor husbands away in the fields or for their children dying of hunger at home – neither for their money nor for all their crowding could they get any after that time; then you would hear sad wailing and weeping all over Paris, sad lamentations and little children crying 'I am dying of hunger!' In the year 1420 you might see all over Paris here ten there twenty or thirty children, boys and girls, dying of hunger and of cold on the rubbish heaps. No one could be so hard of heart as not to be greatly distressed, hearing them at night crying 'Oh, I am dying of hunger!'; yet the poor householders could do nothing to help them – no one had any bread, corn, firewood or charcoal. Moreover the poor people were so burdened with guard duty [on the city walls], which had to be done day and night, that they did not know how to help themselves or others.[20]

These diaries often speak of hardship and famine among the poorest classes. They indicate how the tribulations of warfare, poor crops and inexorable taxation led to what must have been endemic social unrest, insecurity and despair for these classes, frequently leaving them absolutely no recourse but to resort to eating the coarsest of foods.

The account books of a few late-medieval households have come down to us, if not always for a long unbroken period at least with enough regularity that the expenditures for foodstuffs that they detail are of some use as indicators of what was actually eaten in those households during those times for which the ledgers exist. Similarly in the account books of institutions, such as hospitals, for which financial statements had to be drawn up and submitted to a governing authority, we have the chance to trace, week by week, what actually was spent for those provisions that had to be supplied by 'outside' sources. Two fundamental problems that have to be recognized with this sort of information are, firstly, that these expense accounts do not reflect *all* that was eaten in the household or in the institution; and, secondly, that the current size of the household, or the number of mouths

---

[20] *Journal d'un bourgeois de Paris*, translated by Janet Shirley as *A Parisian Journal 1405-1449*, Oxford (Clarendon), 1968, pp.155–56.

being fed from the institution's kitchen, at any given time, is often very uncertain. The first problem arises because kitchen gardens were so common in the Middle Ages, wherever the house or institution was located, and whatever its size. And in the same way that many vegetables and fruits might come directly from these private gardens or farms without any expenses being noted in the daily registers, so fish might be provided from a private pond on an estate, or game and fowl might be furnished from a private forest. Furthermore, meat or some other costly foodstuff could be supplied to a household free-of-charge in exchange for some unrecorded consideration. No matter what caveats have to be attached to their use, at least these account registers reveal that the foodstuffs itemized in them were consumed by the residents in some quantity, whatever else may also have been eaten.

Such evidence as accounts books may afford us seems, then, perhaps disappointingly inconclusive. A remarkable exception to at least one of the limitations of this variety of evidence is found in the account books labelled the *Mensa della Signoria* in Florence over the exceptionally long period from 1344 to 1428.[21] The *Signoria* was, at the time, the municipal executive body whose members lived their term of service in virtual isolation in the town hall. All of their food was purchased and brought in; none was privately grown or furnished. With Italian care for meticulous accounting, the pages in the books record in neat columns, on a day-to-day basis, the type of food, the amount (in number or weight), the supplier's name and profession, and the cost. Although there were at any given time nine members of this council who ate at the Table of the Signoria, food was undoubtedly prepared for a slightly larger number – and, on special formal occasions, for very much larger numbers. However, the accounts which survive do show very precisely what bread, wine, meat, fowl, eggs, cheese, spices, fruit, vegetables, and so forth were handled in the kitchen for the use of the councillors, and frequently they identify as well the actual prepared dish for which these foodstuffs were intended. They provide precious, solid evidence of the food habits of a medieval time and place.

The records of medieval slaughterhouses likewise afford us precise details of another aspect of early food habits. If these records do not unquestionably demonstrate what was actually consumed, they indicate at least the quantities and types of fresh meats that were made available on a particular market at a particular time of the year. What must remain uncertain in these statistics is whether any significant portion of the yields of slaughterhouses was destined to be smoked or salted, that is, to be preserved for consumption at some later date. At any rate, whether those meats went on the retail

---

[21] See Allen J. Grieco, 'From the Cookbook to the Table: A Florentine Table and Italian Recipes of the Fourteenth and Fifteenth Centuries', in Carole Lambert, ed., *Du manuscrit à la table*, Paris & Montréal (Champion-Slatkine & Université de Montréal), 1992, pp.29ff; especially pp.30–31.

market immediately or later, we may assume that all of the produce of slaughterhouses answered a reasonably constant and firm yearly demand for red meats.

The figures that are available on the yields of slaughterhouses are interesting and point to two general conclusions: that domestic meats must have been eaten in moderately generous amounts in towns, and that certain meats predominated over others on the market according to the season. A particularly exhaustive study[22] of the animals processed in Carpentras, a regional town in the south of France, shows generally for the year 1419–1420 that mutton practically drove all other meats from the market in June and July, that beef (oxen and cows) accounted for an amount between 40 and 50% of sales between September and January, and then up to 64% in February, whereas virtually the entire output of the slaughterhouse in March (94%), and most in April (51%) was lamb. Over the years of the first half of the fifteenth century the same market handled a changing balance of animals, in some years mutton being the predominant meat, in other years beef. In terms of actual quantities, there are months, such as September, November and December, in which the slaughterhouse was particularly busy, and others, April to July, in which the average production was half of that amount. Given the presence of the Lenten season in March, this must have been a holiday time for most butchers.

A most interesting revelation in such historic studies is the way in which the processing of meats, and so eventually their consumption, varied in quantity quite significantly from year to year. For the town of Carpentras the numbers for the year 1419 appear to be average; yet 1420 is perhaps 20% lower; 1422 is slightly higher, and 1437 is something like 20% higher. In actual quantities, the more active years turned out and average of 15 tons of meat per month at peak production, and the more slack years saw a maximum of only 10 tons per month. A number of factors can account for variations in the amount of meat eaten by the general population. Clearly these variations must have depended upon the current price for the various meats, which itself, in the simplest of economic systems, would depend upon supply, that is, the availability of the animal for slaughter. Again, relative abundance could effectively be determined by the weather of the current and previous years, the state of grazing lands, any prevailing diseases, the number of young animals born, the number of young allowed to grow to maturity, and the number of animals their owners wished to retain or to dispose of because of personal circumstances or because of some crudely perceived economic outlook.

Such research yields evidence about medieval eating habits that is not merely speculative. As far as domestic meats are concerned it is now clear

---

[22] Louis Stouff, *Ravitaillement et alimentation en Provence aux XIVe et XVe siècles*, Paris/ The Hague (Mouton), 1970.

that meat of one variety or another was certainly not uncommon on bourgeois tables during the late Middle Ages. In provincial towns such as Carpentras butchers seem to have kept busy throughout the year (always excepting the five weeks of Lent, when carcasses may still have been prepared expressly for some sort of preserving treatment and later consumption); they answered a demand from consumers that was more or less constant, but it was a demand that was willing to accept a change in diet as the various meats became relatively more or less affordable. Similar results turn up from similar investigations of slaughterhouses in such larger cities as London, Paris and Lyon, so that our overall picture of bourgeois diet during the later Middle Ages generally has to include a good portion of domestic meats.

A number of illuminating revelations emerge from studies of official records, regulations and judicial sentences that deal with butchers and butchering at this time. A 'paper trail' of various documents through the whole period demonstrates how seriously the population regarded the provision of good, healthy, fresh meat and insisted upon proper cutting and fair weight in its retailing. Professional guilds levied fines on their members for what was ruled dishonest conduct or an activity apt to incur the opprobrium of the public. Strict public officials themselves condemned offending butchers to remarkably ruthless punishment: in London the purveyors of meats.qualified as 'putrid and stinking, an abomination to mankind', 'putrid, rotten, stinking, and abominable to the human race', and 'putrid and corrupt, unwholesome as food for man, and an abomination' were 'without exception punished . . . by being placed in the pillory and having the putrid matter burnt beneath'.[23] Regulations concerning the sale of good meats were universally strict; infractions were punished severely.

The disposal of the wastes of butchering posed a particularly serious problem in most medieval towns. Even in London, with its wide, tidal-flowing river Thames, the problem was such that an endless series of ordinances and indictments throughout the late-medieval period could only keep trying to abate intolerable but recurrent abuses. It was perhaps natural that the operators of scalding houses and slaughterhouses should try to get rid of the large amounts of blood, hair, dung and offal in the easiest, least expensive ways, dumping it sometimes in neighbourhood ditches and gutters, or in slow moving streams, tributaries to the Thames, or dropping it (maybe accidentally) on the king's high road. The citizens always objected strenuously, complaining about the vile, noisome stench occasioned by such criminal indifference to the public well-being. In 1422 'complaint was made

---

[23] Ernest L. Sabine, 'Butchering in Mediæval London', Speculum, 8 (1933), p.339. The same severe punishment was meted out to any grocer who sold adulterated spices or spice powders: fastened in a public pillory, he saw – and felt – his entire stock of debased spices ignited under him. The quotations hereafter refer to this article of Sabine, Ibid., pp.335-353.

both by the Warden and Convent of Friars Minors and by the Rector and parishioners of St Nicholas Shambles that a lane near the Church used by the Friars was full of dung and entrails thrown there at the weekly butchering, so that passage through the lane was prevented and the place filled with horrible stenches'. In the middle of the fourteenth century, the practice of disposing of entrails into Fleet Stream profoundly concerned the Prior of the nearby Hospital of St John of Jerusalem. Conditions around the Fleet Prison on the same property deteriorated to the extent that the Prior petitioned the king on behalf of the prisoners: drought had exacerbated the foul foetor of putrid butchers' filth, and furthermore the prison ditch was filled with the 'output' of various privies built over it and the by-products of a number of tanneries bordering it. The king ordered that this very unhealthy state of affairs be cleaned up forthwith.

The work of butchers in early London remained brisk, but had to be regulated vigilently. In 1361, during a visit of the plague, 'because of blood flooding the streets (running down the open sewers) and the entrails cast into the river poisoning the air with an abominable stench, and so causing sickness among those dwelling in the city', butchers were required to remove their operations to suburbs beyond the city proper. By 1391 the suburban inhabitants in turn protested that the butchers' filth was responsible for disease among them. Even the burying of offal turned out not to be entirely satisfactory, because carts dropped blood and entrails along the way to the rented sites, and large mounds of the refuse tended to pile up on plots where pits should have been dug, much to the disgust and malaise of the local residents. A final solution to the enormous problem of the disposal of the superfluities of butchering was thought to have been found by ruling that all such matter had to be dumped from boats in the middle of the Thames at ebb-tide. In the fifteenth century complaints continued, that the river banks downstream were covered with rotting entrails! Such is the usefulness of civic documents in letting us recreate, even partially, the reality of the activities of the 'food industry' in the later Middle Ages.

As a good basis for our understanding of actual food use in the late Middle Ages, we have further solid evidence that is afforded by commercial treatises written for their colleagues by merchants experienced in long-distance trade. The extensive handbook of Balducci Pegolotti, traveller and merchant, a native of Florence who was active between 1315 and 1340, is a descriptive list of all of those items that were dealt with by Italian importers of his day.[24] Concerned as he was with advising fellow merchants about the nature of the merchandise they were likely to be handling, and how to identify the best

[24] Francesco Balducci Pegolotti, *La Pratica della mercatura*, ed. Allen Evans, Cambridge, Mass., (Mediæval Academy of America), 1936. The full name of this highly detailed manual is the *Libro di divisamenti di paesi e di misuri di mercatanzie e d'altre cose bisognevoli di sapere a' mercatanti*: 'A Setting Forth of Lands and Mercantile Measures and other Matters Necessary for Merchants to Know'.

and freshest shipments of a whole range of products, Pegolotti provided exhaustive information, in particular for our purposes about spices and their most common grades and varieties: anise, pepper (white, black and long), ginger (six distinct species of this), tumeric, cinnamon, cassia buds, cassia, caraway, grains of paradise, sugars (including, specifically, that from Cairo and from Damascus, loaf sugar, powdered sugar, candied sugar, refined sugar, rose sugar, violet sugar), alum, mastic, zedoary, cloves, clove stalks, clove leaves, nutmegs, cubebs, cardamoms, galingale, mace, cumin, carobs, aloes, saffron.[25] His handbook describes as well a wide variety of other exotic foodstuffs: many grape wines from outside western Europe, quince wine, pomegranate wine, honey, molasses, carob syrup, dates, figs, currants, pistachios, genet, purslane, both sandalwood and red sanders[26] spikenard, fennelseed, potash,[27] salt herrings, salt sturgeon, pickled tunny fish. Pegolotti also offers information on how these goods are packaged, on how the merchant should handle them, on standard names for such trade items, on costs, on normal packing methods, on import duties, on the principal trade routes followed in the fourteenth century, and on an astonishingly wide range of foreign currencies, weights and measures. By reading such treatises closely we may form an even more accurate picture of the historic use of those foodstuffs that were not produced locally. A thriving commerce in imported foodstuffs put a broad variety of foods at the disposition of the relatively affluent household. The cooks in these households must have handled many such exotic foods quite routinely.

And, for visual illumination, we have firm iconographic evidence to help us understand what medieval people ate. A particular genre of health handbook known (in Latin) as a *tacuinum sanitatis* – that is, roughly, a 'medical almanac' – methodically examined all elements in the human condition that were apt to exert any influence, whether for good or for bad, upon the state of a person's health. A typical one of these books would study, and carefully define the nature and all the effects of, everything a person was apt to experience, from the air he breathed and the season of the year in which he breathed it to the act of coitus he engaged in, from the foods he ate and the water he drank to the vomit he disgorged. In the fourteenth and fifteenth centuries it became common to reproduce these encyclopædic compendia accompanied with detailed miniatures in which the reader could examine some aspect of the subject or thing being defined. The illustrations

---

[25] The dissertation by Luise Bardenhewer, *Der Safranhandel im Mittelalter*, Bonn (Hauptmann), 1914, may still usefully be consulted on the very wide distribution of this last substance.

[26] Sandalwood, used as a reddish-brown food colouring when finely ground up.

[27] Properly, 'clavellated ashes', used for soaps and to treat 'sick' wine. In its wine section, the *Viandier* (§179) makes use of these ashes in a 'recipe' designed to keep wine from becoming slimy or cloudy. Pegolotti's commercial treatise describes two varieties of clavellated ashes according to their source, Soria or Alexandria.

of the most commonly consumed contemporary foodstuffs are especially interesting for our purposes, in part because they demonstrate that each of the foodstuffs detailed was indeed in current use to a serious extent, and also in part because the illuminations shed quite a bit a light upon the circumstances of the production and retail distribution of these foodstuffs.

The *tacuina sanitatis* show us, for example, a view of an orchard in which cherries are being harvested by one peasant climbing among the limbs with a basket, another on the ground spreading her gown like a chute to gather the falling fruit, and another bearing away full baskets on a shoulder pole. Or in a field we see a peasant and his wife each flinging a flail on a carpet of spelt stalks and ears; in the background stooks of mown spelt stand drying under the protection of a thatched shed. Other peasants harvest asparagus into similar all-purpose baskets, and still others figs, pine-nuts, crocus flowers (for saffron), truffles, partridge eggs, melons, rue and anise. We see the itinerant peddlers, whose raucous cacophony we heard above, now actually stopping at the front doors of houses to urge a series of housewives to buy their sour or coagulated milk, turnips and olive oil. From contemporary reality an artist sketches the shopper bending over a deep tray that is crawling with live crayfish and crabs in order to make the best selection; he reproduces a large beam-operated wine press to illustrate the making of must; he takes us into a cheese 'factory' so that we may appreciate the sequence of processes that milk undergoes in order to become ricotta cheese; and then for a nearby article on *Old Cheese* he shows us a storeroom in which a lady on a ladder stacks shelves to the very ceiling with rounds of fresh cheese being laid away for aging.

Our artists seem to be most concerned with the activity of the food market. Their preferred locale, especially for illustrating the availability of various meats, is the shop stall. Normally in these miniatures the shop consists of a counter behind which, and occasionally in front of which, the tradesman or merchant is busy plying his particular craft. Butchers are shown cutting up kid, mutton, ram-meat, veal, pork, beef and the meat of gelded animals.[28] Certain shops seem to have specialized in animal viscera, for we see a table covered with animal heads (of calf, sheep, goat and kid), and another bearing a bowl of brains,[29] others variously with animal hearts,

---

[28] To be complete we should also mention the illustrations that a few artists provide for articles on gazelle meat and on camel meat: much of the basic inspiration for these *tacuina* is clearly Arabic, even if the illuminations, added later, depict Europeans.

[29] The writer of one *tacuinum* notes that while brains are difficult to digest and spoil easily, if properly seasoned (in order to counter their naturally cold and moist temperament) they are a fattening food and will increase the cerebral matter of the person who consumes them. He particularly recommends eating the brain of small birds, especially mountain birds, presumably because such wild creatures of the air (warm, dry) will by nature have brains whose temperament is less phlegmatic (cold, moist) than normally is the case for any viscera.

udders, testicles and fat. Sundry fishmongers deal in fresh fish, pickled fish and salt fish. Other shops trade in almond oil (interestingly the back shelves of this establishment are filled with amphoræ of a whole range of sizes), in raisins, dried figs, butter, sugar, vinegar, salt, starch, and an assortment of breads (brown wheat, bran, millet, and so forth: see below). A pharmacist offers among his many wares the wonder food/medicine known as theriac.

Then there are the interiors. Illustrations in the *tacuina sanitatis* let us see into private houses and to glimpse a bit of the life going on there. Where the subject matter being analysed is food, we are allowed to examine a good deal of kitchen activity: women making pasta, first by rolling balls of dough flat, slicing it into long strings, and drying these on an angled rack; two women processing tripe, by slitting it, scraping it clean and boiling it in a cauldron over a centrally built fire (two children at a table in the background seem eagerly to be stealing a foretaste of the women's work!). In some lower room, housing an active henhouse, a wife gathers hen's eggs, and in another interior she ventures out among some very spirited geese to fill a basket with their eggs. The medicinal properties of *Barley Soup* are illustrated by means of an interior scene of a comfortably panelled bedroom where an invalid, sitting up against thick pillows in his sickbed, has been served a bowl of this standard sick-dish by two women attendants, one of whom bears a pot of the concoction which she has just brought from the kitchen fire. In what may well be a tavern, five enthusiastic drinkers standing about a flask-laden table give a convincing demonstration of the meaning and function of the article enscribed beneath the picture: *Robust Red Wine*. The authors and artists of these manuals seem concerned above all with teaching by reproducing scenes of daily life, scenes that incorporate actual foods in actual circumstances.

These views, quaint perhaps because of the exiguity of the shop space or the kitchen interiors, possess nevertheless a huge amount of realism. These are down-to-earth peasants, housewives, merchants and shop keepers that we see here, men and women handling food products as they would today, for families or a local populace who are looking for quality and economy the same as we do today. These are real people who, at the middle and end of each day, sit down to meals composed of foodstuffs that are in many respects very similar to what we eat today.

Cookery

One further, final source of information, about both foodstuffs and the dishes that were actually prepared from them, is available to us from contemporary witnesses: written recipes. Because recipes refer to real culinary practices and gastronomic customs, because they apply to a specific time and region, and because a relatively large number of such recipes has survived to this day in manuscript copies that were produced at the very time at which the dishes described in them were without any doubt being made and eaten, it is upon this final historic source of information that we shall be most dependent throughout the present study.

The history of late-medieval cookery would be virtually impossible without the body of food recipes that we possess. With them to use as our fundamental resource for factual data about ingredients, about processes, about finished dishes and even the manner of their formal presentation at table, we can put together a broad and fairly accurate picture of early European food. Because many of the manuscript recipe collections – in a certain limited sense, the 'cookbooks' of the Middle Ages – have come to light, been published and carefully studied only in very recent years, the picture is more complete than it has ever been possible to make it since the fourteenth and fifteenth century themselves.

We cannot here examine the actual contents of these recipe collections in any great detail. It is enough to observe that at least seventy-five collections have been identified to date, in languages representative of most European nations, and that the size of these collections varies in length from a handful of recipes up to three and four hundred, although a good average collection might number perhaps one hundred recipes. Among the various collections there is, understandably, a considerable amount of repetition and echoing of material, although significant variations in ingredients and procedures do exist and are historically interesting.

Generally speaking, the culinary 'style' adopted by medieval recipe writers anticipates the generic terseness of their modern counterparts. Yet even though the language is far from chatty,[30] the individual recipes do list the ingredients for a dish, normally mention how they are to be prepared, mixed and cooked, direct that particular kitchen utensils and containers are to be used, and, where the question is crucial, try to indicate the length of cooking time and the relative intensity of the heat to which a preparation is to be exposed. The recipes further advise on the manner of garnishing and serving the finished dishes.

What is frequently lacking in these early recipes is a precise indication of quantities, times and heats. Before becoming dismayed that we cannot consult a medieval recipe in the same way as we pick up and follow a modern one, finding in it explicit instructions to guide the novice, we should be reminded that the cookery manuscript was not a popular book intended to be universally useful to 'everyman'; popular cookery, if there has ever been such a thing, is a much more recent phenomenon. Late-medieval cookery was in every sense a professional matter. The cook, whose vocational entity

---

[30] A most notable exception to the generally sparse style in the recipe books is that of Master Chiquart whose *Du fait de cuisine* occasionally reflects its author's own tendencies to grandiloquence.

we shall examine later, was a qualified tradesman who exercised a craft. A good part of that craft involved *knowing* how to prepare a good number of standard dishes. It is entirely arguable that recipe books were not compiled *for the use of* the professional cook in the Middle Ages, but only *by* him; the recipe collection may have functioned in large measure as archival material that documented the practice and experience of an important household. In any case, the professional cook did not need precise directions in order to arrive at the suitable *relative* balance between the condiments and the principal ingredient, or to recognize when a *Pastello di sardelle* was properly cooked, or to judge the appropriate heat to play on the bottom of a pot with *Mortrews Blank*.

What perhaps the professional cook may have looked for was to be reminded about *all* of the ingredients that he should include in any given preparation, or that one cooking step was preliminary to another, or perhaps that the appropriate sauce for a dish was such and such. As time went on in the fifteenth century, and especially in Italy, the normally laconic directions in recipes do become a little more helpful for the uninitiated. A few writers will establish a quantitative basis for a recipe, specifying that for twelve diners the dish should be made in such and such a way. Similarly these later writers will condescend to attempt to indicate absolute cooking times – always a most difficult question in the medieval kitchen – by telling the amateur that the right time is that which it would take to say three *Pater nosters*, or to walk around a certain size of field. The nature of cooking fires of coal, peat and, particularly, wood precluded the possibility of precision where heat was concerned. Because it was not feasible to define exactly what heat would be produced by flames from a piece of unknown firewood in an unknown fireplace in which unknown equipment was installed from which to suspend an unknown pot, later writers occasionally resort to writing that the preparation should be cooked over a 'sprightly' fire or a 'low' fire, or else over live coals or swung entirely from the direct heat of the fire.

Most of early European recipe collections have been edited and published in the twentieth century and are available in academic libraries.[31] The major gaps in this available material occur in the area of German collections, where scholarship has not kept up with an increasing awareness that a good

---

[31] The best general catalogue of medieval recipe manuscripts was assembled in 1991 by a team consisting Constance B. Hieatt, Carole Lambert, Bruno Laurioux and Alix Prentki and published under the title 'Répertoire des manuscrits médiévaux contenant des recettes culinaires' in *Du manuscrit à la table*, ed. Carole Lambert, Montréal and Paris (Université de Montréal and Champion-Slatkine), 1992, pp.315–388. The major difficulty with this listing is that it is concerned primarily with identifying manuscript sources rather than with the recipe collections as such. A general 'synthetic' review of the contents of all major recipe collections of this time is still to be undertaken.

amount of culinary material exists in German manuscripts.[32] A considerable proportion of the total German material has never been edited, published or studied.

The Present Study

A variety of historic sources, then, afford us quite a good understanding both of what was eaten in the late Middle Ages and how it was eaten. These two fundamental questions, the what and the how of late-medieval food, will be the subject of this book.

The sequence of chapters that follows attempts to present the complex matters of foodstuffs, cookery and eating – their theory, practice, practitioners and vicissitudes in the late Middle Ages – in a sequence that has some sort of order imposed upon them. Chapter 2 presents a thesis (if there is one) in this study, and that is that in several important respects over the twenty generations that intervene between 'us' and 'them' our perceptions of what makes good eating have not really changed. Chapter 3 attempts to show certain peculiar attitudes and tastes that *do* account for late-medieval taste and practice being in reality different from our own; the ideas about food that are seen here will be referred to continually in most of the remainder of the book. The following three chapters, 4, 5 and 6, examine the specifics of food preparation in the fourteenth and fifteenth centuries: the foods that were eaten and how they were handled in the kitchen; how and when dishes were made and served; and what was normally drunk at mealtimes. Chapter 7 continues the question of eating by a survey of the nature of formal dining. The two chapters that follow are devoted to special considerations about food, both raw and prepared: Chapter 8 looks at foods for the sick and sickly; Chapter 9 considers the very broad matters of national taste and its opposite, internationalism, in late-medieval food practices. The final chapter, though it tries to be a summary, concludes the book by pointing to what the reader may already have seen as thoroughly obvious, the supreme role played in the best of medieval food by the professional cook.

The proof of the medieval pudding is always in its taste. A book about food, no matter how evocative its descriptions, can never do more than merely suggest the substantive nature of its subject matter. This is not an

---

[32] See in particular the unpublished thesis of Alix Prentki, *Les traités culinaires du sud de l'Allemagne à la fin du Moyen-Age*, Mémoire de D.E.A., école des Hautes études en Sciences Sociales de Paris, 1985. Though concerned only with southern Germany, this scholar has located some thirtymanuscripts containing culinary material in German, of which only a very small amount has been made available to modern readers.

apology for the present undertaking, but a recognition that language and historical studies have their limits. Food, that cultivated element that we are examining of a past civilization, is above all a sensual experience, and as such it has a reality that is intimately personal.

In most unacademic fashion we would urge the reader to consider *really* making the acquaintance of medieval food by experiencing it personally. As we have pointed out, a good number of important recipe collections from the late Middle Ages have been published in recent years; the Bibliography offers data on these editions. Two drawbacks to a 'functional' modern use of these editions must be acknowledged: if the editor has not provided a modern English translation, then the reader will have to be prepared to tackle Old English, fourteenth-century Catalan, Middle High German, and so forth; and, secondly, most of the old recipes do not take their reader by the hand through the various processes.

Later on in this book, in Chapter 9, we will transcribe a small number of typical recipes from several national collections. The criteria guiding our somewhat capricious selection of these recipes have been those of Chapter 9 in general: to illustrate, on the one hand, instances of dishes that were common and 'universal' across Europe and, on the other, ways in which medieval food habits tended to differ slightly from place to place, to have developed regional particularities. We hope that your culinary curiosity will have been piqued by the time you reach Chapter 9. These extracts from several recipe collections may suggest grounds for experimentation to the verturesome modern cook. Almost without exception it is the different foods and the different preparations of the European Middle Ages that offer the most satisfying gastronomic rewards for the modern diner.

TWO

Similarities in Medieval Foods and Cooking

Foodstuffs

Generally

The foodstuffs that were brought into medieval European kitchens were neither identical in all respects to those with which a modern cook normally works nor totally different. Some, such as caviar, might surprise us because we think of this as somehow 'modern'; others, such as marijuana, though perhaps equally known to us, might surprise us for other reasons.[1] Some fruits and vegetables, some cuts of meat and some liquids would be quite familiar to cooks in either period. Once they arrived in either kitchen, then or now, they would be handled in very similar ways, too. In some cases, by flavour and texture alone a blind-folded time-traveller eating the dishes prepared from these foodstuffs would find it difficult to distinguish whether he or she were in the fourteenth or the twentieth century. These are the foodstuffs that seem to have enjoyed more or less universal popularity in the western world since the time that recipes were first written down in the Middle Ages.

Other foodstuffs, however, were used much more commonly in the earlier period than they are today. Certain of them were looked upon as staples to a much greater extent then than they would be by most cooks in our generation, or in our century. Some were in fact so commonly resorted to in the cookery of medieval Europe that they are largely responsible for giving that earlier cookery some of its unique qualities. We shall examine later the ways in which they imbue that cookery with its *cachet*.

On the whole the similarities between medieval and modern foods are more numerous and more fundamental than the ways in which we cook or eat differently from our forebears in the fourteenth and fifteenth centuries.

---

[1] Caviar is used, for instance, in Martino, Recipe 258 for *Per far el Caviaro di Storione* and in the Neapolitan Collection, Recipe 184 for a *Fritata de Caviaro*; hashish turns up in the Neapolitan Collection, Recipe 34 for *Senipa di canepa* which uses *Cannabis sativa*, a recipe which recurs in Martino, Recipe 95, and Platina, *De honesta voluptate*, Part VII, Recipe 49.

Yet dissimilarities clearly do exist: some are obvious, and can be understood or guessed at by reading an historic account of medieval cuisine. On the other hand, however, some differences are remarkably subtle, though nonetheless just as real, and even fundamental. Though many of these latter differences have to be experienced – their reality often exists most forcefully on the palate alone – we shall attempt to represent them in cold, rational prose in Chapter 4.

Specifically

By the end of the Middle Ages virtually all of the vegetables that we use were prepared and eaten. Even more recently accepted vegetables such as asparagus, carrots and parsnips became handled fairly regularly in the kitchens of the wealthy.[2] Fruits such as currants, quince and pomegranates were entirely common. On the basis of evidence presented in the wide range of documents referred to in the previous chapter, we can state with a fair amount of assurance that *in general* medieval vegetables and fruits were the same as modern vegetables and fruits. With certain exceptions in these food groups, people ate then what we eat now.

Meats, poultry and fish that are prepared for the table today were likewise routinely handled by late-medieval cooks. Nothing in these domains would surprise him, although he or she might be a little dismayed that we do not avail ourselves as much as he did of the broad diversity of fishes and crustaceans. While most foodstuffs tended to be seasonal, depending upon their maturity and harvests that were normally made of them, some meats and fish could be had throughout the year. When out of season these meats and fish were available to cooks only in a 'preserved' state – that is, either smoked, pickled in brine, set in gelatin, or much more commonly, salted and dried, or simply dried. Fruits and nuts could be candied in order to prolong their life as a food beyond the brief season in which they happened to ripen.

Chicken and chicken eggs were, then as now, vital staples. In part this was due to a perception that both of these foodstuffs were endowed with qualities that made them both nutritious and readily digestible. In part, too, their popularity derived from their ubiquitous availability, and hence their relative affordability. Every peasant's yard had these fowl, and the peddling of eggs and birds afforded many individuals the chance of a modest cash income. Undoubtedly many townspeople with even the smallest plot of land likewise raised a chicken or two. In the early cookbooks more recipes involve chicken than any other meat. And despite the difficulty of storing eggs over

---

[2] Concerning the tomato's sixteenth-century importation from the New World, see Rudolf Grewe, 'The Arrival of the Tomato in Spain and Italy: Early Recipes', *First International Food Congress*, ed. Feyzi Halici, Ankara (Kültür ve Turizm Bakanligi Yayini), 1988.

any length of time, the frequency of their occurence in early recipes points to a very active egg trade at the humbler levels of medieval commerce.

It is likely that domestic production – that is, the kitchen garden – was able to supply most of the common herbs that are called for in the cookbooks. Parsley and sage, easily grown virtually anywhere, were the primary cooking herbs; as well, bay (or laurel) leaves, sorrel, herb bennet, hyssop, basil, tansy, marjoram, rocket, rue, water and garden cress, dill, mint, spikenard, pennyroyal, even violets and rose petals were valued by medieval cooks for the variety of flavours and colours they could bring to their dishes and to liquids in which they were infused.

In much the same way, spices enjoyed high esteem in early kitchens. Some were in such common demand, for even standard preparations, that cooks kept supplies on hand, ready-ground if necessary in leather pouches, of perhaps a dozen of the most common. Spices and herbs were thought of generically as varieties of drugs. In larger households, those houses that were affluent enough to maintain the office of an apothecary or pharmacist, to that office was relegated all responsibility for the procurement, storage and dispensing of all drugs *and* spices, including sugar. A cook in such a house had to submit a requisition for any of these substances he would need, on a meal-by-meal basis, and provide the household comptroller with a strict regular accounting of their use.[3]

In large measure these spices, most varieties of which were imported by foreign merchants from distant, mysterious sources, were imbued with occult, barely fathomable properties. Medieval physicists were content to glean information about them wherever they could, reproducing even the most wondrous of 'facts' and embroidering on them with seeming fantasy. Even the most common spices, such as cinnamon, became encrusted over the years with a lot of folklore. 'Pliny speketh of canel [cinnamon] and seith that of canel and of cassia men tolde fables in old tyme, [that it] is yfounde in briddes nestes and specialliche in the fenix [phoenix] his nest, and may nought be yfounde but what falleth by his owne wight or is ysmyte down with leded arwes [arrows].'[4] It seems to have been believed for a time, if we in

---

[3] In 1416 an apothecary of Amadeus VIII of Savoy entered into his ledger an accounting for spices delivered to the Duke's cook, Chiquart. Specifically and explicitly these spices were destined for the elaboration of a lamprey sauce in the Duke's kitchens, in the *Du fait de cuisine*, Recipe 4. *Libravit Iohanni Belleni appothecario pro specibus suprascriptis ab eodem emptis pro dicta salsa lampree facienda et tradictis dicto magistri Chiquardo. Et primo pro una libra zinziberis albi, .I. flor. .VI. gross.; dimidia libra cinnamoni, .VI. den. gross.; uno quarterono grane paradisi, .III. den. obl. gross.; uno quarterono piperis, .II. den., .I. quart.; uno quarterono garioffilorum, .IIII. obl. gross. dimidio quarterono gallericorum, .IIII. den. obl. gross.* See Mara Castorina Battaglia, 'Notizie sui farmaci usati alla corte di Savoia dal 1300 al 1440,' *Minerva Medica*, 69 (1978), p.511, n.32. It may be noted in passing that the modern Italian word *droga* still has the sense of 'spice'.

[4] *Plinius . . . de cinnamomo inquit, et cassia, fabulose narravit antiquas, quod invenitur in nidis avium, et speciliter phoenicis, nec habeti potest, nisi quod cedit proprio pondere, vel quod*

turn believe Bartholomew the Englishman, that black pepper resulted from fire having scorched white pepper. The peppercorn was the fruit of a tree that grew on the south slope of the hill Caucasus; the peppertree forest seems to have been the wonted habitat of a breed of snakes that had to be driven away by fire in order for the pepper to be harvested. It was this fire that transformed white pepper into the wrinkled black variety. Such lore served to imbue spices generally with an aura of the exotic which made their use all the more tentative.[5]

Because most spices were indeed of distant origins, they were generally costly; cooks knew they could not be profligate in their use of spices. In the fourteenth century, and for some decades before, pepper was the king of spices. Supplies of pepper must always have been kept on hand and must have represented a serious investment in the account books of any household. The 'popularity' of pepper appears clearly to have waned toward the end of the fourteenth century, though, and to have been replaced by a new aromatic wave of preference as grains of paradise became the flavour in favour. But this exotic condiment, whose proper name is meleguetta pepper but which is more commonly, and universally, known as grains of paradise, is the only exception that we have to make in order to be able to say that the elements of medieval spicing are really not fundamentally different from those that we know and use quite normally today. Cinnamon and ginger are called for in many recipes; cloves, nutmeg (and mace), galingale, cumin, mustard seed, mastic, cardamom, cubeb, caraway and anise were usually within the cook's reach, ready to be ground up and to release their pungent or mellow zest. These remain the spices at hand in the modern kitchen.

Salt, too, served as a seasoning, in the same way as it does today. A considerable industry was devoted to evaporating salt from sea-water and shipping it to specialty shops in towns whence it was retailed. It is true that the demand for salt must have risen in the autumn each year as some households prepared tubs of a thick saline bath and undertook to preserve fresh meats for the coming winter, but its use in general cooking remained constant. After combining all other ingredients for a dish, a great many

---

exeutitur cum plumbatis sagittis. Bartholomæus Anglicus, *Liber de proprietatibus rerum,* Book 17, Chapter 26. The early English translation is by John Trevisa, *On the Properties of Things,* 2 vols., Oxford (Clarendon Press), 1975.

[5] In the thirteenth century the origin of even the more common foreign spices remained somewhat of a mystery, at least for those who were not involved directly in their commerce. In his biographic *Life of Saint Louis* (completed in 1309), Jean, Sire of Joinville and Seneschal of Champagne, could still write of the Nile that 'before this river enters Egypt, the people who usually do such work cast their nets of an evening into the water and let them lie outspread. When morning comes they find in their nets such things as are sold by weight and imported into Egypt, as for instance ginger, rhubarb, aloes and cinnamon. It is said that these things come from the earthly paradise . . .' *Joinville and Villehardouin, Chronicles of the Crusades,* trans. M.R.B. Shaw, Harmondsworth (Penguin Books), 1963, p.212.

recipes conclude with the simple, universally understood direction: 'Then salt to taste.'[6]

A word should be said about water, at least as it is used in cooking. Any kitchen, then and now, makes very great use of water. It is necessary for washing, of course, and for general cleaning, but also in cooking. Most of us today rarely give a second thought to this clean, pure liquid that moistens our dry ingredients into a paste, or that helps make a stock base or a stew, or that boils a pot roast. Water was just as commonplace an ingredient in medieval cookery but, unlike most of us, the medieval cook had to ask, 'What water?' He had a choice of sources for his water, and in reality the choice he made was literally vital. Time after time cookbook writers and physicians specify that for such and such a preparation the cook must use fountain water. The alternative was water drawn from a well or water scooped from a pond or lake, from a stream or river.

The problems inherent in water taken from an open source, whether a standing body of water or a running stream, were certainly recognized though not too well understood in the Middle Ages. The nature of the problems was simply polution. In an age when it was perfectly normal to wash clothes in the local pond, to dump animal offal into a nearby stream and to empty and rinse chamber pots there, people came soon to realize that it was better to avoid using that same water in the kitchen for purposes other than the ordinary cleansing of utensils and furnishings. Even when a town was blessed by having a site alongside a sizable fresh-water river, its citizens customarily availed themselves of their good fortune by using it to dispose of every sort of garbage. At the local castle some of the latrines almost invariably opened directly over that river; the ones that did not open directly onto the river usually helped fill the castle's moat, but naturally enough this moat had periodically to be flushed of its accumulated putrifying garbage, carrion and excrement – again, inevitably, into the river. A medieval river was much more a handy sewer than a source of potable water.

Wells, too, became suspect over time. Most wells were relatively shallow and, where inadequately sealed, were subject to ground seepage and surface infiltration. At the times of the great plagues that repeatedly swept over Europe throughout the Middle Ages, and particularly during the Black Death of the mid-1300s, rumours were rife that poisoned wells (presumably coincidentally and all the way right across Europe) were largely responsible for the infection. Undoubtedly in many cases leaching cesspools did contaminate well water, and some wells must in fact have caused serious inexplicable illness and death. In the midst of so much uncertainty about the

---

[6] A most interesting variant on this common directive is a phrase that regularly concludes recipes in one or two German collections: . . . *und versalcz ez nicht* – '. . . and do not salt it too much'. See, for example, the recipes edited by Alix Prentki in *Les traités culinaires du sud de l'Allemagne à la fin du moyen-âge*, Thesis, Paris, Ecole des Hautes Etudes en Sciences Sociales, 1985.

purity of water, careful cooks insisted that the only safe source was a spring or fountain. Where water rises fresh and cool out of the earth of its own accord, that water must be pure. For the medieval cook, of course, the problem was how to identify safe water; in 1256 the Sienese physician Aldobrandino offered practical advice in this matter.[7]

> Water which is good to use must be clear, tasteless, odourless and colourless, for it cannot have such qualities [of turbidity, taste, odour and colour] without having been contaminated by something . . . . You can tell which water is lighter and purer by this means: get two pieces of cotton or linen of the same weight, soak them in different waters, weigh them again and they should be equal in weight; then set them in the sun to dry, and the lighter one will have been soaked in the better water.

Just what the cook was to do who had no immediate access to such a spring on his master's estate is never explained, although Aldobrandino does approve of a stream (of water with the above qualities) that flows in an eastward direction at some length over a sandy bed. Physicians and cooks were clearly aware of the prime need to ensure that cooking water be clean.

In conclusion we can repeat the general observation we have already made, that foodstuffs five and six hundred years ago were much the same as are in common use today. There are some notable and important exceptions to this observation, and we shall come to them in the next chapters. But our conclusion here is sound, and important: today's cook would find few ingredients in medieval recipes with which he or she is unfamiliar. Medieval Europe of a dozen generations ago was no cultural backwater; those who were well enough off to afford both the services of a professional cook and the foodstuffs that this latter might want to use could enjoy carrots, brussels sprouts, squash, quince, oranges, lemons, pomegranates, deer, pheasant, perch, lobster, rice cakes, walnuts and a wide variety of cheeses. Many nobles did, and so too did an increasing number of affluent townspeople. The foods eaten in the Middle Ages hold few surprises for us, though the combinations of the foodstuffs and eventual dish preparations might. Furthermore, the basic methods by which these foods were cooked are still entirely familiar to all of us, though we might think reasons for using the various cooking methods a little strange.

---

[7] *Le régime du corps de maître Aldebrandin de Sienne*, ed. Louis Landouzy and Roger Pépin, Paris (Champion), 1911, pp.17–18.

Preparing and Cooking Foods

Preparations

The standard dishes that were habitually prepared in the late-medieval kitchen, borne into the dining hall and served to the privileged classes of the day were in many respects similar to those with which we are still familiar in the twentieth century. Any aristocrat or affluent bourgeois might sit down to a menu that was composed of a variety of roast meats (with a corresponding variety of sauces served in bowls separately), fried fish fillets (again with their appropriate sauces), stews of chunks of boiled meats or fish, sops (or soups) of bread and thickened meat- or fish-broths, pies of meat or fish, stewed vegetables, stewed fruits, poached eggs, porridges, biscuits, and so forth. Such preparations constituted the basic fare of a good board in late-medieval Europe.

The principle behind the preparation of a dish was that the diner had to be able to feed himself or herself from the prepared food means of (a) a knife and the knife's point, (b) a spoon, and (c) the fingers. What the fingers or knife-point could not manage, a spoon had to. This principle imposed few constraints upon the medieval cook, and would impose very few upon a modern cook. In fact, anyone from the fifteenth century who might be dining in a restaurant today would encounter few, if any, difficulties in consuming everything on the menu. He or she might complain about the limited variety offered by the restaurant, and perhaps a tendency toward blandness in the fare, but the restaurant's chef would probably not be faulted for presenting outlandish or unmanageable preparations.

As generic preparations these broths and pies and porridges sound quite recognizable to us. And in fact they are. No class of dish preparation which is common in medieval recipe collections has disappeared from the menu of any good neighbourhood restaurant nowadays. Very generally the elaboration of medieval dishes calls merely for adaptations of procedures and techniques that are within the ambit of the average modern cook. The real differences are appreciated as the medieval dishes are eaten!

Cooking

If, for whatever reason, you consider that a foodstuff is preferable in a cooked state, you can boil it, fry it, roast it or bake it. Or you can try a sequence of any of those four procedures. If you are a truly modern cook you can add pressure cooking and microwaving – although both of these are actually just varieties of boiling – to that gamut of choices. Cooking transforms a foodstuff chemically and physically by subjecting it to heat, and the four principal methods of applying heat to a foodstuff were devised very long before the

Middle Ages could be said to have begun. Essentially the choice for any cook is between a moist transmission of heat and a dry transmission of heat. For the first, naturally, you need a cooking medium: the most common such medium is water, but the use of an oil or any other liquid is certainly feasible; a pot or a pan holds both the foodstuff and the cooking medium and is placed over the heat. For the second, a dry type of cooking, there is no medium, or more correctly the heat is transmitted to the foodstuff through air: here the problem of 'container' is a little simpler, because it comes down to a question of determining the intensity of the heat that is most practical, given the foodstuff to be cooked. For the Middle Ages this in turn is partly a matter of location – the proximity of the foodstuff to the heat source.

All of this is commonsense knowledge, and such an abstract analysis as we have just indulged in does little to help us understand why, with his or her raw scallops in hand, a modern cook will almost instinctively choose one cooking method over another. The medieval cook had just as good a sense of the relative suitability of the various cooking methods for the final effect that he wanted. He could have recourse to exactly the same cooking methods – boiling, frying, roasting and baking – as the modern cook. Unlike his modern counterpart, however, he took another set of data into more or less conscious consideration. In the next chapter we shall see just how the medieval understanding of the physical nature and composition of all foodstuffs – and of those of human beings as well – had a profound influence upon what was done in the kitchens of the fourteenth and fifteenth centuries.

Breads, Biscuits and Pastries

We saw above, in the anonymous *Parisian Journal*, how much the uncertain availability and cost of bread preoccupied Parisians of the beginning of the fifteenth century. In England in the thirteenth century the fluctuating price of bread caused such anxiety and hardship, particularly among the poorer elements of the population, that efforts were made to regulate this price closely. The Assize of Bread and Ale of 1266 fixed the price of a loaf in extensive tables that related weight and allowable price to the cost of wheat. So attentively monitored was the baker's profit that 'in 1303 an allowance of ½d was added [to the allowable net profit] to cover the costs of a dog, and later the London Bakers' Company successfully lobbied for the allowance to cover not only wood, candles, journeymen and apprentices, salt, yeast, and the millers' charges, but also the costs of the baker's house, a cat and even a wife.'[8]

---

[8] W. Duncan Reekie, *Give Us This Day* . . . (Hobart Paper 79), London (Institute of Economic Affairs), 1978, pp.24–25.

Bread was the absolute food staple, for all classes in society. Other foods – cabbage for brewets, beans for purees, raw apples, the meat from small game – could be eaten along with the bread if those other things were available, but even when they were, even on the tables of the wealthiest potentates of all of Europe, a round loaf of bread was also present for eating as well. Rather the difference between the poor and the wealthy in the matter of bread was in its quality.[9]

During the Middle Ages a wide range of cereal grains was ground into flour, kneeded with a liquid, with or without a yeast to lighten the dough by fermentation, allowed to rise and finally baked into bread. Some of these grains, such as wheat, millet and barley (which yielded a coarse bread), could be used alone; some, such as oats, produced such a dense bread as to be practical normally only in a mixture with rye and wheat. *Meslin* or *maslin* (the French *metail*) was a common bread-grain mixture, especially of wheat and rye. Even the generic term 'wheat' encompassed several varieties of grain including spelt, a valued hard wheat. Other substances than the familiar cereal grains were on occasion ground and used by themselves or in mixtures to make a bread: rice, peas, beans, vetches, lentils, chestnuts, acorns, various ferns and so forth. The recognized standard of excellence among breads, however, the bread traditionally ranked as best by physicians, and prized above all on the medieval dining board as finest *paindemayne* ('hand-bread' or table-bread), was a pure white, leavened bread made from the flower of flour of wheat, alone.

Recent historians have found enough data to let them estimate the usual consumption of bread in the late Middle Ages, and their figures for various countries are surprisingly similar. In lordly English households at this time, for instance, a standard daily food ration allowed every individual between roughly two and three pounds of wheat bread and about a gallon of ale.[10] Interestingly, the same allowance applied in the provisioning of castle

---

[9] A number of studies in recent years may usefully be consulted about medieval breads. Heinrich Eduard Jacob, *Six Thousand Years of Bread*, Garden City (Doubleday), 1944; Françoise Desportes, *Le pain au moyen âge*, Paris (Olivier Orban), 1987; Robert Delort, 'L'aliment-roi: le pain', *L'Histoire*, 85 (1986), pp.96–102. Félix Lecoy briefly sets out the weights and costs of different types of French breads in 'Pain bourgeois, pain faitiz, pain de retrait', *Mélanges A. Lombard*, Lund, 1969; repr. in *Critique et philologie* (*Le Moyen Français*, Vol. 12), Montréal (CERES), 1984, pp.129–34. Philippe Wolff studied the medieval grain trade, especially in Mediterranean Spain: 'Un grand commerce médiéval: les céréales dans le bassin de la Méditerranée occidentale', *VI Congreso de Historia de la Corona de Aragon*, Madrid (1959), pp.147–64.

[10] Christopher Dyer, 'English Diet in the Later Middle Ages', in T.H. Aston, P.R. Cross, Christopher Dyer and Joan Thirsk, *Social Relations and Ideas*, Cambridge (Cambridge University Press), 1983, pp.192–93. The same figures hold for the lower clergy as well. In another study the author translates these English quantities into metric measures: 1–1.3 kg of bread and 4.5 litres of beer: 'Les régimes alimentaires en Angleterre, XIIIe–XVe siècles', *Manger et boire au moyen âge*, Paris (Les Belles Lettres), 1984; II, pp.263–74.

garrisons and for inmates in hospitals. In France for each of the 3500 residents of Chambéry the amount of wheat that entered the town – to be consumed ultimately and mainly, we have to assume, in the form of bread – was 24 litres per month, that is to say approximately .8 litres of wheat (enough for a two-pound loaf of bread) per citizen per day.[11] Florentines of the fourteenth century likewise averaged about two pounds of bread per day.[12] Françoise Desportes[13] has found that even by the beginning of the thirteenth century Paris had seventy water mills alone, without counting the windmills sited on the summits of its hills! Such figures as these support the observation that bread was the basis of the medieval diet.

Generally speaking the making of bread was a commercial enterprise in late-medieval towns. That is to say, bread was not normally baked in aristocratic or bourgeois kitchens. Often enough both the mill in which the grain was ground into flour and the bakery itself were owned by the lord of the territory himself or by the municipality. The output from this bakery would likely satisfy the demand of the owners and the immediate neighbourhood. Where a bakery was an independent exercise in free enterprise, the operational rules were very clear. The history of bakers' guilds, and the numerous, unending regulations by which their trade was regulated, are well documented. The grave official concern of municipalities about the size, quality and price of bread reflects the paramount importance of this staple in the daily diet of their citizens.

Apart from their use in breads, cereal grains could be boiled into porridges and consumed after having been roasted and perhaps only partially ground into flour. Kasha, normally made from rye or buckwheat, remains a modern variety of such porridges. While recipes for these gruels and porridges do occasionally turn up in manuscript collections they are extremely rare, for the simple reason that no detailed recipe for boiling a cereal grain is really necessary. Chiquart does write out directions for making a fairly straightforward barley broth (On Cookery, 78: Orjat) with almonds and sugar, but only because it is to be included in his section of dishes appropriate for the sick.

Oats have a culinary use particularly in England – although even there only in three recipe collections.[14] Elsewhere cooks have recourse to oats only

---

[11] Réjane Brondy, *Histoire d'une capitale vers 1350–1560*, Lyon and Paris (Presses Universitaires de Lyon and Centre National de Recherche Scientifique), 1988. Chambéry was at this time the seat of government of Savoy.

[12] E. Fiume, 'Economia e vita privata dei Fiorentini nelle rilevazioni statistiche di Giovanni Villani', *Archivio Storico Italiano*, 111 (1953), p.208.

[13] *Op. cit.*

[14] In the *Diversa servicia*, Recipes 11, for a *cullis*, and 49, to remove excess salt from a dish – a process for which the German Eberhard (Recipe 19) recommends *Furmenty*; in the *Cure cocorum*, Recipes 27, for an almond gruel, 42, again a *cullis*, and 133, in a rayfish preparation; and in *Stere Hit Well. A book of medieval refinements, recipes and remedies from a manuscript in Samuel Pepys's library*, ed. A.J. Hodgett, Cambridge (Cornmarket Reprints), 1972, Recipes 15, for black pudding, and 19, for Buttered Worts.

to prepare a sick-dish that generally is known as *Avenast, Avenat* and *Avend*.[15] Outside of England the use of oats in everyday cookery is very limited: Chiquart has a *Gruel Broth for Capons* (59) that calls for oats. And the Latin *Liber de coquina* distinguishes between two varieties of potherb preparations: one which the author qualifies as being 'in the English fashion', with sliced apples and oat flour (I, 9); the other 'in the French fashion', with white chicken meat and oat flour (I, 9).

Of all the boiled cereal dishes the most common is undoubtedly the universally known *Furmenty*. This is merely a plain, thick wheat porridge – although some modifications are possible – and is described in English (*Forme of Cury*, the first recipe in the whole collection), French *On Cookery*, 6), and Italian (*Anonimo meridionale*, 'A', 22) collections. What is peculiar about this dish is that it is frequently paired for serving with another preparation, whether venison (stag or salt boar, as in the *Menagier*, 91) on meat days or porpoise (as in the *Forme of Cury*, 70 and 119) on fish days.

A surprising assortment of wafers were available, commercially, across Europe at this time. Known variously as *cialdone, nevole, nelles, neules, lozanges, oublies, hosties, waifurs, wafron* and *wastels*, they have some limited use in the kitchen, mostly in layers as an alternative means of forming the lower or upper crust in a pie.[16] Biscuits likewise are baked commercially, but little used in cookery itself. The biscuit, its name literally describing it, resulted from a double baking (*cuit bis*) of a wafer, small cake or thin loaf of bread; being doubly dried, it was intended to be durable, to remain edible over several months.

Pastry was made within a noble or bourgeois household to the extent that the kitchen had need of crusts for turnovers or pies. In the most affluent households a distinct kitchen division, under the immediate direction of a pastry chef, was responsible solely for preparing this pastry and for making it up into the sort of pie shell required by the cook. Late-medieval recipes distinguish between two genres of pastry, a richer variety with eggs in it and the run-of-the-mill variety compounded merely of flour, salt and water. Colourants, particularly saffron, could be added, as could sugar or rose-water.

Conclusion

By the end of the Middle Ages, those who possessed the means – the relatively affluent bourgeoisie of which there were increasing numbers, virtually all of the aristocracy and upper hierarchy of the clergy – could manage to eat very well. Even the middle classes in German states at this

---

[15] See the *On Cookery*, 75; *Sent sovi*, 99; Mestre Robert, *Libre del coch*, 119; *Anonimo meridionale*, 'A', 112; *Tractatus*, II, 20 and IV, 9.

[16] See, for instance, the *Libro de arte coquinario* of Maestro Martino, Recipe 146.

time seemed to have been guaranteed enough to eat: an ordinance promulgated by the Dukes of Saxony in 1482 declares,

> Let it be understood by all that the craftsmen must receive a total of four courses at their midday and evening meals; on a meat day: one of soup, two of meat, one of vegetables; for a Friday or a meatless day: one of soup, one of fresh or salted fish and two of vegetables. If the fast has to be extended, five courses: one of soup, two sorts of fish and two vegetables. And in addition, bread, morning and night.[17]

After examining a variety of evidence bearing upon the availability and relative cost of food and the consumption of meats, Fernand Braudel concludes very cautiously that 'from 1350 to 1550 Europe probably experienced a favourable period as far as *individual* living standards were concerned'.[18]

One of the criteria necessary in order to develop taste (of any sort in any field) is the possibility of choice. For the most part diners in these classes at this time were indeed able to choose what they wished to eat and to enjoy what they liked to eat. The period could boast a true gastronomy.

When late-medieval cooks placed their orders for foodstuffs, the raw materials of the dishes upon which they intended to work would be almost entirely familiar to us. There would be little to surprise us in these orders. And, furthermore, if we were to look into a medieval kitchen we would see that really there was nothing 'foreign' about the various cooking processes that these foodstuffs normally underwent. Were we to sit at a medieval table and a server bring in and set out actual dishes for us to eat, we would find that, perhaps even more remarkably, we would be able to recognize, at least in a generic sense, a good number of these preparations. Yet when the time came that we actually cut into a *Letelorye* or dipped our spoon into a *Souppe jacobine de chappons* we would realize that a dish that may look familiar on the surface can actually contain quite exceptional pleasures.

The following chapters will try to show why medieval cookery really *is* different.

---

[17] A generous ration of beer was likewise stipulated. Wilhelm Abel, 'Wandlungen des Fleischverbrauchs und der Fleischversorgung in Deutschland seit dem ausgehenden Mittelalter', *Berichte über Landwirtschaft*, 22 (1937), p.415, as translated in Fernand Braudel, *Civilization and Capitalism 15th–18th Century*, 3 vols., London (Collins), 1981; I, p.192.

[18] *Op. cit.*, p.193.

THREE

The Theoretical Bases
for Medieval Food and Cookery

Generally

Through his kitchen door the cook received foodstuffs that in most cases were identical to what we pick, gather or buy today. He subjected them to a set of operations quite similar to those to which a modern cook might have recourse. He cooked them in ways generally familiar to any experienced modern cook – and that would be entirely familiar to any modern cook without access to electricity or gas. He served them up as dishes that were prepared, for the most part, in ways that his modern counterpart would certainly recognize even if he or she might not normally choose to use them.

There are, of course, certain exceptions: some of the foodstuffs that we know today and in a few instances have come to depend upon as staples are completely absent from the medieval menu, and unknown in the medieval kitchen. The are also certain preferences which the medieval palate demonstrates for particular flavours and textures or colours, preferences that have with the centuries passed out of common favour.

That medieval cookery is not entirely the same as modern European or North American cookery is not owing entirely to a change in available foodstuffs, or simply to a change in what technology lets us do to the foodstuffs we now have at our disposal. A very important difference between medieval and modern food and cookery derives as well from quite fundamental differences in the area of ideas *about* food.

It is a commonplace to hesitate to say whether the cook exercises an art or a craft. Does cookery belong to those activities where a sense of what is needed in a given gastronomic context is more important than knowledge of those rules of nature by which the inevitable is defined. The Savoyard cook of whom we have spoken, Chiquart, did not hesitate when he came to classifying his work: he wrote to his master, the Duke, that, as the Duke's Chief Cook, he exercised *both* an art *and* a science.[1] When faced with the

[1] He modestly protests to the Duke that, as his Chief Cook, he is unable adequately to

professional obligation to produce a satisfying meal consisting of a number of appetizing dishes, the medieval cook's decisions and choices – ingredients, preparations, cooking methods, garnishes, combinations of dishes, and so forth – frequently involved considerations that went beyond any transient, personal notions of culinary 'art'. Unlike his modern counterpart, he had to weigh another set of data more or less consciously. This data was felt to possess such absolute, objective accuracy that today we would have little hesitation in qualifying it as 'scientific'. It had to do with theories about the fundamental nature of the ingredients the cook was handling, and particularly about the four essential qualities of all foodstuffs. In short the cook had to know what was good or bad to eat, and how to go about making dangerous foods safer.

Different Concepts and Attitudes

Since the time of the Greek physician Galen, and probably before, there existed a concept of the nature of universal concrete reality, a concept that posited that all existing things were composed of a combination of two pairs of elements, warmth and cold on the one hand, and dryness and moistness on the other. These four elements, combined and in infinitely variable amounts, accounted for the 'temperament' that was, in theory, unique to every single species of thing in the world. This was the theory of the four humours.

In humans the humoural or temperamental agents were blood, choler, phlegm and melancholy. The sanguine temperament combines warmth and moistness, and is the essence of the air; the choleric, or bilious, temperament results from a mixture of warmth and dryness, and is realized by fire; phlegmatic persons are both cold and moist, as is water; and the melancholic temperament mixes coldness with dryness, the qualities of earth. Medieval scientific systems were encyclopedic and aimed to do nothing if not account for the totality of existence, both the basic elements of life and absolutely all of the circumstances that affect it. And so in order to understand a human being, we must begin, along with medieval thinkers, by weighing the relative influence upon him of each of the four elements: earth, air, water and fire. The first three of these provided the source of man's food, and determined its essential qualities; the last element, fire, was the determinant factor in modifying the temperament of the foodstuffs, by cooking, in order to make them suitable and safe for human consumption.

fulfil the Duke's command that he compile an exemplary cookery book: '. . . mesmement . . ., comme vous dictes et affermiés, que je soye instruict et suffisant en celle science et art . . . .' The preamble of the On Cookery: Du fait de cuisine, folio 11v.

This elemental theory of humoural temperament became much elaborated in the Middle Ages, particularly as physicians (properly, scholars whom we might be tempted to call physicists) saw in it a rational means to define human temperament and health, and any modifications to which these states might become subject.[2] If all things have their own peculiar temperament, then all foodstuffs certainly must have, too; and the influence of the temperament of everything in a person's environment and of everything that he or she consumes, is logically bound to influence his or her own personal temperament. Everything, consequently and quite logically, becomes a question of mixtures, of how the combining of different things with different temperaments produces a change, in things or in a person. As far as a person is concerned, that change, accidental or deliberate, may be either harmful or beneficial.

For the medieval physician the principle of humours and the modification of temperaments was fundamental in identifying disease and in treating it. Wealthy householders put a lot of faith in the vigilence of full-time doctors whose function was to ensure that the respective tempers of their employers and family remained stable. Nowhere was the learned knowledge of the household doctor more important that at the dining board. The late-fourteenth-century English cookery book, the *Forme of Cury*, indicates that this collection of recipes was 'compiled by assent and avyssement of maistres of phisik and of philosophie' who were attached to the court of Richard II.[3] A vital aspect of the responsibilities of the six physicians who enjoyed appointment to the court of the Duke of Burgundy bore upon the Duke's food. Their presence, singly or together, was required behind the Duke when he was at table in order that they might examine each dish presented to him and to advise him on its suitablility for his continued good health.[4]

An indication of the close logical rapport between medicine and food in the late Middle Ages is offered by the juxtaposition in several manuscripts of medical treatises and collections of food recipes. In some instances it appears

[2] For a good review of these concepts see Per-Gunnar Ottoson, *Scholastic Medicine and Philosophy. A Study of Commentaries on Galen's* Tegni (ca. 1300–1450), Naples (Bibliopolis), 1984; especially Chapter 3, 'The Conceptions of Health and Disease,' pp.127–194.

[3] Richard Warner, ed., *Antiquitates Culinariæ: Curious Tracts on Culinary Affairs of the Old English*, London (R. Blamire), 1791; repr. London (Prospect Books), n.d.; p.1. 'One of the duties of Edward IV's physician was to "stond muche in the kynges presence at his meles, councellyng his grace whyche dyet is best." Besides consulting with the steward and master cook as to the day's menu, the royal physician would also sit at the king's table to see that he ate nothing harmful to his health'. Colin Clair, *Kitchen and Table*, London, New York, Toronto (Abelard-Schuman), 1964, p.63.

[4] Charles Commeaux, *La vie quotidienne en Bourgogne au temps des ducs Valois (1364–1477)*, Paris (Hachette), 1979, p.215; Commeaux refers to the first-hand evidence of Olivier de la Marche, *Mémoires*, ed. cit. Together with these six physicians there were a further *four* surgeons whose responsibilities covered the whole of the Duke's household.

that the person who ordered the compilation of a manuscript, or the copy of one, whether this person was a physician or an aristocrat, saw no reason to distinguish between culinary and medical materials. It must have seemed appropriate that anyone concerned about health and well-being be able to consult either a medical treatise or a recipe collection, both of which embodied the respected principles of sound health. When, probably in the 1330s, a Milanese physician called Maino de' Maineri composed a health handbook and dedicated it to his master the Bishop of Arras in France, Andrea of Florence, he devoted a good proportion of its pages to analyses of the physical properties of all foodstuffs.[5] In Part 3 of this work, Chapters 10 to 21 consist of a thorough survey of everything a person of the time was apt to eat, from cereal grains, through leafy vegetables, fruits, roots, mushrooms, meats, fish, animal products (milk, cheese and eggs), herb and spice mixtures (that is, sauces and condiments), and beverages. An Italian physician, graduate of the University of Paris, attached to a potentate's court in a cosmopolitan milieu, Maino was familiar with the best thinking of his time about health. As he compiled his *Regimen sanitatis* he was content to follow the general lines of many other such learned handbooks of his own and previous generations, though his treatment of foodstuffs may be a little more detailed than in other similar works. What remains highly significant is that food was always a central element in the thinking of medieval physicians.

The practical involvement of medical practitioners in food preparation was well established and continued into at least the fifteenth century. Another Italian physician who, unfortunately, signs himself merely 'N., a doctor of Assisi', was responsible for a collection of 141 culinary recipes in Latin, recipes he seems to have gleaned from several venerable traditions in his homeland but which he undoubtedly was proposing to his reader as composites of a good, healthy, *safe* regimen.[6] As with the health handbooks themselves, the purpose of this recipe collection, according to its physician-author, was 'to maintain the body in health and in good appetite and relish

---

[5] *Regimen sanitatis Magnini Mediolanensis medici famosissimi Attrebatensi Episcopo directum*, Louvain (Johannes de Westfalia), 1482. One portion of this work, Chapter 20, *De saporibus et condimentis* seems to have known a life of its own in the late Middle Ages under the title *Opusculum de saporibus* and warranted the modern edition that Lynn Thorndike gave it in 'A Mediæval Sauce-Book', *Speculum*, 9 (1934), pp.183–190. For a study of the theory underlying each of these specific sauces, see Terence Scully, 'The *Opusculum de saporibus* of Magninus Mediolanensis', in *Medium Ævum*, 54 (1985), pp.178–207.

[6] In the preamble to this unpublished collection, now held in the Municipal Library at Châlons-sur-Marne (MS 319), the author has his scribe write that the book was *compositus et scriptus per me, N., medicum de Assissio*. The sense of the word *scriptus* is debatable. At the conclusion of the manuscript the scribe signs his own name - a highly exceptional procedure: *per me, Reimboldus Filinger de Argentina*; and he dates the conclusion of that particular copy: the 18th day of December, 1481.

in accord with the proper times for all foods as required of all the faithful
. . .'.

Considerations about food had a consecrated place in the total review of
the factors in man's health. The medieval physician was concerned about
the seasons, air, sleep, bathing, exercise, coitus, blood-letting, purgation and
vomiting, as well as with normal anatomy and body organs, and finally with
the pathology, diagnosis and therapy of diseases. In the medical idiom a
regimen was a term of broad application and designated the circumstances of
human existence. It may be because of the medieval insistence upon the role
of food among these circumstances that the term has now come largely to
refer primarily to diet. In large measure the medieval physician was
attempting to do the work of a modern nutritionist.

The humoural principles certainly held in cookery as everywhere. For
instance, theories distinguished different humoural effects wrought by
different cooking procedures. Roasting – since the food sits directly over a
flame – dries a food as it warms it. Boiling warms a food, though not as
intensely as does roasting, but it also adds moisture to the food because of the
liquid cooking medium. Baking warms moderately, but dries only moderately
as well. When he chose a cooking method, the medieval cook had to be
conscious of the consequences of his choice, not solely in a gastronomic
sense but in a physical sense as well. His choice of cooking method was
determined primarily by the necessity of 'correcting', or 'amending' as much
as possible, the natural humour of a foodstuff that might potentially be
harmful to the person consuming it. Beef, being perceived as a relatively dry
meat, should always be boiled[7] (and never roasted); pork, as moist as beef is
dry, should always be roasted; fish, somewhat cool and moist (as is the
temperament of the element in which they live), generally are fried, at least
as a first step in their preparation.

Certain foods possess qualities whose excessive degrees of coldness or
dryness, or whatever, make them actually dangerous for human consumption
unless they are subjected to extreme countermeasures: the lamprey is a
curious case in point, perhaps because eels as a species were highly valued by
the gourmets of the time. A difficulty arises in that the lamprey was defined
as cold and moist in the second degree. It was felt that the logical strategy to
adopt in order to combat this markedly phlegmatic temperament of the
lamprey had to begin from the moment any lamprey was killed: a practice
was consequently long-established of killing lamprey by submerging it in
wine, so that this warm and dry liquid (both warm and dry in the second
degree) could infiltrate into all of the parts of the lamprey and begin
immediately the necessary process of tempering its undesirable qualities.[8]

---

[7] As a practical and very useful consequence, beef bouillon seems to be ubiquitously
available in medieval kitchens for use in moistening dry ingredients and as the base for
a sauce.

[8] See, for instance, the recipe for lamprey at folio 76r of the Neapolitan cookbook.

The physician Maino de' Maineri furthermore warns his readers quite clearly about the hazards posed by the lamprey: 'With all due respect to those who are habitués of [the lamprey], this fish is very dangerous, even though it is tasty in the mouth. It is analogous in water to the snake on earth, and so it is to be feared that it may be venomous. . . . And so because of its viscosity it is good that it be immersed alive in the best wine and remain there until dead, then prepared with a galentine made with the best spices, just as the cooks of the great lords are knowledgeable about how to make. I recommend, further, that it first be parboiled twice in wine and water and then thoroughly cooked. . . .'[9] Subsequent treatments of a dead lamprey almost invariably involved a hot and dry roasting at some stage, and the admixture of warm and dry herbs or spices.

For much the same reasons it is recommended that eels be killed by burying them in salt.[10]

The pastry shell of a pie protects the moisture of those foods that had only moderately moist temperaments (meats such as veal, poultry and certain wildfowl) from the dessication of a long exposure to the drying heat of an oven. The food's natural moisture would be further safeguarded if lard as well was cut into the pie, as was normally the procedure in cases of such meats. Only rarely can a pie be made with a meat which is by its nature quite dry: for his recipe for Beef Pasties (Recipe 4) Chiquart expressly stipulates the use of *fat* loins of beef (*lomblos de beuff d'aute gresse*).

Most vegetables, whether leaves or roots, were chopped, ground and cooked by boiling. The logic of this cooking method lay in the tendency of vegetables, being products of the earth, to be dry in their nature;[11] the action of stewing vegetables lent them the moisture they lacked by their nature. Members of the onion family, however, being moist in the third, and even fourth – or most dangerous (even mortal) – degree, were usually fried, thus removing a little of their superfluous moisture.

Because the moisture 'content' of fruits such as apples, apricots, cherries, dates, grapes, melons, peaches, pears, plums and pumpkins is rated at 2 (high) or 3 (extreme), it was normal to use them as food only if they had been roast or baked, or combined with ingredients whose dry nature could overcome some of the excess humidity of those fruits. An instance of the latter procedure can be seen in the Neapolitan collection where an interesting recipe for fried beans (*Fava in padella*) calls for figs and apples to be mixed with the very dry herbs chervil, sage, mint and parsley before being wrapped into a bean fritter.

The principles governing a cook's choice of cooking method for his foodstuff were well understood in the late Middle Ages. Supposing he were

---

[9] *Regimen sanitatis*, Ch. 18, 'On Fish'.

[10] See the *Menagier de Paris*, Recipe 26.

[11] The exceptions here were the marrows and melons, and chard, all three of which were held to be rather moist.

not simply following a recipe he had learned as a very young apprentice, a cook could make that choice of cooking method for any foodstuff with relative ease, in large measure because he was quite familiar with conventional thinking about the humoural nature of every single foodstuff that was likely to pass through his hands.

We may think that this conventional thinking of five and six hundred years ago is sufficiently different, alien, even weird, that we are justified in being rather wary of its practical effects on medieval cooking. Why should we make any effort to appreciate, let alone recreate, dishes from this period when the purely rational theories that contributed to producing them have so little to do with our modern scientific understanding of what happens to lamb or mutton when someone boils it – a medieval cook might say, if anyone were *foolish enough* even to consider boiling it. We might think rather that the finished dish, its texture, certainly its flavour, its appearance perhaps, was more important in deciding cooking method than some dubious theory about undemonstrable 'qualities'. Humours, good and bad, are what cooks have, not the ingredients they use.

Good, Bad and Moderated

Theories of what is Good/Bad, Beneficial/Harmful

We have outlined the long-standing ancient and medieval ideas about the properties of all physical matter, ideas that constitute what is known very generally as humoural theory. It is enough to understand that human beings, too, had a specific humoural nature, that nature being a delicate blend of slightly warm and slightly moist qualities. Of course an individual might have a peculiar temperament that differed slightly from the norm; this personal temperament or complexion – sanguine, choleric, phlegmatic or melancholic – resulted from a singlar, 'abnormal' proclivity in a person toward moistness or dryness, warmth or coolness. But the mean nature for all human beings, the base mark from which most sickness was measured and therefore termed an abnormality or ill temper, was slightly warm and slightly moist.

It followed with absolute logic that the most useful, safest foods any person could eat were those whose nature most closely resembled that of the person in his normal healthy state. And so the health handbooks and physician's guides of the Middle Ages usually set out a list of *preferred* foods, invariably those that were considered to have natures ideally suited to the normal human temperament and that therefore offered no dangerously excessive properties in the sense of moistness, dryness, warmth or coolness. The fourteenth-century *Regimen sanitatis* or Health Guide of Maino de' Maineri exemplifies a good compendium of the thinking about foodstuffs in the late

Middle Ages.[12] Divided into chapers according to the standard categories of foods, the book's Part Three opens with an explicit statement that our health is necessarily determined by our exposure to one or another of the four elements that compose all things in the world. Consequently, we are, in effect, what we eat; the idea seems to be as old as the hills. Then there follow the succession of chapters on the various food groups.

In most of these chapters on food and drink Maino is at pains to rank the foodstuffs whose qualities he describes, declaring their relative 'desirability' for human sustenance. Among the meats he says that goat kid is entirely praiseworthy,[13] as is veal, but limits his stamp of approval for pork to those pigs that are between one and two years of age, adding that one should in any case prefer *wild* pig (that is, wild boar) over its domestic counterpart.

These last distinctions, between young and old animals and between domestic and wild meats, were well recognized by anyone at this time who attempted to analyse physical properties or who laboured under the onerous responsibility of choosing and preparing food for an important lord. The porcine species is cool and moist by nature, but the young of any creature tends to be even more moist than the adult. For this reason one should prefer pork that has had time to dry slightly with age – but not with too much age, because (a further general principle) the old of any species become by nature progressively more dry. Merely by looking at many of their elders, the youth of the Middle Ages could, of course, vouch for the obvious evidence of this simple principle. A similar exercise of logic leads to a similar incontrovertible conclusion about game animals: wild animals get more exercise and are more exposed to the sun, therefore their natures tend generally to be warmer and drier than those of their domestic counterparts; as a consequence, given the cool nature of the swine species, wild pig is in this respect preferable to domestic pig as source of human food. Contrarily, stagmeat frequently is larded for cooking in order to enhance its meager moisture content.

A common, generic preparation, with many variations, is the *larded-boiled* dish; the name describes the preparation and cooking procedure. The meat that is so prepared is usually veal or venison (deer or stag). Hare and rabbit, their flesh tending to aridity, lend themselves likewise to a similar treatment. Depending upon the nature of a specific meat, an initial larded-boiling could be followed up with a dessicating roasting.

And so on. Because of the moderate warmth and moderate moistness of their species, chickens and chicks are recommended as food, but capons only

[12] This fascinating Latin text, mentioned earlier, is unfortunately still available only in fifteenth- or sixteenth-century editions.

[13] Learned opinion continues to approve of kid throughout the Middle Ages. Of all of the members of the goat family, kid alone is normally eaten at aristocratic tables. Platina praises kid meat above all other meats of domestic animals. Platina (*alias*, Bartolomeo Sacchi, 1421–1481), *De honesta voluptate et valitudine* (c.1450), Book IV, Chapter 24, ed. Mary Ella Milham.

if they are young; if old, capons must be fat.[14] The last bit of reasoning here is again entirely logical: females are universally more moist than males of the same species; by castrating a rooster, for instance, that drying process that always sets in from youth onwards is mitigated, even to the extent that an older capon is acceptable only provided it is plump – that is, if it retains the moisture inherent in the fat of its flesh. Repeatedly, we find that recipes direct the cook to begin a dish by selecting *fat* pullets and capons.[15] In a similar way, for any young animal of naturally moist flesh, castration will tend to maintain that moistness of youth and will be desirable if otherwise, with age and because it is male, its meat will become too dry to be healthful. The castrated male sheep (a wether), for instance, is a valued source of food. And the moreso with the young of the species: 'The meat of these [castrated] male lambs is healthful and better than female lamb, for it is considered warm and moist, tending toward a balance but having the property of more moistness than dryness. Do not set your teeth into ram, for its meat is not good and is even really very bad.'[16]

Wildfowl tend to be warm but, unfortunately, slightly too dry, partaking as they do of the nature of the element in which they live, the air. However, Maino makes it clear that within the general class of 'fowl' a wide variety of temperaments are found, and of this variability the cook should be fully conscious: 'Some fowl,' he writes, 'are of a temperate complexion, whereas others are removed from the temperate [*distemperate*].'[17] Because most wildfowl escaped constant daily observation, a lot of folklore grew up about various species. At a place in Asia, for instance, storks 'congregate and murmur among themselves and tear to pieces the last one to arrive'; 'swans predict their own deaths with a mournful song'; 'when her mate is lost, a female turtle-dove does not touch a green tree in flight'; 'the food most pleasing to quail is the seed of poisonous plants'; the female partridge 'has so much lust that it can even conceive from the smell alone of the male, or from hearing his voice.'[18] Among these wildfowl, after pheasant the best and most preferable are, naturally, waterfowl such as ducks. When Chiquart refers to a Latin couplet, which he probably learned as a young kitchen apprentice, on the methods appropriate for the cooking of wildfowl, he considers this to be the expression of a long-established culinary law.

---

[14] Chiquart's large *Pasté coquart* (Recipe 41) calls for a section of the pie to be filled with *chappons de pallier gras*: 'fat grain-fed capons'.

[15] Even in the sixth-century letter of Anthimus, *De observatio ciborum* (Chapter XXIII), we find an assimilation of hens with fat pullets (*pullus pinguioris*) and that the author recommends this variety of meat: 'These nourish the better humours and good blood'. Ed. Shirley Howard Weber, Leiden (E.J. Brill), 1924, pp.21–22.

[16] Platina, *De honesta voluptate*, IV, 23.

[17] *Regimen sanitatis*, Chapter 17. In part these differences in 'complexion' spring from the different habitats of fowl, some living sheltered lives in domestic pens, some being forest creatures, and others waterfowl.

[18] Platina, *De honesta voluptate*, V, 5, 6, 9, 13 and 14 respectively.

Si volucris verrat, qui torret eam, procul errat;
Sed procul ab igne volucrem de flumine torre.[19]

Chiquart and his professional fraternity had access to a broad range of authoritative knowledge which might be classified under the general rubic of 'natural science'. Much of this knowledge had to have a direct bearing upon good cookery.

Fish demand great care in preparation for the table because, like their element, water, they are by nature both quite moist and cold. Of fish the best are what Maino de' Maineri qualifies as 'bestial' fish, that is, apparently, those most resembling land animals in their qualities: porpoise, shark, dolphin, cod. Following these, his ranked order of fish examines and analyses red mullet, gurnard, plaice, sole and whiting. Salmon, turbot, mackerel and conger appear much further down the preferred list, among species not to be recommended (*even* for robust, active young men, the author says) because of their superfluous viscosity (that is, their excessive moistness).

Melons, pumpkins and cucumbers are in themselves dangerous to eat, being so cold and moist that they are difficult to digest; they tend rather to putrify in the stomach and generate chronic fevers. Raw pears are occasionally condemned outrightly by medical authorities as tantamount to poisonous; even prudently cooked, they should still be eaten with wine, itself warm by nature.

Animal milk is good: its properties are identical to those of the human body. But almond milk shares the same properties, and so is equally desirable – as well as being much longer lasting. New cheese is cold and moist: care should be taken in is use. Old cheese is warmer but dry (in part because of the salt added to it, Maino points out): it should likewise be avoided. The conclusion: prefer a medium-aged cheese. And so on; Maino follows the general outline of most of the health handbooks of the time and evaluates a long list of possible condiments and beverages.

All of this doctrine was an integral part of medieval cookery. Everything that entered the kitchen had its own particular properties. As Martino writes repeatedly of a meat or fish, . . . *il suo naturale e de frigerlo* . . . , or *questo pesce per sua natura et qualita vole esse rostito* . . .: 'its nature calls for it to be fried . . .', 'this fish because of its nature and properties should be roasted . . .' – and so on. The cook had to be thoroughly familiar with these natural properties, to know what would be safe to set before his master and what would require some sort of special treatment in cooking or in saucing. This knowledge constituted a large part of the cook's profession.

---

[19] 'If the bird is at home on the land, he who roasts it will go far; but if it is a water bird, it should be roasted far from the fire.' *On Cookery*, p.13, n.22.

Mixtures

In order for one ingredient efficaciously to modify the nature of another, the two must come into intimate contact. They must mix in such a way that, as much as possible, the two ingredients become one, a mixture. The best way to ensure this close mixture is to reduce each ingredient to particles. And so the medieval kitchen had its rasp, its mortar, its colander, its sieve and its yards and yards of boulting cloth.

Modern critics tend facilely to characterize medieval cookery as consisting of a lot of mush. A basis exists for this gross over-simplification, but only insofar as condiments and sauces are concerned. There was perhaps no more common and more valuable culinary tool in any medieval kitchen than the mortar-and-pestle. Estate inventories on the occasion of a death almost invariably list a mortar of some sort among the property of the deceased, even though other kitchen utensils of any value may be rare.[20] A mortar was almost the *sine qua non* of medieval cookery.

When were ingredients reduced to particles and powder and when not? The principle that seems to have been followed was still that of the need to moderate any harmful humoural qualities present in the major foodstuff of a dish. The stronger the undesirable qualities of that prime foodstuff, the more closely the corrective ingredients should be bound to it, immixed with it. The corrective compound could be 'applied' in the form of a spiced cooking broth or basting, or a serving sauce or dressing. Or the foodstuff itself could be reduced to a fine-particle state and the moderating ingredient mixed directly with it.

Whatever the procedure used to render a food safer for human consumption, this procedure goes very largely to make medieval food what it was. The consequence of the medieval cook's concern not to disturb his client's or master's health is that the combination of all of the ingredients in his finished dish was not merely the result of a casual whim on his part. What he prepared is a deliberate and learned combination, and its texture – chunky, granular or smooth – depended necessarily upon concepts of the values of each item of food in the preparation. For us what is frequently

---

[20] See, for instance, the studies by Pascal Herbeth, 'Les ustensiles de cuisine en Provence médiévale (XIIIe–XVe s.)', *Médiévales*, 5 (1983), pp.89–93; and by Marguerite Gonon, *La vie familiale en Forez au XIVe siècle et son vocabulaire d'après les testaments* (Publications de l'Institut de linguistique romane de Lyon, No. 17), Paris, 1961. See also Alicia Rios, 'The Pestle and Mortar', *Oxford Symposium on Food & Cookery, 1988*, London (Prospect Books), 1989, pp.125–135. For a general survey of kitchen utensils see Margaret Wade Labarge, *A Baronial Household in the Thirteenth Century*, London (Eyre & Spottiswoode), 1965, pp.116–28; Rosemary Weinstein, 'Kitchen Chattels: the Evolution of Familiar Objects 1200–1700', *Oxford Symposium, 1988*, pp.168–182; and the useful picture-book of Raymond Lecoq, *Les Objets de la vie domestique. Ustensiles en fer de la cuisine et du foyer des origines au XIXe siècle*, Paris (Berger-Levrault), 1979.

remarkable is that the medieval mixtures and textures seem so very *right* that we may wonder whether in fact the rationalization of the nature of foodstuffs might not actually have followed *after* the inspired elaboration of some of the dishes. In looking at medieval cuisine we may be justified in speculating whether art might actually have preceded science.

Flavours

The notion of deliberately seeking out ingredients which, in a mixture, would check the dangerous effects of another ingredient can be seen to have at least one most curious, and lasting, consequence: the combination of bitter and sweet tastes in a single dish.

A rational understanding of the physical nature of sweetness and sourness can be read in the ratings that medieval physicians accorded to the single most common source of each taste. Vinegar had long been a staple in the kitchen, valued in part undoubtedly for the piquant tang which, in moderation, it could instil in the blandest preparation. In part, too, the favour vinegar enjoyed in medieval kitchens derived from the fact that wines that had accidentally turned vinegary still represented too costly an investment simply to discard into the cess with the slops. But not just any 'turned' wine would do: cooking vinegar had to be strong. Aldobrandino da Siena describes a test for a vinegar's goodness: drop a little on the ground, and if it 'boils and froths' it is good; if it doesn't, it isn't.[21] This strongly acidic vinegar was a esteemed liquid in medieval cookery. It was potent enough to dissolve the bones of a pigeon that was left to steep one full day in it.[22] However, it did have one very serious drawback: vinegar was held to have a nature that was cold in the first degree and dry in the third, qualities that rendered it unfit for human consumption in an unmodified state. A solution to the cook's dilemma lay in the admixture of a sweetener, and so the sweet-and-sour taste in medieval European cookery was born. Or at least justified.

[21] *Régime du corps*, op. cit., p.120. 'Se vous volés savoir s'il est boins, si en gietés sor le tere, et s'il bout et escume, sachi'es qu'il est boins, et s'il ne bout, il est malvais.' The soil where Aldobrandino observed his test must obviously have been alkaline. Incidentally, Aldobrandino's first recipe for making vinegar is curiously simple: leave a quantity of wine in the sun for three or four days in a container that is not full. Should the householder be in more of a hurry to have his or her vinegar, the learned doctor's alternative, more rapid method consists of inserting a hot iron rod or a heated river-stone into the wine: an infallible procedure, he claims.

[22] This is the essence of the 'marvellous' dish described in Recipe 66 of the *Neapolitan Collection*: the bird is eviscerated, steeped for 25 hours in vinegar, then washed, stuffed with a mixture of cheese, eggs, spices and raisins, and roasted on a spit. The author assures his reader that, after the vinegar bath, no bones will remain in the carcass.

Traditionally the premium sweetener in early medieval kitchens had been honey, and to some extent this naturally produced substance remained in use in the cookery of the fourteenth and fifteenth centuries. Particularly in the kitchens and on the tables of the German states and England its use seems to have been ingrained, and its relished taste was not wholly abandoned with the growing availability of sugar. The important activity of bee-keepers in the earlier century is recorded in the *Tacuina santitatis* where artists show beehives that are homes to enormous swarms of bees. 'There are many excellent qualities to be found in honey,' the *Tacuina* write: 'it cleanses the chest and the stomach; it purges the abdomen; it keeps the humours of the flesh and the mouth from decaying. It heats the blood and is suited to those with cold, moist temperaments, and to the elderly.'[23] Honey had very early found its way into a good number of therapeutic medicines, candies, preserved compotes and, of course, into that aristocratic beverage of northern Europe, mead.

Into southern Europe, though, came an alternative sweetener, sugar. This substance, relatively exotic although known and used in pharmacological compounds in Europe from the first century onwards, became increasingly common on the fourteenth-century marketplace, thanks wholly to the enterprise of Mediterranean merchants. Produced first in Asian cane-fields and then from the eleventh century on Mediterranean islands, sugar syrup was extracted from crushed cane, clarified, solidified and transported by Arabic dealers to European ports on the Mediterranean. During the fifteenth century European householders seem almost to have become addicted to the flavour that sugar lent their foods. Recipe collections of the time attest to the increasing reliance upon sugar in dishes that were concocted for the wealthy. Some later Italian collections, for instance, call for some amount of sugar in almost half of their recipes.

The inclusion of sugar in a recipe was entirely justifiable in the mind of the medieval cook or physician. He rationalized that the nature of sugar, being warm in the first degree and moist in the second, made it one of the safest, most appropriate foodstuffs for a human being. These very qualities had from time immemorial ensured for sugar a pre-eminent place on the shelf of the pharmacist: virtually all medicines, therapeutic potions, syrups and theriacs prescribed a basis of sugar. By the fourteenth century, sick-dishes – intended for invalids or those recuperating from a disease – can be distinguished in recipe collections from all other dishes intended for those who were healthy, primarily by the presence in the former of sugar. But if sugar were good for the sickly and convalescent, surely it was only reasonable to see it as

[23] Judith Spencer, *The Four Seasons of the House of Cerruti*, New York/Bicester, England (Facts On File), 1984, p.26. This modern reproduction and translation of the late-fourteenth-century north-Italian handbook is based upon the manuscript that is now found in the Oesterreichische Nationalbibliothek of Vienna.

potentially good also for the healthy. After all, the *Tacuina sanitatis* vouched for its almost universally beneficial properties: 'Ask the grocer for refined sugar which is hard, white as salt, and brittle. It has a cleansing effect on the body and benefits the chest, kidneys, and bladder. . . . It is good for the blood and therefore suitable for every temperament, age, season and place. Artificially white, it is very effective for tightness in the chest and when the tongue is unusually dry.'[24] It would be remarkable if everyone who could afford to in the fifteenth century did not indulge what was quickly becoming a very sweet tooth.

Here, in sugar, was the perfect gastronomic and humoural antidote to that other predilection of the medieval palate, vinegar. A combination of a substance which was warm in the first degree and moist in the second, with another which was cold in the first degree and dry in the third, was almost perfect. It is perhaps not surprising that, as far as the phenomenon is concerned in Europe, this novel 'taste sensation' of bittersweet seems to have been developed in Italy first, but it soon spread to all of Italy's neighbours. In the course of the fifteenth century we find a large number of recipes in which the writer explicitly requires that a dish have a bittersweet taste. An Italian collection, for instance, the *Dilicate vivande*, concludes its directions for making a fish dish (Recipe 91) by directing that it must be *agradolcie*; here this contrast is obtained by mixing vinegar with sweet raisins and dates. Elsewhere[25] a Italian recipe for chicken explicitly instructs the cook that the nature of a particular dish is to be both bitter and sweet. In English collections the same result is had by similar mixtures, and the dish is named for it: *Egge dows* (*Diversa servicia*, 51): vinegar and raisins; *Egerduse* of fish (*Diversa servicia*, 60): vinegar and sugar; *Egurdouce* of meat (*Forme of Cury*, 23): vinegar, sugar and currants; *Egredoucetes* (Austin, p. 113): vinegar and sugar.

Preservation

A constant problem clearly recognized by all those who handled foodstuffs in the Middle Ages concerned the freshness of those foodstuffs. We are today perhaps not sufficiently aware of how blessed we are to be able to depend upon refrigeration and freezing to extend the useful life of our foods, both before and after preparation.

Medieval society had to be much more vigilant about spoilage, and particularly of course in the matter of meats. Municipalities enacted laws

---

[24] *The Four Seasons of the House of Cerruti*, p.15.

[25] In the *Frammento* edited by Guerrini, p.42. There, Recipe 80 (for a delightfully named *Ambrogino di polli*) states: *E questa vivanda vuole essere agra e dolce*. The effect is obtained by combining ground prunes and dates with vinegar.

requiring butchers to bring their animals into town 'on the hoof' for slaughter, in order for it to be wholly manifest that the meat they sold was not already of some venerable vintage; the i'luminated *tacuina sanitatis* contain striking representations of animals being slaughtered, and their blood drained, in the public street immediately in front of a butcher's stall. Without refrigeration, animals were butchered only as the daily, perhaps hourly, demand for meat made that necessary. Laws further prohibited butchers from holding any cuts of meat over the two lean days that concluded each week: at the end of business hours every Thursday evening a butcher had to dispose of every piece of fresh meat that he still happened to have on hand.

Although various meats, poultry and fish had their respective 'seasons' in medieval Europe, many could still be obtained without too much difficulty throughout the entire year. However, when out of season these meats and fish were available to the householder only in a 'preserved' state, that is, either smoked, pickled in brine, or much more commonly, salted and dried. Merchants were diligent in answering a demand for such off-season foodstuffs, offering the preserved items in their shops; alternatively the provident householder by himself or herself quite regularly 'put down' carcasses, joints or cuts of meat using one of the standard means of preservation.

That the consumption of such preserved meats and fish was common is evident in contemporary manuals. Techniques for de-salting a piece of meat or fish, for instance, are frequently found toward the beginning of cookbooks, and are usually titled, quite practically, 'How to remove the salt [understand, *excess salt*] from your meat or fish'. Similarly, a recipe which allows the use of salt meat or salt fish invariably opens with a phrase directing the cook to soak or boil the piece of preserved meat or fish at great length in order to dissolve the salt from within it. Residual traces of that quasi-universal preservative, salt, may have given cooks some concern when they had to rely on preserved foodstuffs, but the effectiveness of this method of preserving foods meant that there was rarely a season in the whole year, and rarely a place in Europe so distant from the sea, in which cooks could not prepare meat and fish dishes when they or their masters wanted them.

Animal milk was subject to a short life, but the life of its secondary products products, butter and cheese, could be extended by means of an admixture of salt, in the same way as salt could protect meats and fish from early corruption. It is true that almond milk by and large replaced the milk of cows, sheep and goats in medieval cookery because of its durable qualities, and almond butter, churned from almond milk, was not unknown among medieval recipes.[26] But heavily salted butter could be kept for a

---

[26] Chiquart's *On Cookery* has a recipe for Almond Butter among its dishes for the sick: Recipe 67.

comparatively long time; recipes such as the two that the *Menagier de Paris* contains (in §354) for de-salting butter before using it prove that kitchens did depend to some extent upon butter from animal sources.

> To take salt out of butter. Put it in a bowl on the fire to melt and the salt will precipitate out of it to the bottom of the bowl (which salt is good in a pottage), and the rest of butter will remain sweet. Otherwise put your salt butter in fresh sweet water and knead and rub it there with your hands and the salt will remain in the water. *Item, take note* that flies will never swarm on a horse that is greased with butter or with old salt lard.

We may be able to guess why salt was understood to be able to preserve a food. The medieval cook was quite clear about the mechanism of the process of drying and of preservation. 'The virtue of salt is fiery so that it contracts, dries and binds whatever bodies it touches. If dead flesh is salted in time, it is very well preserved, as we can see in hams and other salted meats.'[27] As is the general case in medieval cookery, what cooks had to appreciate was the action of one foodstuff upon another. The nature of salt was that it was very warm (in the second degree) and extremely dry (in the third). It must necessarily tend to warm and particularly to dry any other foodstuff with which it is combined. The nature of corruption (rot or putrefaction) was essentially an excess of moisture, and perhaps also of warmth in connection with the high moisture content. The surest method of preserving a food was naturally enough seen to reside in the elimination of this superfluous moisture, or at least in removing as much of it as possible. Salt was, then, simply an agent, one agent among several good possibilities, to accomplish this dessication.

Pickling in a salt brine was the standard method of preserving meats and fish. The operation must have been widely practised in ordinary households, right down to our own day, probably in the late fall or whenever a particular meat or fish was in abundant and cheap supply on the market.[28] The process ensured that these foodstuffs could be kept usable over a relatively long term.

---

[27] *Salis vis adeo ignea est ut quae attigit corpora astringat, siccet, alliget. Mortua si salitura tempori fiat optime conservantur ut de pernis et de aliis salsamentis licet cernere.* . . . Platina, I,13: *De sale.* The *De honesta voluptate* goes on to list the various other recognized properties of salt, its benefits and its dangers: 'It is especially effective against certain ills, since it burns, combats, diminishes and dissolves; however, it is not good for the stomach except for arousing the appetite. Its immoderate use also harms the liver, blood and eyes very much.'

[28] Platina gives us a glimpse of the technique: 'Pork meat is so moist that it cannot be preserved except with much salt. . . . When a pig becomes a year old, it is fit for salting. The day before it is butchered, it is best to keep it from drinking because its flesh will be drier; then it should be salted carefully so that it will not rot or taste withered nor be damaged by worms or grubs. When you make a brine, put salt in the bottom of a pot or jar, then lay the pieces in with the skin down. The meat should remain in the jars until it absorbs the salt, then it should be hung up on a meat-rack

55

Over the short term, though, jelly performed a similar service since the nature of gelatin was likewise dry. The fact that gelatin was also slightly cool in nature meant that it was advisable always to prepare it for use with particularly warm foods. 'Gelatin is a highly refined food of a cold and dry nature, as we are told by the best authors [read: *authorities*], and hence highly suitable and useful for [consumption by] those with hot and moist temperaments, for young people and adolescents, and in the torrid season of southern regions. The blood that it produces is in some ways coldish, but it is particularly good for the secretion of bile which is the special property of gelatin. For this reason cooks should prepare it with skill and care, preferably from the flesh of pigeons. Take care, as it can cause colic and is harmful to the nerves, for which reason it should be served with a well-aged, aromatic wine.'[29] A natural gelatin was known to be available from certain specific sources (such as sheep's feet) and could be added to stewed meats, especially pork and chicken, to prolong their life a little. Apart from animals, cooks knew they could turn also to any of those fish, such as pike, perch, tench, carp, eel and lamprey, whose skin bears a mucous coating, rich in protein. The fish, along with their skins, were thoroughly boiled and then finely strained. When pieces or fillets of other cooked fish were immersed in the resulting gelatinous liquid and the mixture was cooled and allowed to set, this jelly would retard corruption for a a useful time.

A variety of jelly that was very common throughout the late-medieval period was known as Galentine, a name derived more or less directly from the root 'gelatine'.[30] However, the 'active ingredient' in Galentine, apart from the animal gelatin, probably the ingredient that was held to be the essential or vital ingredient, was its spice mixture. Today the mixture would undoubtedly be the object of a multiplicity of patents by manufacturers in the food industry. In the Middle Ages each cook undoubtedly had his or her own idea of what constituted the most effective and most savoury Galentine.

Here, however, 'savoury' was of less significance than 'effective'. The role of the spices in this type of preservative was essentially identical to what salt was known to do for meats and fish; Galentine functioned in a way analogous to brine. Empirically, cooks had some evidence of the bacteriostatic effect which spices exerted upon foodstuffs, but a scientific definition of their action was provided by the early physicists. Spices, being with only a

---

where the smoke may penetrate it. From it you can take lard at will, ham, shoulder, sowbelly, tenderloin.' *De honesta voluptate*, II, 21.

[29] *The House of Cerruti*, p.50. Bile, the essence of the melancholic temperament, results from a harmful combination of dry and cold.

[30] 'Gelatina,' says the *Alphita*, 'is any coagulated muscilage that issues from meat or fish when they are boiled and served cool with vinegar.' The text is a medieval technical vocabulary, edited by Salvatore de Renzi in his *Collection Salernitana*, Vol. 3, Naples (Filiatre-Sebezio), 1854, p.283: *Gelatina est piscium sive carnium quaedam mucilago coagulata, quae nascitur de illis, quando post alixationem servantur infrigidata in aceto.*

few exceptions uniformly warm and dry – these qualities ranging from temperate in some right up to an extreme and dangerous degree in others – were seen as offering a good alternative to salt as a means to 'super-cook' and dessicate already cooked meats and fish; such treatment would render them longer lasting. This durability depended not so much upon the jelly in the Galentine as upon the presence of the spices which were held in long-term close proximity to the meats by means of the jelly itself. One advantage of Galentine was that virtually any meat, fowl or fish could be preserved by means of it. One had only to make sure the spices in it were of a warm and dry nature, to soak the flesh in it and to let it set completely encasing the flesh.

Of course the occasional meat was blessed with a sort of self-preservation feature. Such, for example, was the flesh of a peacock. It seems to have been general knowledge that, should you for some reason – perhaps just negligence – leave the carcass of a roasted peacock hanging for one month in your larder, you will have wasted nothing: even though the surface of its flesh may have taken on a mouldy appearance (quite understandably, one might observe, given the circumstances), if you cut beneath that unsavoury surface you will find the meat still to be good, white and tasty![31]

Fruits and nuts were regularly preserved in the Middle Ages in either sugar or honey, just as they are today. Sugar offered two advantages as a preservative: it was itself manifestly durable, it did not corrupt other foods or become corrupt over time; and, when liquified, the manifest fineness of the particles that composed it allowed it to mix intimately with other foods and in some sense to bond closely to them. 'By melting [sugar] we make almonds (softened and cleaned in water), pine-nuts, hazelnuts, coriander, anise, cinnamon and many other things into candies. The quality of sugar then almost crosses over into the qualities of those things to which it clings in the preparation.'[32] For the same purpose some cooks suggest using a sweet wine that has been boiled until most of its liquid has evaporated. The resultant syrup coated and permeated the foodstuff, warming and drying its complexion. Honey was the original preservative in this procedure, since it had been attributed a hot and dry nature. At any rate, whether from honey or sugar or a rich red wine, the thick syrup was proven to conserve the fruit or nut or else, if the syrup continued into a hardened, throughly dried state, it candied them. Entire books, such as the Catalan *Libre de totes maneres de*

---

[31] See, for example, recipe 50 (Vatican manuscript version) in the *Viandier*. The precept is likely inspired from St Augustine who writes in the *City of God* (Book 21, Chapter 4) about the incorruptibility of peacock flesh.

[32] Platina, *De honesta voluptate*, II, 15. Honey afforded similar virtues: 'Summer honey is better than autumn honey, for it agrees with bodies which are cold and damp, it heals many ills, it does not allow bodies to decay and it is considered best in preserving apples, gourds, citron and nuts.'

confits,[33] were devoted to an exposé of the techniques of preserving by means of sweet substances.

For fresh meats and fish whose high oil content made them particularly subject to 'corruption', it was known to be efficacious to saturate them thoroughly with wood smoke. Smoked hams are by no means a recent invention. One staple of fine Roman cuisine, a sort of sauce or condiment known as *garum* and consisting primarily of the oil of deliberately fermented anchovies, sprats, mackerel or scomber, did not make its way into late-medieval Europe,[34] even though this sort of fermented fish sauce is today a delicate staple in south-east Asia. Fatty fish such as anchovies and herring were enjoyed at table throughout the medieval year after an intensive smoke treatment had thoroughly penetrated their flesh. The term 'kipper' may refer literally to the coppery hue with which this treatment imbues the appearance of fish.[35]

Religious Strictures

Lean Foods

A fundamental influence upon food habits in medieval Europe was exercised by the Christian Church. It is appropriate to deal with the question of lean foods here in this chapter because the theological rationale underlying the various regulations governing fasting seems to derive in some measure from the same thinking that lay behind the humoural theories of Greek and medieval medicine.

---

[33] L. Faraudo de Saint-Germain, ed., '*Libre de totes maneres de confits*. Un tratado manual cuatrocentista de arte de dulcería', *Boletín de la Academia de Buenas Letras de Barcelona*, 19 (1946), pp.97–134.

[34] There existed in Roman antiquity an entire industry devoted to supplying the food market with *garum* or *liquamen*. The customary use of this sauce amounts to one of the distinctive features of Roman cookery. Varieties of it evolved by adding different spices or by making it tangy with vinegar. The *De re coquinaria*, with which the name of M. Gavius Apicius (25 B.C.–A.D. 37) has been attached, cites a number of variations on plain *garum*, incorporating rue, pepper or honey among diverse possibilities. See the interesting comparative study by Alan Davidson, 'Nuoc Mam: the Fish Sauces of Vietnam and South-East Asia', in *A Kipper with My Tea. Selected Food Essays*, San Francisco (North Point Press), 1990, pp.223–28.

[35] *The Random House Dictionary of the English Language*, Second Edition, 1987 (p.1059a): '. . . Apparently deriv. of *cyperen* of copper, i.e. copper-colored'. With regard to KIPPER *substantive*, the *Oxford English Dictionary*, Second Edition, 1989 (Vol. 8, p.456c) notes only: 'Etymology uncertain; it is also doubtful how sense A.2 [the cured fish], which goes with KIPPER *verb*, is connected with A.1 [a male salmon], and indeed whether it is the same word.' It seems arguable in this case that the verb may well have been at the origin of the noun.

By the time the Roman Empire collapsed, Christian doctrine had adopted, or simply maintained, certain attitudes that were long-established in other religious thinking concerning the need to distinguish between foods that were relatively 'clean' or 'pure' and foods that were relatively 'unclean' or 'impure'. For early Christians the question of the purity of foods was complicated by long-established Jewish concepts about what was suitable for human consumption. In Jewish thought blood, for instance, represented an animal's soul. When the Israelites sacrificed an animal, its blood and grease were reserved for God. All meat destined for the faithful must therefore be thoroughly drained of blood in order to be approved as 'kosher' or fit for the mere people of God.

The distinction between clean and unclean, undoubtedly physical and sanitary in its origins, readily became a moral one as theologians sought out all of the ways by which an individual could make himself or herself purer, and so more acceptable to God, better able to please God and worthy to commune with Him.[36] The learned doctor of the Church, St Isidore of Seville (c.560–636), praised the moral usefulness of fasting and expressed what he believed to be indisputable scientific fact when he wrote that eating meat breeds lust of the flesh: in effect, meats over-heat the person who eats them and so feed every vice[37] Isidore's clearly enunciated Christian 'fact' is based upon the Galenic theory about humours, and upon the consequent understanding of the ways in which foods operate to determine a person's temperament. He himself stated that 'the human body is made up of the four elements: for earth is in the flesh, air in the breath, moisture in the blood, and fire in the vital heat.'[38] It was enough for theologians to realize that most meats partook of a warm nature, and that the sanguine or choleric temperament produced by such food usually lent itself to lechery and other excesses of the most heinous kind. Logically, then, the virtuous Christian should eschew foods that were overly warming in their effects. Above all, this meant that red meats, and anything related to them that partook of their nature, creatures of the Earth and the Sun, could be dangerous to one's *moral* health; it was, even if only on occasion, a good, Christian thing to avoid such foods in one's diet.

[36] At the beginning of the third century A.D., Tertullian, in his *De jejunio adversus psychicos*, expounded the principle of fasting as this had been merely sketched in the Gospel of St Mark (9:29). Later Christian thinkers, from St Benedict, in his monastic rule, to St Thomas (2-2ae:147:7c), merely elaborated on the ascetic and penetential reasons for the devout Christian to observe the current ecclesiastic laws on fasting.

[37] *Isidori Hispalensis episcopi Etymologiarum sive Originum libri XX* (Scriptorum Classicorum Biblioteca Oxoniensis), ed. Wallace Martin Lindsay, 2 vols., Oxford (Clarendon), 1962, Vol.2; XX.2,22. The author arrives at his conclusions by relating *caro*, *carnem* ('flesh') and *elixum* ('boiled') to *luxus* ('carnal lust'): *Elixum, ea quod in aqua sola coquitur. Lixa enim aqua dicitur ab eo quod sit soluta; unde et solutio libidinis luxus, et membro loco mota luxa dicuntur.*

[38] *Ibid.*, II.1,16.

When was the proper occasion, then, to strive for such purity? Needless to say, the definition of meat-free days, or days of so-called qualified fasting, was not uniform across Christian Europe or constant throughout the Middle Ages. Certain periods were from time to time and from place to place deemed appropriate for purification and penitence; in general the penitential days were those that preceded significant feasts or high moments in the ecclesiastical calendar. At one time the Church insisted upon four periods of fasting, each lasting up to forty days: Advent, Lent, Epiphany (Ascension) and Pentecost. In England in 1256, Ralph of Lenham (Kent)[39] stated that

> Four fasts have been fixed
> which are called the 'four Ember days'
> because they fall in the four seasons.

According to the same Ralph of Lenham the obligation to fast fell on three days during the first week (alone) of each of Lent and Pentecost: Wednesday, Friday and Saturday. During the week following Holy Cross Day (September 14) and again immediately after St Lucy's Day (December 13) the same three fast days must be observed. Apart from the fact that Ralph does not explicitly tie the last two of these fasting periods to the normal penitential calendar, what is particularly interesting is his justification of the fundamental principle of fasting. We must fast, he says 'in order to pray God that he temper that humour that we have within us, that temperament which most closely resembles each season and *its* temperament'. With explicit care he then details the moist, warm nature of spring and the need to temper the excess of blood that we have in us at that time; then in summer it is our choler which must be combated because of the dryness and warmth of that season; autumn's fast must counter our melancholy, both human and seasonal temperament being dry and cold at that time; and in time moist, cold winter brings the need to fast away those specific, excessive humours. To conclude this exposition of the beneficial effects of seasonal fasting, Ralph summarizes:

> We must needs fast four times
> in order to temper these four humours,
> for they hold the greatest sway
> over the disposition of every individual:

---

[39] Rauf de Linham, *Kalender*, ed. Tony Hunt, London (Anglo-Norman Text Society), 1983, lines 986ff.

> *Quatre junes sunt asis,*
> *ke quatuor tempre nomé sunt,*
> *pur ceo ke as quatre tens charrunt.*

> whoever shall temper those humours
> shall be less inclined to sin.[40]

This usage declared by Ralph of Lenham, of twelve fast days in the year, may be strictly local. What we may guess is that when Ralph writes 'fast', he really means *fast*, a total fast: no substantial food whatsoever is to be eaten on those twelve days. The sole exceptions that he recognizes to this rule – a hard and *fast* rule, we might call it – apply to those who are sick and to the very young. It seems that for Ralph fasting was a serious matter that was truly rooted in starvation. It still reflected its original intentions: the cleansing from the body of any corrupt elements that had managed to accumulate there. The scientific argument that can be elaborated by the mid-thirteenth century in order to rationalize a long-established religious practice shows just how thoroughly a learned understanding of the physical nature of man could be incorporated into theological doctrine.

Some form of modified fasting was certainly practised each week throughout the year in late medieval Europe. Originally Friday and Saturday seen generally to have been designated as fast days. In a manuscript copy of the *Viandier* (Recipe 195) from the beginning of the fifteenth-century,[41] however, the days of the week on which it was licit to eat meat are identified as being limited to Sunday, Tuesday and Thursday. Implicitly, therefore, no fewer than *four* days in a week – Mondays, Wednesdays, Fridays and Saturdays – were to be meat-free days, at least according to the author of this late version of the *Viandier*. When these weekdays are added in with the regularly prescribed fasting *periods* of penance during the Christian year, more than half of a person's meals might well be designated as subject to some form of abstinence.

The pious Christian, then, was expected more or less constantly to prepare himself or herself for the joyous feasts of a Sunday or of the Easter or Christmas holy-day mass by, at the very least, abstaining from flesh meats and from the warming by-products (fat and grease, milk, butter, cheese) of animals.

While such abstinence might seem to entail only a slight modification in the normal diets of medieval Christians – with little change in net gastronomic effect, people could still cook using nut oils, for instance, rather than lard – the strictures and prescriptions of fasting were sometimes complex and did in reality have wide-ranging consequences. Not only did

---

[40]
> *Ben devum quatre feiz joner*
> *pur ces quatre humurs temprer,*
> *kar il unt la greingnor summe*
> *des corages chescun homme,*
> *e ki ben tempré les ust,*
> *meins coragus de peccher fust.*

[41] This version is now held in the collection of the Vatican Library.

fasting determine what could be prepared and set on the medieval table but it also shaped what today we would call the food industry of the time as a whole. These wide-ranging effects were due in part to the very importance of meat in the diet of the medieval aristocracy and wealthy bourgeoisie, and in part to the very frequency of fast days in the medieval Christian calendar.

The Lenten Debate

A curious result of the enormous role that Christian dietary rules played in the lives of the medieval European population is seen even beyond the kitchen and the dining hall. Scholastic education set great store by academic debates as a means by which the rational faculties of students could most effectively be honed. Over the generations of the thirteenth and fourteenth centuries a huge number of topics became standard, commonplace bases for debate, the student or master marshalling all of the logical arguments for or against one of the proposed positions. Most topics were remarkably abstruse and usually theological in significance ('Whether the predestined can be damned', 'Whether angels possess knowledge that is innate or acquired'), but by the time the graduate left his university he was often so thoroughly trained in the techniques of dialectic and disputation that it seems to have been common practice to amuse oneself with parodies of serious debates, pastiche arguments, as it were. The burlesque contentions dealt with subjects that were, if not simply ridiculous, at least patently unworthy of earnest scholastic attention. A few of these topics made their way into the literature of the time: 'Whether water or wine is the nobler element'; 'Whether the military man or the ecclesiastic makes the better lover'; and, of interest to us, 'Whether Lent or Carnival has right on its side'.

As a literary motif, the 'debate' between Lent and Carnival was famous throughout Europe. Even Pieter Bruegel the Elder continued the joke in 1559 by painting a version of the *Battle between Carnival and Lent*. His canvas incorporates an enormous amount of culinary detail in the activity that surrounds the jousting figures of corpulent Carnival and gaunt Lent. Doubtless intellectually playful students had subjected the topic to some sort of facetious treatment from the earliest scholastic period, but only as opposing sets of abstract arguments, an excuse for an amusing exercise in logic and dialectics. In the hands of skilled writers, however, the conflict in this pseudo-debate became quite real: we can follow the development of a quarrel between two medieval potentates, Lord Lent and Lord Carnival, as it escalates into a full-fledged, deadly combat on the battlefield. In this quite funny rendition of human sensitivity and stubbornness we can see quite clearly a marked resentment against the severe Lord of Lent[42] who attempts

---

[42] In a Spanish version of this *topos*, the allegory personifies Lent as a straight-laced, altogether fearsome dame, because the Spanish word *Quaresma* ('Lent') is feminine.

to impose his authority upon the Lord of Carnival.[43] For his part Lord Carnival, overweaning in his self-assurance and hedonism, resists this insidious subversion of his power. At Pentecost, as Shrove Tuesday approaches, the dissension between the two feudal lords becomes acrimonious; the messages they exchange by their ambassadors (Lent's envoy is a herring, Carnival's a pigeon hawk) leave less and less room for amicable compromise in the resolution of their differences. At last by Ash Wednesday a state of war is declared between them, their respective vassals are summoned in a general ban, and the lines of battle are quickly drawn up.

To set the scene we have a deft portrait of each of the two principals, fully armed for combat, of course: Lent's battle gear consists of a roach (his breast plate), fresh salmon (coat of mail), pike (helmet), plaice (shoulder pieces), lamprey (doublet); he wears fish-bones as spurs, and carries a long thin sole for a sword. For his part Carnival puts on pork and mutton (his doublet), partridge and quail (coat of mail) and a bore's hear (helmet). Lent humbly mounts a mule; Carnival's saddle is cinched onto a great antlered stag.

The amusing, and illuminating, battle scenes occupy a good portion of this moderately long poem. Gone now is any suggestion of a parody of a merely academic *disputatio*; in this fictional narrative the time is past for any carefully constructed, rational argument for and against Christian abstinence. Unabashedly the author makes a direct sensual appeal to the audience's taste buds!

To begin, the two potentates come together in single combat. Just as it seems that Lord Lent is about to gain the upper hand, or perhaps the upper fin, the two armies *in toto* close in a general melee, and we have a chance to see in real, concrete terms just what consequences Lent (and Advent, and Mondays, Wednesdays, Fridays and Saturdays) must have had upon the average European diet, and how the lean rules determined what was set on the wealthy dining tables of Europe for eating at those times. We see that the first attack of Lord Carnival's army is delivered by roast capons against Lent's fresh whitings. Then the halibut and mackerel contend valiantly against the beef. Eggs measure their prowess with herrings, and a fresh salmon grievously wounds a *brochette*. Olive oil fights lard and, interestingly, almond milk combats animal milk.

These first combatants are among each lord's most noble knights, some of the principal foodstuffs upon which the cook in an affluent household depended for the basis of his meals either on lean days or on meat days. But the battlefield is covered with an huge variety of foods, prepared dishes and sauces; the struggle is grandiose – and mouth-watering. Herrings in White

---

See Juan Ruiz, the Archpriest of Hita (d.1350), *Libro de buen amor*, ed. Julio Cejador y Frauca, 2 vols., Madrid (Espasa-Calpe), 1959; II, pp.76–123.

[43] The word *carnival* derives from *carnem*, 'meat': a time when the eating of meat is allowed.

Garlic Sauce contend with a Pork in Green Sauce; Eel Broth matches itself with Carbonados; Cretonnée of Beans combats Pepper Sausage; Fritters and Rishews meet *Feves frasées* and Roast Flounder in Fennel. The narrative is truly a 'gastronomic epic' as the editor of its French version terms it.[44]

The eventual (though temporary) defeat of Lord Lent afforded a double cause for celebration. Easter reminded the faithful of the joyous theological message; the arrival of Easter Day, appropriately a 'high feast day', also allowed European Christians at last to throw off the dietary constraints of the last forty days and again to indulge voluptuously in the most savoury and satisfying of foods.

This long-awaited restoration of Lord Carnival, in decadently glorious full estate, gave rise to a peculiar custom that illustrates the popular elation that came to be associated with Easter – as it had always been associated with the return of Spring itself, of course. Because eggs were one of the most important foodstuffs covered by the dietary injunctions of Lent, in certain regions the end of this long period of purification and abstinence, Holy Saturday, was celebrated by a blessing of eggs in church. These eggs, stained and gaudily decorated with the happiest of bright colours in anticipation of their return to the dining board, were exchanged as gifts among friends and relatives; quite naturally they became known as Easter Eggs.

Conclusion

Despite our natural reluctance to see much virtue in an art that claims to be scientific in its basis, at least in part, we should not be too hasty in rejecting its results just because we know now that this basis is only *pseudo*-scientific. What medieval cooks may have thought they were doing and what they were actually on to are perhaps two different matters. As always, the test of the pudding is in its taste. We have to begin by admitting that, whatever the reasons, medieval cooking produced dishes that must be qualified as gastronomically successful. These dishes may have disappeared from the tables of subsequent generations in part because the theoretical notions that led to their making had faded out of intellectual favour. More likely, though, there were other, more important considerations, such as costs, availability and taste (in all its senses), that accounted for a change in food habits over time. They usually do, as the fast-food chains know quite well today.

The material point is that it does not really matter whether or not we accept that the flesh of pheasant is temperately warm and temperately moist, or even that we agree with Averroes that pheasant is the supremely preferable fowl for eating, in order to enjoy a good English *Mawmenee* made

[44] Grégoire Lozinski, *La bataille de Caresme et de Charnage*, Paris (Champion), 1933; p.52.

with shredded pheasant meat, wine, sugar, rice flour, pine-nuts, dates, ginger, cinnamon and cloves. We don't have to be aware that crayfish are both warm and dry in the second degree in order to be convinced that the Italian *Pastello de gamari* is delectable when it combines the meat of crayfish, that is first boiled and then fried in olive oil and onion, with pepper and saffron, ground walnuts and filberts, and sugar, and then baked all together in a pieshell. And why should we care that sorrel is held to be cold and dry in the second degree if the Latin *Succum acedule viridis*, by making an entirely logical combination of ingredients also makes such an absolutely delightful sauce for capons? Or that the same sorrel verjuice is rationally combined with (bitter) orange juice in a delicious French dressing for fried sole? Or that barley is held to be cold and dry in the first degree when, boiled until thick with warm-and-moist almond milk and warm-and-dry honey, the Catalan *Ordiat* is such a simple yet mouth-watering delicacy? In short, whatever the careful reasoning that went on in the medieval kitchen as various ingredients were artfully combined and then deliberately cooked in particular ways, the outcome was remarkably palatable. And it still is so.

When nobles sat down to table in the late Middle Ages, most of what went into the dishes they consumed would be largely familiar to us. As we saw before, there is little to surprise us as far as the normal culinary ingredients are concerned. Furthermore, there is not much that is clearly 'foreign' about the various cooking processes these foodstuffs would normally undergo. A good number of theoretical ideas about foods and eating did, however, exert a significant influence upon what and how people ate in the fourteenth and fifteenth centuries. Questions of theory account indeed for most of what we may perceive as being unique about medieval food and cookery.

FOUR

The Distinctive Nature
of Medieval Foods and Cookery

Dissimilarities of Foodstuffs

As we saw, the vast majority of foodstuffs used in the Middle Ages continue to be among the everyday choices of modern cooks. Likewise, in the medieval kitchen these foodstuffs were carved up or chopped in similar fashions, and then cooked in ways that we could hardly call alien. Yet the dishes that were prepared out of these foodstuffs and set on the medieval table are sometimes patently *not* modern. These medieval foods possess something that is unique to them.

In order to identify the substantial reasons for that *cachet*, we must take into account other factors. Along with the influence of certain preferred ingredients in the early period, we have to consider the consequences of the absence, at that time, of several of today's more common foodstuffs. From our modern viewpoint we can then distinguish between what we might call both the positive and negative influences upon the nature of early European cuisine: foods commonly used at the earlier time, but no longer quite so prominent in our cuisine; and foods not used at the earlier time, but fairly common now. Those later foodstuff items that were unknown to the medieval cook – and we should include those (such as rhubarb and the banana) that might have been known but were not normally sought out by him as potential ingredients for his culinary preparations – are relatively few in number. However, some of them are very important in determining the nature of the food habits in our own day.

A few edible things have been 'discovered' since the Middle Ages, of course. To the extent that the medieval cook was *not* handling the foodstuffs that we know and use today, he could be said to be doomed to prepare 'only' medieval food. And the absence in his kitchen of these more recently available items undoubtedly determined that his cuisine must have had a certain peculiar flavour.

The list of such modern foods (that is, normal European and North American foods which were generally unknown in the Middle Ages) is not, in fact, very long.[1] Among vegetables we can mention potatoes, yams, artichokes, green peas, 'indian' corn (the white, yellow or brown kernels growing on large cobs), the red, green and yellow peppers, chilies – and tomatoes. Fruits from the tropics, such as bananas (known *about*, but still exotic), pineapples and kiwi, were not universally imported into Europe even by the end of the Middle Ages, although the pomegranate, cultivated in Italy and in the Hispanic peninsula, was well known and well used. Ignorance of peanuts did not hamper medieval cooks, because anything a peanut can do today an almond seems to have done just as well then. Among today's more popular seasonings the European Middle Ages were never to use allspice (*Pimenta officinalis*, also called Jamaican pepper) or the product of the vanilla bean. However, with the notable and famous exception of the turkey, none of today's domestic meats were yet to be 'discovered', although in the more modern period some of the domestic animals, such as the pig, would undergo significant genetic modifications in order to improve their 'yield' in meat.

In the general category of fowl, there is, of course, the famous North-American turkey which remained unknown in Europe for a century or two more. Of the fishes, from both the sea and fresh-water sources, medieval cooks and diners had a broad acquaintance with the edible species, making use of a good range (though far from all) of flat and round sea-fish as well as crustaceans from the waters around Europe, and of lake- and river-fish from inland waters. In some cases the recognition of significant distinctions within separate species of fish was remarkably discriminating. The elderly *Menagier*, for instance, advises his young bride that in Paris the efficient housewife needed to be able to distinguish between no fewer than five varieties of pike, depending upon their maturity and size.[2] Such discrimination may indeed be common in other civilizations today, but modern Europeans and North Americans are rarely concerned with distinguishing other than among the major fish species.

Artificial compounds, such as margarine and shortening, had to wait for the modern food-chemistry industry. As beverages, coffee, tea and cocoa assumed their preeminent places in the popular diet only after the earlier period. And, having alluded to medieval Europe's ignorance of the cocoa bean, we must also point out that medieval gourmets managed to survive

---

[1] On the contribution of the New World to the food habits of the Old, see Raymond Sokalov, *Why We Eat What We Eat*, New York, London (Simon & Schuster), 1991; and Sophie D. Coe, *America's First Cuisines*, Austin, Texas (University of Texas Press), 1994.

[2] These are, in the French of the day: *lanterel, brochet, quarrel, lux* and *luceau*. The generic term including all of these pike was simply *brochet*. The *Menagier de Paris*, p.173, line 17. Fish merchants in England drew a similar distinction between a *hurling pick, pickerel, pike, luce* and *lucie*, again, depending upon maturity and size. Frederick J. Furnivall, quoting Randle Holme, in *Early English Meals and Manners* (EETS, 32), London (Oxford University Press), 1868, p.99.

without all the ubiquitous chocolate upon which we moderns depend for so many desserts – and other things – nowdays. The lowly peanut was likewise foreign to medieval gastronomy.

There were, however, very few edible substances commonly used as foodstuffs today – vegetables, fruits, meats, fats and liquids – that were not known and so used in the late Middle Ages. Where significant differences do appear, though, is in the emphases within the various food groups. Some foodstuffs enjoyed a preference they have lost today; and some were in much more common use then, relative to other foodstuffs of the same major group, than they are today. In large measure it is these differences in emphases, rather than the non-use (or use) of an unknown (or now-forgotten or -disused) foodstuff, that account for what is unique in medieval cookery.

Grains

All of the common cereal grains were in use somewhere in Europe for grinding into flour and, at least potentially, the making of bread. In virtually all cases the flour was what we would call 'whole-grain', unboulted, without the bran normally having been separated from the kernel. The *tacuina sanitatis* and health handbooks provide useful analyses of the diverse properties of barley, millet, sorghum, oats, rye, buckwheat and spelt as well as of rice and 'ordinary' wheat. Rice flour is frequently called upon to thicken liquid mixtures, especially where the final dish should be as white or as clear as possible. As today, starch was commonly relied upon as a dependable thickener, although this starch seems to have been produced in the cook's kitchen itself. Several English and French cookbooks offer their readers directions for making a domestic supply of wheat starch which could be drawn upon whenever a mixture had to be thickened. In the fifteenth-century *Noble Boke of Cookry for a Prynce Houssolde or eny other Estately Houssolde*, for instance, we may see the procedure for making wheat starch, a process which remained more or less the same in every book since the earliest versions:

> To mak amydon, take whet and step it in water x [ten] dais and change the water evry daye; then bet [beat] it smalle in a mortair and sethe [boil] it with water and mylk and sye [strain] it throughe a clothe, and let yt stond and setelle; and pour out the water and lay it in a clothe and turn it till it be drye.[3]

While the moderately cool and dry nature of most cereal grains meant that their use in porridges was highly appropriate, wheat and wheat starch, being temperately warm and dry, were valued in a particularly wide variety of functions.

[3] Page 101.

Vegetables and Fruits

One remarkable peculiarity of the medieval use of food has to be guessed in the recipes that come down to us, and that is just what was understood by the term 'vegetable'. Even today the definition of this food group is not at all clear. The easiest procedure, in order the better to grasp the nature of what is meant by 'vegetable', is to draw a nice neat line between vegetables and fruits. The difficulty, though, is that there are places where the line is not easily drawn. For instance, in a modern grocery store, where properly should we look for the squashes (called *vegetable* marrows' in recognition of their identity problem) and sweet peppers? Among the fruits or in the vegetable section? In the Middle Ages neither the shopper nor the cook worried overly about such classifications. The physician merely read what the ancient authorities had declared.

Even with a different sort of scientific help today, grey areas still remain. 'Vegetable . . ., *substantive* 2. A plant cultivated for food; *especially* an edible herb or root used for human consumption and commonly eaten, either cooked or raw, with meat or other article of food.'[4] Such a definition as this covers a lot of ground; specifically, the distinction between vegetable and fruit is not immediately apparent. We even have what looks like the odd hybrid, for instance 'vegetable pears'. And that most famous (and post-medieval) fruit, the tomato – possessing all of the characteristics of any typical fruit except in the way it has been incorporated into our meals – appears from an historical perspective to owe its place in the family of 'vegetables' merely by adoption. The same fate has been allotted the lowly cucumber.

Furthermore, on first blush it seems to be a simple matter to speak of vegetables as being edible plants, and then go on quite naturally to distinguish between the leaves and the roots of these plants. Some vegetables are leafy, some are rooty. But where does that leave 'herbs'? Should mint leaves, sorrel or lovage be classified as vegetables? On occasion they are certainly used that way. Perhaps it is usage alone, or at least primarily, that defines such foodstuffs: if a plant is used as a vegetable, it *is* one.

As we mentioned, the problem is not a recent one. In the Middle Ages science could not offer the sharp, lucid distinctions that we trust to guide our understanding today. The categories of foodstuff which we believe, a little naïvely, to be clear were neither quite so clear nor even the same in the fourteenth and fifteenth centuries. In particular the distinction between fruits and vegetables tended to a little muddy.

---

[4] *Oxford English Dictionary*, Second Edition, Vol. 19, p.474c. A primary definition of 'fruit' in the same modern authority is 'the edible product of a plant or tree . . .', *Ibid.*, Vol. 6, p.229a. The secondary definitions are hardly more helpful.

If the theoretical distinction between the various sub-species of plant foods was obscure in medieval times, the practical culinary uses for fruits and vegetables were subject to even less clear a differentiation. An Italian recipe collection includes a dish called a *Chomposte di pere o di rape*: if the cook didn't happen to have any pears on hand, he could simply substitute turnips, with no perceived change in the fundamental nature of the dish.[5] In much the same way another collection juxtaposes recipes for Quince Pie and Cabbage Pie, stating that they are to be treated analogously.[6] The modern cook seems to have accepted the limitations on culinary possibilities that are imposed by a more or less firm distinction between vegetables and fruits. If convention today calls for a vegetable at a certain point in a meal, then one ought not normally to serve up peaches at that point. The medieval cook, even though he was working within other, scientific restrictions (viz., the humoural nature of each foodstuff), did not have to worry whether such assimilations as between pears and turnips were reasonable in our modern sense. What mattered more were in part the scientific 'parity' of the two foods, and in part the gastronomic consequences of such a substitution.

In whatever category of foodstuff contemporary students of natural science felt inclined to place nuts, it must be observed that they played an enormous role in the medieval diet. Walnuts, filberts (hazelnuts), pistachios, chestnuts, pine-nuts and almonds were all kept on hand in the larger kitchens. Almonds, in particular, seem to constitute the *sine qua non* of medieval cookery: there is perhaps no more common ingredient in the dishes of the day than almonds, in some form or other. Usually ground very finely in a mortar, mixed with a liquid and then strained, almonds yielded a so-called almond milk whose culinary uses appear to be close to infinite in number.

It is tempting to say that, generally speaking, fruits were delivered to the medieval aristocratic table in cooked form. Certainly there are innumerable recipes for fruit pies, compote of fruits, candied fruits. These recipes could offer delightful alternatives to the humdrum of the modern table. But there are really no grounds for making out that apples, pears, quince, medlars, peaches, plums, cherries, dates, figs, grapes, raisins and nuts were *never* served and eaten in a 'raw' state. What we do have, and what medieval physicians and cooks had, was a well known doctrine that stated that most fruits were of a moist nature, often possessed in fact an excessively moist and cold nature, and so would tend readily toward 'corruption' and to make bad blood whenever they were ingested raw. So, we must ask: did the medieval

---

[5] This recipe is in the Italian collection *Dilicate vivande*. The manuscript containing this work, from the fifteenth century and as yet unpublished, contains a remarkable assortment of such 'composts'.

[6] Recipes 139 and 140, for *Torta de codogne* and *Torta de caule*, respectively, in the Neapolitan Collection (New York, Pierpont Morgan Library, manuscript Bühler, 19). Each is boiled in a fat broth, ground and strained and put into a pastry shell with cheese, pepper, saffron, eggs and butter.

noble or bourgeois really pass up the chance to gnaw at delicious fresh apples and pears, or to bite into plums and peaches when these fruits came newly onto the market every year? It seems highly unlikely. But we cannot really tell with any certainty just how much *fresh* fruit was regularly consumed as a matter of course. The problem is that our main source of information is the medieval cookbook, and, naturally enough, cookbooks deal primarily with food-preparations that are cooked.

In a sense it may be seriously misleading to rely overly upon recipe collections as a main source of evidence about what was actually eaten in the Middle Ages, or at any time. And this is particularly so if we conclude from a close scrutiny of these recipes that the people of the fourteenth and fifteenth centuries must have eaten little in the way of fresh fruits and vegetables. Again, there is ample evidence from the illustrators of the various *tacuina sanitatis*[7] that a variety of such fresh foodstuffs was peddled daily in urban streets. Other historic texts (mentioned in Chapter 1) demonstrate clearly that a rich assortment of both vegetables and fruits were commonly marketed for general consumption. Some townsfolk were not even restricted to only the produce that was available commercially: these had their own backyard gardens and orchards; others again, the more affluent bourgeois, possessed plots or actual farms out in the country. The author of the *Menagier de Paris* instructs his young wife how to handle both the labourers and the livestock on their farm; he provides her likewise with advice on the grafting of fruit trees and with a detailed calendar on the planting and harvesting of garden crops, together with instructions on when, and how, to lay down a wide variety of preserves of their own garden produce.

It is not usual to find such a clear distinction between market-bought produce and domestic produce in a contemporary cookbook. As the author of the *Viandier* writes, quite condescendingly, about the common-place or 'lesser' preparations of stewed vegetables for which he will not bother to provide recipes: '. . . Stewed chard, cabbage, turnip greens, leeks, . . . plain shallot pottage, peas, split beans, mashed beans, sieved beans or beans in their shell, . . . brewet of pork tripe – *women are experts with these and anyone knows how to do them*; as for tripe, which I have not put in my recipe book, it is common knowledge how it is to be prepared.'[8] It is likely to be precisely *because* vegetables and fruits were so commonly served at mealtimes, and in a fairly plain state, that medieval recipes books remain relatively silent about them.

---

[7] See above in Chapter 3, p.**.
[8] *The Viandier of Taillevent*, Recipe 154, pp.217 and 295; my italics.

Meats

When talking about meat today it is rare to distinguish whether the living animal was native to the wild or raised in the barnyard or pen. Modern societies depend overwhelmingly upon domestic livestock for their meats. Even fish are more and more the product of a carefully controled cultivation, so that breeding, nourishment and harvesting, whether of meat-animals, fowl or fish, are no more haphazard than a carefully managed manufacturing process. In the late Middle Ages, however, hunters, trappers and fishermen still provided much of what was cooked for the table.

Written records are scarce which might document the actual numbers of game animals and game birds that were incorporated into aristocratic meals. We do possess a large number of recipes for deer or hare or heron, but without evidence on the 'supply' side of the kitchen it is difficult to judge accurately for any milieu and for any period to what real extent late-medieval cookery depended upon wild animals. A researcher recently reported, with great regret, that even the household account books that he had been able to examine were either incomplete or insufficiently detailed to allow him to draw any but the most general conclusions about the use of the meat of game animals and fowl relative to that of their domestically raised counterparts. For noble courts in Brabant and Artois, in present-day Belgium and the north-east of France, he concluded rather tentatively that stag, deer and wild boar represented a relatively minute proportion of meats consumed, while the numbers of hare seemed quite considerable, and the numbers of game birds large but still uncertain.[9]

Master Chiquart lets us understand how very important this wild source of meat was at the court of Savoy – but of course the vitality of the fauna of Brabant and Artois may not have been that of the mountains and forests of Savoy. To prepare for the two-day banquet whose recipes form the bulk of the material in his *On Cookery*, Chiquart insists on the need to scour the countryside for *everything* that the local hunters and fowlers can provide.

> Your purveyors of game should be able, diligent and foresighted enough to have forty horses to get to various places for deer, hares, rabbits, partridge, pheasants, small birds (whatever they can find of these, without number), doves, cranes, herons, any wildfowl, whatever sort of game they can get. . . .[10]

And this during a period of up to two months ahead of the projected banquet. The fact that Chiquart does not specify quantities for his game

[9] J.-P. Sosson, 'La part du gibier dans l'alimentation médiévale. L'exemple des "pourvances" de Guillaume d'Ostrevant au Quesnoy (23 sept.–23 juin 1398', *La chasse au moyen âge*, Paris (Belles Lettres), 1980, pp.347–364.

[10] *On Cookery*, p.9.

animals and game birds, whereas he explicitly states the number of carcasses of sheep, piglets and chickens he will need, means only that the actual numbers of such wild animals and wildfowl that might be available in any region or season could never be known much in advance. Even with two whole months of 'lead time' ahead of a grand event like a banquet, a cook such as Chiquart could only order, as he does, *as much as is possible* of such meats – and then simply stand ready to make good use of whatever quantities should come in.

It has become commonplace to say that the medieval diet consisted primarily, if not overwhelmingly, of meat; that the average individual embodied a definition of a carnivore. The picture of the barely civilized medieval diner, draped in animal furs, tearing with his teeth at dripping joints of semi-roasted meat is an easy one to draw and a simple one to retain. The image serves for both the prehistoric era, about which we know little but deduce much, and the medieval period, about which we really do understand a very good deal more. Yet as with most generalizations the easily evoked image is only partially accurate. Meat was indeed central in most meals of the time, *if* we consider only the meals of those members of society who could actually afford to provide themselves with enough meat to give it this central place in their diet.[11] In a sense this 'truth' about medieval life is true only because it must be so heavily qualified as to define only itself. The simple picture needs a good number of specifics added: it is true that a large proportion of a meal on an aristocratic table did consist of meat from a variety of the dozen or so animals normally butchered for food, but in most cases these meats *entered into* dishes that were prepared, with considerable skill, for this table. The meat delivered to the kitchen door was, as it were, merely the initial raw material for the cook's professional labours – of which we have spoken earlier.

Early Christian authorities repeatedly suggest that it is good for the soul to abstain from the eating of meat. This accepted doctrine on abstinence, which concerned the consumption of meat, is not really that of fasting, which involved a total abstention from *any* food. In the late Middle Ages, the term fasting normally came to have the sense merely of abstinence, so that, as far as food was concerned for a Christian, moral cleansing had to do solely with meat and when one might or might not properly eat it. As we have seen, a very considerable portion of the ecclesiastical year was, from time to time, declared to be periods of fasting. At such times the meats,

---

[11] Yet in the diet even of the bourgeois population of a town such as Chambéry in Savoy meat did enjoy a relatively important place. Réjane Brondy has estimated that over one year (1375–1376) between 160,000 and 165,000 kilograms of red meat was consumed, which amount she calculates to mean the equivalent average of 45–50 kilograms per inhabitant per year. *Chambéry. Histoire d'une capitale vers 1350–1560*, Lyon (Presses Universitaires de Lyon), 1988, pp.108–109.

whether domestic or wild, upon which the cook depended for much of his cuisine could not enter the kitchen door; the pork roasts, hare civets, mutton mortrews, the deer *chivrolees* and veal pies which usually covered the medieval table were simply not admissible on fasting days.

As a consequence, a good part part of the cook's professional knowledge had to concern the options available to him on those instances when he could *not* make use of certain meats or certain animal products because of religious prohibitions. Fortunately, both for him and for his master – for his entire master's household – an interesting range of choice remained into which those meats and animal products did not have to enter. If, as was generally speaking the case, four-footed animals and their products were forbidden, fish and fowl were not. And so it was upon the creatures of the water and, in some places, of the air that medieval kitchens depended in order to see them through those periods of 'abstinence' that recurred with such frequency in the ecclesiastical calendar. Fish and fowl became standard lean fare, in part because they were not explicitly outlawed as were animal meats, in part also because because religious philosophers could defend the physical natures of fish and fowl as being less imbued with 'earthy' qualities and so less prone to nourishing the sinful nature of man. And in large part as well fish and fowl became the lean staples in the medieval diet simply because they were readily available to the kitchens of the day.

Owing to the enormous, and more or less constant, demand for fish and fowl throughout Christian Europe, two extensive industries, parallelling that of agriculture, developed to serve the food market: a fishery of both fresh- and salt-water species, and a fowlery whose techniques derived from long, practical experience. The fishing industry relied primarily upon nature, of course, to supply stocks of edible fish and crustaceans in the seas around Europe and in inland lakes and streams. There was a busy fish market that supplied both fresh and preserved fish (salted, smoked or dried).[12] But many large landowners supplemented what could be had on this commercial market by maintaining fishponds which were well stocked with the most useful varieties of fresh-water fish.[13] The fishponds of the Count of Flanders are noteworthy: in the year 1187 alone they yielded no fewer than 264,000 eels, surely a figure that points to commercial enterprise on the part of the Count.[14] Fish husbandry became a very important business in seeking to satisfy the demand for alternatives to meat.

[12] During the six-week Lenten period of February 9–March 22, 1417, the relatively small town of Chambéry in Savoy (population, c.3500), passed through its gates provisions of 3800 carp, 1000 eels and 20,000 salted herrings. Réjane Brondy, *Chambéry*, p.110.

[13] The noble House of Savoy possessed *two* fishponds, and seems to have preferred to ensure a fresh supply in particular of carp, tench and pike for its table. T. Chapperon, *Chambéry à la fin du XIVe siècle*, Paris (Dumoulin), 1863, p.98.

[14] See Raymond Delatouche, 'Le poisson d'eau douce dans l'alimentation médiévale', *Comptes rendus de l'Académie d'Agriculture de France*, June 22, 1966, pp.793–798.

A feature of many medieval cookbooks is the number of recipes devoted to fish and to wildfowl. In the *Viandier* of Taillevent, for instance, we find separate recipes for pike, pickerel, barbel, bass, carp, perch, tench, bream, roach, loach, chub, eel, trout, pimpernel, waymel, small fry, lamprill, lampern, bleak, crayfish, fresh-water shad, dace, gardon, porpoise, gurnard, conger, whiting, dogfish, mackerel, salmon, grey mullet, cod, haddock, whale, garfish, brett, coalfish, salmon trout, sea shad, seal, smelt, sturgeon, cuttlefish, oysters, cockles, mussels, lobster, lamprey, red gurnard. Yet even here, in the *Viandier*, the list of common alternatives is not exhaustive. For some reason the chief cook of Charles V has forgotten or passed over skate, plaice, limanda (or dab), sole, rayfish, turbot, hake, flounder and a number of other varieties of fish that are dealt with, at roughly the same time and in the same country, by recipes copied in the *Menagier*.

In order to impose some order upon the mass of recipes for fish in fourteenth- and fifteenth-century collections, it was customary to try to organize them according to whether they were fresh-water fish or sea-fish, and, if the latter, whether they were round sea-fish (e.g. mackerel) or flat sea-fish (e.g. sole). Such categories tended to break down a little when the compilers of the books came to deal with crustaceans and mollusks (both normally classified just as 'fish'), particularly those like crayfish that were taken both from inland rivers and lakes and from the sea. And some fish, such as salmon, sometimes turn up under both sea and fresh-water categories, betraying a reluctance on the part of the compilers to let the facts destroy a perfectly rational system.

By natural association, fish partake of the nature of water. Their temperament is conceived, therefore, to be generally both humid and cool in varying degrees. For the cook this nature had implications in two areas: fish should be cooked in such a way as to increase its warmth and to dry it, both to an appropriate extent depending upon the particular fish; and the sauce prepared for fish should take the same nature into consideration and be designed both to warm and to dry it. For this reason fish are customarily roasted (on a grill) or fried, and, in the elaboration of a suitable sauce, warm and dry herbs and warm and dry spices usually enter into the mortar. Some fish call for extreme measures in order to dry them. Lamprey, for instance, was generally held to be a particularly moist creature whose flesh required a potent treatment designed to dry it sufficiently for safe consumption. The *Viandier* stipulates that a cooking sauce for lamprey be composed of very warm and dry spices, carefully ground, of course. A health handbook of an earlier generation, the *Regime tresutile pour garder santé*, goes so far as to direct that lampreys should even be killed in wine, itself warm and dry:

> To remove their viscosity it is good to immerse them live in wine and let them die there, and then to prepare them with a galentine sauce,

which is an extremely good seasoning; that is how the cooks of the great lords prepare lamprey.[15]

It is not enough for this author to warn of the lamprey's perilous moistness; the resemblance that lamprey bear to snakes makes the author of this work fear that the former may even be poisonous! The preferred treatment for lamprey at this time is Lamprey in Galentine, a jelling preservative sauce whose basis is a remarkably rich mixture of warm, dry spices, all of them so finely ground and filtered that they are invisible except as a colouring in the galentine.

According to the *Menagier de Paris* (Recipe 26) eels, which are likewise of a dangerously humid nature, should be killed *in a bath of salt* and left there for three whole days, this patently in order to begin a necessary drying and warming process as soon as possible. Platina continues to propagate the learned lore about this perilous nature of eels: with the typically acerbic tone he uses for the caustic comments with which he interlards his recipes he says of the Eel Pie (Recipe VIII,42) for which he has just copied the recipe, 'When it is finally cooked, serve it to your enemies, for it has nothing good about it'(!). Eels are never boiled, of course, but either fried or roasted; a common serving sauce (Chiquart, Recipe 34) is a claret red wine (itself warm) mulled with finely powdered dry spices and salt. As rare as the use of black pepper had become in Chiquart's day – it was rated as dry and warm in the maximum (and mortal) fourth degree, according to the physicians – he still insists on grinding it up, finely, to counter the harmful nature of the eels he had to prepare. The highly influential health handbook, the *Régime tresutile*, confirms the dangerously humid nature of an eel, stating that '. . . it bears a great similarity to mushrooms in taste, in viscous humidity and in evilness of nourishment'.[16]

A third order of foodstuffs, after those that live on the land and take after it, and those whose basic nature is identified with water, is the birds of the air. The strictures against red meats on days of abstinence seem, from time to time and from place to place, to have borne upon fowl as well as upon four-footed animals. The logic of ruling out the meat of fowl on lean days was strained somewhat in the case of poultry because young chickens, pullets and capons were deemed by physicians because of their moderate temperament to offer an ideally restorative food to anyone who was sick or 'out of humour'.[17] Furthermore, domestic fowl afforded the most readily available

[15] 'Pour oster leur viscosité est bon de les bouter en vin toutes vives et illec les laissier mourir et puis les preparer avecques saulse et galentin [sic] qui est espisse fort bonne; et ainsi les preparent les cuysiniers des grans seigneurs' (*Le régime tresutile et tresproufitable pour conserver et garder la santé du corps humain*, ed. Patricia W. Cummins, Chapel Hill (University of North Carolina), 1976; p.77).

[16] Ed. Cummins, folio 66v.

[17] Fowl are generallly of a temperate nature and certain poultry are the most temperate of fowl: *Inter carnes volatilium laudabilium in regimine sanitatis quedam sunt temperatiores et*

meat of all; there were few households in medieval Europe, in towns or across the countryside, where even a small number of chickens was not raised in a coop or a limited run. For a daily ration of grain a few chickens could regularly provide the household diet with a cheap supplement of eggs, to say nothing, on periodic gala occasions, of the freshest supply of chicken flesh.

Medieval recipes distinguish between several varieties of domestic fowl. Reference is made to hens, to cocks and roosters (very rarely), to chicks, chickens, pullets, cockerels and capons. The case of this latter is curious because the castration of a male chicken when young represents an attempt to limit the drying effect of age in a male. Frequently recipes will insist further that the capons selected for such and such a dish should be plump.[18] The presence of fat in a capon is considered additional insurance that this fowl, when older and larger, will possess an adquately moist nature.

Wildfowl of one variety or another seem always to have been available in the kitchens of wealthy households. Of course a long tradition of fowling existed in the upper classes of European society. Its techniques had so attracted the interest of aristocrats that among the favourite 'sports' of many nobles was that of hawking. As a pastime, equivalent to the hunting of forest game animals, hawking allowed the aristocrat and his lady to play at doing what their game keepers and fowlers did in earnest in order to set food on their master's table. Most professional fowlers made use of only the lowly net spread as a trap on the ground or swung through the air on a light frame. Pigeons and turtle-doves were raised in the dovecots which were commonplace features of urban as well as of rural houses. In these dovecots it might be usual as well to harbour an assortment of less significant wildfowl which were called simply 'small birds'. The surprising frequency with which such miscellaneous minor wildfowl are called for in medieval cookery seems to indicate that they had considerable value in early cookery, particularly in a pie ('four-and-twenty blackbirds . . .') or on a shish kebab . The *Forme of Cury* contains, for instance, a dish called *Drepe* in which 'smale bryddes' are dressed in almond milk, pellitory, salt, a little grease and 'a grete quantite' of onions.[19]

The larger game birds, pheasant, partridge, quail, mallard, stork, heron, crane, bittern, bustard, cormorant, spoonbill and teal usually make some appearance in the recipes of the time, even though the basic culinary treatment of them tends not to vary a great deal from one species to the

---

temperamento propinquiores. Alie sunt minus temperamento propinque. Temperatores quedem sunt galline juvenes, galinarum, pulli et juvenes pingues capones que tamen ad aliqualem caliditatem et humiditatem declinant. Magninus Mediolanensis, Regimen sanitatis, ch. 17.

[18] The *Viandier*'s Recipe 40, for *Chappons de haulte gresse en pasté*, is an example of this culinary precaution.

[19] *Forme of Cury*, ed. Hieatt and Butler, Part IV, Recipe 21, p.102.

next: generally they are merely roasted, occasionally while coated with a basting sauce which will limit the dessicating effect of the open flame. In this list the wildfowl of choice are undoubtedly pheasant and partridge, caught, prepared and served universally right cross Europe. Among the twenty-eight meats, fowl and fish for which Magninus specifies particular sauces, he devotes four substantial paragraphs to these birds. For them he explicitly lists ten sauces, the most appropriate to be selected according to the way in which the birds are to be cooked and depending upon the season of the year in which they are to be eaten.[20] An interesting grouping of fowl in these recipes combines (domestic) capons with (wild) pheasant in one case, and capons and hens with pheasant in two other cases. What this grouping indicates is that the physician Magninus understood that these three fowl shared a common nature, viz., somewhat warm and somewhat moist. As it happens, dove, partridge, pigeon and quail are also perceived as being likewise moderately warm and moist. All of these fowl can therefore be subject to several manners of preparation, provided always, of course, that the mixture of ingredients composing the sauce possesses a net absolute warmth and moistness that is appropriate for the season of the year[21], suitable for the cooking method that has been used. Capons and pheasant may, for example, be boiled, but if this procedure is followed in winter, the cold, damp season, the sauce must incorporate three very warm and dry herbs in order to ensure that the dish not produce any superfluous phlegmatic humours: bouillon, spice powder, hyssop, sage, parsley. In summer, however, to the bouillon bases of the sauce need only be added sorrel juice, ground almonds and white sugar: these last ingredients are only slightly warm and moist, and offer a reinforcement of the effect of boiling which is appropriate for the warm, dry season. Other sauces specified by Magninus confirm the ideal nature of the flesh of these fowl: if they are roasted (the most common treatment), then a garlic, wine or spice sauce is suitable, depending on the season; if they are in a pie, then spices, verjuice and wine should be included in the pastry shell in variable amounts, again according to the season.

Greater use was made of animal 'parts' than may be the case generally in the western world today. The offal and giblets – the whole head or muzzle of large animals, brains, tongue, cock's comb, gizzard (throat), sweetbreads (pancreas and thymus gland), lungs (lites), organs or entrails (including the stomach, liver, kidneys and bladder), intestines, mesentary, marrow, udder, testicles, feet and tail – all may end up in one dish or another, cooked and sauced in some proper fashion. Little of the medieval animal, bird or fish was

---

[20] Thorndike, 'A Mediæval Sauce-Book', p.187: *Assature autem turturum* . . .. The multiple recipes are analysed in Scully, 'The *Opusculum de saporibus* of Magninus Mediolanensis', pp.190–2, §§9–12.

[21] Winter is cold and moist; spring, warm and moist; summer, warm and dry; autumn, dry and cold.

discarded. While some of these cuts and pieces may not have been common fare everywhere in the late Middle Ages, master cooks were usually familiar with ways to render them most appetizing for eating.

Certain cuts were recognized as the property of the aristocrat. Stag's testicles, for instance, were so esteemed a delicacy that at the end of a successful hunt a sacrosanct convention reserved them for the noble hunter who (or whose hounds) had brought the animal down. Certain other cuts pose interesting questions about the gastronomic value of both the cuts and certain combinations of them, such as one finds, for instance, in the Pie of Cock's Comb, Liver and Testicles.[22]

When preparing a fish dish the cook could eliminate the bones if he wished, using only a fillet of the flesh, or he could choose to include the bones in the dish. In the latter case a customary procedure after the fish was cooked was to reduce the bones in a mortar, along with some or all of the flesh. In the same way recipes sometimes direct that the shells of crustaceans be ground up and mixed with their meat and other ingredients. Fish roe and milt (not *everyone* partakes of caviar these days) are not foreign to the medieval kitchen, and a few preparations incorporate fish intestines as a main ingredient.[23]

Liquids and Greases

The liquids that began on the grape vine had a place of honour in every medieval kitchen. Today we cook with wine (of several varieties) and, in special cases, with vinegar (white or red), and that is about all. In the Middle Ages the choice was broader and lay not only among wines and vinegars but included verjuice and must as well. In all cases the decision, as to the appropriateness of whichever liquid, was founded upon a clear sense of the physical qualities of each. Must, which we can assimilate to grape juice, is understood to be warm and moist, both in the second degree. Verjuice, the early juice of a particularly tart variety of grape, is cold in the third (or extreme) degree and dry in the second. Vinegar is generally as dry as verjuice but a little less cool.[24] And though the temperament of wine differed

---

[22] Martino, *Libre de arte coquinaria*, Recipe 38; *Neapolitan Collection*, Recipe 73; and Platina *De honesta voluptate*, Recipe VI,38.

[23] See, for instance, the *derme van vysschen* in the *Mittelniederdeutsches Kochbuch*, Recipe 9, the *Guter Spise*, Recipe 58, and in Platina's *De honesta voluptate*, Recipe VII,36: *Cibarium ex intestinis trutæ*.

[24] Because the bubonic plague was considered to be a sanguine (hot and moist) disorder or type of disease (the infected person had a fever and sweated), a common precaution whenever one left the protected atmosphere of one's house and feared contamination was to cover the nose and mouth with a cloth soaked in vinegar (or perhaps in verjuice). Platina states that, 'In this year of pestilence, we are ordered to use [vinegar] in food in place of spices, to apply it to our pulses and nostrils and to sprinkle it in our houses.' *De honesta voluptate*, II, 25.

according to its colour, its fundamental nature was, like must, warm in the second degree, and, like vinegar, dry in the second degree. White wine tended to be viewed as less warm than red.

To this list of the four standard grape liquids we might also add reduced wines and spiced wines. The first was a wine syrup, generally called simply 'boiled wine,' whose initial volume had been reduced by up to two thirds. The second is the ubiquitous product of mixing a virtual infinity of spice combinations with wines. The mixture was most commonly known as 'hipocras'; although it was universally served as a beverage at the conclusion of a meal, a few recipes call for it also as an ingredient. And there were as well flavoured wines such as *vinum salviatum* (with sage) and *vinum rosatum* (with rose petals).

Wine, vinegar, verjuice and must, then, afforded the medieval cook with a useful range of tasty liquid ingredients for sauces and broths. The tang of verjuice and vinegar in particular, a quality that was interpreted as emanating from their cold natures, was a very important element in this early cookery. Any large kitchen would almost certainly be able to draw on barrels of these liquids laid up in their stores or larders.

A major difficulty accompanied the extensive dependence upon must and verjuice at this time – at least on the continent. The fermented juices, vinegar and wine, had the chemical means to survive over a good number of months without serious deterioration. Because must and verjuice had not yet fermented to any great extent, they were always readily subject to spoilage, or simply to losing their inherent 'spirit.' They were products with a relatively short life, and it must have been rare, if not unheard of, for must in particular to last the year round until the next must-grape crop and pressing. Even in Roman antiquity, Cato realized that it would be useful to pass on to his readers a recipe that purported to ensure a long-lasting must:

> If you wish to keep grape juice (*mustum*) through the whole year, put the grape juice in an amphora, seal the stopper with pitch, and sink in the pond (*in piscinam*). Take it out after thirty days; it will remain sweet the whole year.[25]

Neither must nor verjuice was very common in English cookery, perhaps because the juices did not travel well yet had to be a relatively long time in transit from the continent. For verjuice, French writers often distinguish between *new* verjuice and *old* verjuice: 'Note,' writes the *Menagier* (Recipe 279), 'that in July old verjuice is very weak and the new is still too sharp. After this time, during the harvest, a mixture of half old and half new is the

[25] Marcus Porcius Cato (234–149 B.C.), *De agricultura*, ed. and trans. William Davis Hoopter, in *Marcus Porcius Cato, On Agriculture, Marcus Terentius Varro, On Agriculture*, London and Cambridge, Mass. (Heinemann and Harvard University Press), 1967, pp.106–07, ¶CXX.

best.' The new product becomes available, then, in some regions in July – in fact, for his *Brochette of Pork Viscera Eaten in July* (Recipe 266) the *Menagier* does explicitly specify *vertjus nouvel*, unmixed. In other regions a cook would normally have to wait until the middle of August for deliveries of fresh verjuice.

Alternatives, if not substitutes, for verjuice had to be on hand in most kitchens. Recipes are common enough in the course of which the writer gives advice on how to make an ersatz verjuice, '. . . if it is the time of year in which you do not have any'. For instance, in the Tuscan *Libro della cocina* the author advises, 'Should there be a want of verjuice, you can use lemon juice, orange juice or rose-water.'[26] It should be remembered that the oranges of this period were almost as bitter as lemons, and could provide much of the tang of verjuice, though with a different flavour, of course. Another recipe[27] requires a liquid base of one part wine to two parts verjuice – or, failing the latter, the juice from gooseberries. Occasionally, as here, an author will suggest using a mixture of a variety of fruit juice (such as orange juice) and vinegar. Alternatively, and quite commonly, an infusion of ground-up sorrel leaves in water will provide an adequately tart substitute. The *Menagier* even provides a recipe (270) for making this Sorrel Verjuice. Any sort of verjuice could, of course, be coloured green by adding ground parsley, young wheat or vine sprouts.[28] Then at the end of his recipe collection the Tuscan author appends a brief recipe entitled 'To Make Verjuice': 'Get the lees of white wine – that is, the argol of white wine – grind it up, boil it with wine or water, and you will have verjuice.'[29] The Latin manuscript at Châlons-sur-Marne contains a recipe for Sauteed Pullet (*De pullis gratinatis*, Recipe 35 at folio 22v) in which a sauce of beaten egg yolks, verjuice and pullet bouillon is poured over the frying pullets; 'and,' adds the author, 'should you not have any verjuice, make it using tartar deposits . . .'.[30]

As was always the risk with any storage of food, even wines could spoil over time. Barrels of wine represented a considerable investment for any household, so that any sickness to which a whole cask might fall demanded serious efforts to remedy. The long study and treatment of the various types

---

[26] Recipe 126.

[27] Stag's Testicles Broth in the *Menagier*, Recipe 193.

[28] In Recipe 206 of the *Viandier*, 'he who cannot obtain verjuice' should have recourse to almond milk instead. This alternative is so surprising, lacking as it does all of the tang which would be the *raison d'être* of verjuice, that we must seriously wonder whether a scribe has misread something here: such 'scribal errors' are, unfortunately, always a hazard in old cookbooks.

[29] Recipe 183. The old Italian term in the manuscript is *groma*, which translates *argol*: 'Tartar depositied from wines completely fermented, and adhering to the sides of the casks as a hard crust' *Oxford English Dictionary*.

[30] *Et sucum agreste non habes, fac cum tartura vegetis sive caprio surtaso sive rasia vegetis.* The tartar left on the inner walls of a wine-cask is to be scraped away and dissolved in wine or water.

of spoilage to which wines were subject had lead empirically to an assortment of possible procedures that were passed from household to household and from generation to generation. These were considered to be useful practical suggestions and were copied in recipe collections in the same way as procedures for removing the burnt taste from a pottage that has sat above too hot a fire[31] for extracting excessive salt from a stew or from butter, or for making hand-washing water scented with sage, camomile, marjoram, rosemary, orange peel or bay-laurel leaf.[32] With the chemical and thermal treatments that commercial wine undergoes nowadays such recipes for the cure of sick wines may at last be superfluous.

For those who, through improvidence or some other reason, find themselves short of vinegar at the last moment, it was always possible to improvise. In his *Book on Wine* Arnaldus de Villanova (1235?–1311) offers several recipes for making vinegar relatively quickly from wine. One of these reads:

> Dry grape seeds with the skins of the grapes, grind them into a powder, then mix this with the best vinegar [that you still have on hand]; repeat the preceding three times; finally, after having dried the resultant mixture for a last time, put a little of the powder into your wine and it will become vinegar immediately.[33]

Aldobrandino provides his reader with not only a choice of three quite straightforward recipes for the making of vinegar but a quick test for the householder to 'prove' the quality of that vinegar or of any vinegar that happens to be on hand. You can make [vinegar] this way: get good wine and put it into a vessel, but not to the top, and leave it uncovered, and it will become vinegary; and you can put it in the sun for three or four days; and if you want to make it more quickly, get a hot iron rod or a heated river-stone and shove it in, and it will become vinegary. And if you want to know if [the vinegar] is good, drop some on the ground, and if it boils and froths you can tell that it is good, and if it doesn't it is bad.[34]

To these grape liquids for cooking we may also add orange and lemon juices, pomegranate juice and apple juice or cider, as well as the juices and

[31] The *Menagier de Paris* offers the following advice: 'Before your pottage burns, and to keep it from burning, stir right to the bottom of the pot often and leave the spoon on the bottom so that the pottage won't stick there. And, *nota bene*, as soon as you see that your pottage is burning, stop stirring, but remove it from the fire and pour it into another pot.' (*Ed. cit.*, p.172, ¶8).

[32] The Latin *Tractatus*, for instance, contains in its Part I (pp.381ff of the edition by Mulon) a series of prescriptions for 'sick' wines. Similar recipes are offered in the *Viandier* (p.234f) and the *Menagier* (p.133f), as does an early Italian publication, the *Edificio di ricette*, Venice, 1541.

[33] The *Liber de vinis*. See H.E. Sigerist, *The Earliest Printed Book on Wine* (1478), New York (Schuman's), 1943, p.43.

[34] Aldobrandino, *Le Régime du corps*, ed. cit., p.120.

ciders of a wide range of other fruits. For the most part these juices appear to be used primarily as alternative sources for the bite of verjuice. The oranges that were grown in the mediterranean regions of Europe at this time were still of a bitter variety, somewhat akin to lemons in their tartness. The pomegranate, domestically grown in the same regions, travelled well and was not at all exotic, in the sense that northern European cooks or diners would not recognize its colourful and tasty seeds. Apple juice, rarely fresh and much more often in a more durable fermented state as cider, was generally limited in culinary use to English and Germanic traditions. Pears and even ripe acorns yielded a 'cider' for early cookery.

Cooking oils were, then as now, quite common. They were of two sorts, animal and vegetable. Animal fats, particularly pork fat, rendered into oil or grease, were a staple as both ingredient and cooking medium. Normally these fats are called simply grease. Generally speaking, though, any mention of oil in a recipe is almost certainly a reference to olive oil, throughout the Middle Ages a customary alternative to animal oils and particularly on lean days. If the term oil is qualified, most usually the oil comes from some sort of nut, mostly walnut, sometimes hazel or filbert.[35] Almond oil is certainly used as such, but it would likely be termed an 'almond milk' that has not been diluted with water or a meat broth, as was most usually done. Almond oil was rarely used as a frying medium, though very often foods are boiled in it or in almond milk.

Butter and animal fat seem to have been preferred in more northerly countries for frying. The latter medium, grease from fat and, in its refined form, lard, afforded the advantage of being almost a by-product of the slaughter of large domestic animals. Frequently recipe writers saw the need to specify that any fat to be used for frying should be 'good' pork fat.[36]

Spices and Herbs

And finally we come to herbs and spices, and to the much vexed question of their role – especially the importance of that role – in medieval cookery. We have already suggested the short answer to this question: the medieval physician and cook were quite familiar with all of the herbs and most of the spices that we cook with today. Furthermore they believed they knew the real physical qualities of these natural products and understood just how and why they should be used, or rather 'prescribed' for use, in a mixture.

[35] English recipes alone regularly qualify olive oil as such, as if the product were not common enough to do without explicit identification. In the *Diversa servicia*, for instance, we read: *Fry hem in oyle dolyf.*

[36] For instance, in the second recipe collection edited by Austin, Recipe 24: . . . *Fry hem* [pies] *in faire grece fressh* . . . ; and in the *Guter Spise*, Recipe 1: . . . *Nim denne ein rein smaltz oder spec und smeltze daz in einer phannen* . . . .

83

With our increased knowledge about medieval cookery it is no longer necessary to refute that tired old, utterly groundless statement that spices were used to mask the flavour of spoiled meat. The kitchens of late-medieval European potentates had absolutely no reason to handle tainted meat in the first place. A good variety of meats, of domestic and game animals, of freshwater and sea fish, were available fresh throughout the year; methods of preserving these meats, though rudimentary, were effective and universally practised. Nor would the potentates themselves, who had reason to pride themselves on a certain growing gastronomic sensitivity, have tolerated being presented with dishes whose objectionable basic taste was compounded by the adjunction of seasonings that were even stronger.

Late-medieval cooks used spices in their cookery quite conscientiously, with professional deliberation. In manuscript recipes we read numerous passages in which the writer – presumably in most instances a practising cook – cautions that spices should be added 'with care': *specie a discretione* says the Neapolitan Collection (Recipe 136), for instance. In another recipe of the same Collection (2), the writer actually *counts out* the spices and herbs to be incorporated into a dish: 30 grains of pepper, 5 or 6 cloves, 5 or 6 sage leaves, 1 bay-laurel leaf. This is *not* a cuisine in which a huge miscellany of spices is dumped nonchalantly into the stewpot!

In terms of quantity, given the relative costliness of some of them, the cook used only what was strictly necessary of herbs and spices. His reliance upon such condiments was, in the fullest sense of the word, judicious.

Historians who study the account books of noble households are occasionally surprised at the relatively large proportion of the expenses devoted to condiments. For this they offer two quite reasonable explanations. In the first place food was always the most important element in the costs of running any household, yet large estates were normally able to provide for most of their victualing needs – meats, vegetables, fruits, grains – from their own resources, whether directly out of the demesne's fields or woods or streams, or indirectly through barter with neighbouring estates. As a consequence there is rarely any bookkeeping entry for these staples. What especially had to be imported, *purchased*, were wines, salt and spices, with the result that these 'foodstuffs' take on a relatively large importance in the household's accounts. A second explanation for the documented quantities of spices purveyed to great medieval houses is simply the very size of those households. Firm figures are not easily calculated for most houses across Europe, but where those figures exist they surprise and impress. The court of King Richard II of England (1367–1400), wherever it happened to be, normally numbered ten thousand mouths, to prepare food for which the more or less constant labour of three hundred kitchen staff was required.[37]

[37]   Came every daye for moost partie alwaye,
         ten thousand folke by his messis tould,

Given these numbers we may perhaps begin to appreciate why the *Forme of Cury* declares Richard II to have been *the best & ryallist vyaunder of alle cristen kynges*. Naturally few numbers varied as radically as of those present in a noble house at any given time. However, the relatively stable numbers of those who were directly dependent upon lord for their sustenance, those retainers who by virtue of their appointments were entitled to wear their lord's livery and to eat his food, constituted only a fraction of the grand total of family, noble attendants, temporary servitors and guests (with *their* suites) who might come and go from time to time and for whom the lord's kitchen had always to provide two substantial meals a day. There was a very good reason why food in general and spices in particular composed so significant a part of the noble budget.

What ingredients in this category of 'spices' did the cook use that made his cookery different from ours? It has to be repeated: very few. Taillevent furnishes a sort of overall spice-list for the user of his *Viandier*. Interestingly it is both short and unsurprising: ginger, cinnamon, cloves, grains of paradise, long pepper, mace, spikenard, round (or black and white) pepper, a finer cinnamon, saffron, galingale, nutmeg and cumin.[38] Up into the fourteenth century black and white pepper dominated the kitchen spice shelf, but then, over several generations, the old taste clearly must have given way to a new taste. Pepper certainly did not entirely disappear from fifteenth-century cookery, but to a large extent it was displaced by a preference for grains of paradise. These seeds look very much like grey pepper corns but yield a distinct gingery flavour.

Two other condiments should be singled out as exceptionally preferred in the late Middle Ages. These are saffron and sugar. Neither needs much comment except to say that each had a role as an ingredient in prepared dishes that is greater that what is usual in modern western cooking.

The king of all medieval colourants was undoubtedly saffron. A pouch of the reddish-yellow powder was never far from a cook's reach, and is called for, explicitly and solely in order to lend its hue to a dish, in an overwhelming number of the recipes of the time. And just as saffron was so highly valued for the cheerful hue it lent a preparation, so a variety of herbs is incorporated into numerous mixtures in order to give some food a greenish colour. In the same ingredients list (Recipe 170) we just referred to, the *Viandier of Taillevent* enumerates, *pour verdir* – 'as green colourants': parsley, herb bennet, sorrel, vine sprouts, currants and newly sprouted wheat. It is

that folowed the hous aye as thei would,
and in the kechin three hundred servitours.

John Hardyng (1378–1465?), *The Chronicle of John Hardyng. Containing an account of public transactions from the earliest period of English history to the beginning of the reign of King Edward the Fourth*, ed. Henry Ellis, London (F.C. & J. Rivington), 1812, p.346.
[38] *Viandier of Taillevent*, Recipe 170, p.230.

remarkable that sage is overlooked here because it is used consistently as a colourant along with parsley throughout the *Viandier*. The fascinating question of medieval food colours will be considered in the next Chapter.

To be incorporated into a mixture most spices and even most herbs have to be chopped or ground up. A cook today will insist that any condiments requiring grinding should be so prepared only as they are needed. The medieval cook usually managed to attend to this chore a little ahead of time, reducing his dry spices to powder in the mortar and storing them over the short term in leather pouches which he hung near at hand.

It is above all the mixture of spices and herbs that characterizes medieval cookery. There are very few recipes, from England to Naples, from Portugal to the German states, in which only one spice or one herb is called for. Even in those pottages and sauces in which the predominance of the main spice or herb accounts for the dish's name, there is nearly always an additional or complimentary herb or spice to make a compound blend of the condiments. Such, for instance, is the Catalan Mestre Robert's *Jolivertada* (Recipe 159), whose principal ingredient, the *jolivert* or parsley, is mixed with cloves;[39] and the *Menagier*'s Yellow Pepper Sauce (Recipe 281) combines pepper with ginger and saffron (this last for its colour). Very frequently in medieval cookery it is the clever admixture of herbs or spices that makes all the difference, that exquisitely determines the nature of the dish.

Preparation and Cooking

The Kitchen

The kitchen of a late-medieval castle, palace or palatial town mansion was a room or series of rooms spacious enough to allow five to fifty persons to work at once at their tables and sinks and mortars. The main room had to be ventilated enough to provide oxygen for the flames of one or more fires in fireplaces or open hearths, and to allow a flow of air to carry smoke up chimneys or out roof louvres. Because of the noise, smells, heat and smoke associated with the early kitchen, as well as of the very real danger of conflagration, a kitchen was preferably located away from the main living quarters of the house. A corps of servitors was normally required to transport the finished dishes from the kitchen to the hall.

In the kitchens of this period that still exist, physically, down to the present day, it is clear that a designer or builder has taken the room's function into account in its layout. At Dijon in France, in the palace of the Dukes of Burgundy, the fifteenth-century kitchens gave the chef six wide

---

[39] Mestre Robert, *Libre del coch*, ed. Veronika Leimgruber, Barcelona (Edicions Catalanes), 1982.

stone-hooded hearths, built in pairs against three walls of a large, high-ceilinged room. Fresh air, always a problem in an enclosed area in which a number of vigorous fires are blazing, is provided down a 'chimney' in the centre of the room. The fourth wall has a large window whose advantage was multiple: its shutters can be opened to allow even more fresh, cooling air; bulky supplies, whether of fuel or of foodstuffs, can be delivered through it; and, of course, during the daytime hours those wielding sharp knives and cleavers at the massive tables, or scrubbing used pots at the sinks, can enjoy a little natural light on their work. Light is a precious commodity which we tend to take a lot for granted nowdays; in their hot, smoky kitchens most medieval cooks and their assistants normally had only the flickering glow radiated from the cooking fire; only if absolutely necessary could the glimmer of a cooking fire be aided by the much more feeble, flickering glow of torches or candles. Of the environmental essentials in a kitchen – space, air and light – the cook was probably resigned to working with only the bare minimum.

Along that fourth wall in the Dijon kitchen, under the large window, are the remains of what must originally have been several sinks. Hollowed out of large blocks of stone and fitted with drains to a cesspool, these sinks were vital to the operation of this or any kitchen. In them foodstuffs were cleansed, utensils, vessels and dishware (for kitchen use and for serving) were scoured, and cloths (for filters and general sanitary purposes) were summarily laundered. A good fifty percent of the personnel in any kitchen functioned as scullions, labouring in the unglamorous tasks related to cleaning; throughout any extensive meal or a banquet, these yeomen of the ewer were kept very busy, hauling water – if a piped supply was not available – and perpetually scrubbing. A serious chief cook such as Chiquart insisted almost fanatically upon cleanliness in his kitchen: the scullions under his direction probably *did* have their fingers worn to the bone!

Garbage was always a problem. We may say today that it has merely remained a problem that medieval households of all sizes faced up to with much the same degree of inventiveness – or lack of imagination – as is used in our own times. The medieval household dumped its garbage only as far away as to ensure that its smell did not immediately or seriously discommode the dumper. For the grand, moated castle, the midden was conveniently close at hand, right under its walls, as it were; when the stench grew overpowering – which tended naturally to happen in the dry season – orders were issued that the moat was to be cleaned out. (What happened to this refuse, the destination of the medieval honey-wagon, as it were, is a matter of conjecture, but the peasants' countryside was vast.) Fortunate was the castle or town situated on a flowing river, for into it went the superfluities of the kitchen very easily. The officials of towns tried to combat a tendency on the part of householders to resort to the street as a garbage dump; they promulgated ordinances and, admitting the futility of mere law, they periodically had recourse to engaging street cleaners. The town dump, again maybe, but only barely, beyond the scent of its citizens, was usually located on the far side the town walls – in someone else's backyard.

For fuel the fourteenth-century cook had to depend upon wood. It complicated his job immeasurably. Early recipes abound in directions about the heat needed for a preparation: hoist the cauldron over a 'pretty little fire', set the pan on a 'gentle fire', insert the pot into 'bright' embers. The recipe writers recognize the difficulties the cook faced normally even in preparing the simplest dish: a fire of wood cannot easily be regulated to a given, even temperature. For a dish, say of eggs or milk, requiring a sensitive application of heat, the cook's difficulties became acute. A switch to coal as fuel in affluent kitchens in the fifteenth century was undoubtedly motivated in large part by a quest for more control over the intensity of the heat under the pot and pan.

In either case, whether the cook was burning wood or could afford the luxury of coal, enormous quantities were required on a daily basis. For even an ordinary meal the supplies of fuel consumed were considerable: for a large banquet the cook had to ensure that he had entire cartloads of dense, dry wood lined up at the kitchen door, or a 'barnful' of coal. Once a meal was begun he could not take the slightest risk of running out of fuel. Keeping the fires burning at the just right heat was only one of the cook's many worries.

The Dijon kitchen has exceptionally broad doorways in its corners to facilitate movement to and from the outside, the palace courtyard and the dining hall, and to and from the more specialized rooms within. Servers would take up the large platters of prepared food from the dishing-out tables and bear them through a covered walkway to the lord's hall. On the other side of the kitchen the cook and his assistants had access to the pantry (storage areas for a large variety of foodstuffs), the bakery, and perhaps a butchery. The wide, relatively low doorways allowed the free passage, on the one hand, of barrow-loads of logs for the fires and, on the other, of large carcasses for the chopping block, and of wicker trays or baskets of semi-prepared food from room to room.

In late-medieval cookery the bakery was far more important than just a source of breads. The baker did endlessly turn out several grades of table bread and trencher bread, but the room with its deep ovens and fire chambers was home as well to that almost-equally-eminent personage, the pastry chef. (The two functions could, of course, be exercized by the one individual.) The latter person was responsible for the making of pies, tarts, turnovers, anything encased in dough and either baked or deep-fried. In the kitchen the cook concocted his 'filling' by hacking, grinding, cooking and combining, but then he sent this off to the pastry chef where it was placed into the required casing of pastry and, usually, baked. From the bakery, pies were returned to the kitchen proper for any final garnishing, and then served on the cook's authority.

Occasionally in the later Middle Ages there is evidence that a cook was allowed to dream of an ideal kitchen layout, and to transmit his ideas to a builder. Such a case is the elegant kitchen at Fontevrault Abbey in Anjou, France. With a basic floorplan of an octagonal shape, this tall, separate structure had eight semicircular bulges, much in the manner of apsidal chapels of a church. Five of these remain intact today and were clearly intended as fireplaces; the other bulges, now taken away by subsequent construction in the Abbey, may have contained either storage or work areas. Each fireplace is surmounted by a cone and a chimney; other chimneys flues received smoke from fires set in hearths further out on the kitchen floor, so that there are in all twenty chimneys projecting at various locations around the circumference of the building. At the peak of the central pinnacle, high above all the chimneys, a pierced basket funnel fed cooling ventilation down to the centre of the kitchen, and ultimately supplied a good draught of air to the fireplaces round about. The whole design incorporates a great deal of functionality with grace, and does it with remarkable architectural skill. We can imagine the pride the chef at Fontevrault must have taken in his (or her) professional premises.

Food Preparation

We have seen briefly the determining influence that the Church exerted upon medieval European food customs. Canonical requirements, with which the cook was thoroughly familiar, led to a formulation of the first modern 'lean cuisine': the rules concerning abstinence laid down quite explicitly which foodstuffs could be consumed when. As he selected his foodstuffs the cook had also to keep in mind what cooking processes were scientifically appropriate for them, and what combinations were proper, necessary and allowed.

And so on lean days when the cook wanted to moisten the dry ingredients of a ground spice mixture, he automatically reached for the pot containing his pre-prepared pea puree, rather than for the jug in which the meat broth (usually beef bouillon) was stored. In choosing a source of yellow for the dish know as Ginestrada or Geneste (named after the brilliant colourant yielded by the flowers of the plant Genista tinctoria, or Dyer's Broom), he knew that egg yolks were not an option, but rather instead he took a pinch of crocus stamens, ground up and sieved – saffron. To thicken a sauce or pottage on a lean day he resorted to ground bread or toast, thick almond milk or starch, rather than depend upon egg yolks, ground liver or blood. At the beginning of a civet he fried his onions in olive oil rather than in pork fat. Over time, Christian culinary tradition had established fairly rigid rules about what ingredients were admissible and what were not. In a sense every day came with its own set of possibilities in the kitchen, and in the matter of lean-day and meat-day cookery the professional learned at the very outset of his career in a house just how much latitude his master would allow in the interpretation of ecclesiastical injunction. An important measure of his professional ability lay in the creative imagination he could use to satisfy the demands of both Church and master.

In meeting the requirements of lean cookery, the medieval cook became very adept at making substitutions. But occasionally, too, he showed a real sense of gastronomic art. Such is the case, for instance, of the *Flans and Tarts in Lent* which were passed down from the earliest versions of the *Viandier* (Recipe 152): 'Flans and tarts in Lent which will taste like cheese'. Rather than a cheese custard tart, however, the cook uses fish roe and milt along with almond milk so that Lent has been tricked. In a similar fashion the *Menagier de Paris* (Recipe 260) describes Rissoles made of chestnuts, eggs and cheese, but then notes that in Lent one should substitute finely chopped small cod and parsnips for the eggs and cheese. The diner need not be puritanically conscious that his or her regular diet is being restricted by religious rules. Obeying the letter of the law did not mean that one's spirit had necessarily to suffer; piety did not necessarily demand gastronomic pain.

If the cook had only to substitute one ingredient for another on lean days, as clever and as gastronomically satisfactory as these substitutions may have been, he would face no more difficulty than would be posed by reading a hand-written list of alternatives, laid out like a set of equations. The *Menagier*'s recipe that was referred to above concludes with advice of a very general sort: 'Also, lobster meat is a good substitute for animal flesh in these rissoles.' Such a universal list of alternative ingredients for lean dishes might be little more than a compilation derived from the learned experimentation of many generations of professional cooks; undoubtedly it would fit, along with other fundamental principles of their craft, quite easily and securely in their individual memory. To obey Christian dietary laws, however, and to obey them elegantly, with honour and in a way to do both himself and his master proud, more was involved for each cook than simply to refer to a facile set of substitutions for a number of proscribed ingredients.

Because a cook was preparing not simply a sauce or a pottage but a whole *meal*, his first thoughts on a lean day had to be of his menu. What must the total offering of food be that he and the Steward would set in a series of courses before his master, his master's guests and all his household? From serving to serving, through each *mets* and *entremets*, from appetizers down to 'desserts', the lean menu could not be just a makeshift job of minor adjustments, driven only by the need to avoid certain foodstuffs. It had to constitute an homogenous whole whose character, while avoiding any charge of having infringed the laws governing abstinence, nevertheless possessed of itself a distinct and worthy integrity. This character is certainly related to what Chiquart in his book constantly refers to as 'honesty'. It is a sort of self-respect, a sense of honour or dignity that in this case comes from the conscientious exercise of one's profession. It is the basis of professional pride. In setting out a lean menu the good cook owed it to himself and to his profession to compose just as appetizing and gastronomically harmonious a meal as he would be able to do on any day on which ecclesiastical strictures were not in force and the choices he could make of foodstuffs were completely unfettered.

Rare among medieval cooks who have left a written trace of their activities, Master Chiquart bequeathed to posterity a record of his answer to the obligation to create good lean menus. His were certainly worthy of his position as chief cook in a duke's household. They involve counterparts – not merely lean adaptations – to each of the many dishes and courses prepared for two dinners and two suppers of large formal meals on 'normal' meat days. Where great roast joints of meat would constitute the first serving in a normal meal, the lean meal began with large fish; where chitterlings and sausages were served on meat days, salt herrings appeared on lean days; porpoise replaces venison and, assimilated in its physical properties to venison, is prepared and served in virtually the same ways; a Partridge Tremolette becomes a Brown Sorengue of Eels, the two dishes bearing a certain culinary resemblance to one another; a Chyvrolee of Stag, in which the meat is larded and boiled, is replaced by a Larded-Boiled Dish of Tench, in which the fish are 'larded' with long slices of eels and then boiled. A supper's *pièce de résistance* on meat days might be the elegant and complex Parmesan Pie, composed of chicken and pork, herbs, spices, fruit, cheese and egg – to say nothing of a generous dose of wine; on lean days the equivalent dish could be a Parmesan Fish Pie which incorporated fillets of carp and of pike, and eel, together with herbs, spices, fruit, almond milk and rice flour. For a lean *entremets*, in place of the highly decorative Boar's Head, there could be a particularly impressive large pike, divided into thirds, variously boiled, fried and roasted, sauced as was respectively appropriate for each third, and reassembled. In a sense there was a certain irony in the way that the Church's insistence upon 'abstinence' led medieval cooks to develop dishes whose gastonomic appeal lost nothing in comparison with those of their greatest creations that were licit on meat days. The cooks' inventiveness and mastery of their craft must have made 'abstinence' quite a bit more enjoyable for the wealthy Christian.

Cooking Methods

Until the relatively recent use of electricity, with its filament wires and microwaves, the source of heat for cooking food has always been the flame coming from some combustible material. By the late Middle Ages the nature of various sorts of fires had been so well observed, and the techniques of best using the heats produced by these fires so carefully and fully worked out, that the hit-and-miss job today of frying fish over a campfire in the woods, or of barbecuing steak in the backyard, has very little in common with the ways in which cooks used their fireplaces in the fourteenth and fifteenth centuries.

Certain difficulties existed then as now. For instance, a fire can vary widely in intensity, whereas a cook often must know exactly to what heat his foodstuff is being exposed; furthermore, he must be able to regulate this heat closely and immediately. In the Middle Ages the professional cook, in the employ of a wealthy lord or bourgeois, could afford to select his firewood with a view to its burning qualities. He could, as Chiquart does, specify to the woodsman who had secured the firewood contract for the castle that the kitchen would purchase only wood that was perfectly dry and would burn well and evenly. By the beginning of the fifteenth century, as much use was being made of coal – in those areas of Europe where coal was normally available – as of wood. The value of coal's durable, intense heat had been recognized for a very long time in the smelting of metal ores; some cooks chose it over wood when a pot needed a relatively constant heat during a long time.

One of the more serious problems associated with a dependence upon open fires was and has been the difficulty of defining for someone else just how hot a fire should be. For the master cook, the person who has enough experience to know empirically, almost intuitively, at what heat to cook, say, calves' brains, there is no difficulty: if they are in Cameline Sauce he simply *knows* that this should boil at such-and-such an intensity; if in a Garlic Jance Sauce, perhaps it should just be barely warmed, though over a longer time. Even that question of time, the length of time that a preparation should cook, is another difficult matter, though it had a somewhat readier solution. In an age when mechanical clocks were huge, cumbrous affairs and, because of their cost, were extremely rare, and when sand hour-glasses were not really dependable, cooks regularly defined cooking time by referring to the duration of universally familiar activities: boil and stir the sauce for the time it takes to say three *Pater nosters*; let the solid particles precipitate from the mixture for the time a person would take to walk two leagues. As a practical temporal measure, this seems to have worked quite usefully.

But how does the profession cook pass this knowledge on to anyone else? How does he write it down. And particularly, with regard to the blaze in the firepit or on the kitchen hearth, what does the writer of recipes for a cookbook do in order to indicate to the neophyte the *absolute* heat to which a foodstuff in a pot or pan is to be exposed?

It appears that no satisfactory solution was ever found for defining heats. The measure that the recipe writers commonly fall back upon is a descriptive one: heat the pot with a 'fine little fire';[40] place the pan over 'coals without flame';[41] warm the preparation on a 'graceful' fire.[42] None of these directions

---

[40] . . . *a beau petit feu* . . . : *Recueil de Riom*, Recipes 12 and 23.
[41] Icelandic Collection, Recipe 7.
[42] . . . *sur gracieux feu* . . . , in Chiquart, Recipe 33, folio 59r.

is particularly useful except in a relative sense: the contemporary reader, even if he is another experienced master cook and not merely a raw apprentice, will be able to guess that a heat should be relatively more or less intense than the norm, should be relatively more or less even and constant that the norm. It is only after he has had some experience making a wide variety of fires, and after he has himself found out what happens to a foodstuff or a mixture cooked over the wrong fire, that rather by process of elimination he will come to understand what heat is proper. By then, of course, he will not have any need of a recipe book to tell him how to go about cooking the dish!

Along with this minor problem, of course, that of *describing* heats, other difficulties persisted that arose from the nature of flame-cooking. The design of firepits, fireplaces and kitchen equipment had gone a long way toward exploiting the advantages of an open fire and limiting its disadvantages. The central hearth, an indoor version of the ageless circular bonfire emplacement, had been the standard hearth in modest houses throughout the Middle Ages, occupying the middle of the main room's floor, the site of a fire for both heat and cooking. In some noble kitchens this fire in its more or less central location remained useful when the cook could install finely adjustable grills and tripods there to heat both small frying pans and very large cauldrons of meats and fish. The heat and the smoke with which the open fire filled the room were undesirable by-products of such cooking, but ones which people had learned over innumerable generations to tolerate in their homes. A large vent was invariably located at the peak of the medieval kitchen's roof, and performed the same function as the roof vent in a medieval house.

When the firepit was moved over against one of the kitchen's walls – or even *into* a very thick wall, becoming properly a mural fireplace – a projecting stone hood at the beginning of a chimney could channel some of the smoke and surplus heat up and away. This hood, which over time became a massive projection, further facilitated the installation of a variety of devices designed to regulate the amount of heat to which the contents of a pot or pan might be exposed. A bracket or trammel let a cooking-pot or kettle be suspended over the fire and did away with a fixed table or the legs of a tripod set in or beside the fire; an ingeniously conceived system of hooks in the suspension chain let the cook estimate fairly accurately how close his pot should be to the flame under it; and a ratchet built into the links or hooks let him adjust the height of a heavy iron pot even after it was fully charged. Mounting the horizontal arm of the bracket on a vertical pivot gave the cook the means to swing a pot immediately from the heat in an emergency, as well as a safe and labour-saving mechanism to locate a ponderous cauldron in an optimum position over the flame, to vary that position minutely, and so vary the heat the food received during the cooking process, and at the end to remove a hot pot from the fire altogether. Such a fireplace and such equipment afforded the medieval cook in some respects more control over what was happening to his food than a modern electric range.

Tripods, of iron, came in all sizes, right down to a low trivet to set over, or in, glowing coals. Some iron braising-pans were cast were short feet so that they could be set directly into the embers of a fire. The upright posts of some andirons were topped with small metal baskets designed to hold a small quantity of hot coals under a pot or pan. In this way a cook could apply a slight but contolled heat to a preparation, either at a certain stage in its cooking or in order to keep it warm until the Hall Steward called for it. Chiquart speaks of setting a cooked pot upon a particular type of stone (presumably of a dense substance that held its heat) in order to maintain its warmth. An eternal difficulty, faced by cooks everywhere and in all ages, was how to keep food nicely warm after it has cooked but is not yet needed for serving. Then as now a great deal in the art of professional cooking depended upon timing.

For the roasting of meats and fish the cook could use a variety of spits and grills. Depending on the size and weight of the meat, the cook chose a heavy or light spit of various lengths. The longest spit that Chiquart mentions is of thirteen feet, although at this length several thickness of iron are available to the cook. The choice the cook made of thickness of spit depended, of course, upon the weight he wished to load upon it. The spit was normally mounted in clips on a pair of heavy metal stands designed to hold the spit at a variable height before or directly over the fire. Alternatively the spit could rest in clips on the fireplace andirons themselves so that the meat was not directly over the heat but somewhat to the side of the flame. Before the days (in the sixteenth and seventeenth centuries) of experimentation with various mechanical contrivances for turning a spit, the unfortunate spit-turner might be at least partly protected from the blaze by a low metal shield.

As well as spits forged of iron, wood must have been in fairly common use for for this purpose, and not just as skewers. Chiquart cautions against the use of wooden spits; he advises his reader that it might be false economy to try to make do with a cheaper wooden spit only to lose the cost of a joint of meat.[43] The meat that was mounted on a spit normally had the spit run through it; some recipes exist for early shish kebabs in which various fowl and fat meats and vegetables alternate along the length of the spit. Otherwise meat could be bound onto a spit by cord; this procedure was particularly used for small birds. As Platina shrewdly observes at one point in his De honesta voluptate, if you were to push a spit through such tiny creatures there wouldn't be enough left to eat!

A large number of medieval recipes direct, with seeming indifference, that such and such a meat should be either roasted (that is, on a spit) or grilled.

[43] Folio 15r.

Grills were in very common use. Relatively flat items of food, such as fish before or after filletting, that were too thin to be mounted on a spit, could be roasted by being placed on a metal grill above the flame. Where large joints of meat on a spit were attended by the ever-present turn-spit, so the recipes remind the cook not to forget to flip and baste the food he has cooking on a grill. The distance of the grill from the flame could be adjusted in much the same way as for a spit.

Roasting, whether on a spit or a grill, was perceived, quite logically as we have seen, as a process that heated and dried a meat to the highest degree. Thus roasting was the ideal method of cooking a cool and moist meat such as pork and some waterfowl. Should the dry or warm nature of a meat – wild animals such as stag and hare tended toward this nature – preclude roasting, then cooking by boiling could be useful. A third and fourth method still remained as possible choices, procedures ideally suited for meats of moderate temperaments: these were heating in a hot liquid (frying and deep frying) and heating in hot air (baking). The first should cook the foodstuff while moistening it without excessively heating it; the second should cook while heating but without significantly changing the moisture content of the foodstuff.

Again, as with the spit and the grill, the frying pan was a standard utensil in any medieval kitchen. Always flat-bottomed (to sit securely on a grill), it came, like the ubiquitous pot, in a multiplicy of sizes and depths. The cooking medium used in the Middle Ages for frying was generally either oil – which for France and southern Europe usually meant olive oil – or butter, or animal fat.[44]

The medieval cook used fire directly, setting his joint of meat or his pan more or less in direct contact with the flame. He also had ovens, as had many generations of bakers before him. The principle of baking goes all the way back to the time when men buried foodstuffs under hot coals or put hot stones on top of their pot as well as under it. A number of late-medieval recipes still call for a preparation in a covered dish to be cooked in live coals; the writers tell the cook to spread hot coals over a pot. One of the most elementary of recipes consists of setting an egg in hot coals until you guess that it is cooked. In that recipe the writer directs, in all seriousness, that the egg should not be broken open before it is cooked in this way – in all seriousness, because another recipe tells the cook to *break* eggs directly onto hot coals, and later when they are cooked and taken up onto serving plates to brush any trace of ash off them, perhaps anticipating the fastidious taste of the patron.

The medieval oven is simple and fundamentally that of much more modern periods: it is a stone cavern that is heated by a fire within it; when the stone of the structure has become hot enough, the coals are removed,

[44] See section d. Liquids and greases, above.

perhaps to a smaller chamber beneath it, and the food to be baked is inserted where the fire was. The heat radiating on all sides from the stone is even and moderate.

Not all wealthy households baked their own breads. A peculiarity of medieval recipe collections is the disappointing absence of directions for the making of any variety of bread. This certainly does not indicate a disinterest in bread, but likely points to an assumption either that *everybody* in charge of an important kitchen knew how to make this fundamental staple, or that interest in bread-making properly lay outside of the kitchen and exclusively within the domain of the bread baker, a distinct profession in its own right and one that was very closely regulated by the civic authorities of each locality. All large kitchens seem, however, to have had the facilities for baking the innumerable pasties and pies that the cooks of the day turned out and whose contents were delightful mixtures of meats, fowl, fish, fruits, vegetables, herbs and spices. All in all, the bakery was one of the most active areas in the kitchen complex. The cook or pastry chef learned very early in their careers, and fairly precisely, what constituted a low, moderate or high oven heat.

Despite an inability on the part of cooks in the late Middle Ages to regulate the heats which were the very essence of cooking for them – in the sense, an absolute sense, that they could have no recourse to thermometers and accurate timepieces – the problems posed by an exclusive reliance upon fires for cooking were largely overcome by vast empirical experience and remarkable ingenuity.

But the enormous quantities of both wood and coal that were needed to be consumed by a busy kitchen must have posed their own problems. When Chiquart lists the items that a cook must be certain of securing in order to produce a two-day banquet, a vital element in his inventory is the fuel for his kitchen's fireplaces and ovens. He doesn't estimate his quantities in terms of bushels, bags or baskets; he speaks of cartloads and *barnfuls*. The foreseeable appetites of the cook's fires will, for just the four meals, consume *one thousand* cartloads 'of good, dry firewood' and a large barnful of coal. For any modern reader who has ever had the exquisite delight of shovelling coal for any length of time or of lugging 80-pound bags of this heavy fuel, the significance of an entire barnful of coal (and a 'large' one, at that!) is impressive, to say the least. And those are just the foreseeable quantities. Chiquart, the cook with a great deal of practical experience, warns his neophyte professional of two things: that the natural prerogative of his master is to decide whenever he wishes, on a whim perhaps, to prolong his banquet beyond the number of days and meals that was originally planned; and that the most horrendous situation any cook can find himself in is for any reason to run out of fuel. His fuel estimates must always be on the generous side.

When a medieval kitchen was at its most active – preparing the multitude of dishes served at a banquet, for example – a great deal of fuel was being consumed, a lot of heat was being produced in a variety of fireplaces, firepits and ovens, and much of the smoke from the fires rose around the pots and out of the oven ports and into the room. Drafts and flues, windows and vents were a very important consideration in the mind of the cooks, who worked very long hours in this kitchen, and of the builders who designed this highly specialized structure. Even if the fireplaces that lined a kitchen wall had effective projecting hoods that captured most of the smoke of the blazing hearth beneath, almost invariably cooks and builders insisted on providing the room as a whole with a central flue through which smoke and steam from other sources could readily be carried away.

If hot, smoke-laden air were to escape up several broad flues, then there had to be a good access for currents of fresh air into the room, preferably as close to the ground as possible. The kitchen of the Burgundian Ducal Palace at Dijon offers a striking illustration of how this need for fresh, relatively cool air was foreseen and satisfied: almost an entire wall of this spacious square room is given over to a very tall window. There would have been no glass in this window, but simply a series of superposed shutters at various heights and of various sizes, perhaps very tall at the top, medium in the middle and squat at the bottom; by setting some combination of these shutters in some arrangement of openness, the individual responsible for the fires could both determine the strength of the draft that fed the combustion in the fireplaces, and limit the amount of smoke, heat and humidity that could build up in the space where the cook and his helpers were working. Beneath this window at Dijon were located the all-important kitchen sinks, with a supply line and drains through the wall. Doorways normally being quite narrow and low, as they are in the Ducal kitchen at Dijon, the window served a secondary purpose by allowing large, awkward items, foodstuffs, fuel and kitchen furnishings, to be passed directly into the kitchen from the courtyard beyond.

The provision of daylight may rarely have been a worry in early kitchens, with the number of fires illuminating the principal cooking area perhaps quite adequately. However, Chiquart does list among the items necessary for a banquet the provision of a supply of 'sixty torches, twenty pounds of tallow candle, and sixty pounds of suet tapers', these last apparently to be used by the cook or his deputy only when inspecting the sundry activities involved in the preparation of the Duke of Savoy's food. These activities, carried on in areas apparently removed from the glow of the main fireplaces, included the butchery, the pastry kitchen and the fish kitchen. In any case, whatever the windows or vents that Chiquart may have been able to open to provide fresh air for his fires and his men, much of his work and theirs must have taken place at a time of day or at a time of year when natural outdoor daylight could not afford adequate illumination by itself. The smell of candles made from grease, tallow and suet must have furnished a very large element to the daily atmosphere in which the people of the time lived. In the kitchen the odour wafting from burning tallow and suet must have combined with the scents of spices and woodsmoke to make an interestingly thick *mélange*!

Smoke was an undesirable by-product of wood- and coal-fires. This was for a much more serious reason than simply that it made eyes water, choked the lungs and may have led over time to the odd, strictly incidental case of emphysema among the kitchen staff. Smoke could also contaminate the delicate aroma and taste of a dish that was being cooked over an open fire. With an earnest tone the author of the *Sent soví* warns his reader to keep his semolina porridge – to which the exquisite flavour of almond milk has been given – from being touched at all by smoke.[45] Platina warns his reader continually to mind the smoke: for the Catalan Whitedish he must mix the best rice flour with two measures of goat's milk in a pan near the fire, but far enough from the flame that the mixture does not absorb any smoke. And again, for Saffron Sauce: 'Take care in this, that [the sauce] cook down on the coals, away from flame, so that they do not absorb any smoke . . .'. [46] The danger of smoke contaminating the taste of his Rice in Almonds is so great that Platina even goes so far as to provide a 'recipe' for removing a smoky flavour from the preparation:

> . . . Because this dish quickly absorbs smoke, if that should happen get rid of the smoky flavour like this: transfer the rice from the pot into a clean pan in such a way that you touch none of what clings to the bottom and sides; then fold a linen cloth, preferably a white one, which has been folded into three or four layers, or dampened with fresh water which has been squeezed out of it; place the cloth tightly over the opening of the pan. Repeat the same procedure after a little while. There is no more effective remedy for drawing out smoke.'[47]

---

[45] *Sent soví*, Recipe 109. The aroma of this dish must have been particularly prone to contamination: Chiquart betrays a similar preoccupation when he admonishes his neophyte cook to 'watch [the Semolina Pudding] carefully that it doesn't burn'. For an Applesauce several recipes earlier in the *On Cookery*, he advocates the use of 'bright, clean, *smokeless* coals'.

[46] *De honesta voluptate*, Recipes VI, 42 and VI, 44.

[47] *De honesta voluptate*, Part VII, Recipe 54. As is the case in much of what Platina wrote, this whole passage, and the recipe for Almond Rice itself, is lifted more or less *verbatim* from Maestro Martino's *Libro de arte coquinaria*: 'Et perché simele menestra pigla volenteri il fume, quando ne pigliasse, il modo da cacciarlo è questo: caccia fore la menestra de la pignatta, et guarda non toccare il fundo, et ponila in un'altra pignatta netta; dapoi togli una pezza biancha et doppiala in tre o quattro doppie et bagnala d'acqua frescha, dapoi premi fore l'acqua; et mitti la pezza così doppia sopra la pignatta de la menestra, et lasciavella stare per un quarto d'ora; et bagniala un'altra volta et rimittila sopra la pignatta se serà necessario. Et in questo modo il fume si cacciar'a fore. Né trovo miglior remedio par cacciare questo fume.' (Ed. Faccioli, p.146.)

98

For the medieval cook smoke was a natural element in his environment. As he exercised his profession the effect of smoke was for him just one more professional concern that had to be taken into account.

Mortar and Sieve-Cloth

Pots, pans, kettles and cauldrons, huge stirring spoons, knives, graters, rasps,[48] hooks, hampers, spits, tripods, oven-shovels – all of this hardware, in quantity and in a wide variety of sizes and types, went to make up the everyday working equipment of a respectable aristocratic and bourgeois kitchen of the time. Two further items were fundamental, even vital, to the preparation of food in the medieval kitchen right across Europe. These were the mortar and boulting cloth.

It has been customary, at least up until the middle of this twentieth century to dismiss medieval cookery as consisting merely of a mindless monotonous programme in which foodstuffs were endlessly chopped, ground, brayed, sieved, strained and filtered. Yet even those who are familiar with the food prepared for the medieval table have to admit that a significant amount of it *was* indeed chopped, ground, brayed, sieved, strained and filtered. The important question to be put is: Why? For the answer we have to go back once again[49] to the physical theorists of the day, the physicians who, inheriting from the natural philosophers their notions of the nature and composition of everything in creation, knew as rational corollaries how to ensure that foodstuffs were safe to ingest. Foods that were potentially harmful to any human being had to be modified by an admixture of another foodstuff whose qualities were contrary to those of the dangerous food. Sauces themselves, Magninus Mediolanensis assures us, were first invented in order to effect this moderating influence upon an intemperate foodstuff.[50] But it is not enough merely to place a meat, say, in close proximity to several cloves. In order to operate effectively the contrary temperaments must be brought into the most intimate contact possible; for this a mixture containing the finest particles of one or both foodstuffs is most efficacious because these particles – a solid reduced to granular form or even to a powder – will exert the fullest possible influence when in contact with another substance. And so the need, or at least the perceived advantage, of

[48] A paramount preoccupation of Chiquart is that his kitchen and everything in it always be impeccably clean. He insists that among his standard equipment his cook should have rasps for the purpose of scrupulously scraping from his tables and chopping blocks any trace of residue at the end of a procedure.

[49] See, in particular, Chapter 3, 3b. Mixtures, above.

[50] 'Dico . . . quod huiusmodi saporibus non est utendum in sanitatis regimine nisi in pauca quantitate et ut corrigatur quorundam ciborum malitia seu saltem remittatur.' Magninus Mediolanensis, *Opusculum de saporibus*, ed. Lynn Thorndike, 'A Mediaeval Sauce-Book,' *Speculum*, 9 (1934), p.186.

reducing all condiments, and often meats and fish, to small particles. The chopping cleaver and the mortar rarely sat idle in a medieval kitchen.

And Chiquart advises his reader to order seventy-five yards of fine linen to make strainers just for the jellies of a banquet, and 'enough' fine white fabric to make 'a dozen' boulting-cloth strainers for other purposes. Whenever ingredients were to be mixed, the cook began almost always by reducing them in size under the pestle, by moistening them and then by filtering through a sieve or cloth the ensuing paste or liquid. What he then held in a bowl possessed the fullest potential to affect the physical properties of the dish that was being prepared. Modern cooks and gastronomes will recognize that such a fine mixture of condiments has as well the greatest likelihood of endowing the final dish with all of their peculiar savoury qualities.

FIVE

Medieval Dining

Prepared dishes

Adaptations

To a large extent the diet of a person at the end of the Middle Ages was dependent upon the seasons. While a good variety of fresh foodstuffs could be and regularly was preserved over several weeks or months,[1] the annual revolution of the seasons still played a large role in determining what could be eaten and when. Furthermore, the means of preserving that were resorted to by medieval households (salting, drying, smoking, candying, and so forth) invariably changed the nature of the foodstuff so that, unlike the case of a frozen food, it could not readily be restored to its natural 'fresh' state; a dish made from this preserved foodstuff was different from one prepared when the foodstuff was 'in season', and no pretence could be made to the contrary. One did not eat fresh boar or stag in the spring, or brussels sprouts in summer, or fresh lamb in the fall, or fresh strawberries in winter.

As he made up his daily menus, the medieval cook had to take into account this seasonal calendar of the foods that were on the market and available for consumption. At the same time he had to pay some attention, once again, to those doctrines, worked out by the physicians, that had to do with what were seasonally *appropriate* foodstuffs. Some of the health handbooks actually presented a reasoned, systematically arranged annual programme of foods that could safely be eaten according to the relative warmth and dryness, or coolness and wetness, of the season.[2] In the

---

[1] See above in Chapter 3 concerning the methods of preserving foods.

[2] Such a 'calendar' can be seen, for instance, in the *Provenzalische Diätetik* edited by Hermann Suchier, pp.20–22, lines 255–320. As well, the curious *Grant Kalendrier et Compost des Bergiers* offered late-fifteenth- and sixteenth-century readers a quickly digestible compendium of dietary rules for each of the seasons, again based upon the humoural nature of each season. An edition of this latter work was made available by Editions Siloe of Paris in 1981. The *Kalendrier* purported to present the wholesome, 'natural' life style of humble rustic shepherds – and that well before any late-twentieth-century flight from the unhealthy decadence of hyper-refined society.

temperate spring, one should eat food that is not too warming: fat quail, partridge, eggs, stuffed pullets, goat's milk, lettuce. Summer calls for foods whose nature could counter that season's heat and dryness: pomegranates, acidic apples, cucumbers, vegetable marrows, veal or kid but dressed in vinegar, any meat or fish when dressed in must or verjuice. For the fall, termed in the *Provençal Dietetic* the 'melancholic' autumn because of its combination of cool and dry qualities, warm and moist foods: ripe grapes, figs sweetened in wine, fat two-year mutton, chicken, game birds prepared in a ginger or saffron sauce. And finally, to help the body resist the cold and damp season of winter: game animals, roast hens, cocks or capons, and other roast meats and meat pies, pork if roasted on a spit (i.e., intensely) and cracknels, on all of these to be sprinkled a spice or pepper garnish; eaten with rich wines, plain or spiced.

Contrariwise, the cautious cook and his master should take care to avoid any of those foods whose humoural properties might dangerously reinforce the particular temperament of the season, rather than assist the body to withstand it. During February, for instance, one ought not to indulge in chard; in March, lentils or anything sweet; in April, any root vegetables; in May, the 'head of anything'; in June, lettuce; in August, anything apt to 'stir up the blood or engender black bile' – i.e., whatever might be cold and dry – and avoid beef and pork; in December, cabbage – generative of abscesses, the torment of the sick.

The person who took the injunctions of the health handbooks seriously must have rejoiced when the month of September rolled around: this month 'is harmful to no one, provided he had not fallen ill in August; and [in September] a person may eat any food without harm, more than in any other month of the year'.[3] Really, the month of September seems to have been well worth waiting for!

Just as the medieval cook had to be able to substitute appropriate ingredients when he was cooking on a lean, fasting day, in much the same way he had to be prepared to make substitutions in his recipes according to the seasons. He had to recognize that at certain times in the year he would not normally be able to get certain foods; he would have to be ready to turn to some available alternative ingredient whose use in the dish would not alter its fundamental nature too radically. For instance verjuice, yielded by a particular variety of grape at a date earlier than that of the regular grape harvest, afforded medieval cuisine a sharp, almost bitter flavour. The difficulty was that verjuice did not have a very long life; a twelve-months

[3]   . . . A nuilh home mal non fa,
             si en aost pres non o a,
             e pot hom miels manjar ses dan
             tot condug que en mes de l'an.
Suchier, *Provenzalische Diätetik*, p.23, lines 359–362.

supply was all that any household might sensibly lay in, and that twelve months dated from mid-summer. A supply of verjuice could easily run out before the new grapes were available and pressed. However, from the time that the last batch of 'old' verjuice was either exhausted or no longer serviceable, it was not necessary simply to pass over the many recipes that called for the acrid tang of verjuice: cooks learned to concoct adequate substitutions for verjuice, and so could continue to serve their *Gratonea* and *Grattonata* (*Anonimo meridionale*, 'A', Recipes 129 and 23) or *Brouet de verjuz* (*Viandier*, Recipe 25) throughout the whole year.

Furthermore, clever gardeners or vine-keepers had devised a means to have fresh verjuice grapes even at Christmastide!

> If you want to have verjuice on the trellis at Christmas. When you see that buds are beginning to form, and before the flowers open, cut off the bunch of buds twice in succession [over several months], and the third time let them develop up until Christmas. Master John of Hantecourt says that you should cut off the shoot beneath the bunch, and that that lower sprout will form a new bunch of buds.[4]

On the whole, much imaginative effort seems to have been exerted by cooks to create dishes that pretended to be other than what they were. Several motives occasioned this search for the unexpected.

As we have seen the successive seasons of the year inevitably brought times when certain foodstuffs were either unavailable in their fresh state, or were simply forbidden by the rules of Christian devotion. The cook made substitutions as well as he could, of course, but these substitutions, some of which were simple and others not so simple, suggested in themselves an even more creative solution to the problem of unavailable foods. They may even in the long run have contributed to the origin of the so-called *subtlety* or *entremets*.

There are recipes, for instance, presumably to be used outside of the autumn stag-hunting season, to make beef taste like stag: 'If you want to make a piece of beef seem like stag venison – or like bear if you are in bear country – take a fillet or leg of beef, parboil it, lard it, mount it on a spit and roast it . . .' (*Menagier*, Recipe 86). Similarly, if the cook is unable to obtain the wild boar that his master has his heart set upon, then it is a relatively simple matter to substitute domestic pork, although admittedly the cook will have to plan a little in advance for this one: 'Get a male pig of about two years and in May or June have it castrated, then in boar-hunting season [September, October] catch it, dismember and cut it up as you would a wild boar . . .' (*Menagier*, Recipe 335).

In order to mitigate some of the rigour of lean-day rules, cooks devised a variety of substitutes for those meats and animal products that were banned

---

[4] *Menagier*, p.320.

by those rules. Many a cook must have proven his worth by such counterfeit inventions. The *Menagier de Paris*, for instance, provides the bourgeois housewife the chance to offer her family an *Esturgeon contrefait de veau* – Sturgeon Pretending to be Veal (Recipe 206). In the *Forme of Cury* a recipe for *Hastletes of Fruyt* (Recipe 195) allowed a cook on fasting days to shape counterfeit pieces of 'meat', suitable for roasting on a small *haste* or spit somewhat in the manner of a shish kebab, out of dried fruits and almond paste.

The prohibition of cheese, by virtue of its being an animal by-product, was a serious limitation on normal cooking and refined gastronomy on fast days. The anonymous author of Neapolitan Collection gets around this rule by presenting three substitutes for ordinary cheese: Almond Cheese (from almond milk, pike broth and starch), Fake Ricotta (from almond milk and fish broth – that is, of either pike or tench) and Fake Butter (from almond milk and rose-water).[5] This ingenious writer even carries the subterfuge to the point of directing his cook to mold the almond-milk curds in a wicker basket 'like those carried through the streets by peddlers who shout, "Ricotta! Ricotta!" ' Other taste-alike recipes for a pseudo-cheese include the Flans or Tarts in Lent Which Will Taste of Cheese (*Flaons et tartres en karesme qui auront savour de fromaige*) that was copied by Taillevent into his *Viandier* (Recipe 152); to counterfeit cheese, the cook uses the milt and roe of tench, pike and carp. In these lean dishes once again the obligations of the fasting Christian are met – but with much less penitential distress to the taste buds when they are so cleverly tricked.

A good number of preparations seem to reflect a spirit of playfulness, pure and simple. A cake is decorated very realistically so that what the diner firmly believes he or she will cut into is a baked fish.

The games of pretend-foods helped bring variety to a table where the seasons of the year or the Church calendar were apt to limit it. At the same time, though, those pieces of artifice were very likely found to be amusing by those who eventually bit into them. Whatever its original causes, the sense of culinary playfulness, that in its beginnings probably had a practical function, remained strong throughout the year. And over the decades of the fourteenth and fifteenth centuries, it continued to grow.

Subtleties

The games of pretend-foods grew primarily in the shape of the *subtlety* or *entremets*. The earliest such dishes were designed as mere fillers in the middle of a meal; presented literally 'between' the 'services', their virtue lay in their very simplicity, their lack of ambition, as it were. They constituted a pause

[5] Recipes 166, 167 and 168, respectively.

so that the diner's palate not become jaded with a surfeit of delight and so that the dishes coming in the subsequent course(s) might be appreciated all the more. One of the earliest *entremets* is the so-called *Faugrenon* of the version of the *Viandier* that dates from about 1300 (Recipe 61). It is the first item in a series of dishes explicitly identified as *entremés* in later copies, and is really just a fairly elementary dish of ground meat: 'Cook chicken livers and giblets, or veal, in wine and water, chop the meat up finely and fry it in lard; grind up ginger, cinnamon and cloves, and moisten them with wine and verjuice, beef bouillon or the bouillon in which the meat has just boiled; add in egg yolks; strain all this and pour it over the meat and boil everything together, adding in a little bread and saffron; the dish should be yellowish, and tangy with verjuice; garnish it with powdered cinnamon.'

Garlins, later called *Taillis* or 'Slices', is an equally straightforward preparation in the *entremets* section of the *Viandier* (Recipe 64), whose recipe in its earliest version of this collection reads as follows: 'Get figs, raisins, boiled almond milk, wafers and thinly cut white crusts, and boil everything together until it is thick enough to cut.' It is then apparently just dumped out of the pot onto platters, sliced and served. Later versions of the *Viandier* insist upon a yellowish hue by adding a dose of saffron to the mixture. The following recipe for *Millet Porridge* simply boils millet in cow's milk, again with a little saffron, until it is thick. This dish, too, is classified as an *entremets*.

As time went on, in other dishes that were used in the same way as *entremets*, cooks began to experiment with unusual colourations. To yellows, reds (or pinks) and greens was added the yellow-green of so-called 'gawdy green'[6] or *vergay*. Several colours were presented on the same plate, either two differently coloured preparations that were dished out along side one another, or the same preparation that had been given several colours which were served up together for a strictly visual effect. The Parti-Coloured Whitedish is an example of the latter procedure. Chiquart uses a lean version of the this at the place in his fish-day dinner where an *entremets* would normally occur. In his recipe for it (*On Cookery*, 33) he goes to exhaustive lengths to direct the cook who wants to obtain just the right shades of gold, blue, red and silver that Chiquart suggests for this jaunty creation.

Then, if it were not enough merely to plop variegated mounds of some preparation onto a platter, an enterprising cook might try the imaginative 'Checkerboard' that the author of the Neapolitan Collection (Recipe 90) describes and that we mentioned in the previous chapter. In that recipe the cook isn't restricted to just two colours; he may have a clear jelly, a yellow

---

[6] The term *gaudy* had the sense here not of 'ostentatious' but of its etymon, the Latin *gaudium*, gaiety, joyfulness, an English adaptation of the French *vert gai*. This yellow-green was intended to be a cheery, festive colour in any language.

(saffron), a red (cornel berries), a green (parsley and other herbs), or a peacock-blue (cooked carrot peel, according to the manuscript text).

English cooks seem to have enjoyed playing with pastry, designing *Chasteletes*, for instance in the *Forme or Cury* (Recipe 197), in which carved crenelations along the upper rim of a pie shell made the pie into a miniature cylindrical or square tower; or elaborating the so-called *Hattes*, found in the *Ordinance of Pottage* (112), which fold a round of thin pastry into the form of a cap which could contain a pie filling somewhat like a turnover.

Some dishes were imagined that reproduced animals such as hedgehogs, marmots and porcupines, their quills represented by slivered almonds.

Then as the fourteenth century advanced, cooks at noble and royal courts, and particularly in England, France and Italy, experimented with the idea of presenting a cooked animal in some sort of lifelike pose. The wild boar's head, caught in the act of eating an apple, is of course the prototype of such reanimational or restorative cuisine. Certain fowl, such as the hen, swan and peacock, underwent an elaborate skinning procedure before they were cooked in order to preserve their feathers, in which skin and feathers the cooked carcasses were 'redressed' just before being served in the dining hall. The aim was to make them *look* uncooked. By the fifteenth century such *mirabilia* included a more or less standard trick of supporting a cooked fowl on a frame – in the case of a peacock, its tail would be held fanned out, of course. Well known, too, was the 'dish' found in the Neapolitan Collection (Recipe 70) entitled 'To Make a Cow, a Calf or a Stag Look Alive', or some variant of it. The feat promised in the recipe name is accomplished by removing the animal's skin, as for a hen or peacock, but with the head and hooves still attached to it; then, by means of iron bars fixed onto a solid platform and passed through its shanks, the gutted, stuffed, cooked and redressed animal is made to assume a lifelike posture – up until the time the carving knife must attack it. At the end of this recipe, a note which reads, 'The same can be done with a deer, a sow or a chicken and with any other animal you wish,' makes it clear that no theoretical limits were recognized to this sort of recreational entertainment.

Chiquart uses two variations of the redressing artifice. The first involves the shaping of live creatures out of meat-paste or (on lean days) out of pea- or bean-paste. A mortar could be made to yield the raw material for a realistic fabrication of any number and variety of small game and fowl; all the cook, or some assistant whose artistic talents he might enlist, had to do was to mould the paste into any recognizable shape and to set it into a living pose. Chiquart's second variation made use of the fact that the skin and plumage that had been removed from a fowl while they were still in their natural state need not be 'redressed' around the carcass from which they were taken. Anything could be dressed in the preserved skin. In a number of recipe collections, for instance, we find a dish in which the skin taken from a hen or a shoulder of mutton is stuffed with a tasty mixture of ground meat, herbs

106

and spices. In a variation of this exercise the Neapolitan Collection contains directions for creating two doves out of one (Recipe 67): the single dove's skin is stuffed to its normal form with a mixture of cheese, eggs, spices and raisins, the hole in the skin being carefully sewn up and the new dove then boiled; the skinless carcass is roasted on a spit and, when half done, is coated with a mixture of breadcrumbs and salt and this new 'skin' of the second dove is coloured by being painted with a beaten egg yolk.

Chiquart clearly prided himself on his ingenuity in inventing another trick of the same sort: for an *entremets* he skins a peacock in the usual way but then substitutes a cooked goose for the peacock's carcass, redressing the goose in the peacock's skin and feathers. This trick, or what he himself calls a pleasant subterfuge, will not be discovered until the diners, expecting to find the normally insipid, tough flesh of the peacock, with delight bite rather into the tender, luscious roast goose.[7]

This is the source of pleasure that the *entremets* was becoming. Since one creature could be substituted for another, why not create a combination of two animals? With this inspiration the English author of the *Forme of Cury* describes how to join the front (or upper half) of a cock to the stuffed hind quarters of a piglet (in Middle English, a *gris* or *grise*) and so produce the hybrid bastard marvel known as a *Cokagrys* or *Cockantrice* (Recipe 183).[8] And, carrying this inspiration a step further, why not do what was so commonly done for humourous (and satiric) effect in the mock-epic stories about Reynard the Fox: give animals human characteristics. For meat-days Chiquart has Pilgrim Capons in which each capon pilgrim bears a staff made of a roast lamprey (or a 'large fresh eel' if the lamprey happens to be out of season: Recipe 45); and for the same dish on lean-days he uses glazed pike, each pike still grasping under its fin its pilgrim staff of a roast lamprey (folios 109v and 112v). In a similar spirit the *Viandier* presents an *entremets* in which a a cock is mounted astride a piglet and, to make the parody quite obvious, the vainglorious cock is given a paper lance to grasp under its wing and a paper helmet to wear on its head.

Such culinary representations clearly border on the theatrical. The amusing trick of serving an edible thing in a sort of disguise, that is, in a form in which they represented some other thing, belonged to a tradition that had a venerable history. We find in the *Satyricon* of Petronius, a companion of the Roman emperor Nero, the description of a rabbit that is decorated to appear as Pegasus, the winged horse of Greek mythology.[9] The boundary

---

[7] Though Platina continues to reproduce a recipe for a redressed peacock, he makes it clear that its meat has a number of rather serious drawbacks. 'This food is indeed digested slowly, is of little nourishment, increases black bile, and harms those with liver and spleen problems.' *De honesta voluptate*, VI, 14.

[8] This well known preparation is also outlined in the two fifteenth-century English cookery books published by Austin, at pp.40 (*Cokyntryce*) and 115 (*Cokentrice*).

[9] 'We saw in the well [of the dish] fat fowls and sow's bellies, and in the middle a hare got

between food and *divertissement* is gradually passed when the *subtlety* ceases to be primarily an edible dish but is given over to its function as entertainment. Chiquart's grand *entremets* (Recipe 10), appearing between the two long courses on the first day of a meat-day banquet, portrays a model of the Castle of Love. It must be a fairly large-scale model because it is borne into the dining hall on a platform by four men, but this platform conceals four professional musicians as well. These musicians, we are told, must sing with such sweet voices that they seem enchanting sea-sirens, but they must also have room among the complex infrastructure of the Castle's platform to play a rebek, a lute, a psaltery and a harp! Above them, visible through windows in each of the four corner towers of the Castle are a fire-breathing boar's head, a pike each third of which is cooked and sauced in a different way, a fire-breathing glazed piglet, and a fire-breathing, skinned and redressed swan. In the Castle's courtyard the Fountain of Love gushes both rose-water and spiced wine beneath a dovecot in which 'every species of flying bird' is represented, and beside which our roast goose, redressed as a peacock, struts its glory. On the grounds a hunt is depicted by means of meat-paste hunters, horses, hounds and game animals (the hunt of Love?), while the Castle's battlements are manned by miniature archers under fluttering pennants and banners. Beyond the curtain walls, again fabricated of meat-paste, on a stormy, painted sea that covers the lowest two feet of the structure (and helps conceal those beneath), galeons bring an army which is laying a bloody and ineffectual siege to the Castle of Love itself. Chiquart's creation combines the deliciously edible with the purely dramatic. We can imagine the polite contention among the Duke's guests over which figure would be allotted to which guest.

By the beginning of the fifteenth century the *entremets* was being moved deliberately in the direction of the grandiose spectacle. The latest version of the *Viandier* appends directions for what the copyist terms Painted Diversions,[10] all of them produced primarily by the labours of carpenters, sheet-metal workers and artists: there is the Lady with the Unicorn (of tapestry fame), the latter's head contentedly in the Lady's lap; the Knight of the Swan (called Lohengrin in German mythology), the knight's boat fashioned out of parchment glued together and drifting on an artificial pond whose frame is mounted on wheels and hides the human motive power; a

up with wings to look like Pegasus. Four figures of Marsyas [a flute-playing satyr] at the corners of the dish also caught the eye; they let a spiced sauce run from their wine-skins over the fishes, which swam about in a kind of tide-race. We all took up the clapping which the slaves started, and attacked these delicacies with hearty laughter. Trimalchio [the host] was delighted with the trick he had played on us . . .' *Petronius, with an English translation by Michael Heseltine*, Cambridge, Mass., (Harvard) and London (Heinemann), 1939, p.55.

10 That is, *entremets de paintrerie*, in Recipes 215–219, inclusive. The version in the Vatican Library has more than half a dozen such 'dishes'.

Wild Man and a Wild Boy attacking a castle held by Saracens (by throwing balls of compact wool!); and so forth.

The intellectual taste of the age tended to favour solemn allegory and this often overwhelmed culinary taste in the *entremets*. Moral themes, particularly religious or pseudo-religious ones, lent themselves to such treatment: the ages of man, astrological figues, even mythological animals. Among a series of fifteenth-century English banquet menus documented in a British Library manuscript[11] we find such earnest, perhaps edifying *subtleties* – invariably at the conclusion of one of the three courses: *coronys* [crowns], an *Agnus Dei*, an *Aquila* (the eagle seems to have been a popular motif, rucurring in several banquets), *a Doctor of Lawe, Sent Andrewe*, a stag, a man and a tree.

An inherent tendency in the *entremets* toward the purely dramatic is exploited as the Middle Ages close. In a banquet offered to the Prince of Capua toward the end of the fifteenth century, the *intermezzi* have become nothing less than a series of dramatic tableaux. These present, firstly, Venus, accompanied by Jove and Juno situated, in curiously anachronistic medieval fashion, beside the Fountain of Love; later Diana (the Huntress) appears in a make-believe forest with two wood-Nymphs to announce the course of game-animals; then Neptune, 'drawn by ten silvered sea-monsters,' and after the fish course that Neptune has introduced, three Sirens accompany the Greek musician Arion in an interlude; Pan, the rustic, introduces a course of pseudo-rustic cheese called *gioncata*; and finally Pomona, the Roman goddess of fruit trees, presents a variety of fruits.

The 'four-and-twenty blackbirds baked in a pie' were, indeed, an *entremets*, an historic phenomenon of a most impressive type. A recipe for this very procedure is actually found in Latin[12] and in Italian.[13] In the last version, Maestro Martino directs that when the pie is set before the guest, the upper crust is removed and the birds will fly away. 'This is done,' he comments, 'in order to create more gaiety and pleasure for the company.'[14] But it is difficult to qualify this four-and-twenty-blackbird pie either as a culinary phenomenon or as a gastronomic phenomenon; the birds were not really baked at all, rather they were inserted cleverly into an already-baked pie so that, when it was opened, they could startle and entertain the guests by springing to flight around the Great Hall. We may even imagine that some of the more humble of the retainers present – but certainly *not* the aristocratic diners, whose natural weapon was the sword – may have added to the general entertainment by trying to bring down these fluttering birds by means of their archery skills.

[11] Harleian 279, reproduced in Austin, *op. cit.*, pp.57ff.
[12] *De pastillo avium vivarum*, in the *Liber de coquina*, II, Recipe 29.
[13] In two recipes: *Del pastello di ucelli vivi*, in the *Libro della cocina*, Recipe 119; and *Pastello volativo*, in the *Libro de arte coquinaria* of Maestro Martino, p.204.
[14] *Et questo per dare festa et solazo a la briata.*

The significant characteristic of these last creations is that *none of them contains anything edible*. By the mid-fifteenth century the *subtlety* was no longer exclusively, or even principally, a culinary matter; the *subtlety* had become a spectacle, an amusement introduced into the course of a meal in part for the very reason that it had nothing to do with food. The *subtlety* and *entremets* entertained, they impressed, these later prodigies of invention astounded by the clever ways contemporary reality and romance were portrayed. In two or three generations the humble *entre - mets* had come a long way!

Genres of Dish

When he made up his menu for a meal, the medieval cook worked within a framework of several conditions, whether these were laws or conventions. He had to know whether the day or the season prohibited red meats; he had to know what foodstuffs could be made available to him; he understood, or had been given to understand by the Steward, in how many servings or courses the various dishes were to be grouped and the meal subdivided; he had to know the function of each dish within the meal, and in particular whether a *subtlety* was required; and, of course, he must be able to make types of dish that possessed a temperament safe for his master and that were appropriate for each of the previous four conditions.

The genres of dish that the normally competent cook of the fourteenth or fifteenth century handled routinely would make up a brief list. For the meats, whether of animals, fowl or fish, he could boil or roast them whole or in joints and serve them in or with a sauce;[15] he could stew small pieces in a variety of broths or sops, jell them or incorporate them into a pie; or he could grind the meat into a paste and use this in some preparation. He could puree fruits and vegetables, then occasionally fry the puree (as, for instance, with legumes), or occasionally candy them in a syrup; he could serve fruits raw. Grains (including rice) he might reduce to flour for dough or pastry, or boil them into a gruel. Milks he could curdle into puddings and compress into solids. For egg dishes he cooked eggs in all of the 'modern' ways, boiling, poaching, roasting or scrambling as an omelet.

In sum, then, the late-medieval cook's standard repertoire consisted basically of joints, sops, sauces, pottages, jellies and preserves, custards, porridges, cakes, biscuits and pies – if we leave aside all consideration of the *entremets*. At first glance, such a micro-catalogue of dish-types does not seem to place much of a strain upon a professional's skills or creative imagination.

---

[15] A 'sauce' was merely a deliberate combination of condiments that, in intimate contact with a foodstuff, would season or beneficially modify the temperament of that foodstuff – as well, of course, as render it more appetizing. Some Italian recipes distinguish between *sapori*, which are cooking broths, and *salse*, which are serving sauces.

Yet there were many variations on each of these themes, many ways of modifying flavours and textures, differing processes or garnishes, so as to alter the fundamental dish quite significantly. Really, this has always been the essence of talent, to ring changes on a given motif, so that what is familiar becomes new again. This is an essential source of pleasure, too. The cook, as a sort of gastonomic bell-ringer, worked his variations artistically within the strict limitation of his means, his understanding, and the traditions of the milieu where he worked.

What is medieval cookery other than joints and jellies, sops and sauces, pottages, porridges and pies? What is it that otherwise best defines the food that was set on the tables of the European Middle Ages? A brief answer is that it seems to be the unusual mixtures that many of these dishes contain. While it is certainly true that much of what is unusual in these mixtures involves the condiments, the herbs and spices that ultra-modern cookery is only now re-discovering, it is also true that these condiments account for only a part of what we can call typical medieval taste. The larger part of the explanation lies perhaps in three main areas – to simplify the question enormously: a predilection for certain flavours, not entirely those of the herbs and spices; a willingness to make what we will call unusual mixtures, of foodstuffs as well as of the condiments; and a concern for the appearance of a dish.

Aesthetic Concerns: Flavours, Mixtures, Appearance

Particular Flavours

In the first place, in the matter of the medieval *taste*, we have already spoken of the grape products, that is, wine, vinegar, verjuice and must. These ingredients were in just about universal use. There are few dishes or sauces in which the liquid requirements are not satisfied by grape juice in one of its forms, fermented or not. Two basic reasons probably account for this reliance upon wine and its relatives, their durability and the diversity of their flavours. While generally rich and fruity, red and white wines, vinegar, verjuice and must all possessed a distinct tang in a greater or less degree that was very highly valued by medieval cooks and their patrons. Furthermore, wine allowed an admixture of spices that would enrich its flavour, whether this spiced wine was to be used as a cooking ingredient or as a beverage. With the exception of must, the grape products could generally be depended upon to last, always available in a convenient cask, at least a year. Even if they were subject to some diseases and spoilage, precautions and remedies could be applied that were relatively easy and even customary. And these products were produced across continental Europe, were readily available in season, and were affordable in the normal household. Above all, if properly kept they remained bacteriologically safe for human consumption. No other cooking liquid – especially water in this last regard – could compare or compete.

As a result of this dependence upon wine, vinegar, verjuice and must, medieval dishes often have a particularly fruity, tart taste. In the fifteenth century some cooks began to resort to the citrus fruits for this bitter or sharp taste. Though limes, lemons, citrons and oranges (always the bitter orange at this time) appear in Italian and Hispanic collections, and are squeezed for their juices, vinegar and verjuice are never displaced from their dominant positions, and much less did wine yield any ground at all. The pungent, fruity flavour was desired and sought. Many recipes will, in fact, direct that the cook should judge the amount of verjuice or vinegar to enter a dish by the way it should dominate all other flavours, including any spices, in the dish. While must was richly flavourful, wine, vinegar and verjuice furnished the cooking of the period with its zest.

On the other hand, medieval cooks and their patrons appreciated very highly the flavour of one of the most bland of foodstuffs, the almond nut.[16] The same advantage of durability as we saw possessed by the grape-juice products made of almonds, too, one of the ubiquitous ingredients of medieval cookery. In kitchens across Europe large sacks of shelled and unshelled almonds were kept on hand continuously; over the months there was never any break in their availability and apparently insignificant deterioration in their quality. To that quality of durability almonds could add, in the same way as the grape, a certain potential for producing varied by-products such as roast slivered almonds, pebbly ground almonds, filtered almond oil, almond butter and, of course, the hugely important almond milk. With the latter's purity and freshness, animal milk, though in some places cheaper and obtained without the same labour at the mortar, simply could not compete. Besides, almond milk and breadcrumbs made a useful binding agent where the yellow of egg yolk or the black of liver was not suitable.

Almonds were responsible, then, for the other dominant flavour in medieval cookery. This was a mild, gentle savour and aroma. It mixed well with the flavour of virtually any other foodstuff, effacing itself where necessary, or blending with other delicate flavours such as that of boiled leeks or rice or chicken. If such an exquisitely dainty flavour could be said to dominate, then that of almonds does indeed dominate late medieval cookery. Of all of the ingredients that were handled in the kitchens of the time almonds were probably the most common. At the dining table almonds imbued late-medieval food with one of its most refined and characteristic tastes.

---

[16] This was always the sweet almond that was employed in early cookery. The bitter almond had only medicinal use throughout the Middle Ages.

Peculiar Mixtures

An essence of medieval taste in prepared dishes lies as well in a seeming absence of any prejudice against combining virtually any ingredient with any other. The only condition, in principle, is that the resulting combination possesses a humoural temperament and qualities that may be considered safe for the person who is to consume it. It is for this reason that fruits and meats or fish are quite commonly mixed, with no trace of any modern compunction about the conventional unsuitability of such a mixture. In the *Forme of Cury*, for instance, the *Tart de brymlent* (Recipe 175) combines figs, raisins, apples and pears with salmon, codling or haddock – along with pitted damson plums just under the top crust; and in the *Guter spise* the dish called (simply) *Ein gut getrahte* (Recipe 27) contains an unspecified boiled meat that is ground up with fried eggs, sour apples, pepper and saffron.

Likewise a wide variety of herbs is often ground together or, in the manner of *bouquet garni*, bundled together, often in a bag and immersed in a cooking liquid. Recipes, particularly those written in southern Europe, will often call for, simply, 'all sorts of herbs': we must suppose that the final effect of the dish is apt to depend upon just which herbs the cook happened to have on hand. The *Libre de sent soví* is a little more explicit: the dish called *Frexols* (Recipe 169) is to include sage, mint, hyssop, savory, rue, parsley, fennel, watercress, coriander, anise, 'and other good herbs'. Martino's *Herbolata de maio*, or Omelet of May Herbs, in the *Libro de arte coquinaria* (Recipe 126) uses along with beet greens quite a normal Italian selection of savoury herbs: marjoram, sage, mint and parsley.

It is when the herbs are not to be eaten in the finished dish but are only to flavour it that they remain unchopped and are bound together. For his Savoy Broth, for instance, the Savoyard Chiquart directs that the cook take sage, parsley, hyssop and marjoram; 'they should be thoroughly washed and cleaned, and a *bouquet garni* should be made of them without chopping them up, and put them in to boil with the pottage and the meat' (*On Cookery*, Recipe 3).

Appearance

One of the measures today of a cook's excellence has a lot to do with *gourmandise* but little or nothing to do with gastronomy. That measure is simply of the appearance of the plate that is set in front of the diner. Gastronomy should be concerned with the palate or taste buds, and with all of the other organs proper to the digestive tract. A blind person is potentially just as capable a gastronome as one who is sighted – and perhaps even more qualified. How many cooks today would be utterly dismayed to discover that a judge appraising their products was blind!

The mere sight of food, however, *can* excite appetite, and with appetite the diner naturally eats with all the more relish, sensing that he or she is ingesting something that is more savoury. It is a classic area for the action of sensual transference. With appetite the very ordinary dish becomes delectable, and other considerations than the inherent gustatory qualities of a dish come into play. The appearance of a dish predisposes a diner to think that a dish is gastronomically superior or more satisfying than it might really, or otherwise, turn out to be; by reminding a diner of previous gastronomic delights, sight can trick the saliva glands into doing the work that another dish might more warrant.

The medieval cook knew a lot about the role that the appearance of his dishes played when they were presented in the dining hall. Above all, rich colours were sought in the sauces, broths and pies: reds, blues, yellows, greens, greys and even black. Frequently the dish is even named, defined, according to its colour, and the recipe will conclude with the instruction that enough of such-and-such a colour should be added in order that the dish will have the colour of its name! The recipes of the French collections, the *Viandier of Taillevent* and Chiquart's *On Cookery*, often specify – with much more precision than, for instance, is sought in the instructions to indicate even the quantities of the ingredients to be used – just what the final colour of the dish should be. Dark browns, mid-browns, reddish browns, reds, pinks, reddish yellows, bright yellows, yellowish greens, light greens, dark greens – all of these colours recur commonly on the pages of early recipe books. Even the most common French sauce, the *Cameline Sauce*, is named by comparing its cinnamon-brown hue to that of a camel. Authors of the recipes for these coloured preparations provide quite exacting directions about the colourants to be used, and in what relative amounts, in order to ensure that future chefs reproduce just the colouration to warrant the name by which the dish was known.

Among all of the colours used in medieval cookery, yellow undoubtedly takes the prize.[17] A yellow tint could be had from several sources but cooks habitually turned to saffron. Should a mixture need to be thick then egg yolks could be both thickener and colourant. A so-called cheery green colour – *gawdy grene* in English and *vert gay* in French – resulted from a mixture of yellow and green and was quite popular. Green alone recurs on the dining board in many dishes; in sauces this hue suggests fresh, leafy nature, but in the Green Sausages of the *Mittelniederdeutsches Kochbuch*[18] we may be a little

---

[17] Especially concerning this predilection for a 'gold' hue, see the article by C. Anne Wilson, 'Medieval Food Tradition,' in *The Appetite and the Eye. Visual aspects of food and its presentation within their historic context* (Papers from the Second Leeds Symposium on Food History and Traditions), ed. C. Anne Wilson, Edinburgh (Edinburgh University Press), 1991, pp.5–27; especially pp.18–26.

[18] *Ein mittelniederdeutsches Kochbuch des 15. Jahrhunderts*, ed. Hans Wiswe in the *Braunschweigisches Jahrbuch*, 37 (1956); Recipe 93, p.46.

uncertain just what the effect of this colour might be on a modern diner. Blues seem to to have known some favour in Germany turning up, for instance, in a recipe 'to make *kolde blawe gherychte edder blawe mose* – cold blue dishes or blue mush: to obtain this colour one must pluck columbine blossoms before they open at dawn, crush them and mix them with honey'.[19] Browns are commonly extracted from sandalwood or sanders (a pinkish brown), from cinnamon or ground toast – this latter affording a range of brown tints depending on the darkness of the toasting that the bread underwent; blacks from cooked liver and burnt toast; pinks and reds from rose petals, the plant Dragon's Blood, animals' blood and the root of the plant alkanet (known botanically as *Alkanna tinctoria* or *Anchusa officinalis*).[20] A remarkably useful culinary colourant was discovered at some date in the form of *tornesaut* or *tournesoc* – not the sunflower (French *tournesol*) but an orchil lichen with the botanical name of *Gozophora tinctoria*. While naturally blue in colour this substance turns red under the influence of acids, and blue when mixed with alkalis. Thus the clever cook could obtain variable results from the same ingredient: the *Viandier*, for instance, specifies Orchil for the blue section of its Parti-Coloured Whitedish (Recipe 199), and the same Orchil to give its Pink Dish its proper colour.

Such was the ardour with which the search for colourants was carried on that several substances of dubious salubrity were resorted to: a brilliant blue was ensured by grinding the gemstone *lapis lazuli*, and green by incorporating a mixture of verdegris and pennyroyal into a dish. We must, of course, advise the enthusiastic medievalist against using either of these colourants, no matter how reliable and effective our sources claim they might have been.

The substance of certain preparations, such as the rice or almond paste in the standard Whitedish, lent itself particularly well to being tinctured with as many different hues as the cook's inspiration and means allowed. The only restriction, should the reader wish to serve these different coloured portions together for effect on the same plate, was a technical one: the jelly should always be firm enough that adjacent colours do not run into one another. Another dish that could readily undergo the same colouring process was a meat or fish jelly: the cookbook of Martino and the Neapolitan collection based upon it direct how to make a checkerboard by sequentially slicing out squares from a plate of jelly, melting each, colouring it and, when

[19] *Ibid.*, Recipe 41, p.38.
[20] The *On Cookery*, in its recipe for Pink Broth, explicitly directs the neophyte cook on the extraction of this colourant: 'When your broth has boiled, take a good big frying pan which is very clean, and put very good clear oil into it and heat it up hot; when it is very hot and boiling, throw in some good alkanet which has been cleaned well, and cook it and take it out at the right time; then strain it [the oil into which the root's colour has infused] neatly through a layer of boulting cloth into good dishes, and put it into your broth in just the right amount so that the colour of the broth is more pinkish than reddish.' Recipe 8, pp.27–28.

it has cooled almost to the point of setting again, returning it to the hole from which it was extracted. For ordinary pottages that were to be relatively thick, as opposed to being of a runny consistency, the cook habitually reached for breadcrumbs or toast, starch, egg yolks or roasted liver.

A favourite embellishment of medieval dishes is a coloured glaze that was basted to its surface – usually in the case of a roast or a pie – close to the end of its cooking time or just before it was served. Often the glazing is properly an endoring, that is, a golden yellow glaze. This colour, felt to ennoble any dish, was regularly produced from either egg yolks or saffron, or a combination of these. In fact, while parsley and sage are occasionally ground to produce a green glaze, the use of yellow for such a purpose was so common that the French term for any glaze at all was simply *dorure*.

The top crust of a pie invited decoration. Where the meal called for some degree of showiness, an upper crust could be layered with an actual gold or silver leaf[21] If a noble guest were to be flattered, the cook could call upon the household painters to reproduce the appropriate coat of arms as a decoration on the particular pie that was to be set before him or her. Sticks that supported miniature banners were likewise inserted into the upper crust of a pie as a means to please an important guest.

Food and the formalities surrounding the presentation and consumption of food has probably always carried connotations of generosity. When a person eats, a fundamental human need – *the* fundamental animal need? – is being satisfied. To provide food gives the provider an opportunity both to demonstrate respect for the person being fed and to reflect upon the provider's own position relative to the person eating: the one offering food that is in excess to his or her own personal needs is in a real sense superior to the one who is consuming it. It may be a gracious act, a generous one, to provide food to a guest, but the occasion gives the host or hostess an exceptionally potent chance to claim preeminent status in the hierarchy of his or her society.

The king or the pope had an inherent right to proclaim this preeminent status: the king and pope *were* preeminent. For the security of their positions the king and pope could tolerate no pretenders. In the same way dukes and archbishops, counts and bishops, princes, viscounts, marquesses, barons and prelates of whatever degree were in a sense always looking back over their shoulders to ensure that none of their vassals was getting any ideas about supplanting them. The stability of the whole of medieval society demanded a rigid hierarchy in which one's clear position in the ranking scheme was manifest and recognized.

[21] Both the *Viandier* (195) and the *On Cookery* (6, 21, 51) refer to this procedure; a coating of egg white will ensure that the thin beaten leaf of metal will adhere to the meat or pastry.

A means to regulate this hierarchy in the secular realm, and to discourage any inappropriate, not to say perverse, ambitions, was to legislate any 'show' that a person could put on that might, however intended, make it appear that he or she belonged in a class higher than that of which he or she was actually a member. The search to impose limitations *by right* upon such conspicuous ostentation, to lend juridical force to what might seem merely a regulation of taste, eventually took the remarkable form of 'Sumptuary Laws'. Such laws have been common enough in history, even in the Athens, Sparta and Rome of Antiquity. When Richard II and other English kings promulgated their Sumptuary Laws in the late Middle Ages it was clear that they perceived a need to shore up the decaying structures of feudal privilege. Known in some form throughout Europe,[22] and focussed primarily on two areas, clothing and personal adornment on the one hand, and food and banquets on the other, these laws sought to define what was tolerable in the way of individual displays of luxury. In the city of Cologne, for instance, a series of laws beginning in the thirteenth century aimed at restricting extravagance during family celebrations: at weddings and funerals the maximum number of courses allowed for any banquet was fixed at six.[23] Whether citing or implying political, economic, social and even moral reasons, sumptuary laws invariably had a sole purpose: to prevent a person from exalting his or her standing in the social system.

As wealth came to rival birth as the legitimate key to nobility, ostentation among affluent bourgeois became not merely galling to the 'proper' aristocracy, but was interpreted as a real threat to their existence. In Italy a funeral or a wedding was occasionally an excuse for lavish displays of grandeur.[24] Laws in various cities were enacted to limit or eliminate a family's possibility of offering of a dinner following a funeral; similary a wedding banquet could be severely defined as to the number of guests allowed, the days of the week on which it could be held, the number of courses and the number of dishes composing it. In an attempt to curb a move to circumvent these limitations, there were

---

[22] The phenomenon of sumptuary laws seems to have been most common in Italy, where the social structure and supreme government generally had a municipal base. Bourgeois, and particularly wealthy bourgeois, were the energetic social climbers par excellence.

[23] Edith Ennen, *The Medieval Woman*, Oxford (Blackwell), 1989, p.192.

[24] See particularly Odile Redon, 'La réglementation des banquest par les lois somptuaires dans les villes d'Italie (XIIIe-XVe siècles)', in Carole Lambert, ed., *Du manuscrit à la table*, Montréal/Paris (Université de Montréal/Champion-Slatkine), 1992, pp. 109-119. On women's clothing and ornament as signs of social rank in fifteenth-century Italy, see Diane Owen Hughes, 'Sumptuary Law and Social Relations in Renaissance Italy', in John Bossy, ed., *Disputes and Settlements: Laws and Human Relations in the West*, Cambridge, 1986, pp.69-99.

further ones as well that bore upon the number of such banquets allowable within a given period, and upon the free proffering of food to select persons apart from an actual banquet setting.

Prepared food has long played an important role in proclaiming the social status of an individual or family. Only by having a generally recognized basic standard of excellence in matters of cookery, however, could the wealthy in medieval Europe know what membership in their classes *entitled* them to by way of prepared food. Two hundred years of recipe collections show that there were indeed certain food preparations that constituted an international standard of culinary good taste at the end of the Middle Ages.

Meals

Some foodstuffs in the cookery of the fourteenth and fifteenth centuries are different; some mixtures are unusual; because of different culinary theories and different tastes, both æsthetic and gastronomic, certain prepared dishes even are unique to the this period. Another distinctive element in late-medieval eating concerns meals.

When in the day one ate meals in the Middle Ages, and the order in which one ate what had been prepared, were matters of concern to the physician and to the cook. The upper echelons of medieval society, the most elevated and, by varying degrees of emulation, the somewhat less elegant, accepted very clear rules about when and how it was proper to eat. The rules that governed meals were in a sense merely the implementation of those rules that determined *what* it was proper to eat, rules that professional cooks everywhere accepted as part of the necessities of human existence. Meals constituted the means whereby foodstuffs, cooked, combined and prepared into dishes, could most effectively be assimilated into the body in order to maintain it in the good temper of good health. Nature gave hunger; science determined the safest way to satisfy that hunger.

Usual Daily Meals

Time given over to appeasing the cravings of hunger is time that must be taken from other tasks, whether in the wheatfield, the monastic scriptoria, the craftsman's workshop or the feudal court. Most commonly only two meals were eaten in a day. Normally the first meal of the day was the major meal. This was dinner. It must originally have been prepared to fit into a late-morning pause after the initial activities of one's daily routine. Because this meal required so much preparation, particularly in affluent households, it could not usually be available much before noon, the sixth hour of the day. By that time half of the day's work – or play – could very well be done.

To conclude one's active day a second meal was more easily prepared and served some six or eight hours later, at or just after dusk. Because the original basis for this meal was soup, or sops, it became known as supper. This meal too was subject to elaboration at the hands of professional cooks, but universally it remained a somewhat simpler meal than the midday dinner. According to Platina in the second half of the fifteenth century, at supper 'we must eat food which our stomach can digest easily; however, we must eat rather sparingly, and especially those of melancholy humour whose ills usually are increased by nighttime dampness and food weighing them down with discomfort'.[25]

Following the teachings of the Medical School of Salerno, John of Milan advised:

> Rise at 5, dine at 9,
> sup at 5, retire at 9,
> for a long life.[26]

Why were there normally just two meals rather than three or four? Or, for that matter, rather than just one? The answer to any custom is undoubtedly rooted largely in practical convenience, but for the medieval physician the justification for mealtimes involved in part a perception that one felt healthier if one ate only when one became hungry. To eat, therefore, before a previous meal had made its way completely out of the stomach was declared to be a most dangerous practice. Given that the average 'modern' digestive system seems comfortably able to handle only two *substantial* meals in a day, and given that the professional cook was required to lay on nothing less *than* substantial meals, the two-meal pattern remained the norm for most of medieval Europe.

As cookery became more complex and skilled an undertaking, dinner became increasingly more elaborate and its serving was pushed even past the middle of the day. Supper, in turn, could be delayed until 7 or 8 oclock, when useful daylight was past, but it seems always to have remained a meal of clearly secondary importance, at which the assortment of dishes was both more limited and simpler. Toward the end of the period with which we are dealing, hunger became unwilling to wait until noon or 1:00 pm to be satisfied. Perhaps the delicious odours that began wafting from the kitchen at the earliest light of dawn excited people's appetite beyond reasonable restraint. And so it became acceptable to *break* one's overnight *fast* with a small bite at some time before dinner.

---

[25] *De honesta voluptate*, I, 3.
[26]   *Surge quinta, prande nona,*
    coena quinta, dormi nona,
    nec est morti vita prona.

Breakfast, at first a concession, of an unseemly if not totally dissolute sort, became seen as less disgraceful to the extent that it was just an immaterial trifle. The licence was justified – an excess, which strict medieval morality might judge to be a variety of sin – by designing it on the one hand either to give the peasant and craftsman something to sustain their morning's labour or, on the other, in the case of the aristocrat, merely to hold hunger a while in abeyance until a meal that was really worthy of his or her status could be prepared. We find the morning collation justified in particular in the case of the aristocrat who was forced so often to be on the road visiting the various outlying parts of his estate, but who was unwilling to set out at daybreak on an empty stomach.

The earliest breakfast was undoubtedly just a chunk of bread and a mug of watered wine. Then we have evidence of anchovies and fillets other fish being consumed, these like the famous British breakfast of kippered herring being always in a preserved state ready for eating at any time. The fatter fish, such as herring (and its small relative, the anchovy), salmon and trout leant themselves to particularly well preservation by smoking, and came to be appreciated in certain circles as a tasty means to hold off hunger pangs. Besides, if nibbling a breakfast could be censured as contributing to the sin of gluttony, surely the fact that what was nibbled was fish could only help mitigate the sense of sin!

At the other end of the day, at bedtime, depending upon the habits of the household it may have been customary to partake of a little spiced wine, that great panacea in all circumstances. This night-cup was indeed traditional in the house of Savoy.[27]

To come back to the two main daily meals, then. Except in very general terms it is difficult to define the composition of the 'normal' meal, whether dinner or supper. Toward the end of the thirteenth century Walter of Bibbesworth, of whom we spoke in an earlier chapter, sketches a series of comestibles that we might consider useful as indicating the constitution of a typical repast in a wealthy household of his time were it not for the fact that his *Treatise* (or *Treytez ke moun sire Gauter de Bibelesworth fist* as it is called in its original Anglo-Norman[28]) was intended to function primarily as a pedagogical tool; its vocabulary ranged widely, demonstrating to the moderately cultivated English reader an extensive variety of proper French terminology covering all of the day's normal contexts. We may assume that any contemporary who read Walter's survey of this 'typical' meal might smile and say, 'Well, maybe in your dreams . . .':

---

[27] See the contemporary account of Jehan Servion, *Gestez et Croniques de la Mayson de Savoye*, ed. F.E. Bollati, Turin (Casanova), 1879; Vol. I, p.142.

[28] *Le Traité de Walter de Bibbesworth sur la langue française*, ed. Annie Owen, Dissertation, Université de Paris, 1929); the passage reproduced here was re-edited by C.B. Hieatt in Hieatt and Butler, *Curye on Inglysch*, pp.2–3; the translation is mine.

A fashionable yeoman who came from a great banquet has told us about the feast, how their service was ordered. Without bread and wine and ale, no one at a feast will be at ease, but nought but all three were set out there. But at least he told about the serving they brought in first: a boar's head, larded, with the snout well garlanded, . . . and venison with furmenty; then a great variety of other foods, cranes, peacocks and swans, kids, pigs and hens; then they had rabbits in gravy, all coated with sugar, *Viaunde de Cypre* and Mawmenee, all you could want of red and white wine; and then another lot of roasts, each alongside the other: pheasants, woodcocks and partridges, thrush, larks and roast plovers, blackbirds, woodcocks and throstles and other birds I cannot name; brawn, crêpes and fried dishes, tempered with rose-sugar. And when the table was taken down, sweet spice powder with coarse dragées, candied mace, cubeb, clove and many other candies, and lots of wafers.

Outlines of meals were written out from time to time in early recipe manuscripts, that is, in the fourteenth and fifteenth centuries. Frequently, however, these menus are associated with special events, particular banquets or receptions for visiting dignitaries, or in order to mark exceptional occasions. A few English cookery manuscripts devote a folio or two to the elements of several grand feasts: the Coronation Banquet of Henry IV, the same king's Wedding Banquet, banquets offered to the Lord de Grey and the Bishops of Lincoln, of Sarum, of Bath and of Wells, and so forth.[29] The first of these, the menu for the Coronation Banquet, seems generally typical of noble meals of the period, and typical too of other examples of menus we find for the same high social level in England: it enumerates 43 dishes presented in three servings termed the first, second and third *courses*. These dishes range from a boar's head, large joints of meat, pheasants and Lombardy Custard in the first serving, to venison-and-furmenty, stuffed piglet and great pies in the second, to Blandesore, partridge, rabbits and fritters in the third. Every serving concluded with a *subtlety*.

On the continent, in Italy, the same manuscript in which the Neapolitan recipe collection is transcribed concludes with a series of magnificent banquet menus. The second menu outlines the meal that, at some unspecified date, was set before a certain fortunate Count Jerome (*Convito del conte Jeronimo*): twenty-four courses were served, each of which consisted of between two and seven dishes; the seventh course, mainly of roasted meats and their sauces but with other dishes as well, records thirteen items. The following menu, of a mere 20 courses, consists of seventy-five edible dishes ('edible' because the menu specifies three occasions at which

---

[29] These menus are found in the manuscript British Library, Harleian 279, ed. Thomas Austin, *Two Fifteenth-Century Cookery-Books*, London (Oxford University Press), 1888; pp.57–64.

perfumed wash water was presented for the diners to cleanse their hands). One can imagine with what a collective sigh the various cooks responsible for such a banquet saw their last preparation dished up and borne out of the kitchen!

At the very end of our period a document affords a glimpse of the relatively small gap that existed – at least in one German household – between the table of the master and that of the servants.[30] For his dinner Count Joachim of Oettingen (d.1520) expected eight courses (dishes), whereas his supper consisted of six; for his workers' two meals there were, respectively, just half that number of courses (dishes). What the workers missed out on were dishes comprising rice and several varieties of meats.

The formal dinners in the household of a wealthy bourgeois seem hardly to have been less elaborate. The *Menagier's* list of 15 suggested meat dinner menus contains each an average of 26 distinct prepared dishes which are presented in three, four, five or six courses.[31]

In the Austrian town of Villach in 1486 the wife of the burgher Kaspar prepared a meal of ten courses, whose beginning was recorded by a guest:

> First course: 3 artificial fish moulded of milk, eggs and almonds, and sprinkled in the pan with peeled almonds, raisins and sugared aniseed.
> Second course: a dish of fowl pâté, ground and strained, mixed with cinnamon and ginger.
> Third course: fattened thrushes (?) and a dish of chicken and other meat. . . . [32]

The guest, an Italian, was greatly impressed by the excellence of this meal, declaring it to have been worthy of a Florentine cook.

So much for dinner. Supper was necessarily a come-down, though scarcely a notable one, whether or not it formed part of an on-going banquet. The cook and his master used dinner to impress those who sat at the master's

---

[30] Edith Ennen, *The Medieval Woman*, Oxford (Blackwell), 1989, p.160. The document reproduced in Ennen's study details the actual menus for the various classes composing the household: 'In the morning, soup or a mash of corn or legumes, milk for the workers, soup for the rest. At midday, soup and meat, cabbage, a spiced broth or preserved meat, a mash or milk . . . . At night soup and meat, turnips and meat or preserved meat, a mash or milk.'

[31] These courses are termed *assietes* or *metz*, apparently indifferently. *Le Menagier de Paris*, pp.174–182. It should be noted that the author qualifies the nature of his selection of menus in his rubric to this section: 'Here follow several dinner and suppers for great lords (*de grans seigneurs*) and others.'

[32] H. Hundsbichler, 'Stadtbegriff, Stadtbild und Stadtleben des 15. Jahrhunderts nach ausländischen Berichterstattern über Österreich', *Des Leben in der Stadt des Spätmittelalters* (Veröff. d. Inst. f. mittel. Realienkunde Österreichs, 2), Vienna, 1977; as reproduced in Edith Ennen, *The Medieval Woman*, Oxford (Blackwell), 1989, p. 192. The service is typically German, with each dish being presented alone in its own course.

board; the second main meal in the day was more perhaps just a matter of necessity, a means to tide a person over until dinner at noon on the next day. One exception to the customary primacy of dinner over supper might be allowed in the case where some exceptionally strenuous activity was envisioned for the afternoon. It was, for instance, common to mark a particularly significant moment in court life with both a banquet and a tournament. Chiquart seems to consider that such a coincidence of events might suggest an adjustment on the part of the cook. '. . . If jousts, tournaments or other recreational activities should be held on that day [of a banquet], the cooks would be well advised to prepare all the lighter a dinner, and to make the supper that much more worthy and generous.'[33] Normally only one course of dishes was served at Chiquart's suppers.

For the bourgeois *Menagier de Paris* supper was only slightly less ambitious than dinner: in his three sample menus for meat supper, there are an average of 19 prepared dishes served in either three or four courses.

The late Middle Ages nourished a fine sense of the ways in which mealtime could be used to reflect the glory of the person eating. When we today are impressed by the surprising quantity and variety of preparations that make up some late-medieval banquets, we should bear in mind that the designers of the banquets *intended* to make precisely such an impression upon the guests (and probably as well upon everyone who mattered but who was *not* invited). A banquet was merely a marvellously inflated meal. A potentate offering a banquet succeeded in evoking awe primarily by means of two factors: quantity and the *entremets*. When we examine closely the contents of these fabulous feasts, what we find is that we recognize virtually all of the dishes. All of them turn up here or there in our recipe collections, whether they happen to have been preparations that were current away back at the end of the thirteenth century, or whether they are of the latest, most modern, fifteenth-century invention.

Such a realization may be a little disappointing perhaps. We might expect that such a prodigious event as a banquet, by its very exceptionality, by the very definition of it as a demonstration of precellence, would somehow offer the flattered diner dishes that were extraordinary. But even the most astounding banquet menus are little more than very long lists of quite normal dishes. And, more to the current point, the structure of the banquet menu, when it is boiled down to what we might call everyday proportions, is fundamentally that of the normal daily meal of any aristocratic household.

The grand banquet opens with the same sorts of dishes as the cook prepared for any dinner, builds during the lengthy succession of courses by an accumulation of dishes that would be served at a similar point in practically any regular meal, and concludes in ways that would put no great demands upon the competence of any experienced household cook. Apart

---

[33] *Chiquart's 'On Cookery'*, p.119, n.238.

from any specially contrived *subtleties*, a banquet was in its essence a meal like any other. It was really just more of the same.

Determinant Factors: Ecclesiastical and Medical

The meal in late-medieval times was shaped by two enormous considerations: ecclesiastic and medical. Religious strictures determined what foods could be eaten on what days and in what times of the year; as a consequence a meal in a Christian household on a lean day or during a fasting period was quite different from a meal when such restrictions did not apply. The order of foods served in a meal was to a very large extent determined likewise by considerations which lay outside what today we would call the strictly gastronomical or culinary. As well as the composition of particular dishes, medical authorities prescribed the proper composition of a meal by means of reference to the natural qualities of foods, both in and by themselves and in learned mixtures. While it is true that much of the influence from these two sources no longer plays much of a role in our thinking about food today, certain curious vestiges do remain. At any rate when people sat down to eat five and six centuries ago the effects of both areas of doctrine in their lives, the religious and the medical, were profound in determining what could be set before them.

Religious rules

The injunctions that defined lean periods in the ecclesiastical calendar bore upon foods and not upon dishes or meals. If at those designated times the cook took care not to use the foodstuffs that were forbidden, then as far as the canons of Christianity were concerned he was free to do whatever he and his secular master wanted. As the author of the *Guter Spise* notes very carefully when writing his recipe for salmon (*Lahs*, Recipe 19): *Ist ez aber eins fleischtages.*

It is probable that one of the reasons the faithful accepted with relative docility the doctrinal imposition of dietary rules was that, for the upper classes at least, the alternatives to a normal 'meat-day' meal were not really all that bad. In the *On Cookery*, Chiquart's recipes are arranged in such a way that a kitchen clerk or household steward can find menu suggestions for lean days. With rigorous symmetry the Master Cook of the Duke of Savoy describes lean dishes that are in every case the equivalent of those he lists that might have composed his menu on a meat day.

German Broth of Capons	German Broth of Fish
Savoy Broth of Poultry	Savoy Broth of Fish
Lamprey Sauce of Beef Loin	Tripes of Large Fish
Frumenty & Venison	Rice & Dolphin
Talmoses & Flans	Almond Milk Flans

Partridge Tremollette	Brown Sorengue of Eels
Chyvrolee of Stag	Larded-Boiled Tench
Rabbit in Saupique	Fried Fish in Saupiquet
Jacobin Capon Sops	Georgé Broth on Fish
Buchat of Rabbit	Verjuice Broth on Fish
Parmesan Meat Pies	Parmesan Fish Pies

And so forth. These lean counterparts are in no way less interesting, less appetizing, than the meat-day dishes. They are alternatives to meat dishes only in the sense that they are built around or incorporate foodstuffs that were not prohibited at those times. Clearly Chiquart and his professional colleagues sought to meet the challenge imposed by the Church by using a good deal of imagination and gastronomic sense.

Among supplementary material at the conclusion of the *On Cookery* Chiquart has appended a record of the menu for a grand banquet which he was responsible for preparing some twenty years before he compiled his cookbook. The occasion was the meeting of his master the Duke with that most glorious and mighty potentate of all of Europe, the Duke of Burgundy. In 1403 the Duke of Burgundy handed his eighteen-year-old daughter, Mary, to the man to whom she had technically been married since the age of eight, Amadeus, the then twenty-year-old Count of Savoy. The formal ceremony was held at a castle on the very border between Burgundy and Savoy, and was marked by the banquet of which Chiquart was required to take charge. That the Friday and Saturday on which the banquet fell were, *ipso facto*, lean days probably did not worry Chiquart overly. By the sound of the menu which Chiquart proudly reproduces, none of the noble guests should have been upset.

In the year of Grace 14.., Amadeus, First Duke of Savoy, my most mighty Lord, received my Lord of Burgundy, and because I, Chiquart, who was his cook at that time, fulfilling my duty, prepared and ordered to be prepared several notable dishes for the Dinners and Suppers for that banquet, I ordered, made, or had made by order of my aforesaid most mighty Lord, at the First Serving of the dinner of the first day, and commanded to be written down, what follows here, to wit:

Get big salt fish such as salt mullets along with big pieces of fillet of salt pike and several other salt fish, and set these out in fine dishes; then, with them, get herrings and set them out in another fine dish by themselves; for all that has just been mentioned no other sauce is needed but Mustard. And pea puree and a puree of greens will be the pottage for that serving; as well, a White Almond Broth on fried fish, a German Broth, a Brown Sorengue of eels, and the pasties, and fish tripe carefully cleaned and prepared to make an Arbaleste. For the *entremets* of the first serving, pike cooked in three ways, that is, fried in the middle, the third at the head boiled, and the tail third roasted; as well, other pike boiled in the middle, roasted at the head and fried at the tail;

and because the above fish are called Glazed Pilgrim Pike, they should have over them a good roast lamprey which will be the staffs of those pilgrims – and if you do not have any lamprey, use eel. The staff, that is, the lamprey, should be eaten with Lamprey Sauce, and the eel with Green Garlic Verjuice Sauce; the boiled part of the pike should be eaten with Green Sauce, the fried and the roasted parts with Green Verjuice or with oranges. And fish tripe, well cleaned and properly prepared, to make an Arbaleste, and these tripe should be served before the *entremets*.

At the Second Serving: first get all sorts of sea-fish set out by themselves in great gold dishes; then fresh-water fish – big pike fillets, big carp fillets, big trout, fresh pollacks, dace, big fillets of char, big perch and other fish; lamprey in Lamprey Sauce, a Salamine, a yellow Larded-Boiled Dish of tench, with sops, Rice-and-Venison of Dolphin, and crayfish in vinegar. Of the sauces appropriate for the above-mentioned fish, we need make no mention. For the *–entremets*, Parmesan Pies, each one endored and embanded with the arms of the Lord before whom it is set.

For the Supper:

First: roasts of pickerel and pollack and all sorts of suitable roast fish; they are served with Green Sorrel Verjuice; and White Sops of Almonds, with fish jelly, white sea-fish and white fresh-water fish, Norse Pasties, fried onions, and fried fish in Saupiquet.

For the next day.

For the First Serving of the Dinner: strained peas and turnips, a George Broth, a salt-dish of herrings by themselves in a fine dish, eels, trout and salt pollack, a Violet Broth on fried fish, a Vinaigrette of Fish Tripe on fried fish, a Genista Broth on fried fish.

The Second Serving: all sorts of white fish, either sea-fish or fresh-water fish, a Party Whitedish in four colours, gold, blue, silver and red, together with a Yellow Verjuice on fish, rice, small Almond Flans, Galentine of Lamprey, crayfish, and a Savoy Broth.

For the Supper:

First, white fish, pasties, Green Sops, a King's Broth, Fish-Tripe Sausages, glazed Rissoles, a Chaudumel, and a Camelin Broth.[34]

As an unavoidable fact of life in the Middle Ages, the lean meal seems to have contributed its fair share to the history of medieval gastronomy.

Physical/humoural dogma

When *we* in the twentieth century sit down to dinner, as guests either in someone's home or at a restaurant, we have certain expectations concerning what will be set before us. We are not too surprised if our host, or the waiter, begins by offering some sort of appetizer, then follows successively with soup, a salad, fish and then meat dishes, a dessert preparation, then cheese and

[34] *Chiquart's 'On Cookery'*, pp.116–119.

perhaps nuts; a formal meal concludes with a cordial. The sequence of dishes and of foods seems normal to us; the way the meal proceeds seems to have something natural about it, almost as if it were ordained by common sense.

If there is any common sense in the sequence in which we eat the varieties of foods that make up a normal meal, then that common sense is medieval. The very notion of foods that are appropriate to the beginning and to the end of a meal, the aperitif and the digestive, are rooted in medieval theories concerning the function of the stomach. The stomach is the place in which everything that is ingested undergoes its basic transformation in order to be converted firstly into chyme, then into chyle and then into blood. The image of the stomach was of a sort of flexible cooking pot; the verb used to express the idea of digesting was that of cooking: the stomach 'cooked' what was given to it. However, the problem was that, as with the cooking operation that took place in a pot over a fire, various foods had various cooking times. And furthermore the process of cooking reduced the substance of some foodstuffs to a mush that flowed relatively rapidly through the digestive system, while it toughened that of others to a state that took longer to flow through and sometimes even tended to stop up the digestive course. Horrible things were perceived as resulting from any delay or stoppage in the digestive process.

> What should be eaten first. There is an order to be observed in taking food, since everything that moves the bowels and whatever is of light and slight nourishment, like apples and pears, is more safely and pleasantly eaten in the first course. I even add lettuce and whatever is served with vinegar and oil, raw or cooked. Then there are eggs, especially the soft-cooked kind, and certain sweets which we call *bellaria*, seasoned with spices and pine-nuts, or honey, or sugar. These are served first to guests.[35]

The composition of a meal was a matter of great interest to the theorists. A complex doctrine was worked out to determine the sequence in which it was scientifically most proper to consume various foods. This doctrine was based, as always, upon an understanding of the qualities of foods. On the one hand the doctrine postulated that some foods were by nature more digestible or, rather, more readily digestible, than others; on the other hand the theorists surmised that the function of digestion must involve some sort of cooking procedure. Both notions seemed entirely reasonable. Empiric observation

---

[35] *Quid sit edendum primo. Observandus est ordo in assumendis cibis cum omnia quae alvum movent quaeque lenis ac parvi sunt alimenti ut poma fere ac pira quaedam tutius ac suavius prima mensa comedantur. Addo etiam lactucas et quicquid crudum vel coctum ex aceto et oleo assumitur. Ova praeterea sorbilia praesertim ac tragemata quaedam quae nos bellaria dicimus ex aromatibus et nucleis pineis aut melle aut saccharo condita. Conviviis percommode apponuntur.* Bartolomeo Sacchi (also known as Platina), *De honesta voluptate*, Book 1, Ch. 16.

showed even the most unlettered person that ricotta cheese is difficult to digest, but that most cereals digest quite easily. As a consequence it would be an appalling error to consume ricotta cheese at the beginning of a meal because it would immediately sink to the bottom of the stomach and, sitting there while undergoing its slow digestion, it would obstruct the egress of more rapidly digested foods from the stomach. As these latter continued a superfluous digestion, they would generate excessive moist humours that would tend to be corruptive, to putrefy and to disrupt the body's humoural balance most grievously. Though nourishing, such cheese should be kept until the conclusion of a meal, and preferably eaten with walnuts or almonds in order to warm it and aid in its digestion.

That the action of the stomach was envisioned as analogous to that of a furnace is not really surprising.[36] Since heat is the essential resource of the stomach, according to Platina we should limit after-dinner activity to light humour and games. 'If we have to work at night, we should not do that immediately after eating, but only after the first digestion is finished, for by the activity and excitement of the mind natural heat is drawn from the stomach and it is rendered too weak for digestion.'[37]

Food is prepared for ingestion and useful digestion by a human being by subjecting it to a sort of preliminary cooking in a kitchen, over a fire or in an oven; to further transform a food in order that it become chyle and eventually blood, and so be absorbed into the nature of the human body, the stomach merely continues what amounts to an extensive cooking process. By means of heat and moisture, qualities that are the essence of the human body, the stomach renders food more like that human body: in a quite comprehensible way, cooking is digestion and digestion is cooking. As a consequence of the perception of this principle the best aperitifs are those that warm the stomach up and prepare it for its function; the most easily digested foods are those that are moderately warm and moist to begin with.

These latter are the foods, no matter what their actual nutritive value may be, that commend themselves to the stomach at the beginning of a meal. Conversely, those foods over which the human furnace must labour at length in order to extract all of their nourishment from them should be served toward a meal's end. And so the first course of the medieval dinner most likely contained boiled dishes such as stewed meats or vegetables, while the last *main* course might contain dishes of venison or fish.

Again, the order of dishes in a medieval meal was not at all a random caprice. A cook determined the structure of a meal by a careful calculation and weighing of a number of scientifically known factors. Just as the health of his patron depended upon a cook's decision about the composition of each

---

[36] Throughout his De honesta volutate, Platina uses the Latin verb concoquere ('to cook together' or 'to finish cooking') to express the idea of the stomach's digestive function.
[37] Ibid., I, 4.

prepared dish, so too it depended upon the sequence in which he decided to set out his various preparations on his patron's dining board.

What the knowledgeable diner had, then, to take care to do was, firstly, to make sure that his or her stomach was prepared to 'cook' the meal that was headed its way; secondly, that the foods passed into it arrived in a order such that those that were easier to process came before those that were more difficult, and so were not held up (and consequently overcooked, as it were) waiting to be processed from the outlet of the stomach; and thirdly, that this mini-factory was properly closed down at the conclusion of its functions. The aperitif literally opened the stomach: that is the sense of the word, coming as it does from the Latin, *aperire*, 'to open'. The aperitif could be either a solid or a liquid, provided that its properties were such as to allow foods that passed through the gullet to enter the stomach and and to encourage the stomach to undertake its primary function. Without an efficacious aperitif it must be supposed that chewed and swallowed foods might well remain undigested – or, at the least, that one's stomach would only sluggishly begin to accept small amounts of the food that one was prepared to send down to it for processing. To begin a meal with an aperitif was simply a practical way to ensure that efficient digestion did take place.

> ... Buttir is an holsom mete, first and eke last,
> for he wille a stomak kepe & helpe poyson a-wey to cast,
> also he norishethe a man to be laske and evy humerus to wast,
> and with white bred he wille kepe thy mouthe in tast.[38]

There is no widespread agreement on the best aperitif. Physicians point to the utility of certain confections consisting of seeds, such as anise or caraway, steeped in honey or in sugar.[39] Anise and caraway, along with

---

[38] John Russell's *Boke of Nurture*, ed. Frederick J. Furnivall, p.7: 'Butter is a wholesome food, at the beginning and end of a meal, for it fortifies the stomach and protects it from poisons; it also nourishes by opening the stomach and clears away ill humours – and on white bread will add relish to eating.' In his *Dyetary of Helth*, Andrewe Boorde (c.1490–1549) even goes so far as to advocate beginning the day with butter: 'Butter is made of crayme, and is moyste of operacion; it is good to eate in the mornyng before other meates. ... A lytell porcyon is good for every man in the morenynge, yf it be newe made.' Ed. F.J. Furnivall, London (Kegan Paul), 1870, pp.265–66.

[39] See Magninus Mediolanensis, *Regimen sanitatis*, Part 2, Chapter 3, Paragraph 26, 'De confectionibus et earum usu.' Magninus lists the best *confectiones* then in use 'and the most delicious' as candied ginger, sugar- or honey-coated ginger, candied pine-nuts, pistachios and filberts, candied aniseed, candied coriander, fennel and juniper, crude *dragées*, fine table *dragées*, rose-sugar, *dyacitonium*, marzipan, walnuts candied in sugar or honey, filberts candied in sugar, and dates. A nougat, itself called 'mazapan' (marzipan), was made with sugar, filberts, almonds, pistachios, pine-nuts, along with flour and, optionally, egg whites. Many fruits, including orange, lemon, plum and apricot, could be *confit*, that is, candied. In the fifteenth century an entire work was devoted to recipes for fruit confections made with honey or sugar: L. Faraudo de Saint-

fennel and cumin, were held to be the warmest of seeds, and consequently most appropriate for stoking the stomach to perform its cooking 'function'. According to Aldobrandino of Siena, anise 'strengthens the stomach's power to digest food properly,' as does caraway. Wine, likewise, drunk alone in a moderate quantity on an empty stomach, opens its orifice and arouses the appetite.[40] Wine is recognized by the scholars of the time to be one of the naturally warmest of liquids, especially red wine. (Wine is also held to be the most useful substance one can absorb in order to hold old age at bay – provided, the physicians advise us, it is not used in excess!) The modern tipple of sherry before a meal has a long and respectable history.

> . . . Milke, crayme and cruddes, and eke the joncate,
> they close a mannes stomak, and so dothe the possate;
> therfore ete hard chese aftir, yef ye sowpe late,
> and drynk romney modoun, for feere of chekmate.[41]

The digestive was thought to operate in a way contrary to the operation of the aperitif. After consuming a meal the diner had to close the aperture of his or her stomach. The action was somewhat analogous to fixing a cover on a cooking pot: the cooking processes of digestion occurred best in a closed container. At the conclusion of a formal modern meal the host or hostess might pass a platter of chocolate wafers, and the restauranteur, usually on the same salver as the bill – suggesting that it was high time the client vacated his/her table in favour of the next customer – presents a hard factory-celophane-wrapped sweet. At the origin of this practice is the medieval *dragée*. This small candy is not to be confused with the modern *dragée*, normally a candy-coated almond. Because of their warm nature, spices were valued in cooking, but spices by themselves could be consumed in a more or less pure state in order to warm the stomach. So warmed, the stomach could fulfil its cooking function most efficiently.

This re-warming of the stomach is, in very summary terms, just what both the medieval and the modern diner do when they pop the final sweet. Sugar itself was a highly valued foodstuff – a pharmaceutical product of widely

Germain, '*Libre de totes maneres de confits*. Un tratado manual cuatrocentista de arte de dulcería', *Boletín de la Academia de Buenas Letras de Barcelona*, 19 (1946), pp.97–134.

[40] *Si enim stomacho jejuno bibatur vinum sine omni comestione in parva quantitate, incitabit stomachum ad appetitum sequentis cibi, quo non indigent jejunare volentes . . . .. Idem.*

[41] John Russell's *Boke of Nurture*, ed. Frederick J. Furnivall, p.8: 'Milk, cream and curds, as well as rose "junket", close a man's stomach, as does the "possate"; therefore eat old cheese at the end of the meal, if you eat late, and drink a sweet wine to prevent constipation.' Both *joncate* and *possate* were sweetened milk drinks, relied upon as fortifiers. An Italian recipe for the first is contained in the Neapolitan Collection, Recipe 166: *Jonchada de amandole*. The *OED* defines the second as 'a drink composed of hot milk curdled in ale, wine or other liquor, often with sugar, spices, or other ingredients'.

recognized medicinal qualities – because its warm and moist temperament identified it closely with the healthy human temperament: what better combination for a good digestive than sugar and spices, especially when ginger or cinnamon were blended into melted sugar? The medieval lump of candy – spiced candy–was the original *dragée*; together with candied ginger or a mixture of rose-water and melted sugar, these were the preferred digestives of the late Middle Ages.

In aristocratic households it was customary to stock a fancy box (the French term *drageoire* is found across Europe) with candies, and to pass this box as a genteel offering *after* guests had risen from the dining table and the table was collapsed and removed, in a way similar to the modern custom of serving a digestive of coffee and/or liqueur in the salon.[42]

Of course coffee was as yet unknown in the fifteenth century, and distilled liqueurs were still used a little more for medicinal than gastronomic purposes. But a variety of wine-based drinks were prepared that included very learned mixtures of spices and that functioned in much the same way as our after-dinner drink. The most common of these spiced drinks was the mulled wine known universally throughout Europe as hipocras.[43] This cordial bore a prestigious seal of approval in its own name, a derivation of the name of the Greek 'father of medicine', Hippocrates (c.460–c.375 A.D.). He was presumed to have elaborated the first formula for this beverage. By the late Middle Ages Hippocrates and Galen had assumed almost a mythological status, so that in the late-1200s the author of a *regimen* known today as the *Provençal Dietetic* could claim that his work, which he terms 'a good treatise' – possessed absolute authority because it derived directly from the writing of those much earlier physicians.[44] Although the formulæ for making hipocras that were adopted in the centuries following the heyday of Greek medicine were as many and varied as the individuals who prepared it, hipocras was consistently held to be as close to a universal elixer as anyone who was anxious about his digestion of general health could wish for.

---

[42] So much a commomplace did the dragée box become in the late Middle Ages that it was for a time customary to offer it, and its contents, as a gift to honour a respected visitor, or as an initiatory present to mark New Year's day or a birthday or wedding. Today the gift of a box of dragées remains the conventional token offered by new god-parents or to celebrate a first communion. It also became customary for a litigant to offer such dragées to the judge who found in his favour; King Louis IX (1214–70) had to set a maximum limit – dragées of the value of ten *sous* per week – upon the amount that any one judge could accept, and later Philippe le Bel (1268–1314) limited this further to only what the judge's household could consume per day!

[43] See also Chapter 6, Beverages, below.

[44]   . . . un bon tractat . . . c'ai traig dels libres ancians
       que Ypocras e Galians [Hippocrates and Galen]
       escriuseron per rason fina
       de la nobla art de medicina . . .

Hermann Suchier, *Provenzalische Diätetik*, Halle a.S. (Max Niemeyer), 1894.

The Sequence of Dishes

Before looking at the dishes that actually consituted any formal 'aristocratic' meal, we should return briefly to a feature of medieval dining that has been only implied before here. We have mentioned courses or servings. In the account of Chiquart's banquet that we saw above, it was clear that the major subdivisions of each of his meals were called just that, 'servings'; elsewhere in the On Cookery Chiquart speaks of 'courses' as well. For this professional chief cook the two terms appear to be interchangeable in sense. In the context we are dealing with, 'course' and 'serving' are in fact roughly synonymous.

A serving was what the word says, the action of presenting prepared dishes and setting them on the dining board for those who were to eat them. The meaning of the word course still contained something of its etymology, that is, that the servitor bringing the prepared dishes did so at a 'run' (from a distant outdoor kitchen?) or in a pass. What has to be understood, however, is that what was brought to the table was not just a dish or a preparation. What constituted a serving that was set on the table by the servitor, or by a procession of servitors in one pass, was a number of preparations. During any course in a meal the diners had in front of them a variety of dishes from which they could select what interested them. The actual number of dishes served in a course, the variety and the choice that each diner had before him or her at any given moment, was small or large, narrow or wide, according to the means of the household.

This sort of meal, in which there is a simultaneous serving of several dishes, became called 'French Service'. The procedure seems to have been common at this time all across Europe except in the German states. Before the very irregular, inconsistent and, on the whole, unavailing proclamation of various sumptuary, laws, there appears to have been no firm social rule dictating the number of servings that were appropriate for a meal. By the end of the fourteenth century the Menagier de Paris shows dinner menus consisting variously of two, three or four courses of dishes.[45] Fifteenth-century English practice for banquets, as this is shown in Austin,[46] divided a meal into either two or three courses. In relatively sober noble houses, such as that of the Duke of Savoy (the future Pope Felix V), even an impressive formal banquet could be limited to two servings of dishes, as Chiquart's On Cookery shows. Italian examples of grand, formal meals could go on for eight, ten or a dozen courses.[47] Between the aperitif and the digestive, the proper sequence of foods in a late-medieval meal was, as we have seen, rationally ordered. When we examine menus that have come down to us in

[45] Pages 174–183.
[46] Two Fifteenth-Century Cookery-Books, pp.57–64.
[47] See, for instance, the menu section in the Neapolitan Collection, folios 77r–89r.

manuscripts from the late Middle Ages, the logic of the sequence of servings may not be all that apparent at first glance. In part the seeming heterogeneity of what is served, and when, comes from our modern habit of looking to identify how each dish satisfies the requirements of a sequence of types of dish in a meal: meat, fish, salad, dessert, for example. The medieval logic in organizing a meal did not consider the distinct (modern) phases of a meal, however, but rather the proper relative sequence in which the various foods that constituted the meal should be consumed.

Logically the best order was undoubtedly one in which the most easily digestible foods were consumed first, leaving to a later stage in the meal all those foods on which the stomach would have to spend more time. Among foodstuffs, of easy digestion were cabbage, lettuce, portulaca (purslane) and other 'herbs', all moist fruits (and especially peaches, recognized specifically for their faculty of opening the stomach?47[48]), and light meats such as chicks, chicken and goat-kid. Concerning quinces, Platina observes that 'they are eaten as a first course . . . and are valued since, with anise and raisins or with pure wine or clarified honey, they do not harm the stomach much. Eaten after the meal, they tend to rot in the stomach and bring on phlegmatic humours.'[49] Of more difficult digestion, and consequently those foods that should be consumed later in a meal, were all so-called 'heavy' fruits such as pears and chestnuts, 'heavy' meats, such as beef and pork. Among prepared dishes most sorts of broths and pottages could and should be served first, largely because being warm and moist their nature made them most readily digestible.[50]

Among the dishes that the Menagier suggests to compose the courses of his twenty-four dinner and supper menus we find a variety of 'initial' foods: Garnache [a spiced wine] and toast; veal pasties; beef pasties and risshews; white leek dish; pea puree; bean puree; stewed white vegetables; joints of meat; German Broth [meat fried in pork fat, then boiled in almond milk, with spices]; Seymé [poultry stewed in fried onions, with spices]; capons in herbs; various pottages; baked apples. A few of these initial dishes (such as the pasties and the pea puree) tend to be repeated as favourites from meal to

---

[48] The peach, whose name of *poma persica* or Persian apple reflects its exotic origins, was endowed with rather a complex nature. 'The food value of the peach is considered useless on account of their dampness and coolness in the stomach, for they turn sour quickly and are converted into phlegmatic humours. . . . Eaten ripe . . . and as a first course, they induce appetite, move the urine, lubricate the bowels and remedy bad breath. Dried peaches eaten as a last course, although they have no nourishment, are considered sealers of the stomach because they are astringent.' Platina, *De honesta voluptate*, II, 12.

[49] *De honesta voluptate*, I, 22.

[50] And because they could be composed of foodstuffs whose qualities could excite the appetite. In the Châlons manuscript (folio 6r), the recipe entitled *De modo faciendi brodium appetitivum* of pullets and various herbs, spices and pullet liver is a case in point.

meal, but all of them possess the recognized faculty of being readily digestible. Spices warm the stomach; veal and poultry are temperate meats; pasties are likewise temperate in their physical qualities, since their pastry shell and their method of cooking ensure a moderating influence upon their contents whatever they may be: whether baked or deep-fried, a pasty was necessarily a relatively more moist dish than its contents would constitute if roast or grilled. While peas and beans may cause flatulence, this is in part because they pass through the stomach so easily; in principle pottages are an ideal initial food because they combine warmth with moisture; most fruits, including apples (but excluding pears, as mentioned above), are generally looked upon as useful stomach openers.

If fish is served in a meal, then it should be followed immediately by nuts: being intrinsically dry, nuts will absorb the superfluous humidity which is a natural property of almost all fish.

If meat is served, then it should normally be followed in the meal by cheese, particularly if this was not too aged and too dry. Physicians indicate that this practice of concluding a meat meal with cheese was not merely a matter of convention but was the consequence of an awareness of a particular property of cheese itself. 'Cheese, taken after a meal, makes food descend to the bottom of the stomach where digestion is primarily active, as all those versed in the art of medicine know full well.'[51] The sense of this rationale is just what the author says: the weight of this substance, itself of slow digestion, forces all of the food previously eaten during the meal, and still not processed *out* of the stomach, to fall into the area of the stomach where it will be most effectively digested. As with the vast majority of so many other doctrines about food in the Middle Ages, the rules about cheese were elaborated from dogma codified in the *Regimen Sanitatis Salernitanum*, this durable Latin poem, associated with the medical school of Salerno in the twelfth century, having influenced generation after generation of physicians, students, authors and commentators even past the so-called end of the Middle Ages.

> 'Ignorant doctors say that I [cheese] am harmful, yet they do not know why this should be so.' Cheese brings help to the weak stomach. Before meals cheese is useful since it descends readily into the belly; eaten after other food, it properly ends a meal. Those who are not ignorant of medicine will attest to these things.[52]

---

[51] *Regime tresutile*, p.85.
[52]
> 'Ignari medici me dicunt esse nocivum,
> sed tamen ignorant cur nocumenta feram.' . . .
> Languenti stomacho caseus addit opem.
> Caseus ante cibus confert, si defluat alvus;
> si post sumatur, terminat ille dapes:
> Qui physicam non ignorant hæc testificantur.

Even in the second half of the fifteenth century Platina is still writing much the same things: 'Fresh cheese is cold and moist; salt cheese [that is, preserved and old] is hard, warm and dry. Fresh cheese is very nourishing, represses the heat of the stomach and helps those spitting blood, but it is totally harmful to the phlegmatic. Aged cheese is difficult to digest, of little nutriment and not good for stomach or belly; it produces bile, gout, pain in the side, sand grains and stones. They say a small amount, whatever you want, taken after a meal, when it seals the opening of the stomach, both takes away the squeamishness of fatty dishes and benefits digestion and head.'[53]

Physicians also cautioned that foods of diverse substance (for example, partridge, chicken, fish, beef and pork),[54] should never be combined. The rationale here is that by their nature some foods are more digestible than others, just as different foods have different cooking times. Consequently, if two foods of different natures are exposed to the cooking action of the stomach, their rates of digestion varying, one is apt to be drawn through the stomach either too quickly and thence 'through the mesenteric vein to the liver' whereby crude undigested humours are spread broadside through the unfortunate dyspeptic's body; or else certain of the foods progress more slowly than they should, with the baneful result such foods are overcooked in the stomach and produce equally undesirable superfluities of 'bad' humours.

Some rules, however, such as this particular one about combining different sorts of food, seem clearly to have been blithely overlooked by the wealthy in their concern with variety and in order to impress both their guests and their own palates.

And so we come to what conventionally today we refer to as the dessert. The term means literally an 'un-serving' or clearing away. It represents the stage in a meal when the last foods are brought to the table, preliminary to the table setting being cleared and the table itself dismantled.

A generally accepted tradition required a formal meal to conclude with spices in one form or another. Under the general heading of 'digestive' we saw the theory which underlay the use of such spices, including sugar, at this point in a meal. According to the theoreticians, a compound of sugar and spice, in liquid form as hipocras or dry as in the *dragée* or spiced candy, offered the perfect finishing touch for any carefully planned meal. Furthermore, candied seeds, candied fruits, delicately scented sugar paste – just those confection that physicians and meal planners counted upon as aperitifs – not only helped the stomach to digest a meal but scented the breath nicely as well!

Flos Medicinæ Scholæ Salerni, in Salvatore de Renzi, ed. *Collectio Salernitana*, 5 vols., Naples (Filiatre-Sebezo), 1852-59; Vol. I, p.457, lines 391-97.

[52] *De honesta voluptate*, II, 17.

[53] The example comes from the *Regime tresutile*, p.16, where Avicenna is cited as the authority.

By the end of the Middle Ages sugar in some form was universally relied upon to provide the finishing touches to a meal. Various fruits could be presented in a sugar or honey syrup, or pureed in a sweet paste that had been reduced by boiling. These fruits could be either fresh, or dried like prunes and raisins. Often spices were incorporated into the syrup or puree.

Other 'desserts' included various sorts of fritters and crêpes, all coated with a garnish of sugar, and sweet custards. Of the latter we might mention in particular the family of *dariols* that are found here and there across Europe. These were in their essence a mixture of milk (usually almond milk) and eggs, baked in a pastry shell in the oven. Sub-varieties of the *dariol* included fruit or fish or bone-marrow among the ingredients.

Conclusion

The large number of dishes encompassed by a formal dinner is astonishing to us moderns. While the number of servings seems normally to have been more or less limited, perhaps by common sense, to either two or three, each of these servings heaped the dining tables with a remarkably wide selection of preparations for the diner. Roasts, pottages, jellies, fruit preserves, wafers and pies were laid out together on what must really have been a 'groaning' board.

Several consequences are implicit in this type of multiple-dish service, apart from merely the variety that it afforded the affluent members of society. The foremost of these consequences is that the kitchen must have been an extremely busy place at mealtimes, and very long before. A menu that regularly calls for several different preparations to be ready for serving at the same moment puts enormous demands upon the organizational abilities of those who are responsible for preparing those dishes. There must be a good deal of rigorous planning at several levels of authority in order that all arrangements are at all times coherent. Furthermore, such a menu calls for a lot of concurrent labour from a relatively large body of kitchen help. In turn this means that the kitchen must be of a size to accommodate both a good number of people engaged in a range of different tasks, and so as to provide space, in the form of tables, chopping blocks, pestles, *several* fireplaces, and so forth, in order that all those activities can go on simultaneously. A late-medieval kitchen must have been a bustling place indeed.

SIX

Beverages

We spoke earlier of the important role that tea and coffee play in practically any modern meal. These two infusions have achieved the status of universal, conventional mealtime beverages. But both of these are, of course, relatively recent 'discoveries'. In the late Middle Ages a number of other liquids were at least potentially available to fulfil the same need to have something to drink during a meal along with the food one was eating.

Water

In a previous chapter we saw the various reasons for the care that any cook had to take to ensure that the water he or she used in the kitchen was (more or less) pure. As a mealtime beverage, water did not play as important a role on the medieval dinner table as it does today. The same disadvantages militated against the use of water at table as in the kitchen: only spring-water could be trusted to be free of pollution, and that only with a number of carefully weighed provisos: the discharge from the spring must have a good flow, it must come directly from the ground or a rock, it must be cold, and so forth. According to Bartholomew the Englishman toward the middle of the thirteenth century, the best water was to be had from a spring which flowed northward, for the northern winds will make that water finer and 'lighter'.[1] A further, theoretical disadvantage attached to the drinking of water during a meal lay in a potential danger enunciated by the physicians of the time: if water were drunk as a mealtime beverage, its cool nature (temperamentally speaking, water's humour was perceived as cool and, as even the uninitiated might suspect, moist) would tend to act counter to the desired function of

---

[1] *De proprietatibus rerum*. After spring water, in decreasing order of preference Bartholomew then ranks river water, lake water and pond or swamp water. Concerning these last, very definitely tertiary choices, he cautions against the possibly grave conquences of availing oneself of them, citing Avicenna's advice that their water should always be boiled.

the stomach, the human digestive furnace. In short, it would cool down the stomach's 'cooking' action. As some of the *regimine* put it, it might threaten to extinguish the stomach's natural heat:

> Drinking water while eating is quite harmful;
> water cools the stomach and food remains undigested.[2]

As a clear consequence of these perceptions, water at mealtime was explicitly ruled out for the healthy person who at all valued the efficiency of his digestive faculties.

If, for various reasons, water was eschewed as a mealtime beverage, other liquids could replace it in relative safety and with only moderate cost. Though cheap, water might well be poisonous. Alcoholic beverages, on the other hand, even those of comparatively low alcohol content, were universally recognized as readily digestible – and even beneficial to the digestion – nutritious, and pure. Or at least the diseases to which wines were naturally subject over time could in large measure be rectified. Their disadvantages lay in their cost, and in those difficulties, well recognized by the specialists of the age, inherent in ensuring them a useful and healthy storage life.

Wine

In the qualities of its humoural temperament, wine was ideally warm (as well as being dry, strangely enough) so that this antediluvian fermented juice was heartily approved as a desirable beverage to accompany a meal. Approved after the fact, one imagines, that is after widespread production throughout most European countries had made wine common enough and cheap enough in medieval society that most individuals and households could afford to stock an adequate supply of it for beverage purposes. Physicians helpfully pointed out, furthermore, that wine possessed the faculty of being so subtle (the proof of this was that it vaporized readily) that it mixed with food particles even more thoroughly than did water, and could transport them better to the extremities of the body where the virtues of the food could do the most good. In his *De sanitatis custodia* of 1341, the Piedmontese physician Giacomo Albini was able to cite the great Galen himself for authority when he declared that 'wine nourishes the body quickly', although he does go on to list several moderately harmful side-effects that wine drinking might

---

[2]   *Potus aquæ sumptus fit edenti valde nocivus;*
        hinc friget stomachus, crudus est inde cibus.
Flos Medicinæ Scholæ Salerni, ed. Salvatore de Renzi, *Collectio Salernitana*, I, p.452; lines 246–47.

produce.[3] It was clear that not only were there no really sound arguments *against* the consumption of wine by healthy adults, it was positively a good and beneficial thing – always within the bounds of moderation, of course – to avail oneself of its pleasures. And particularly at mealtime.

For the young, there were always certain reservations. Albini warned that infants under five should not be given wine because it would tend to curdle the milk they were drinking.[4] Further, he advised that until children were fourteen years of age they should receive wine only sparingly, only if watered and only at mealtimes. His reasoning was that wine was simply too subtle, too *vaporosus*, and harmed the growing organisms of younger children.

Eventually all of the learned doctrines about the benefits of wine as a mealtime beverage, and a good number of other laudatory precepts, made their way from medical treatises into the slightly more popular recipe collections of late-medieval Europe. For instance, at the head of a number of recipes it assembled for potables, the Latin collection known as the *Tractatus* praises of virtues of wine.

> We set wine first in our dissertation on beverages because it is universally to be preferred [as such]. For its spirit strengthens members, digests food, modifies bad humoural complexions, removes melancholy and pain, and restores good cheer and gaiety. This is so provided the wine is good and consumed in moderation; corrupt wine works contrarily, impedes digestion, corrupts food, generates little blood, makes a person sad, lazy, sluggish.[5]

Generally speaking the consumption of wine as a table beverage was universal in France, Italy and the Hispanic peninsula during the thousand years of the Middle Ages. By the end of this millennium the urban per capita intake of wine seems to have averaged just under one litre.[6] In the climates of these countries the grape vine was made to flourish without excessive labour or climatic risk; wine could be produced, in quantity, that was

---

[3] Jacomo Albini, *De sanitatis custodia*, ed. Giovanni Carbonelli (Biblioteca della Società Storica Subalpina, 25), Pinerolo (Tipografia Sociale), 1906; Part II, Chapter 7, pp.95–96.

[4] *Ibid.*, p.63.

[5] . . . *De vino primo de potu tanquam meliori ac digniori sermo noster sumat exordium, quoniam ipsum universis potibus preferendum est. Spiritum enim, membra corroborat, cibaria digerit, complexiones malas alterat, aufert tristitias et dolores, et hominem reddit hylarem et jocundum. Et hoc dico si bonum fuerit et non corruptum, et cum moderamine sumptum. Vinum enim corruptum contrarium facit, digestionem impedit, cibaria corrumpit, parvum generat sanguinem, hominem reddit tristem, pigrum et ponderosum.* Preamble to Part I.

[6] Jacqueline Brunet and Odile Redon, 'Vins, jus et verjus. Du bon usage culinaire des jus de raisins en Italie à la fin du Moyen Age,' in Gilbert Carrier (ed.), *Vin des historiens*, Suze-la-Roussie (Université du Vin), 1990, pp.109–117. These researchers have arrived at the figures of 210–390 l. for Carpentras in 1405–06, 286 l. for Genoa in the 15th century, and 248–293 l. for Florence (p.109 and n.2.

relatively cheap, palatable, and above all bacteriologically durable. An advantage of viticulture that was clearly recognized by agriculturists then as now relates to a peculiarity of the grapevine: it thrives in areas where the soils are too gravelly or have too much clay, soils that are in fact generally unsuitable for most other forms of agriculture.

While the cultivation of grapes, the pressing of juice and the processes of vinification were undoubtedly practised across Europe long before the expansion of the Roman Empire, it is generally accepted that the Romans brought significant refinements to all phases of the production of wine in all countries that fell under their authority. As they moved around the mediterranean litoral into Hispania and up the Rhone valley to Burgundia and over Gallia, through the Alpine valleys of Helvetia and into Germania and ultimately across to Britannia, the Romans insisted that the conquered tribes learn to grow the best possible vines according to the locality. In particular they grafted Roman varietals onto the hardier local vine-stocks and so developed hybrids that withstood the northern climates but yielded a richer juice than before.

One important improvement in wine-making had to do with its storage. Where Romans at home had relied upon large earthenware jars in which to keep their wines – the larger ones being installed in the ground up to their necks, somewhat like quasi-permanent household fixtures – when they were out in the farther reaches of their Empire they learned to make use of the native wooden barrels. The nature of wooden containers is that they breathe and this manner of storage, along with the flavour imparted by the wood, especially by oak, enriched the wine's aging process.

As Christianity spread and the various monastic orders multiplied their foundations across Europe, vineyards also multiplied. Every monastery had immediately to have its local source of wine, and of the best quality. Supply of this best wine could come to outstrip internal demand from several dozen brothers and a similar number of lay helpers – and particularly if the usual beverage drunk by these monks and lay helpers was a grain-based product such as beer. Much care was exercised in perfecting agriculture generally in monasteries; prayer and toil in the fields were, after all, the two primary duties of a monk's life. Over time wines became a principal means by which individual monastic houses could earn the worldly cash they needed for any other business they wished to conduct beyond their gates. Coincidentally many monastic vineyards came to be recognized as having developed extremely fine and valuable wines.

It is noteworthy also that traditionally the most highly developed wine-producing areas tended to be situated around episcopal sees, such as at Reims in Champagne, at Florence in Tuscany, at Trier in the Rhineland, or near the papal court at Rome or Avignon. The Pope's vineyard at Châteauneuf on the Rhône, for instance, was famous for producing the finest of wines even in the Middle Ages. And, closer to our own age, the first vineyards of California were established by the Franciscan missionaries to that area.

The best wines were not for everyone, of course. To begin with, the juice pressed from the grape varied in quality according to how 'naturally' it was obtained. The first, gentle pressing yielded a 'natural', full-bodied juice; this was unquestionably the best juice, and in turn produced the best wines. Only the wealthy and higher ecclesiastics could afford these wines. A second, more forceful pressing of the grapes supplied a secondary quality of juice. Then, by adding water to the mash that was left after this second pressing, a final pressing was made possible; this inferior juice ultimately made an inferior wine, quite well known across Europe even though it was identified by a variety of names.[7] Of relatively low tenor in alcohol this lowest-quality wine was, naturally enough, the cheapest and the most common in the municipal markets. It was what most people drank. Though it was alcoholic enough to be safer, potentially, to drink than water, the modesty of its alcohol content meant that it could be consumed in the course of a day in quantities that were large enough to slake one's thirst but not be overly threatening to one's sobriety. Researchers have found that French fishermen sailing to the Grand Banks off Newfoundland in the sixteenth century were allotted a wine ration of between 2.5 and 3 litres *per day*.[8] On reading such figures as these, the picture that irresistibly springs to one's mind is of a number of cheerful ships laying down some very wiggly wakes back and forth across the Atlantic! In actual fact, however, given the customarily low quality of wines available to the lowest classes in society, the level of continual inebriation in such sea-faring crews was undoubtedly very much less than these apparently generous quantities of wine allotment might in themselves suggest.

As with anything that is widely and commonly used, wines were closely studied and classified into numerous categories. Primary among these were, of course, the 'colours' white and red. White wine, whose juice is pressed from either white grapes (in French, the *blanc de blanc*) or blue grapes (in French, *blanc de noir*, or simply *gris*), is the more easily made because the skin of the grape does not enter into the mash. White wine tends not to improve with age and is available for drinking as soon as it has fermented and without having to be kept in order to age – an expensive tying-up of the producer's capital. Red wine results from a pressing of a grape together with its skin; while the skin adds a multi-layered complexity to the flavour of the juice, the

---

[7] In French the term *piquette*, and in Italian *pusca* or *puscha*, by which this 'near-wine' was known, may have been inspired by its natural tendency to bitterness.

[8] See Laurier Turgeon and Denis Dickner, 'Contraintes et choix alimentaires d'un groupe d'appartenance: les marins-pêcheurs français à Terre-Neuve au XVIe siècle,' in *Du manuscrit à la table*, ed. Carole Lambert, Montréal and Paris (Université de Montréal and Champion-Slatkine), 1992, pp.227–239.

making of the wine and the storage for maturing that red wines generally require, calls for a specific expertise that few but the professionals possessed in the Middle Ages.

The ordinary peasant or bourgeois rarely had a choice among wines. He and she normally drank a white or rosé (into which a few grape skins had slipped) from a third pressing. It was a young wine with perhaps a five percent alcohol content – and was perhaps further watered down either by an unscrupulous retailer or by the thirsty but impecunious drinker himself. The poor distinguished primarily between an affordable white wine and an expensive red. However, those who could afford the luxury of a further selection, along with the merchants, both international and local, and stewards and butlers who supplied the the wealthy with wine, made a great many other distinctions among various wines. In Italy some four dozen terms were in current use among the mercantile trades in order to define the specific nature of the wines with which they customarily dealt.[9] The grapevine and wine industry was certainly one of the most highly developed in the Middle Ages, and probably only slightly less so than that of the cereal grains and of bread-baking.

The cost and quality of wine varied radically from vintage to vintage, and provided (and provide) one of the quickest measures of the state of social health, economy, and agriculture at any given time. Between the years 1405 and 1449 a particularly observant resident of Paris kept a diary in which he noted the events and attitudes of the times. In it we find, almost as a sort of structural framework to Parisian life, references to the continual political and military struggles between the various factions – English, Burgundian, Armagnac, royal, noble, bourgeois, peasant, religious and secular. Complicating these ceaseless conflicts and their consequences on the security and prosperity of town life were the vagaries of climate each season. The net effects of Fortune were most readily seen in the marketplace, and our anonymous diarist regularly reports just how sensitive the marketplace was to cause and effect at any given moment.

> [1414] There was fighting all over France at this time, yet food was plentiful and cheap in Paris, both wine and bread. You could get a quart of good wine, sound and clean, red or white, in a hundred places in the

---

[9] We read of wines qualified as *acetus, acutus, afumosus, albus, amarus, antiquus, aquatus, artificial, austerus, bonus, clarus, corruptioni paratus, crassus et nigrus, debilis, dulcis, foeculentus et turbidus, fortis, grossus, limphatus, loira, lucidus, maturus bene, medius, mediocris, miscatus, mixtus, mollis, novus, odoriferus, picheta, potens, primus, purus, pusca, reversatus et marcius, rubeus, ruptus, secundus, subrubeus, subtilis, torgiatus, tornatus, turbidus, vermilius,* and *vetus.* See Anna Maria Nada Patrone, *Il cibo del ricco ed il cibo del povero,* Turin (Centro Studi Piemontesi), 1981, pp.422ff. The same author has found a number of terms by which the wines specifically of the Piemont region of northern Italy were clearly classified: *agrestus, alburganensis, de Bressia, cirisolus, grecus, malvaticus, nebbiolus, muscatellus, revesii, ponticus subtilis, robola, trebianus, vernacius.*

town for one penny *parisis*, and bread similarly cheap. None of all this year's wine went thick or ropy or stinking.

[1419] It was the very heart of winter, the rain never stopped and it was very cold. The weather during the vintage that year, 1419, was the filthiest and the wettest imaginable; the grapes rotted, the wines were the porrest anyone had ever tasted and yet were four times dearer than anyone could remember their ever being before – and all this was because of the evil they[10] were doing everywhere. Anyone who had [a vineyard] five or six leagues out of Paris had to pay five or six francs a hogshead simply for transport, and 16 or 20 *sous parisis* for an escort of soldiers to within a league of Paris, and that not counting harvesting, tilling, cooperage and other expenses. And, when it was all harvested and gathered in, none of it had any strength or goodness or colour and hardly any of it smelt of anything except decay, the reason being that most of it had not been harvested properly because everyone was so frightened of these men and so apprehensive of their treachery.

[1447] Wine was very dear now in Paris; poor people drank ale or mead or beer or cider or perry and suchlike drinks. Then during this time, in about the middle of May, quantities of wine – estimated at eleven thousand hogsheads and about seven hundred *muids* – were brought into the town of St.-Denis-en-France both from France and from Burgundy for the Lendit,[11] which was due next month. After the Lendit a lot of it was brought into Paris, so that now good wine which had cost 12 penny could be had for four *doubles* or 6 penny. Soon afterwards excellent wine was on sale at 4 penny a quart.[12]

A reliable and abundant supply of good new wines was not the only problem. Because the grape harvest was necessarily an annual affair, and fresh wines could not be available the year round, wine storage was an extremely important matter. Large wine producers and retailers maintained huge vats from year to year in an attempt to supply any demand at any season. For all but the smallest households, however, individual houses and estates had their own cellars in which an assortment of various wines were kept in order to see the household through to the next harvest, pressing and 'vintage.'[13] It was this storage in particular that was apt to cause problems for the wine trade and for the householder. Many centuries of wine-making and wine storage had indeed taught many practical lessons about the most practical and effective means to ensure a long life to barrelled wine. There

---

[10] The author has explained that English troops were marauding on one side of the city, just outside the walls, while Armagnac troops were pillaging on the other.

[11] 'Lendit: A great Faire kept (in a field neere to S. Denis) from the second Wednesday of June unto Midsummer Eve.' Randle Cotgrave, A *Dictionarie of the French and English Tongues*, London, 1611.

[12] A *Parisian Journal 1405–1449*, tr. Janet Shirley, Oxford (Clarendon), 1968, pp.89, 143–44, 365.

[13] The word *vintage* is nothing other than the Latin *vindemia* or French *vendange*, meaning the year's 'crop' or 'harvest' of grapes.

existed a large body of popular knowledge that advised how best to care for stored wine and, should the worst happen, how to cure any of the various 'sicknesses' to which stored wine has always been subject.

Wine rectification was, in fact, a very important matter in the Middle Ages. For both the average modest householder and the great international wine merchant, the possible spoilage of any wine being held in their cellars represented the irredeemable loss of a relatively large investment. Only so much vinegar could be used at any one time, even in a cuisine in which vinegar was ubiquitously a substantial ingredient. Sad experience had long since identified each of the varieties of deterioration that wine could undergo, and trial and error had shown what the most efficacious treatments were for each of these eventualities. So important a concern was the possibility of wine spoilage that a list of remedies for the most common wine diseases occasionally made its way into collections of food recipes. Such procedures must have been viewed as recipes similar to any other recipe about food, offering the householder, in fact, much the same sort of practical advice as did the various 'recipes' for removing a burnt taste from a pottage, for instance.

When we look into the *Viandier* we find a series of ten recipes for treating wines (Recipes 178–87). Some of the advice concerns protecting the wine in order to forestall any spoilage. For instance one should always ensure that any amount of wine that has evaporated through the wood of a barrel should be replaced, the barrel literally topped up with the same wine in order not to allow any air at the top of the barrel – in order, we would say today, to prevent air-borne bacteria from growing. Similarly, in order 'To keep wine from becoming slimy and being cloudy', one should 'put into a hogshead of wine a bowlful of red grapeseeds that have been dried and then boiled; then dry lees of white wine, roast them until they become ash', and add that to the cask.[14] The proof of any procedure, whether scientifically understood or not, is that it works; we can only assume that these preventative recipes did on the whole work adequately.

Otherwise, apart from preventative measures, the wine recipes here in the *Viandier* and in other cookery books, direct how to remedy certain sorts of spoilage that an owner may have discovered in process in one of his barrels. Should you, the *Viandier* says, find a 'ropy wine' syndrome, you ought to boil wheat, puree it, cool it, add egg whites to it and stir the mixture into the wine barrel with a short stick – so as not to disturb the dregs at the bottom of the barrel; then the author instructs: 'Hang a pound of ground laser-wort in a cloth bag on a string through the bung-hole of the barrel.' For our slimy

---

[14] Chemically it is likely that the tannic acid of the ground grape seeds, the sulphate of the alum, and the tartar of the burnt wine lees would constitute an effective bactericide working in a way similar to the sulphur dioxide that is used by modern vintners to prevent what they call, believe it or not, 'slimy wine spoilage'.

wine, for wine that is turning vinegary, for woody-tasting wine, and for wine with a 'broken bouquet', similar recipes could be consulted; they must have been practical, effective and, clearly, generally in demand.

The wine trade was one of the most important elements in medieval commerce. Because there are such widely differing wines, and because wine production in different places tends to specialize in different varieties, a lot of money and activity was engaged in buying, transporting and selling large stocks of wines. There were of course local merchants, retailers whose major business lay in handling the production from the vineyards of the region. But money was also to be made in responding to a demand for wines from more distant parts. Sometimes these were specialty wines from quasi-exotic lands such as Corsica, Crete (Malvasia was the origin of Malmsey), Cyprus, Tyre (probably Capri, Ischia in the Tyrrhenean Sea), Greece and Palestine, wines that had caught the imagination and taste-buds of affluent cosmopolitan gourmets.[15] Wines from Cyprus in particular seem to have been held in very high esteem by late-medieval connoisseurs.

Sometimes commerce was concerned simply with supplying a more abundant, better and cheaper wine than what the local vineyards could turn out. The Flemish, in particular, had long experience in importing wines from the west of France into the Lowlands and the northern German states. Throughout the fourteenth and fifteenth centuries the cities of Cologne and Bruges were at the heart of the German wine trade. Bruges in particular (and its port, Seebrugge) was one of the most active hubs in this trade in all of Europe, exchanging German wines with those of Gascony, Spain and the Levant; then in 1491 Antwerp replaced Bruges as the Flemish centre of the wine trade, and this trade continued to grow. Alsatian vineyards exported eastward and westward particularly through Bruges and Antwerp.

For England the wine trade was concentrated in French ports of the Atlantic coast and in the Hanseatic ports. These latter and Bruges handled the Hoch wines of the Rhine in Germany and of the Moselle; all of these wines, from the Rhine, Moselle, Main and Neckar, came to be designated generically simply as 'Rhenish.' Of the former ports, up to the thirteenth century, big wine merchants preferred the fine harbour of La Rochelle. From it were shipped particularly the wines of the Loire Valley, Poitou, Anjou and Orleans, and to some extent those of the Altantic coast as well. However, ever since the day in 1152 when Eleanor of Aquitaine married Henry of Anjou and he became Henry II of England, Gascony belonged to the royal family of England. With the constant expansion of English possessions in

---

[15] The multi-national list of wines in the *Bataille des vins* of Henry d'Andelys illustrates the extensiveness of the wine trade in the thirteenth century. See A. Héron, ed., *OEuvres d'Henri d'Andeli, trouvère normand du XIIIe siècle*, Rouen (Cagniard), 1881; or in Etienne Barbazan and Dominique Méon, *Fabliaux et contes des poètes françois des XIe, XIIe, XIIIe, XIVe, et XVe siècles tirés des meilleurs auteurs*, 2 vols., new ed. Paris, 1808; repr. Geneva (Slatkine), 1976; Vol. I, p.152.

this area, and particularly with the advent of the Hundred Years War between France and England in 1338, it became increasingly necessary politically to shift the seat of the English wine trade further south; eventually Bordeaux assumed all of this commerce. With this choice of the Aquitanian port there followed a consequent shift in the provenance of the wines shipped to England. These were more and more the wines of the English lands in France, Bordeaux wines and other claret wines from the vineyards of the Gascon region.[16] Though generally recognized to be among the best in quality, the wines of Gascony were a little too far removed from the large Parisian market to enjoy much demand from that source as a cheap wine.

The demand for wine in England was enormous. To supply the daily needs of the king's court alone required huge quantities of food and drink. Enumerating the household personnel and courtiers that regularly surrounded King Richard II (1367–1400), John Stow (1525–1605) wrote:

> This hall [Westminster] being finished in the yeare 1399, the same King [Richard II] kept a most royal Christmas there, with dayly Justings, and runnings at Tilt, whereunto resorted such a number of people, that there was everie day spent [slaughtered] twentie eight or twentie sixe Oxen, and three hundred sheepe, besides fowle without number . . .; he was garded by Cheshire men, and had about him commonly thirteene bishops, besides Barons, Knights, Esquires, and other more then needed: insomuch, that to the houshold came every day to meate 10000 people, as appeareth by the Messes tolde out from the Kitchen to 300 servitors.[17]

Along with these volumes of imported wines commonly consumed by the court, a large provision of wines had constantly as well to be purveyed for the royal armies, even when these were abroad.

In the late Middle Ages the wine trade, both domestic and international, ensured that a wide variety of wines was available to those with the means to purchase them. In February of 1476 a banquet mounted in the house of the wealthy merchant Salutati consisted of some twenty-five elaborate prepared dishes which were washed down by the following broad assortment of

---

[16] An effect of this shift of port was the serious loss of market for those wines of the La Rochelle area, especially those of the white-grape vineyards of the town of Cognac. One tale has it that local entrepreneurs hit upon what was to prove a clever solution to the problem both of the oversupply of the region's wines and the cost of their transportation. By making use of distillation, which was thought to remove the water from wine, the volume of these wines could be reduced, along with their shipping charges; the eventual client could in turn reconstitute these local vintages by restoring their water, and so effect a little French economy. Unfortunately, it seems that the clients who bought this Cognac learned to prefer it just as it came to them, and a whole new industry and market came into being!

[17] A *Survey of London* (orig. publ. 1603), introduction and notes by Charles Lethbrdge Kingsford, 2 vols., Oxford (Clarendon), 1971; Vol. II, p.116.

regional wine varieties: Malvagia, Moscadello, Vernacia, Greco, Trebiano, Fianello, Falsamico, Bonagia di Trapani, Cilento, Fassignano, Mazacane, Asprino (bianco), Asprino (rosso). The chronicler reports, without other comment, that during the heavy going of the banquet the Fassignano and Mazacane wines were the most in demand because they were light wines![18] Even back in the fourteenth century, in a satirical examination of the institution of marriage, the French writer Eustache Deschamps lists no fewer than twenty-two wines that the ordinary housewife will certainly feel must be stocked at all times in her wine cellar: they include wines from Auxerre, Burgundy, Beaune, Gascony, Chablis, Givry, Vertus, Irancy, Spanish wine, Rhine wine, German wine, Greek wine, muscat, grenache, *grenachelle*, verjuice and strong (presumably the local vintage) wine.[19] Deschamps' hypothetical housewife is clearly a Frenchwoman and most likely a *bourgeoise*, but still the assortment of wines is impressively broad. *Grenache*, for instance, was imported from the Near East, and elsewhere Deschamps describes wine from the Rhine as arriving in huge barrels. This rich selection implies a highly developed commercial apparatus for buying, transporting and distributing those wines that were most in demand. It implies as well an appreciative and knowledgeable clientele for the local wine merchant; there was at least a segment of the population of the day that cared very seriously about what wines were set out on their dining tables.

Spiced Wines

Spiced or mulled wines enjoyed a favoured status in the late Middle Ages. In a meal, however, this sort of drink normally functioned more as a privileged element – that is, as an introductory aperitif or a concluding digestive of the meal – than as a general-purpose beverage that accompanied the eating of the various dishes. We should be clear that such spiced drinks as hipocras and claret were probably not available throughout a formal meal and in all likelihood were not consumed in particularly large quantities.

The English encyclopedist, Bartholomæus de Glanville, wrote an encomium of all varieties of spiced wines, which he terms 'Prepared Wines' or 'Made Wines':

> Wyne ymade is ymade by crafte of good spicery and herbes, as it fareth
> of the wyn that hatte *salviatum* [with sage] and of the wyn that hatte
> *rosatum* [with roses] and *gariofilatum* [with cloves], & that wyn

[18] Reproduced in Massimo Montanari, *Convivio. Storia e cultura dei piaceri della tavola*, Bari (Laterza), 1989, p.490.

[19] The *Miroer de mariage* (1381–89) is contained in the *OEuvres complètes de Eustache Deschamps*, ed. Auguste Henri Edouard, marquis de Queux de Saint-Hilaire and Gaston Raynaud, 11 vols.; Vol. 9, Paris (Didot), 1894; see pp.126–27.

accordeth bothe in mete and in medicyne [as beverage and medicament]. For vertu bothe of spicerye and of herbes chaungeth and amendeth the wyn and giveth therto a synguler vertu, and therfore suche wynes beth holsome and likynge whan holsome spicery and herbes beth incorporate therin in due manere. . . . Therfore suche wynes with her savour pleseth the taste, and exciteth appetite, and comforteth bothe the brayn & the stomak with here good odour & smylle, & clenseth also the blood, & pureth and cometh into the innere partyes of the veynes & of the membres, as Ysaac seith.[20]

It must have been a real pleasure to drink several goblets of mulled wine after a medieval meal, knowing that it was so good for you!

Arnaldus de Villanova devotes many paragraphs to outlining recipes for types of spiced wine that he calls *vinus odorifer* or *vinus aromaticatus*.[21] These recipes are, however, pharmaceutical specifics for treating a range of human maladies. All of them depend for their efficacity upon the ability of the wine to transport the necessary elements efficiently throughout the body, and upon the qualities of the ingredients that are added to the wine. One preparation is noteworthy, and reflects the close relationship between alchemy, physics and food in the Middle Ages. Chapter 14, *De vino extinctionis auri* ('Wine in which gold has been quenched'), describes how gold is heated and then dipped in wine in order that its qualities can pass into the wine. This drink makes good medicine for the heart because, according to the astrologers, gold was a metal that corresponded both to the heart and to the sun; and the sun – a planet of gold – governed the blood. With such logic as a basis for their production and prescribing, the drinker of Arnaldus' concoctions could have absolute trust in their effectiveness.

A good number of culinary manuscripts contain recipes for hipocras. While there may be no absolute agreement on all of its ingredients, hipocras was always basically a red wine (warmer in nature than white) into which had been blended powders of several of the most common spices: ginger, cinnamon, galingale, sugar; or ginger, cinnamon, grains of paradise, nutmeg, galingale, sugar; or ginger, cinnamon, cloves, grains of paradise, mace, spikenard, nutmeg, galingale, sugar. These hipocras spices normally belonged for the most part to the category known as 'gross spices', which Chiquart at the beginning of the fifteenth century defined as consisting of

---

[20] Bartholomæus Anglicus, *De proprietatibus rerum*, tr. John Trevisa, 2 vols., Oxford (Clarendon), 1975; Book 17, Chapter 187. Isaac ben Honain was an Arabic physician and scholar who died in A.D. 910. He sustained the Greek traditions in the philosophical and medical fields by his translations into Arabic and his work was in turn translated into Latin. It was by these latter versions, especially through his *Isagoge in Artem parvam Galeni*, that medieval physicians generally had access to ancient Greek medical thinking.

[21] Arnaldus de Villanova, *Liber de vinis*. See H.E. Sigerist, *The Earliest Printed Book on Wine (1478)*, New York (Schuman's), 1943.

ginger, cinnamon, grains of paradise and pepper. To the extent that the infusion included any significant amount of the 'minor spices' – nutmeg, cloves, mace and galingale[22] – the drink might not be recognized as true hipocras. The line between household beverage and pharmaceutical preparation was slender.

Recipes for hipocras reflected a personal taste from household to household and from time to time, but its use remained one of the constant and truly international gastronomic practices of the time. Two English recipes for hipocras from the first half of the Fifteenth Century are set to rhyme in John Russell's *Boke of Nurture*. Given the cost of the rarer spices, Russell thriftily distinguishes between proper hipocras (for the wealthy) and a somewhat cheaper variety of the drink 'for the people':

> Good son, to make ypocras, hit were gret lernynge,
> and for to take the spice therto aftur the proporcionynge,
> Gynger, Synamome, Graynis, Sugur, Turnesole (that is good
>   colourynge);
> for commyn peple Gynger, Canelle, longe pepur, hony aftur
>   claryfiynge.[23]

The *graynis* of Russell's text are grains of paradise. The spice mixture for making hipocras, of whatever formula, was customarily ground in relatively large batches and kept in a pouch for future use with red wine. So traditional and customary was the serving of hipocras that local spicers answered the demand by compounding and offering for sale a ready-made hipocras powder which the householder could purchase and to which he or she had only to add the wine. The same spicer stocked dragées of various flavours, so that the affluent, or lazy, householder had little to worry about in preparing the conclusion of a formal meal.

From the late Middle Ages dates a remarkable metal table-fixture which looks rather like a samovar but is surmounted by a ring of small compartments, each with a lid on top and a valve beneath to control the flow of its contents into a main central compartment. With this utensil placed on a sideboard or dresser, any special flavour of hipocras could be prepared, on the spot and to order, as it were, even perhaps in individual quantities, by a servant appointed to the task.

A good variety of other spiced wines was normally available in comfortable households of the late Middle Ages and they were identified by a variety of specific names. In larger towns the demand for such prepared wines might be enough to warrant that the local wine merchant stocked them for sale, along

---

[22] *On Cookery*, pp.10–11.
[23] John Russell, *Boke of Nurture*, ed. Frederick J. Furnivall in *Early English Meals and Manners*, London (Oxford University Press), 1868, pp.9–11, 14. Russell's work dates from about 1440.

with kegs of standard hipocras, among his more exotic wines. However, ordinary households undoubtedly prepared their own mulled (otherwise muddled or mixed) wines. The simplest method for infusing the spices into the wine involved binding appropriate quantities of them in a cloth bag and suspending this directly in the barrel or pitcher.

The substances used to flavour wine seem to have been almost as diverse as the imagination and available flavourants of the day allowed. Wines were flavoured with pepper, ginger, grains of paradise and cinnamon, individually rather than in combination as we saw above for hipocras. But we also find use being made of cloves, nutmeg, cubebs, rosemary, sage, wormwood (for the liquorice flavour of absinthe), aloes, hyssop, myrtle, anise, musk, and so forth. According to local taste, certain of these seasonings could be preferred or used exclusively; clever mixtures could also produce very sophisticated hybrid flavours, excitingly pungent or daintily, mysteriously chaste.

Of all of these artificially flavoured wines, the most common after hipocras seems to have been the drink known as *claret, claré* or *claree*. This beverage is not to be confused with 'claret' in the modern sense of the word, a bright medium-red variety of wine; the medieval claret is a spiced wine. Because of its complex spice content doctors were as familiar with this claret as were cooks and butlers.

Recipes for the making of claret appear in several medieval recipe collections. The Anglo-Norman collection whose title is *Coment l'en deit fere viande e claree (How prepared dishes and claret should be made*, Recipe 28) contains remarkably extensive directions for the elaboration of this spiced drink.

> Here begin the instructions for making claret. Take half a measure of cinnamon, ginger and mace; a third of a measure of cloves, nutmeg and malabathrum [? *fuyle de Inde*]; fennel, anise and caraway seeds in the same amount; cardamom and squinant, a fourth of a measure; and spikenard in the amount of half the quantity of all the other spices. Grind this into a powder and then put the powder into a [cloth] bag;[24] take white or red wine and pour it over the powder, wring it through the cloth and you will have claret. The more you repeat the process, the stronger your claret will be. If you do not have all these spices, take two measures of cinnamon, ginger and mace, with cloves and spikenard to half the quantity of all other ingredients; grind to a powder and strain as described above, and you will have claret.

In the *Forme of Cury* (Recipe 205) a basic sort of *clarrey* is made from white wine with cinnamon, galingale, grains of paradise, pepper and honey. A

[24] The use of a cloth bag for this purpose was so common that the term *vinum saccatum* (*saccum*: a bag) designated any spiced wine that had been filtered through linen. See E.O. Lippmann, 'Zur Geschichte der Destillation und des Alkohols', *Chemische Zeitung*, 37 (1913), p.1313.

prescription for a 'Lord's Claret' (*Potus Clarreti pro Domino*) can also be read in a late-fourteenth-century English medical collection.[25] Given the noble class for which it is destined, ingredients list (apart from the wine, which is not mentioned) for this latter version is appropriately more complex: cinnamon, ginger, pepper, long pepper, grains of paradise, cloves, galingale, caraway, mace, nutmeg, coriander, brandy and honey. The second-last ingredient here, the brandy, is more commonly called *aqua vitœ* and may itself represent a distillate from a highly flavoured wine (see below).

Recipes for other sorts of spiced wines abound in cookery manuals and seem to reflect local tippling preferences. In a brief miscellany of recipes in an English medical manuscript from about 1400 appear directions for making *Pymente*:

> Take a gallon of either red or white wine – for some like it red and some like it white – and put into it 2 pounds of honey and work it up in the same way as Clary is made; then get 2 ounces of root of elecampane, dry, and one quarter of an ounce of each of galingale, long pepper, nutmeg, grains of paradise and cloves, and six pennyweight, dry, of each of rosemary, bay leaves, hyssop, mint and sage; powder all these and add them to the wine.

Such recipes for a remarkably wide variety of spiced wines turn up here and there in cookery collections and quite casually in other types of manuscripts. While physicians perceived certain pharmacological virtues in the mixtures of some of these 'made wines', healthy citizens must certainly have enjoyed them too, unprescribed, because of their rich flavours.

Beer, Ale

The inspiration for most medical and humoural theory in the Middle Ages comes from the Mediterranean area, and consequently such typically southern products as wine and olive oil (to say nothing of more ultra-Mediterranean fare such as camel's milk or gazelle meat) receive extensive study and analysis in the influential *tacuina* and *regimine* of the day. Most of these analytical studies were elaborated by Arab physicists and philosophers who lived by the Mediterranean Sea. Later physicians whose clientele was more accustomed to other, more northerly customs do, however, occasionally write of such pedestrian products as beer, ale and butter – as feasible substitutes for kumiss or olive oil – if one should be considering a choice of beverage or cooking oil.

---

[25] In British Library, Ms. Royal 17.A.iii, f.97v. See *Curye on Inglysch*, V, 4. For another recipe see the *claretum* in the *Tractatus*, I, §18, p.383.

As beverages beer and ale tend to be looked upon in the learned treatises at the least as preferable to plain water, even to pure spring water, at the worst as hardly to be recommended whole-heartedly. Today one might consider such an assessment to be an instance of damning with faint praise, although physicians did, when all was said and done, credit those alcoholic drinks with qualities roughly similar to those of wine. However the learned physician who was responsible for the vernacular commentary on the *Regimen sanitatis Salernitanum* automatically makes an invidious comparison between beer and wine.[26] In particular he cautions that beer should always be drunk in moderation, because the intoxication produced by beer is worse than that produced by wine and lasts longer. The explanation for this becomes rather technical, but its gist is that the fumes and vapours from beer are more difficult to clear from the brain because they are 'grosser' than those of wine. On the other hand the commentator admits that it might be preferable to drink beer rather than wine at the beginning of a meal: in the first place, beer will not attract all of the body's corrupt, putrescent superfluities to the empty stomach, which is what a pleasurable flagon of wine may do; and in the second place, beer has the virtue of cleansing out whatever undesirable humours may actually be dwelling in an empty stomach to begin with. Furthermore, the drinking of wine does possess the well recognized side-effect of creating a 'false thirst' (caused inevitably, the author indicates, by the natural warmth furnished by wine) to which, fortunately or unfortunately, the drinking of beer does not give rise.

The Sienese Aldobrandino is somewhat less charitable to a beverage which in all likelihood remained quite alien to him.

> Beer is a sort of beverage that is made from oats and wheat and barley, though that which is made from oats and wheat is better because it does not cause as much wind or gas. But from whichever it is made, whether from oats, barley or wheat, it harms the head and the stomach, it causes bad breath and ruins the teeth, it fills the stomach with bad fumes, and as a result anyone who drinks it along with wine becomes drunk quickly; but it does have the property of facilitating urination and makes one's flesh white and smooth. And the beer that is made from rye, or from rye bread in which there is mint and wild celery, is far better than any other type of beer.[27]

At any rate, in England and in the Germanic countries beer and ale were served and consumed as *the* regular table beverages. By the fourteenth century in Amersfoort some 350 breweries were actively producing beer for the home market and the immediate environs; Haarlem had 50 breweries.[28] Water was normally eschewed at table for the same sound 'medical' and

---

[26] *Regime tresutile*, pp.52ff and 93ff.
[27] *Le Régime du corps*, p.118.
[28] G.Z. Jol, *Ontwikkeling en organisatie der Nederlandsche brouwindustrie*, Haarlem, 1933.

sanitary reasons as were accepted throughout the rest of Europe. Naturally, the countries of Europe beyond England, the Lowlands and the German states tended to look down on cultures that consumed beer and ale. When, however, in 1420 King Henry V of England married Catherine of Valois, the daughter of King Charles VI of France, his present to his father-in-law of a fine beer mug declared on the one hand that the young English monarch rejected any such contempt for English tastes and on the other that in England beer was certainly good enough for royalty.[29] The French popular drink known as *godale*, seemingly a derivation of the English 'good ale', was a stong beer made without hops from barley and spelt alone.

Andrewe Boorde (c.1490–1549), Englishman that he was, distinguished clearly between ale and beer.

> Ale is made of malte and water; and they the which do put any other thynge to ale then is rehersed, except yest, barme, or godesgood, doth sofystical theyr ale. Ale for an Englysshe man is a naturall drynke. . . . Barly malte maketh better ale then oten malte [malted oats] or any other corne [grain] doth. It doth ingendre grose humoures, but yette it maketh a man stronge. . . .
> Bere is made of malte, of hoppes, and water: it is a naturall drynke for a Dutche man. And nowe of late dayes it is moche used in Englande to the detryment of many Englysshe men . . . .[30]

By 1525, when hops (the plant botanically known as *Humulus lupulus*) were first introduced into England from Flanders, they had been added to beer in Lowlands brewing for several hundred years. Hops increase the durability of the beer and add a slightly bitter flavour to the mixture, a quality which Andrewe Boorde seems to despise. Beer is a cold drink, he goes on to say, which 'doth make a man fat, and doth inflate the bely, as it doth appere by the Dutche mens faces & belyes'. Then, as now, there is a lot of chauvinism bound up with taste.

Boorde also describes a *poset ale* which is 'made with hot milk and cold ale', a beverage which is particularly beneficial for the drinker who has a 'hot liver . . . if cold herbs be sodden in it'.

As was the custom with wine, ale could also be further 'made' by the addition of various spices. In England this drink was known as *braggot* or *brakott*. The ingredients lists for spiced ale tend to resemble those of elementary hipocras and claret, though the processes for making it are a little more extensive:

> *Ad faciendum brakott.* Take fourteen gallons of good fine ale whose malt is doubly mashed, put it into an earthenware vessel and let it stand for

[29] Alfred Gottschalk, quoting Juvenal des Ursins, in *Histoire de l'alimentation et de la gastronomie*, 2 vols., Paris (Hippocrate), 1948; I, p.306.
[30] *A Dyetary of Helth*, London (Kegan Paul, Trench, Trübner), 1870, p.256.

three or four days until settled. Then add in a quart of fine malt and half a quart of unclarified honey, and set it to boil on the fire, skimming until it is clear. Add in a pennyworth each of ground pepper and ground cloves, and boil everything well together. Take it off the fire, let it cool and pour off the clear liquid into [a] vessel; put the remaining grounds in a bag, put this into the vessel along with fresh yeast, and stop it up air-tight with a linen cloth for three or four days before you drink it. Stir in brandy.[31]

Other Table Beverages

Mead

From time immemorial honey had been dissolved in water by northern European, and particularly Celtic, societies in order make the palatable beverage known variously as *medo* and *mellicrattum* (Latin), *mede* (English and German), and *bochet* (French). According to a late-fourteenth-century English recipe copied in a medical manuscript, mead resulted merely from boiling honey and water.

> To make mead. Take honeycombs and put them into a large vessel, set weighted wood to press on them until as much honey as possible has run out: this is called 'live honey'. Then boil those combs thoroughly in pure water, and press out as much honey as possible into hot water in another vessel, boil it, skim it and add in a quart of the live honey; then let it stand a few days covered tightly. This is a good drink.[32]

As one might expect, however, given its somewhat greater popularity in the Germanic states, the making of mead there required a much more studied process.

> For those who want to make good mead, warm pure water from a well, only as warm as you can bear your hand in it, and for each two *maß* [each about two pints] of water take one *maß* of honey; stir this with a stick, let it sit for a while and afterwards strain it through a clean cloth or through a hair sieve into a clean barrel. Then boil the usual mead spices for as long as it takes to walk around a field, and do that again, and skim the spices using a bowl with holes in it so that the foam stays but not the spices; then pour the mead into a clean barrel and cover it, so that the steam cannot escape, leaving it there until [it has cooled to the point that] you can bear your hand in it. Then get a pot the size of half a *maß* [roughly one pint], fill it half with hops and a handful of sage

---

[31] British Library, Ms. Royal 17.A.iii, f.123r, in *Curye on Inglysch*, V, 8, pp.149–150. For the brandy, a distillate of a spiced wine, see below.

[32] See the series of miscellaneous recipes to which Hieatt and Butler have given the name *Goud Kokery*, Recipes 9 and 10, in *Curye on Inglysch*, p.150.

and boil that together with the spices for [the time that it takes to walk] approximately half a mile, and then pour it into the spice-mixture; take the amount of half a small nutshell of fresh hops and add that and mix it in order to make it ferment; cover it up so that the steam cannot escape and leave it for a day and a night. Then strain the mead through a clean cloth or a hair sieve; keep it in a clean barrel and let it age for three days and three nights, topping it up every evening; after that drain it, minding that no yeast gets into it, and let it sit for eight days so that it drops, topping it up every evening. After that pour it into a resinated barrel and let it sit for eight full days; [even so] don't drink it until after six or eight weeks – then it tastes its best.[33]

At a little later date in Paris the *Menagier* wrote out directions for the making of mead that called for yeast to initiate the fermentation process. The householder should boil good, sweet honey until it yields bubbles of dark steam, stir it, then add in water and reduce the mixture by about one-fifth, stirring constantly. Then he/she should cool it, strain it and barrel it, and at that point add in either beer yeast (which the writer recommends) or bread yeast (which he says is just as tasty, although the colour of the mead will be less rich).[34] The same recipe in the *Menagier de Paris* continues with instructions for making a spiced variation of basic mead, apparently what the *Das Buch von guter Spise* was aiming at. Known to the French of the day still as simply *bochet*, the *Menagier* appears to consider the spiced treatment preferable to the plain variety: he begins this part of the recipe, 'And if you wish to make it very good . . .', and continues with instructions to suspend a bag of ground spices (ginger, long pepper, grains of paradise and cloves) in the cask for two or three days, squeezing the infused spices as you remove the bag; the same bag of spices can be used to flavour three or four such casks of plain mead. In the sixteenth century the Englishman Andrewe Boorde declared that a drink called metheglyn, consisting of honey, water and herbs, was more wholesome than ordinary mead.[35] The ratio which modern makers of mead generally use is four lbs (1.8 kg) of honey to a gallon (4.5 l.) of water.

Although honey continued to be accorded a modest role as an ingredient in late-medieval cookery, mead seems to have declined in popularity as a beverage among the aristocracy. The reason may perhaps be related to a perception that mead was an ideal medicinal drink. In its general preamble, the *Tractatus* declares that the reader should know the different effects of the various foodstuffs, and, among other things, which beverages should be viewed 'as medicinal, of a nature to strengthen the weak or sick person, such

---

[33] *Das Buch von guter Spise*, Recipe 14. This German collection dates from the first half of the fourteenth century.

[34] *Menagier de Paris*, Recipe 299. The author specifies quantities in terms of the *sextier*, a measure whose precise volume at that time is somewhat problematic.

[35] *Op. cit.*, p.257.

155

drinks as *mellicrattum* [i.e., mead], *oxizucara*, *sapa*, *mulsa*, *syrupi* and *tysana*'.[36] The inclusion of the incidental English recipe for mead among medical texts is probably significant. In the *Menagier*'s book his mead recipe appears in a section whose rubric is 'Beverages for the Sick'. A beverage with a long and noble tradition seems to have eked out its life on the bedside tables of sickrooms.

Cider, Perry, etc.

The juice of virtually any fruit can potentially be extracted from the pulp and used as a beverage. In the late Middle Ages a few of these juices were commonly so used, either fresh or, wherever their juice was sufficiently rich in sugar to allow its conversion to ethyl alcohol, in fermented form. As with practically all other undistilled beverages that we are examining, these were familiar to diners in Roman antiquity. Such fruit wines included perry from pears, a fermented liquid cotignac drawn from medlars or quince, and wines from pomegranates, cornel berries (or cornelian cherries), sorb-apples (or service-berries), and mulberries (or blackberries).[37] For obvious reasons a date wine that was drunk and prescribed in Greek antiquity had no popular currency in the rest of Europe in the late Middle Ages.

The existence of apple cider (*cidre* or *pommé*) is mentioned somewhat vaguely by Isidore of Seville,[38] but seems to have been used only as a medicine. Throughout the Middle Ages, for more northerly countries wherever apple trees grew naturally, if not entirely wild, cider was a common enough beverage. The *Tractatus* mentions it both in its preamble, in a brief listing of beverages, and in its Part I, which surveys the nature and production of all common beverages. In Recipe 20 at this latter location we read the following:

> Cider is made from softened pears and acorns (*esculiis*). It provides a drink full of cold and flegmatic [i.e., cold and moist] humours. It can also be made from good apples, and is useful for the choleric temperament [i.e., warm and dry] of men who work outdoors. First the fruit is crushed, then it is squeezed in a press; boiling water is added to the fruit residue of the press and the mash squeezed.

In medieval Europe cider is found as a culinary ingredient only in the early French recipe collection known as the *Enseignements* (Recipe 36). There it is used as an alternative to unfermented grape juice in which a roast pike is to be boiled.

[36] *Tractatus de modo preparandi et condiendi omnia cibaria*, ed. cit., p.380.
[37] An interesting study of these medieval wines in German states is afforded by Eero Alanne, *Die deutsche Weinbauterminologie in ahd. u. mhd. Zeit*, Helsinki, 1950.
[38] *Etymologicon*, XX, 3, 11: *hydromelum*.

From the twelfth century comes a 'recipe' for giving cider a sparkling body.

> To make cider, beer or wine frothy, throw a chunk of sugar into the jug
> at the moment that you are stopping it up; as the sugar is dissolving it
> expresses the molecules of air it contains; overly compressed and
> because of their natural elasticity, these molecules tend constantly to
> separate [from the liquid]; when the jug is opened, they spring out
> immediately, bearing in great effusion whatever of the liquid with
> which they are in contact.[39]

Perry (and *poiré* in French) was a pear juice. Like cider perry could be
drunk fresh or after having undergone the process of fermentation. As, too,
with cider the use of perry was not universal, being limited to the localities
in which the fruit was grown and in which the taste for its juice had
developed.

Similarly *prunellé*, made from wild plums, blackthorn berries or sloeberries,
and a wine from black mulberries or blackberries (called *murrey* in English
and *muré* in French) were popular in those regions of Europe, particularly in
England and France, where the juices could readily be produced. The first
survives today, distilled, as slivovitz; the second is still drunk as mulberry gin
or blackberry wine. Pomegranate juices and wines, from the ground and
strained seeds of the fruit, seem to have been fairly commonly made in
Italy.[40]

One final beverage does not really belong in this category of 'fruit juices',
but then it tends to lie outside the taste of the countries and the time we are
examining. Kumiss, a beverage of fermented animal milk, was certainly well
known among eastern peoples, but was prepared in Europe only on a doctor's
prescription. We may suspect that this drink, originally made from the thin
milk of mares and camels, owes its use in Western Europe only to its
presence in Arabic medical treatises.

Syrups and Distillates

As well as being drunk 'straight' or mulled, as a beverage, wine and various
sorts of beer were also operated upon in two distinct ways in order to produce
two other sorts of drink. There was a wine syrup from which some of the
liquid had been evaporated; and there was a distillate of grain or grape
beverages.

[39] Gottschalk, *op. cit.*, I, p.305. Gottschalk is quoting LeGrand d'Aussy, though without
indicating his precise source.
[40] See the article by Jacqueline Brunet and Odile Redon, 'Vins, jus et verjus. Du bon
usage culinaire des jus de raisins en Italie à la fin du Moyen Age,' in Gilbert Carrier
(ed.), *Vin des historiens*, Suze-la-Roussie (Université du Vin), 1990, p.113 and nn.32
and 37.

Wine syrups in the late Middle Ages were not commonly available on the public market for the simple reason that every household could make its own. A syrup was in its essence merely what was left in a pot of wine after two-thirds of its volume had been boiled away. Although this syrup, called *vin cuit* or *vino cotto* and which Italian recipe books also term *saba*,[41] had an end use in the kitchen more often than not as an ingredient, its medicinal properties were very broadly recognized by physicians as well. The passage from the *Tractatus* that we referred to above places *syrupus* alongside mead and *oxizucara* (a mixture of sugar and vinegar) as standard beverages appropriately prepared for the sick. The recipe for making *vino cocto* which is copied in the Venetian *Libro per cuoco* (Recipe 120) shows an apparently general-purpose beverage, in the elaboration of which honey is mixed into a good red wine in a proportion of one to four, a little cinnamon is added, and the whole reduced by boiling to one third.

The process of distillation seems to have been known as far back as 800 B.C. when the Chinese were distilling rice beer in porcelain stills in order to make an early form of whisky.[42] Aristotle (384–322 B.C.) was interested in its use in order to desalinate sea-water. Toward the beginning of our era there is evidence of a Roman drink produced by a the process of distillation, and both the Roman historian and encyclopedist Pliny (A.D. c.23–74) and the Greek physician Dioscorides (A.D. c.40–90) write of extracting distillates from tar.[43] Both of these writers also describe how sailors held a sponge over a kettle of boiling sea-water in order to obtain potable water. The natural cycle of water by means of evaporation and precipitation – from sea to clouds to rain – seems to have been quite well understood at least as a principle in Antiquity. However, there seems to be no solid evidence that, apart from the Chinese, anyone used the technique of distillation to refine alcohol.

The earliest precise reference to the actual mechanism by which liquids can first be volatilized and then condensed describes what is still – not to pun

---

[41] The Roman agricultural scientist Cato (234–149 B.C.) refers both to *sapa*, a reduced wine, and to *defrutum*, a reduced must. *Marcus Porcius Cato, On Agriculture, Marcus Terentius Varro, On Agriculture*, ed. and trans. William Davis Hooper, London and Cambridge, Mass., (Heinemann and Harvard University Press), 1967; e.g., pp.42–3, §§XXIII and XXIV. In Book I of his *De vita populi Romani*, Varro (116–27 B.C.) gives the name *sapa* to wine that has been boiled away to 50%, and *defrutum* to wine that has been reduced to one-third. See also Pliny, *Historia naturalis*, XIV, 80.

[42] A good survey of the whole matter of distilling is available in Robert James Forbes, *A Short History of the Art of Distillation*, Leiden (Brill), 1948.

[43] According to Dioscorides, 'Of Pitch [tar] is made *oleum picinum*, the watery matter of it which swims on ye top as whey doth of milke being separated. This is taken away in ye seething of the Pitch by laying clean wool over it which when it is made moyst by the steam thereof ascending upon it is squeezed out into a vessel and this is donne as long as the Pitch is seething.' Quoted in Forbes, *A Short History of the Art of Distillation*, p.16. These early experiments may be seen as the origin of the petroleum and gasoline industry!

– the most elementary apparatus: a pot, in which the original liquid can be boiled; a head, on the inner surface of which the steam condenses; and a delivery tube, by which the distillate is led off to a second container. The apparatus is the alembic.[44] The invention of this equipment is attributed – clearly erroneously – to a certain Mary the Jewess – to whom Arnaldus de Villanova also attributed the invention of heating a vessel in a hot 'bath' which he naturally called a *balneum Mariæ* or *bain Marie*. This first attribution, of the alembic, is found in several manuscripts of the ninth and tenth centuries and is interesting in that this Mary is historically associated with an alchemical school located in Alexandria, Egypt, between the first and third centuries: for the West the practice of distilling had supernatural, mystical and occult implications from quite an early time.

It seems that the earliest stills were made of earthenware, copper and tin, and occasionally of lead – this last substance perhaps yielding an output that was all the more potent. Even in 1366 Bonne of Bourbon at the court of Savoy was distilling rose-water and other substances in a lead alembic.[45] Toward the end of the fourteenth century flasks of glass generally replaced the lead vessels in alchemical and medical laboratories. Arabic technology in glass-making and in glazing vessels is particularly credited with this eventual development, although the glass industries of northern Italy in the late Middle Ages, especially at Murano and Venice, greatly facilitated it.

The term *aqua vitæ* ('water of life'), which was applied generically to all distillates,[46] points to an early and almost Platonic perception that such liquids somehow realized a refinement or purification of the substance from which they had been extracted. In the case of an alcoholic liquid such as wine, the concentrate – its relative purity could be tested by trying to ignite it on a piece of linen; it should burn without immediately scorching the cloth. The Franciscan Vitalis of Furno reported this testing technique in the health handbook that has been attributed to him.[47]

---

[44] *Alembicum, id est vas distillatorium, ut in quo fit aqua rosata et aqua ardens et cœtera*: 'The alembic, that is the distilling flask, in which rose-water, fire-water, and so forth, are made.' The thirteenth-century *Alphita* (or *Synonima herbarum* was a medico-botanical glossary which defined the term that designated a 'still'; ed. J.L.G. Mowat, *Sinonoma Bartholomæi*, Oxford (Clarendon), 1882; also ed. Salvatore de Renzi, *Collectio Salernitana*, Naples (Filiatre-Sebezio), 1854; Vol. 3, pp.271–322.

[45] C.G. Carbonelli, *Come vissero i primi conti di Savoia*, Monferrato (Miglietta, Milano), 1931, p.30. The danger posed by the lead may have been more apparent to us than real: usually the inner surface of a lead vessel was deliberately coated by the operator with a layer of salt or of hard loam.

[46] The results of the distillation of grain alcohol in Scotland and Ireland were similarly dubbed 'water of life'. The gaelic *uisge beatha* is at the origin of the modern word *whisky*.

[47] Vitalis Albanensis, Cardinal-Bishop of Albano, *Pro conservanda sanitate tuendaque prospera valetudine ad totius humani corporis morbos et ægritudines salutarium remediorum curationumque liber utiliss*, Mainz (J. Schoeffer), 1531.

Vitalis, who died in 1327, having become successively Bishop of Basel, Cardinal (1312) and Bishop of Albano (1321), illustrates the close connection between medicine, chemical and physical theory, alchemy and the Church in the later Middle Ages. His own recipe for *aqua vitæ* reasonably called for a dose of sulphur to be added to good red wine before this latter was distilled.

Distillation represented a mysterious sublimation of matter. Such transmutation was close to the heart of what alchemists were striving to accomplish throughout the Middle Ages.[48]

Available by means of repeated distillation, the *aqua vitæ rectificata* ('purified water of life') approximated pure alcohol. John of Rupescissa, another Franciscan monk in the middle of the fourteenth century, composed a pair of solid tomes in which he declared what was universally accepted as a double undisputed truth: that this spirit of alcohol was recognized as the fifth essence, after the theretofore acknowledged prime essences of air, water, fire and earth; and that this *quintessence* in turn must constitute an absolute remedy against any and all corruption occasioned (as any morbidity necessarily would be) by abnormally excessive occurences of any of those other four essences.[49] And still in the fifteenth century the renowned physician Michael Savonarola (grandfather of the Florentine friar and reformer Girolamo Savonarola) continued to claim the most impressive properties for various alcohols in his *Art of Making Simple and Composite Artificial Waters and of their Wonderful Virtues in Preserving Health and Curing the Diverse Illnesses of the Human Body.*[50]

While East Indians had been drinking their arrack, which was distilled from sugar and rice, for more than a millenium, and the Arabs had produced a brandy from wine for almost as long, in the European Middle Ages the products of distilling tended at first to be quite limited in both quantity and use. Initialy, too, the site of the production of alcohol was the home and the monastery; what dripped very slowly from the still-head of the earliest rudimentary aparatus was more a marvellous curiosity than anything else. The functional properties enthusiastically attributed to it remained firmly in the domain of the physician and druggist. By the first century A.D. both distilled mead and distilled wine were known. It was only after eighth-

---

[48] On the whole question of alchemy and distillation the study by Suzanne Colnort-Bodet, *Le code alchimique dévoilé. Distillateurs, alchimistes et symbolistes*, Paris (Champion), 1989, provides a useful survey.

[49] *La vertu et propriété de la quinte essence de toutes choses*, published in Lyons (Jean de Tournes), 1549; and *De consideratione quintæ essentiæ, liber de famulata philosophiæ*, Basel, 1561 and 1597.

[50] *De arte confectionis aquam vitæ simplicem et compositam et de eiusdem admirabili virtute ad conservandum sanitatem et ad diversas humani corporis ægritudinis curandas*, Hagenau, 1532 and Basel, 1561, 1597.

century contact with Arabic practice[51], and particularly after the introduction of water cooling around the head of the alembic or still in the twelfth century, that significant quantities of liquors could become available.

The distillation of alcohol from a liquid that contains it requires a canny use of heat in order to distil as much of the alcohol as possible but as little as possible of the water that is in that liquid. In his *Secretis mulierum*[52] Albertus Magnus (1193–1280) offers two recipes for distilling alcohol, which he calls *aqua ardens* or 'fire water'. In his book on *Waters*, by which he means the whole range of possible distillates and normally called artificial waters, Peter of Spain (1215–1277; he became, briefly, Pope John XXI) describes both *aqua vitæ* (the so-called 'elixir of life') and *aqua ardens* ('fire water', relatively pure alcohol). Normally, with comparatively crude stills, the second can be had only by lowering the water content of the distillate to something in the range of 30% through repeated distillations.

It should be stressed, however, that these distillates were not normally consumed freely as beverages in the course of a meal. Their function remained primarily pharmaceutical, just as the laboratory techniques used in their production were absorbed into the sphere of the apothecary and were developed there. Where originally in early medieval Europe distillation was practised in the monastery and in the home of the private artisan, by the end of the Middle Ages, when the craft had been refined to the point of producing commercially useful quantities, the trade became concentrated on the one hand in a few industrial centres[53] and on the other in the chemist's shop. A recipe for *aqua vitæ* appears in the English medical collection that was referred to above.[54]

> *Aqua vite*, that is to say, 'water of life'. Fill the flask full of the lees of strong wine and add in the following ground spices: cinnamon, cloves, ginger, nutmeg, galingale, cubebs, grains of paradise, long pepper and black pepper. Then get caraway, laser-wort, cumin, fennel, smallage, parsley, sage, mint, rue, calamint and oregano – about half an ounce or so as you wish; pound them a little, to make it better, and mix them with the spice powder. Then set the flask on the fire, set the head on top of the flask, being careful not to let any heat on it, and put another flask under to catch the [artificial] water.

[51] See Al-Râzı̂ (865–925), *Madkhal al-Ta'lı̂mı̂* ('Instructive Introduction') and *Kitâb sirr al-asrâr* ('Book of the Secret of Secrets'). These were edited by J. Ruska, in *Al Razi's Buch der Geheimnisse*, Berlin, 1937.

[52] Published London, 1566, and Amsterdam, 1669.

[53] Especially in Italy: Salerno, Venice, the Po Valley; and in Germany: Hara, Saxony, Bohemia and the Hanse towns. Increasingly distilled products were exported from Flanders and Holland in the fifteenth century as Italy and Germany were subject to social and political uncertainty.

[54] British Library, Ms. Royal 17.A.iii, f.99v; *Curye on Inglysch*, Part V, Recipe 7; p.149.

As a medicine *aqua vitæ* enjoyed almost as many specific uses at spiced wines and wine syrups. A doctor of anatomy and medicine at the University of Bologna, Thaddeus Alderotti (1223–1303) did for alcoholic distillates what Arnaldus of Villanova did for spiced wines: a survey and analysis of the various sorts of distillate was made available to the practising physician in his *De virtutibus aquæ vitæ*.[55] This work shows the latest practices of double distillation (in order to obtain a higher percentage of alcohol) and of a water-cooled discharge tube (in order to increase the output).

This water of life had several profane, non-medicinal uses: as an ingredient in English claret and spiced ale (see above); and, most curiously, as the combustible substance whenever cooks had to mount a marvellous fire-breathing dragon or boar for a particularly impressive *pièce de résistance* in a banquet. Among his *entremets*, Chiquart has examples of no fewer than four lifelike, cooked animals (two boars, a piglet and, a little bizarrely when one tries to imagine it, a swan) equiped so as to be able to breathe fire. By soaking cotton in *aqua ardens* and igniting it at the right moment, the animal could continue some time to do the impossible while it was paraded on a platter around the dining hall.[56]

It was especially the superfine particle structure and the volatile nature that physicians valued in these spirits. In the medical thinking of the time, concerned as it was with the need for permeating the body as wholly as possible with various efficatious influences, the faculties that were discerned in liquors were bound to facilitate a rapid and thorough penetration to the source of any superfluous humours. The renowned physician Arnaldus of Villanova saw in these distillates a marvellous panacea for virtually any ailment. In 1309 he wrote:

> This liquor, extracted from wine but with neither its nature, nor its colour, nor its effects, is worthy of the name 'water of life' for it gives one a long life. . . . It prolongs good health, dissipates superfluous humours, reanimates the heart and maintains youth. Taken alone or along with some other appropriate medicine, it cures dropsy, cholic, paralysis, quartan fever, gallstone, ...

Significantly, this encomium on the potency of *aqua vitæ* appears in Arnaldus' work about prolonging life, *On Maintaining Youth*,[57] although he did write a *Tractatus de aquis medicinalibus* or 'Treatise on Alcoholic Medicines' in which the almost magical virtues of alcohol as a medicine are

---

[55] Published by E.O. von Lippmann, 'Thaddäus Florentinus (Taddeo Alderotti) über den Weingeist', *Archiv der Geschichte der Medizin*, 7 (1914), pp.379ff.

[56] 'To instruct the master cook who will have the charge of those [fire-breathing boar's] heads, to make them give out and breathe fire by their mouths, take a double-wicked wax candle and wrap it around with cotton which has been moistened in alcohol in which a little camphor has been dissolved.' *On Cookery*, Recipe 6.

[57] *De conservanda juventute*.

extolled. The quest for an elixir of life had always been dear to philosophers, alchemists and physicians. For a long while it seemed that the clear liquid yielded by the alembic might very well be that magic potion.

Though the alembic was apparently known, and used, in some late-medieval kitchens, cooks must have been clearly aware of its function as a generator of vital, quasi-miraculous substances. The Catalan author of the *Libre del coch*, Mestre Robert, writes out a recipe for a *Torta destillada* in which a still is used. A mixture of raw chicken (with the bones), spices and herbs is chopped and ground very finely, mixed with water and boiled in a still. 'Let all of that, mixed and chopped, be put into an alembic of bronze or lead to distil fully. You should know that what comes out is a thoroughly transparent water. This liquid is so healthful a thing that it will transform a man from death to life.'[58]

Even in the late-thirteenth century the eminent Spanish natural philosopher, mystic and poet Raymond Lull declared that *aqua vitæ* was 'an element newly revealed to man but hid from antiquity because the human race was then too young to need this beverage, destined to revive the energies of modern decrepitude'.[59] Occupying as it did an important shelf or two in the drug cupboards of European apothecaries, liquor was already marked clearly 'For medicinal purposes only'! But any substance which was so much in favour among physicians, to say nothing of alchemists, could not be withheld from the general public for long. If, as Raymon Lull had put it, modern decrepitude could be succoured with liquor, then modern decrepitude owed it to itself to seek succour.

Then as now domestic distilling continued, perhaps still modestly but undoubtedly benefitting from successive developments in technology. In Germany late-medieval moonshine satisfied the demands of the immediate household for a good heart and good health, but by the thirteenth century home-brew (the term of the time was close to literally that: *Hausbrand*) was regularly retailed by vintners and inn-keepers.[60] Even the apothecaries came at this time to maintain a stall in the marketplace at which they distributed distilled products to the public, sick or well, at large. In Nürnberg in the thirteenth and fourteenth centuries municipal regulations indicate that apothecaries were the principal tradesmen in refined alcoholic products, selling various sorts of brandy: *gebrannter wein, bernewein, brandwein*. The consumers of these products were by no means restricted by class, nor were

---

[58] *E tot asò bé mesclat e capolat vaja en un alembich de aram o de plom a destillar molt bé. E sàpies que·n ha de exit una aygua tant clara com lum. E aquesta ès una cosa tant cordial que tornaria un home de mort a vida.* Mestre Robert, *Libre del coch. Tractat de cuina medieval*, ed. Veronika Leimgruber, Barcelona (Curial Edicions Catalanes), 1982, Recipe 137.

[59] Ramón Lull (Raymundus Lullus), *Libri XII Principiorum Philosophorum contra Averroistas.* Lull died in 1315.

[60] See A. Maurizio, *Geschichte der gegorenen Getränk*, Berlin, 1933.

the prices of the liquors such as to deter or discourage their purchase by 'ordinary' citizens.

By 1496 the city fathers of Nürnberg felt themselves obliged to make the following proclamation: 'As many persons in this town have appreciably abused drinking aquavit, the town council warns earnestly and with emphasis that from now on, on Sundays and other official holidays, no spirit shall be kept in the houses, booths, shops or market and even the streets of this town for the purpose of sale or paid consumption.'[61] The partial prohibition which this harsh official measure represents comes on the heels of shrewd advice which a solicitous Nürnberg surgeon had offered his fellow citizens three years earlier: 'As at present practically everyone becomes accustomed to drink aquavite . . ., one should remember how far one can tolerate it and learn to drink it [only ?] as far as one should.'[62] As the Middle Ages were drawing to a close liquor was clearly beginning to ingrain itself into the daily habits of the general population.

The case of one distillate in particular, rose-water, is a somewhat exceptional. The word rose-water designated in reality two sorts of liquid, one of which was a dew or juice that was scraped or expressed from rose petals, and the other of which was a distillate. In the first case the 'water' could be taken more or less directly from the flowers, a manner of making rose-water that is described in the *tacuina sanitatis* along with a statement of its properties, benefits and danger:

> At the right moment during the summer, the women of the house will have prepared rose water, which is made from the most fragrant of the flowers in the rose garden and without adding water but using only their natural moisture. In this way the finest results are achieved. It provides relief in the summer heat because it does good to the efficacy of the sensory mechanisms which, due to the high temperature, become sluggish; it comforts the heart, prevents fainting, and resolves it. Drinking rose water will irritate the respiratory passages, which can be soothed with a white julep.[63]

The yield of pure rose-water from this technique would surely be very small, and the labour involved quite extensive for 'the women of the house'. The *tacuina* disclose a considerable degree of faith in the virtues of this liquid, though, however limited the quantity available of it or however much work went into its gathering. A cheaper rose-water could also be produced merely by taking rose petals, grinding and steeping them in water. Not a beverage,

---

[61] Quoted and translated in Forbes, *A Short History of the Art of Distillation*, p.97.

[62] *Nach dem und nun schir jedermann gemeincklichen sich nimet an zu trinken den geprannten weyn . . ... Darumb was er an idem schafft merk einer selber an im das und lern in trinken dester pas. Idem*, p.97.

[63] Judith Spencer, *The Four Seasons of the House of Cerruti*, New York (Facts On File), 1983, p.64.

this variety of ordinary rose-water, after being filtered, would be used for such purposes as hand-washing at a formal dinner, or for scenting a room or clothes by being sprinkled on them.

The other principal genre of rose-water was a distillate. Produced from the ordinary sort of rose-water (and most likely making use of the quantities that came from the infusion process), it was really an essence of rose-water. Explicitly Vitalis of Furno identifies rose-water as an 'artifical water' – i.e., a sort of *aqua vitæ* – made by distillation. This spirit seems to have had at least three main purposes: as a medicine, as a culinary ingredient, and as a perfume. This last function may have been inspired by Arabic usage, for it is known that long before the end of the European Middle Ages the Arabs in Persia were producing distilled essences from a variety of fragrant flowers for the purpose of creating perfumes.[64]

In medieval recipes rose-water is far from unknown as an ingredient. For some reason its use is much more common in fifteenth-century Italy than elsewhere. However, only the word 'rose-water' is used in these recipes: nowhere in medieval cookery is a distinction ever clearly drawn between 'plain' rose-water and distilled rose-water. It seems to be safe to assume that what the name always implies when it appears as a culinary ingredient is the distilled liquid, essence of rose-water. This assumption is given some solidity by three recipes found toward the end of the *Menagier de Paris* (at Recipe 326), each of which is covered by the rubric which reads 'How to Make Rose-water without an Alembic'.

> To Make Rose-water without an Alembic. Get a barber's basin and bind over its opening a kerchief that you stretch as tight as a drum; then put your roses on the kerchief, and on top of your roses set the bottom of another basin in which there are hot ash and live coals.
>
> To Make Rose-water without an Alembic. Get two glass basins and set them out as instructed on the back of this page. And instead of ash and coals put everything out in the sun, and in its heat the water will be made.

Unfortunately one of the original copyists of this book seems to have ignored the sketch with which the *Menagier* accompanied his second, short-cut recipe for rose-water. Despite this gap in the text, however, what is clearly implicit here is that the usual rose-water of value in the *Menagier*'s day and world, in the kitchen and generally, was precisely the variety that was distilled by an alembic. These recipes in the *Menagier* are found in a chapter of helpful hints for scenting clothes and for making dyes and home medical remedies. A recipe that follows at this point in the same book (Recipe 328) refers to an *eaue distilee* which the context again makes clear is rose-water.

---

[64] They were busy as well distilling crude oil to be used with other ingredients to make the sticky inflammable compound known as Greek Fire. When ignited and cast against an enemy, this Greek Fire made Byzantine and Arabian fleets and armies the scourge of the Mediterranean.

SEVEN

The Hall, Table and Manners

The Hall

Foods prepared in the smoke, heat and noise of the kitchen were borne to a room where, inevitably with some degree of set formal procedure, they were presented to the head of the house, together with his or her family and any guests who had been granted the favour of eating with the head of the house.

The table at which formal meals were served and eaten in the late Middle Ages was different from ours in several ways. In a strictly physical sense it did not have the same sort of permanence as we give all of our 'dining-room furniture' today. In point of fact there was no such thing as a dining room or even dining hall at that time; no room was set aside as a site specifically or exclusively for the function of eating. Even if he were eating with the members of his immediate family, the master of a large household might choose normally take his meals in the intimacy of his own chamber or apartment.

In any noble castle or manor or spacious townhouse there was, however, customarily one room that was designed to be capacious enough for relatively large public assemblies.[1] In that room the lord or affluent bourgeois would hold court, dispose of public business for which he might be responsible, dispense any justice within his jurisdiction, and receive the visits of special friends or dignitaries who deserved some formal, ritual recognition of their status. This was the Great Hall – or perhaps just the Hall. When the lord or affluent bourgeois invited others than his immediate family to come and eat with him, in state, as it were, the Great Hall was the

---

[1] Recent archeology has shown that, depending upon the number of major households inhabiting the place, some larger castles may have had more than just a single 'hall': see John R. Kenyon, *Medieval Fortifications*, Leicester and London (Leicester University Press), 1990, Chapter 5, pp.97-124, 'Halls'. On furniture and the hall see also the article by C. Anne Wilson, 'From Mediæval Great Hall to Country-House Dining-Room: the Furniture and Setting of the Social Meal', *Appetite and the Eye. Visual aspects of food and its presentation within their historic context*, ed. C. Anne Wilson, Edinburgh (Edinburgh University Press), 1991, pp.28-55.

appropriate venue. It alone could adequately accommodate relatively large numbers at table.

In most respects the Hall was much the same as any other room in the building – except that it was larger. If possible, its ceiling was also higher. Up into the twelfth century the Hall might have been of heavy frame construction, as the rest of the townhouse, manor or castle likely would have been. From the twelfth century on, stone was the preferred construction material. If the Hall occupied its own building, or wing of a castle, its roof was almost certainly still of frame rafters. If the Hall was merely one storey, or even a part of one storey, in a multi-storeyed castle tower (a so-called dungeon or keep), then an arched stone ceiling, whether or not this was supported by one or more central stone columns, could have been the floor of the next storey above.

In many cases the Hall was located within the most defensive part of a castle. If the Hall shared a masonry wall with the castle itself, any window openings through that wall would be quite narrow and, inside, the natural light that made its way through the thick embrasures quite dim. Because dinner, the main meal of the day, was served near noon, this relative obscurity was not such a great problem. Except in summer, supper probably required candles or torches to be lit. Before the last centuries of the Middle Ages glass did not close up window opening from the weather: by the time in which we are interested either small panes of glass were set in leaded frames, or semi-translucent sheets of oiled paper were fastened across a wooden frame. Frequently the glass was painted (as were the inside walls of many Halls), but this tinting, in geometric designs and sinuous vines, further limited the light penetrating to the rooms of a castle. In all instances a shutter of wood was used to stop up a window opening completely at the end of the day or whenever the weather was bad.

In winter a fire in the central hearth of a large Hall warmed the room, its smoke filtering out through vents at the peak of the roof. For a Hall of modest proportions, particularly within a tower where a central smoke vent was precluded, masons usually made provision for a fireplace along with its chimney in the thickness of the wall. Such a mural fireplace was less efficient in terms of the warmth it radiated into the room, but in a small Hall floorspace was very much at a premium.

Though the kitchen might not be adjacent to the Hall,[2] there clearly had to be some more or less direct connection between kitchen and Hall by which servitors could bring dishes that had not become completely cold. This might be a straircase from a lower floor in a tower, or a covered passageway from a wing on the other side of the castle courtyard.

---

[2] For reasons of fire and accidental conflagration, the preferred location for a kitchen was in fact at some distance from the main living quarters of a castle. Sensitive noses and ears may also have insisted that kitchen activities be carried out in a separate structure, or at least in a relatively distant location.

Since the Hall was the ceremonial room of a manor or castle it had to function well to that end. It should have some sort of dias from which the lord and master, occupying perhaps the only chair in the room, could be seen physically to dominate his vassals and retainers. Near to where the head table would be set up for a formal meal was located one of the few other pieces of furniture in the Hall, the buffet.[3] This sideboard was literally a place where the beverages were held, in large pitchers in order to fill and replenish the diners' goblets. These pitchers were often of a valuable metal such as silver, so that it became customary to set out on the buffet and on the open shelves of its hutch all of the silver and gold vessels that might be used in the course of a meal. The buffet became in effect an aumbry or dresser where precious table service could most impressively be displayed.

Manuscript miniatures of the period show various sizes and shapes of buffet, always against a wall and usually near to the end of the head table at which the master is dining. In all cases the buffet bears an assortment of wine-pitchers, ewers, basins, bowls, platters, plates, saltcellars and spice-candy dispensers, all presumably worked out of some precious metal and likely engraved. In was partly in the ostentatious pomp of such an exhibit that the glory of the master's house was enhanced.

The articles of table service set out on the buffet did not include linens or common dishware of wood. These were stored in the kitchen or pantry: they did not reflect upon the opulence of the household and might have nothing to do with the ceremonial of service. In particularly affluent households even pewterware might be considered altogether too common and functional to be worthy of display on the sideboard.

Depending on its size, and the pretentions of the house, the Great Hall might have a musician's loft built into it. Several illuminations show a small band of minstrels with wind instruments standing in a sort of balcony, entertaining the host and his guests as a banquet progresses. Doubtless such a corps of musicians had a set of fanfares in its repertoire that could appropriately be called for by the Steward to mark the serving of each new course.

The stone walls of a Hall were likely either whitewashed or decorated with frescos or paintings of one sort or another, in much the same way as the interiors of the stone churches of the day were completely covered with ornamental patterns in cheerful colours or with edifying illustrations. Around the perimeter of the Hall tapestries might further adorn the walls, affording both visual pleasure and some protection from drafts. As well, the lord might hang banners and fix old shields, both emblazoned with the arms

---

[3] In German, this was the *Trysoer*. See Edith Ennen, *The Medieval Woman* (trans. from the original *Frauen im Mittelalter* by Edmund Jephcott), Oxford (Blackwell), 1989, p.189.

of the family in order to recall past exploits and to perpetuate their consequent honour and dignity.

In affluent aristocratic households all of the servitors would certainly wear the lord's livery, much as a jockey today declares in his colours the house he represents. It was normal for such a lord to announce a new set of livery once or twice in a calendar year for each of those in his household who were entitled to wear it. A cook was honoured, for instance, by being on the livery list. Such livery identified the servant as authentically a member of the household, of course, albeit at a somewhat less than exalted level; manifestly also it offered a demonstration to any visitor of the relative size and prosperity of that household.

The Great Hall was the public centre of a grandee's life. Much of the success of any banquet he offered would depend upon efficient operations in the Hall. The Hall amounted to the scenic decor for a demonstration of nobility.

The Table

In such a multi-purpose room as the Hall tables were not a permanent fixture. When the room was to be used for eating, tables had to be set up; these were merely a wooden surface of glued boards that spanned collapsible trestles. In width the surface was somewhat narrower than the standard modern table since in aristocratic households those eating usually sat along only one side of it. In the same way benches were opened up for the guests. The one or two chairs, maybe themselves, too, of the folding variety, were set in position behind the head table for the lord, his lady and any important guest. In many manuscript illuminations it is apparent that even the master and mistress of the house are sitting on a bench, although this often has a tall back and may be covered with elegant tapestry or have a cushioned seat. Behind the head table a tapestry could be hung from a frame whose top might project a canopy; the Italian term *baldachino* eventually came into general use to designate this suspended fabric. The function of the tapestry backdrop was twofold: it clearly set off the host, perhaps along with the guest of honour and their respective consorts in a potentially dramatic fashion; and it could protect the host and head table from any uncomfortable backdrafts which were apt to circulate at the end of the Hall.

If the guest list was long enough to require more than a single table, additional trestles were usually set up so that they extended from each end of the head table in the shape of an angular 'U'. A arrangement with all of the diners seated on the outer sides of this 'U' allowed unobstructed, rapid service from the inner area. At the same time it promoted formal ceremonious procedure in the actual presentation of successive courses, and afforded an excellent focal point for any divertissement that the master of the household might care to have offered. Not the most insignificant advantage of the layout was that lines of sight between guests and host were clear.

The tables were covered with a white cloth – possibly in part to conceal the ingrained grime and stains which the boards may have accumulated in previous use and that could not be scoured or rasped away. A refinement might include the use of a second cloth which was displaced to the side of the table where the diners were to sit and half of which would cover their collective lap. It was quite correct to use this cloth to wipe one's fingers or mouth as the meal progressed. The main cloth was, in French, the *nappe*, and the sanitary cloth was properly the *longière* or 'runner'; the modern English *napkin* seems to derive its sense from this use.[4]

In all likelihood a place setting consisted simply of a spoon and a round (or square) of trencher bread. A plate might or might not be provided as a support for the bread trencher. Depending on the dishes that were proposed for a meal, even that spoon might not really be necessary and was in fact rare on a table before the fourteenth century. The important contents of any prepared dish that was served in a bowl were the solids; the liquid part was in a very real sense merely the sauce. The diner normally had no desire to scoop out or drink any remaining liquid as we would a modern soup. The liquid served to impart a flavour to the foodstuff and to correct its humour; it also effectively kept the food warm between the stew-pot and the table.

A knife, however, was an indispensable implement at a medieval meal. To demonstrate extraordinary affluence and hospitality a host might provide a knife, perhaps from his own large household set of dining cutlery, at each place setting. However, any host could confidently assume that all of his guests, women as well as men, had their own personal knife with them, on their persons. This personal knife was generally everyone's constant companion, an invaluable possession, pointed and sharp-bladed, whether dainty and ornate or sturdy and plain, that served everyone *inter alia* as a defensive weapon if the need arose but always as an eating utensil. For a wealthy host to offer his guests a knife from his own set of cutlery could be seen as a gesture of signal honour.

Trencher bread was of a coarse dough and old enough to have a firm consistency. Set out before each individual it fulfilled a twofold function: it served to identify food that the person had selected from a shared bowl or platter, had bitten into but not finished; and by soaking up some of the excess juices or sauces it saved the tablecloth a little. According to an individual's social status this trencher might be replaced by a personal plate of wood or of pewter, or even of silver or gold. Forks had of course been well

---

[4] In mid-fifteenth-century England this runner was called a *surnappe*: Richard Warner, *Antiquitates Culinariæ, or Curious Tracts Relating to the Culinary Affairs of the Old English*, London (Blamire), 1791, p.10 and Note.

known for a very long time in the kitchen, where with long handles and a few long tines they were useful in removing chunks of meat from a cauldron. At table the fastidious might select their meat from a common bowl or platter by spearing it with their knife, but it was much more normal, safer and entirely acceptable just to use the fingers of one's right hand.

To ensure the peace of mind of others who shared from the same bowl or platter, provision was made for washing one's hands, both initially in a meal and during its course. For the initial washing one servant would tender a bowl while another would pour water from a ewer over the guest's hands, and then pass him or her a towel. For clean-up during a meal smaller finger-bowls were set out along the table, and perhaps occasionally changed during a meal. A fifteenth-century Italian banquet makes use of three varieties of finger-water successively as the meal progressed: lemon-scented, myrtle-scented and muscat-scented.[5]

'The table needs salt so that the food will not seem bland, for which reason we call men who are fatuous, stolid and insipid "without salt," that is to say, without wit. . . . Salt which is going to be used on the table ought to be white and clean like that from Volterra in Tuscany.'[6] To make this vital element available to all the guests at a formal meal it was set out in a variety of holders along all of the tables. The simplest saltcellar consisted of a cube of old bread with a depression or hollow on top. Alternatively, and a little more elegantly, small vessels resembling miniature metal stemware could be dedicated to holding salt. At the head table one of the host's most prized table pieces was conventionally the salt 'boat' or *nef*, a valuable work of silverware designed to offer salt graciously and to suggest its origin *in* the sea and perhaps also its provenance from *across* the sea.[7] Socially the guest could measure his or her status according to the distance his or her assigned place was *below the salt* contained in the lord's saltcellar.

The behaviour manuals of the time instruct the refined diner never to dip his or her food into the salt; we can imagine, with the authors of the behaviour manuals, the rather unpleasant appearance of any saltcellar where this practice was common. Rather salt should be lifted daintily with the tip of one's knife – always assuming, of course, that the knife itself had been adequately wiped just before being so used. An alternative procedure allowed

---

[5] Outlined in the last folios of the manuscript, New York, Pierpont Morgan Library, Bühler, 19.

[6] *Salem requirit mensa ne insulsa videantur obsoniis unde fatuos homines dicimus stolidos et insipidos quod nil salis hoc est ingenii habeant. . . . Sal quo usurus in mensa albus et mundus ut Volaterra in Etruria.* Platina, *De honesta voluptate et valitudine*, Book I, Chapter 13: *De sale.*

[7] The use of this particular table ornament remained fashionable long after the end of our period. In 1545, the Florentine artist and silversmith Benvenuto Cellini (1500–1571) fabricated a golden saltboat for the French maecenas, Francis I. See the *Memoirs of Benvenuto Cellini*, trans. John Addington Symonds, Garden City (Doubleday), 1948, p 278.

a person to take a pinch of salt with the fingers of his or her right hand; again, though, the considerate diner would always take care to ensure that his or her fingers were scrupulously clean before dipping them in the salt.

Table bread was set out by the Pantler, but it was normally a much finer, or at least fresher, whiter variety of bread than that which was sliced into trenchers. A so-called *manchet* loaf, or *pain de main*, was baked from better grades of flour and – as always – shared among several diners. Presumably the expression 'the upper crust' originated in a custom that apportioned to the lord the best part of any table loaf.

Sharing was indeed the essence of a medieval meal. Not only did the master of the house share his food, hence in that sense his 'board', with his guests, but those guests were expected normally to share among themselves. In twos or fours they shared platters and bowls, they shared finger-bowls and flagons. To such a degree was this sharing looked upon as a measure of friendship, that the word *companion* meant literally the person with whom one shared bread.

Even the sanitary runner or napkin was shared as a matter of course. This sort of communal sharing amounted to a sort of material declaration that the guest was indeed assimilated into the group. Contrariwise, not to be allowed to share was tantamount to being outcast, publicly banished from the group. The Constable of France, Bertran du Guesclin, was at a particular moment in his life excluded from the monarch's good graces; at mealtimes his ostracized status was doubly signalled by, firstly, being seated at the very foot of the royal table, and, secondly, by having his tablecloth cut off from that of the other guests 'above' him. Thoroughly humiliated, he ate in reality alone.

Prepared dishes were borne from the kitchen into the Hall in large bowls or on platters. The term 'charger' designated such a platter which was loaded or *charged* with a serving of a dish. Such a serving was normally sufficient for at least two individuals, and perhaps four or six depending upon the social importance of those persons. With very few exceptions 'courses' consisted of several compatible dishes grouped together into a single 'serving' or 'service'.

Where a boiled or roast joint of meat was part of a course, it was normally presented already cut up into 'gobbets' or bite-sized pieces in order to facilitate the diners' job. For any further cutting the diner could hold the meat in his or her fingers under his or her knife. At the head table alone a carver might exercise the honour he had been awarded with his office, that of reducing the host's meat to smaller, more manageable chunks. In medieval courtly treatises many pages are devoted to describing exactly how various meats were properly to be carved at table.

If a sauce was to accompany this meat it could either be poured over the joint just before this was served, or it could be made available to the diners in small bowls placed on the table beside the meat; anyone could thus dip his chunk of meat as he wished into the sauce.

Almost all food was prepared in such a way that it could be picked up and eaten either with the fingers, with the point of one's knife or with a spoon. Pies and tarts could be handled neatly with the fingers. Pastes of meat or peas required spoons; the liquid part of broths and brewets, after the meat was extracted by fingers or with the tip of a knife, could quite properly be taken up in one wished with a chunk of bread. What today we call 'soup' was originally merely a sop, a preparation in which bread or toast is coated or soaked with something else, whether a semi-solid, such as a cheese fondu, or a semi-viscous liquid; like a tart it could be eaten with the fingers.[8]

The meal's beverages were served by the Hall Butler, an officer whose appointment made him responsible for overseeing all of the potables consumed during a meal. He or an assistant would be available throughout the meal to refill the bowls, hanaps, cups, goblets or tankards that host or guests had drained. Given that such bowls, hanaps, cups, goblets and tankards were normally shared between neighbours, the Butler's task must have kept him busy.

A further responsibility of the Butler might be the maintenance of a wine fountain. This mechanical marvel formed in a few exceptional households a wonderful centrepiece for the banquet table. Made of silver or pewter it channelled wine from a manual pump or gravity feed and spewed it from spouts or spigots into the basin which formed its base. From the flow the Butler's assistant could replenish his pitchers. As the banquet progressed the Butler would change the variety of wines that the fountain supplied, and make sure there was a good hipocras in the pipeline for the final refill of the diners' cups.

Toward the middle of the fifteenth century the Italian gourmet Platina laid down definitive regulations concerning the physical circumstances in which one should eat.

> One must set up the table according to the time of year: in winter, in enclosed and warm places; in summer, in cool and open places. In spring, flowers are arranged in the dining room and on the table; in winter, the air should be redolent with perfumes; in summer, the floor should be strewn with fragrant boughs of trees, of vine and of willow, which freshen the dining room; in autumn, let the ripe grapes, pears and apples hang from the ceiling. Napkins should be white and the tablecloths spotless, because, if they were otherwise, they would arouse squeamishness and take away the desire to eat. Let a servant scrub the knives and sharpen their points so that diners will not be delayed by dullness of iron. The rest of the dishes should be scrubbed clean,

---

[8] For an instance of dish prepared as a sop, see the recipe for *Suppa a la Catelanesca* (§260 in the Wellcome manuscript) which is reproduced in Chapter 9, below. This dish amounts really to a thick, mixed sauce served over bread or toast.

whether they are earthen or silver, for this meticulous care arouses even a sluggish appetite.[9]

The table was the object of much attention in well-to-do medieval households. Even though, as far as cutlery, dishware and drinking vessels went, the choice may not have been as ample as the host or hostess has to cope with today, there were indeed a number of other considerations whose determination was equally demanding, and in which a 'good' or 'bad' decision reflected well or badly upon the house, its master or mistress and its servants.

Table Manners

Until fairly recently modern dilettantes, secure in their rather contemptuous condescension toward the Middle Ages and its supposed food habits, claimed that *everything* then was chopped, ground, brayed, sieved and filtered. This seemingly universal love of homogenous mush used to be advanced as proof that few adults retained even a working set of teeth by the age at which they might have been honoured by an invitation to sit at the lord's board; these worthies could only gum their way through bowls of meat paste and pottage.

At the same time a few moderns were loath to abandon the so-eloquent picture of the medieval banquet – the one that is attended by a mob of uncouth louts (disguised as noble lords) who, when not actually hurling huge joints of greasy meat at one another across the banquet hall, are engaged in tearing at them with a perfectly healthy complement of incisors, canines, bicuspids and molars.

Its hard to have it both ways. The truth of the matter is that neither image has much historic basis. In or out of their cups, with both meat-paste *Faugrenon* and roast breasts of pheasant before them, noble lords were able to bite into and fully enjoy the very wide range of prepared dishes that their cooks prepared for them. And to enjoy them without abandoning a conventionally and widely accepted decorum: the wealthy of the late Middle Ages knew very well the refined manners that their peers and betters expected of them. Food-fights are not, of course, even mentioned in the

---

[9] *Pro tempore anni paranda est mensa. Hieme locis clausis et calidis, aestate frigidis et apertis, vere in triclinium et mensam sternantur flores. Hieme fiat suffumigatio odoramentorum, aestate sternatur pavimentum frondibus odoriferarum arborum vitis ac salicis quae conclave recentent, autumno uvae maturae pira poma a laquearibus pendeant. Albae sint mappae candida mantelia ne si secus fuerint fastidium generent et aviditatem edendi tollant. cultros tergat servus eorumque aciem prolixet ne in mora sint convivae ob ferri hebetudinem [. Parata sint reliqua] vasa tersa nitida sive illa fictilia sint sive argentea, haec enim lautities etiam residentem appetentiam excitat.* Platina, *De honesta voluptate*, Book I, Chapter 12: *De paranda mensa.*

medieval cautionary books of good manners, though elbows on the table, talking with food in your mouth, and scratching yourself while at table, are – and such horrendous lapses in elegant etiquette are roundly condemned.

It has always been the assumption that the manner of eating demonstrates one's relative level of refinement. The manner of eating has come almost to define social 'manners' in general. The graces with which a person shows at table that he or she is endowed have always been those graces deemed among the most significant in any society. They amount to nothing less than the ability to govern one's basic appetites, and by this mastery of self one is measured as a social person.

In actual historic fact the legislators of social behaviour in the Middle Ages were quite definite in their insistence upon a code to which anyone with pretentions to membership in the more refined classes must adhere absolutely. From relatively early times writers compiled and copied lists of 'dos' and 'don'ts' intended to guide those who had been invited to partake of food at their lord's board. The very number and variety of these short social treatises, and their persistence from generation to generation throughout the final centuries of the Middle Ages point to them generically as being one the best-sellers of the whole period. They belonged to a type of composition that clearly enjoyed a great popularity.

While some of the injunctions contained among the body of rules in these pieces on table manners seem to have been inspired by similar behavioural advice offered here and there in Antiquity, the counsel that was offered the medieval diner often forms a meticulously detailed and coherent system of regulations. These could cover everything that a worthy and respectable guest should do from the moment he entered the Hall, and before he was even invited to take his seat, to the time when he stood again from his place on a bench in order to allow the boards and trestles to be cleared away.

In one of the earliest such treatises, the *Disciplina clericalis*, or *Training for a Gentleman*, written in Latin by Petrus Alphonsi at the very beginning of the twelfth century,[10] a son naïvely asks his father how he ought to eat if he should happen to to be sitting at dinner before the king. In response, the father first lays down a firm, sort of universal rule-of-thumb to guide the lad in determining proper table manners. 'My son,' the father replies, 'you ought always to eat the same way, no matter where you are: there is no difference between eating here or there; even when eating by yourself you should behave as if you were before the King.' Whereupon the son persists with a further request to be instructed in specific elements of good manners. The father obliges.

> When you have washed your hands, you should touch nothing but
> what you will be eating. Don't immediately gobble up your bread,

[10] A late-medieval French translation appears as *Le Chastoiement d'un pere a son fils*, ed. Edward D. Montgomery, Jr., Chapel Hill (University of North Carolina Press), 1971.

rather wait for the first course to be served. It is not proper to cram such large chunks into one's mouth that bits fall right and left; this amounts to boorishness and gluttony. Chew your food thoroughly before swallowing it, for fear of choking yourself. If you don't want to drink like a churl, make sure your mouth is free of food; only the peasant makes such sops in his mouth. And be aware that it is boorish to speak with a full mouth. . . . Do not reach to the bowl in front of your neighbour to take a morsel that seems better than what you have in front of you: *that* is churlishness. After eating, ask for hand-water, for this is required by medical teaching and it is the decent and easy thing to do.

It is apparent here to what an extent proper table manners were seen as able to establish the necessary distance between the 'boorish' peasant class and a more dignified aristocracy. In fact most of the admonition, moral and practical, contained throughout this work finds its way later into a parallel genre of 'instruction-for-princes', a genre already well developed but which came very much into its own during the Renaissance, in Italy and elsewhere.[11]

A century and a half after *Disciplina clericalis*, a 200-line poem on table manners by a Milanese in the thirteenth century organizes its much more detailed advice according to the sequence of events in a meal. Bonvesin de la Riva was addressing not merely the aristocracy of Milan, a relatively small audience at this time, but the whole of the affluent bourgeoisie, all of those of his fellows, in fact, who were apt to invite, or to be invited out, to a formal dinner.[12] Whether host or guest, we are advised that our first thought as we move to the dining table should be piously of the poor, because the charitable gesture of feeding the poor is tantamount to feeding Christ, to whose table we all hope eventually to be invited. Then we are counselled not to rush to sit down but rather to engage first in a little gracious conversation with our fellow guests. Before beginning to eat we ought to ensure that each dish that is set in front of us be blessed, whether by us or by our neighbour with whom we shall be sharing. Then there follow a succession of earnest injunctions: behave properly, be courtly, well attired, cheerful, alert, affable; avoid dourness; don't slouch, cross your legs, squirm, lean your elbows or arms on the table; eat neither too much nor too little; don't fill your mouth too full, or speak with a full mouth, or drink with a full mouth; don't offer the cup to your neighbour unless he or she asks for it; hold the cup with two hands when you drink; avoid becoming drunk; don't schlurp from your spoon; if you sneeze or cough, turn aside; never criticize the dishes served to you; don't eye some other plate further down the table, but busy yourself

---

[11] See, for instance, *Il Cortegiano* (*The Book of the Courtier*, 1528) of Baldassare Castiglione.

[12] See the edition of the *Cinque volgari de Bonvesin de la Riva*, by G. Contini, Modena (Società Tipographica Modenese), 1937, pp.53–63.

only with what has been served to you; don't rummage around in the platter of meat or eggs – a practice which is apt to disgust your neighbour; don't dunk your bread in the wine cup – another practice which is similarly apt to disgust your neighbour; should you be sharing a platter with a lady, you should cut up meat for her as well as for yourself; don't ask your neighbour questions while he or she is drinking; in your table conversation don't relate distasteful news or raise any contentious issue; don't draw your neighbour's attention to a fly or any dirt you should happen to notice on a dish; and so on and so forth.

From the same thirteenth century in Germany a very similar assortment of rules defining proper courtly table manners for the well-bred was being offered in the *Hofzucht* of a certain Tannhäuser.[13] It is clear that good behaviour at table was recognized quite early and right across Europe to be one of the fundamental measures of social class.

In the second half of the fourteenth century the Catalan Francesc Eiximenis spelled out an exhaustive list of dos and don'ts for the self-respecting diner.[14] While the majority of the precepts in this canon bear strangely enough upon drunkenness and gluttony (see the section of *moral considerations*, below), a series of chapters, 29 to 37, deal with table manners strictly speaking. In this section we find the long-standing rules that have been repeated in more or less the same form from treatise to treatise and from country to country: wash your hands thoroughly; sit where the host directs; keep your eyes from wandering during a meal, especially when you are drinking; don't speak with your mouth full, because it is not pleasant for others to see what is going on in a person's mouth while he is eating; when speaking don't turn directly to your neighbour in case, despite the previous rule, you should accidentally splatter him or her with what may be in your mouth; don't pick at your teeth with your fingernails; don't speak of repulsive things, such as enemas or diseases; wipe your mouth by raising the napkin to your lips rather than by lowing your head to the napkin. But we also find a number of new injunctions, interesting ones perhaps because they represent further refinements on standard good manners: take particular care never ever to sit opposite a lady or girl of the host's household, but only beside her; don't be overly fulsome in praising your host's food, only once or twice voicing such compliments as: 'So help me God, how very good this wine is!' or 'How very fine this bread is!' or again 'How very tasty this meat is!' – also taking great care that the tone of these compliments be moderate so that no one may see any hint of sarcasm in them. And it is here (in Chapter 33) that we find this delightful precautionary advice: before going in

[13] A modern Italian translation of these injunctions is available in Montanari, *Convivio*, §198, pp.371ff.

[14] See *Com usar bé de beure e menjar. Normes morals contingudes en el 'Terç del Crestià'*, ed. Jorge E.J. Gracia, Barcelona (Curial), 1977.

to a meal, be sure to visit the toilet; it is good to purge your stomach at this time, but even more this will reduce the chance that you might happen to break wind in the dining hall!

These are in large measure what we might characterize as rules of civility. They help ensure that a meal will be as pleasant an experience as possible for everyone. In a certain very real sense they constitute an extension of the rules of social comportment that were elaborated for the aristocrary in the twelfth century and that were known as *cortesia*, *courtoisie* and *courtesy*. Such notions of 'courtliness' – the proper behaviour expected of those frequenting a noble court – were closely related to the basic principles of chivalry, or at least to such principles as generosity to the destitute and service to the helpless, most especially, as we know, to widows and orphans. In these earlier times the aristocracy genteelly accepted a host of moral duties – summed up neatly for everyone in the expression *noblesse oblige* – as the price of being recognized as superior. Toward the end of the Middle Ages, and particularly in the various city-states of Italy, the bourgeoisie became wealthy, self-sufficient, proud and perhaps vain enough that its members could begin to take on certain aristocratic airs. They, too, felt the need for manners.

Some of the rules for behaviour at table bore upon strictly sanitary matters, perhaps what we might aseptically call hygienic concerns. Curiously it is the French and English treatises that tend to emphasize these concerns.[15] Wash your fingers frequently during a meal, we are instructed; keep your fingernails pared, and especially keep them cleaned of any muck that might accumulate under them; wipe the grease from your lips before you drink from the cup you are sharing with your neighbour (it's not pleasant to see grease-rings floating on the wine!); don't scratch yourself, don't pick your nose, don't belch, don't try spitting across the table; wipe your spoon clean; don't dip your meat directly into the salt, but furthermore when you take a pinch of salt make sure that your fingers are clean; don't eat from your knife, don't pick your teeth with the point of your knife or rub your teeth with the napkin; don't slop a mess onto the tablecloth – or down your front; deposit all your scraps into a dish; if you rinse your mouth at the end of a meal, don't spit into the basin; and so forth.

Here, as well, in the French and English manuals we find advice of a somewhat more courtly sort: during a meal avoid swearing or telling risqué or ribald tales; if someone passes you a note, just slip it discretely into your bodice; and the always-useful: take care not to doze off in your host's presence.

---

[15] Interesting examples of this literature are found, for instance, in the *Stans puer ad mensam*, an English poem further done into modern English by Edith Rickert in *The Babees' Book: Medieval Manners for the Young*, New York (Cooper Square), 1966; and in Stefan Glixelli, 'Les contenances de table', *Romania*, 47 (1921), pp.1–40.

The medieval diner had no excuse for not knowing how to conduct himself or herself at table. The demeanor of a guest was closely observed, and any offence against the canons of propriety was censurable. The most telling penalty for negligent or unorthodox behaviour was clearly the judgement of one's peers, a judgement declaring that one was no longer worthy of the esteem of one's peers. Even today such disapproval remains probably the strongest form of censure in social matters.

The Catalan moralist we referred to above, Eiximenis, seems particularly concerned with safeguarding the reputation of his country as the home of supremely good manners in all of Europe. He uses an entire chapter (29) to sing the praises of Catalonia, enumerating no fewer than thirteen reasons why his nation unquestionably takes the prize for civility among all other European nations. Repeatedly in this list Eiximenis cites as irrefutable proof of his claim the habitually excellent table manners of his countrymen. And just as he applauds Catalan customs, so he doesn't hesitate to denigrate the usage of each of the other countries.

For instance, in both ordinary daily meals and special banquets, Eiximenis declares, the Catalans drink their wine in good measure and never excessively, whereas the English and the Germans drink only [horrors!] beer or mead or cider or other beverages inferior to wine, and the French and Lombards drink wine always far too much to excess. When Catalans carve up their meat they do it cleanly and neatly, and eat this directly from the trencher plate; the French, German, English and Italians merely hack their meat into chunks, slicing it a little with their knives, handling it with their hands, putting it on a bit of bread in front of them, with their salt in another bit of bread, with the foreseeable result that the bread and the whole of their tables invariably become disgustingly filthy. Catalans eat only twice a day, whereas other nations have no rule, some, like the Germans, getting up in the night to eat, and some, like the French, drinking at any time whatsoever. Catalans eat graciously and decently; in other countries the people eat with such vulgarity that to see them is disgusting in itself. When they eat, the French and Germans end up having their sleeves dip into the serving bowl, and the Spanish bare their arms, whereas Catalans avoid either abhorrent practice by wearing sleeves of appropriate length to dinner. Spanish, Portuguese and French servers, with the short skirts of their jerkins, repulsively display bare legs, but on the other hand hide their face in too snug a hood; Catalan servers avoid both of these offenses to good manners by covering their lower limbs and baring their head. Only Catalans and Aragonese recognize the need to carve each meat according to its variety, and take care to do so; other peoples carve barbarously, as if quite haphazardly.

So much for rowdy food fights in the Great Hall!

Moral Considerations: Sobriety and Gluttony

The earliest work to treat of food in what we may properly term the 'Middle Ages' dates from about A.D. 530 and is entitled *A Letter of Anthimus, the Illustrious Man, Count and Legate, to the Most Renowned King, Theodoric of the Franks, Concerning the Observance of Foods.*[16] In this epistle Anthimus warns the king most earnestly about the need to eat and drink only in moderation.

> ... We who trifle with different foods and different delicacies and different drinks must regulate ourselves so that we are not disordered by overindulgence, but that by living more moderately we may keep our health. If any one pleases to eat any food soever, let him at least eat food well prepared, and of other things sparingly . . ..

This urging to temperateness and sobriety when faced with gastonomic temptations, as even a sixth-century monarch might be from time to time, is in keeping with the most instant counsels for good health laid down by Greek medical dogma. At the same time it accords very well with that prime directive of what will be medieval morality: Nothing in Excess. The doctrine of temperance at the table seems to have been preached continually throughout the Middle Ages.

The health handbooks that we have mentioned before propagate a good number of rules connected with food and eating, and most tend to have to do with restraining one's natural appetite. One must be sober in one's eating and drinking, 'because to eat and drink excessively makes a person dull, sleepy and lazy, and instils weakness in the members and stomach.'[17] One should be particularly careful not to eat too much at supper, the evening meal, because this will inevitably cause stomach pains and interfere with sleep. A walk after a meal is useful 'because by this means food will descend to the bottom of the stomach where the digestive power is located'. Furthermore, we are told on the authority of Avicenna that the mouth of the stomach is the site of appetite: true hunger can be identified (and distinguished from deceptive, imaginary pangs, to which some medieval people seem occasionally to have been subject) by the contraction of the

---

[16] *Epistula Antimi viri inlustris comitis et legatarii ad gloriosissimum Theudoricum regem francorum de observatione ciborum*: ed. Shirley Howard Weber, *Antimus, De observatio ciborum* Leiden (E.J. Brill), 1924; the passage quoted is at p.9.

[17] Though these ideas recur in a number of such handbooks, my specific source here is *Le regime tresutile et tresproufitable pour converver et garder la santé du corps humain*, ed. Patricia Willett Cummins, Chapel Hill (University of North Carolina), 1976. In all likelihood, this treatise is a translation of a Latin commentary by Arnaldus de Villanova (d.c.1313), a Catalan physician who was perhaps the most widely respected member of his profession both during his lifetime and long after it.

'veins' in the orifice of the stomach. The stomach's bottom is, again, where digestion takes place.

Several rules bear upon wine. Anyone with a hangover should drink wine first-off the next morning – we will recognize here the proverbial hair-of-the-dog. That revered authority, Hippocrates, advises that everyone should indulge his or her health once a month by quite deliberately becoming drunk: a good, rip-roaring intoxication will induce vomiting, and this vomiting is in itself supremely useful in cleansing out all of the month's accumulation of ill humours! Furthermore, if anyone finds that drinking in the evening leaves him or her queasy simply because the individual is not used to wine, then the sure solution to that unpleasantness is for the person *to become* accustomed to wine by drinking it in the morning as well! (The author of the *Regime tresutile* then adds rather righteously that custom can be depended upon to render everything harmless!)

An area in which medieval health handbooks offer much advice concerns excessive eating or drinking. It was of course more or less clear to everyone, and not just to the compilers of medical treatises or to certain moralists, just what the effects of overdrinking could be: too much wine or beer makes a person dull, sleepy and lazy, along with a host of other rather undesirable consequences. When the physicians studied overeating, they found a frightening variety of effects, physical consequences grave enough to gladden the heart of any sober, ascetic moralist. Overeating harms the brain; overeating harms eyesight and hearing; overeating impedes digestion and generates gross humours and fumosity – which in turn stops up the hearing channels; and, for good measure, overeating 'makes a man heavy, sleepy and lazy, and weakens the fabric of the stomach.'[18]

Furthermore, if all that were not enough to frighten the gourmand, overeating makes it difficult for a person to breathe, makes undigested foods come back up into the mouth, gives one an inflated, noisy stomach. Starting in to eat again before the previous meal is fully digested and the stomach is once again empty will eventually cause undigested food particles to be carried along with digested food through the mesenteric veins to the liver, whence the person's whole body is apt in consequence be horribly filled with coarse, unrefined humours. Overeating is defined by Aldobrandino as continuing to eat past the stage at which one still has the appetite to eat more: medieval thinkers were nothing if not rationally precise in their definitions. As a result, the cardinal medical rule that must govern any diner was that one should always rise from the table while still at that stage, that is to say while still hungry.

Although continuing to eat beyond the point at which one has satisfied one's hunger had numerous physical consequences, all enumerated and detailed at charming length in the health handbooks, this was looked upon

18 *Ibid.*, p.2.

essentially, and perhaps more seriously, as a moral question. Gluttony was one of the principal or so-called Capital (or *Cardinal*[19]) Sins. All of these major sins in the Middle Ages are in reality sins of excess. If it did nothing else in the area of general morality, the Middle Ages promoted the moral virtue of moderation. There is, for instance, no more persistent theme in early European literature than that of the tragic consequences of excess, excess in any form.

The universally recognized golden rule for the time was that security of any sort, whether in social, political, military or ethical matters, could lie only in the Golden Mean: neither too tall nor too short, neither too big nor too small, neither too much nor too little. Among the Capital Sins of pride, envy, anger, sloth, avarice and lust was numbered the seventh, gluttony, and it, too, like the others, resulted clearly from a lack of moral control over selfishness or one's appetites. In order to live the morally virtuous life one had to learn to limit – if not absolutely master – all of those weak human tendencies that are innate with the sinful human condition.

In a section evoking the horrible seriousness of the Capital Sins, the *Grant kalendrier et compost des Bergiers* of the late fifteenth century purports to relate the endless punishments that Lazarus observed in Hell being meted out to all of the sinners of each sort. When Lazarus comes to the gluttons, his description and consequent sermon take on a seemingly increased relish.

> In a valley I saw a filthy, stinking river on the shore of which was a table with dirty tablecloths at which gluttons, men and women, were being stuffed with toads and other poisonous animals, and filled with water from that same river.

Then the writer continues sententiously:

> The throat is the castle gate of a person's body. When an enemy wishes to seize the castle, once he wins the gate he will soon after have the castle itself; likewise the Devil who once wins a man's throat by gluttony will easily have the rest and will enter into his body along with all other sins. For the gluttonous readily give way to all other sins, and therefore a good guard is necessary on that gate so that the Devil may not win it. For when you hold a horse by its bridle you can lead it wherever you wish; so does the Devil to the glutton, leading that man wherever he wishes. The servant who is fed too freely becomes mutinous against his master, and the body that is too filled with wine and food becomes mutinous against the mind, so that it is no longer inclined toward good works. By gluttony many have died who should have lived long lives, so that in effect they have been murderers of themselves: for excessive eating and drinking corrupts the body and

---

[19] The qualifier *cardinal* derives, not as we might think, from the primary colour red, but rather from the Latin word *cardo*, meaning a 'hinge'. These were the 'pivotal' sins upon which all others, and perhaps all eternal life, literally hinged.

engenders disease by which one often cuts short his life. And those who feed their body too well only prepare food for worms, so that the glutton is but a cook for the worms. Those who drink at any hour and without check follow the swine's rule: so the swine is their abbot and they but follow his rule.

This Dantesque glimpse of Hell is anticipated even in the thirteenth century in the *Libro delle tre scritture* by the Milanese Bonvesin de la Risa whom we mentioned above. In Hell the eighth punishment is the one that awaits gluttons. On the other hand, though, we may nourish some hope in an eighth glory of Paradise – a very neat parallel calculated to encourage the virtuous – which consists of the heavenly joy that will be the reward of those who fast regularly and according to ecclesiastical doctrine.[20]

The guest at a medieval table was well aware of the rules – social, medical and moral – that should govern comportment at that table. He (or she) understood the need at that time to govern every appetite and impulse most carefully, especially if they were what we might apologetically call natural appetites and impulses. To know how to behave oneself at table meant learning how to control oneself, and this was, and is, undoubtedly one of the paramount signs of any civilization. Europeans at the end of the Middle Ages were learning the lesson well.

Conclusion

Historians claim that there is a certain type of *negative* evidence of the otherwise obscure existence of habits or practices in the past. If a rule or a law was formulated, say against bourgeois citizens wearing pointed shoes, then the very act of that formulation must surely indicate that there was a substantial reason for legislative action in this regard: some bourgeois citizens were actually in the habit of wearing pointed shoes when they should not. That moral strictures were endlessly levied against gluttony, in the grand corpus of the Cardinal Sins, in moral treatises, in art[21] and in sermons, seems to indicate that there were people of some significant status in society who did tend to over-indulge from time to time.

But from the distance from the Middle Ages that we are perhaps privileged to enjoy we may be so bold as to ask: Were these individuals in the days of Taillevent, Chiquart, Martino and their cohort of other great chefs really to be blamed, execrated, damned? Could medieval diners really help themselves? When sitting at a four-, five- or six-course meal, consisting of some

---

[20] *Il Libro delle tre scritture*, Pisa (E. Spoerri), 1902, pp.23-5 and 65-7.
[21] See, for instance, the lush treatment given to Gluttony by Hieronymous Bosch in his wheel of the Seven Cardinal Sins.

twenty or thirty ingeniously contrived dishes, each more delicious than the last, is it any wonder that the mouths of some happily favoured persons tried to take in as much as their stomachs could hold? After all, if blame must be fixed somewhere, why not lay it all on the cook?

The medieval cook took virtually all of the foodstuffs known to his world and he did marvellous things to them. With imagination and skill he carved and ground, he mixed and strained, he sauteed and baked, he basted and garnished, and he produced some exquisitely palatable things. On an ordinary day or for a banquet, on a meat-day or a lean-day, out of his kitchen came a succession of dishes that might tempt the archangels themselves with gluttony. In some respects in terms of sin and evil the cook is perhaps indeed the Great Tempter of the Middle Ages.

EIGHT

Foods for the Sick

Foodstuffs Appropriate for the Sick

Sick-dishes

If the medical profession accorded so central a role to diet in maintaining the good healthy balance of humours of any individual who was in reasonably stable good health, all the more so did it insist upon the consumption of proper foods when its members were responsible for the treatment of the sick.

For any healthy individual who wished to engage the learned counsel of a physician, that physician could prescribe a suitable daily and seasonal regimen that included in particular a specification of the foods he or she should eat. The physician's prescription ensued from a close analysis of the individual's natural temperament. When a person was afflicted with some sort of a disease, physicians considered that the person had undergone some sort of disruptive influence (an *influenza*, as the Italians would say) that disturbed the person's natural balance of humours, his or her natural temperament. Due to some cause – from among the many that had been rationally sorted out into neat categories labelled either 'natural' or 'unnatural' – that person had lost his or her good temper. To be in ill health was, really, in very large measure to be upset, in ill humour or, simply, out of humour.

To restore a sick person to his or her natural temperament, and once settled in it, to maintain him or her there, was the professional aim of the medieval physician. Though in the Middle Ages the notion of diet went far beyond the modern concept merely of food intake, and included virtually every factor (such as the orientation of one's house, or the frequency of sexual intercourse) that might modify an individual's natural balance of humours, food was certainly central. And food remained central in the physician's complex of potential prescriptions for restoring good health.

We cannot here examine the specifics having to do with food in medieval medical textbooks. In a typical medical treatise, various chapters analyse the nature of particular diseases, the symptoms, etiology and pathology of each, and prescribe its logical therapy. In every case any food that is prescribed as appropriately therapeutic for a patient is determined quite rationally as a corrective of whatever has influenced the person to the detriment of his or her normal state of good health.

Because of their concept of the nature of illness and of health, medical practitioners in the Middle Ages were concerned as much with the healthy as with the sick. It may be, of course, that they had a little more professional success with the healthy than they happened to have with the sick. Whatever the reason, though, whether in their positions in affluent noble or ecclesiastical households, or as renowned independent consultants, they did wield considerable authority in determining the foods that were prepared for and eaten by the lord, his retainers and his guests. It is certainly in that capacity, as general guardians of the household's health, that physicians determined more or less directly the make-up of a certain variety of quite commonplace culinary preparation, the sick-dish.

The Sick . . .

As did many compilers of recipe collections in the Middle Ages, Master Chiquart assembled a distinct section of sick-dishes. In a brief preamble to that chapter of his book he writes the following justification of a practice that was common enough at the time: 'Since, in such a grand and worthy banquet as you, my lord, are planning, attended by large numbers of noble and valiant lords, there are bound to be some sickly persons or individuals who are suffering from various diseases or sickness, for that reason, I, Chiquart – always making allowance for any specific orders and presciptions stipulated by the honourable physicians – wish, within the limits of my modest understanding, to set forth directions for preparing dishes that are good and that offer sustenance for the sick.' In writing this cautiously diplomatic passage Chiquart is most careful to state that he is not at all usurping the role of the medical establishment in the household. He is simply fulfilling a part of his job as court cook, discharging a legitimate function that required any cook to know how to make *general-purpose* sick-dishes for anyone in the household, lord, officer or retainer, who might have particular need of them.

Even the convalescent, those whose constitution was still weak from a recent malady, required special foods that were both readily digestible and nutritious. The need for such foods by the sick, the sickly and the convalescent helps explain the existence of the so-called 'sick-dish'.

What was the sick-dish? It was primarily a preparation of a foodstuff (or a canny mixture of nourishing foodstuffs) that was (were) carefully selected and cooked so that the quality of the final dish might be as close to the normal healthy human temperament as possible. That is, the sick-dish had to be nutritious, but above all in terms of temperament it had to be moderately warm and moderately moist.

Certain of the foodstuffs employed in sick-dishes had enjoyed a long-standing reputation in this function. Even in the times of the Greek physicians, for example, barley was regarded as an ideal food for anyone who was out-of-sorts. Because barley was understood to possess a temperament that was cool and dry in the first degree, a warm, moist broth of it was seen as lending itself ideally to the treatment of those who were recuperating from a fever. The chapter that Antimus devoted to 'Tisane' describes the virtues of a barley broth specifically:

> Tisane which is made of barley, should you know how to make it, is good for well people and for those with a fever. There is also made out of barley a good dish that we Greeks call *alfita*, the Latins *polenta* and the Goths in their foreign tongue, *fenea* – a great remedy. Diluted with warm wine, a teaspoonful of it well mixed should be sipped slowly on an empty stomach. It nourishes well a worn out stomach. It also does marvellously for those with dysentery if warmed up with pure wine, a spoonful be mixed with it in this way and it be taken on an empty stomach, whether in the night after cock crow, or whenever the sick man pleases, provided that when he has taken that, he take no other food until he has digested that. We usually give this to those with a fever, not thick, but diluted with clear warm water.[1]

In the *Tacuinum sanitatis* that was copied in the Po Valley at the end of the fourteenth century, the illuminator chose to illustrate the substance 'Barley' – on f. 44 – by showing a barley soup being administered in a bedroom to an invalid by two attendants. The accompanying text repeats the essence of what Antimus had already written, informing us that 'Cream of Barley Soup . . . is very suitable for sick people.' And in the same book the subsequent article on 'Barley Water' likewise states that it 'is cleansing. Nutritious and easy to digest, it is given, with favourable results, to feverish patients to slake their thirst; it alleviates coughs and cleanses the lungs.'[2] In his *Canon of Medicine* the learned Arab physician Avicenna (980–1037) had written that 'barley water cools and moistens the feverish. To treat hot fevers it is even used alone, and for chills with honey and fennel. As a drink furthermore barley that is cooked with figs mixed with boiled honey is given for flegmatic

---

[1] Ed. Shirley Howard Weber, *Anthimus, De Observatio Ciborum*, Leiden (E.J. Brill), 1924; Chapter 44, pp.40–41.

[2] Judith Spencer, *The Four Seasons of the House of Cerruti*, New York & Bicester, England, (Facts on File Publications), 1984, p.53. The original of this particular study of the nature of all foodstuffs, known generically as a *Tacuinum sanitatis*, was written by Ibn Botlan, or Ellbochasim, an Arab doctor who lived in the middle of the eleventh century. His science springs directly from the tradition of ancient Greek medical and physical theory.

[i.e., cold and moist] fevers.'³ Medieval physicians continued to prescribe barley broth or barley porridge for their sickly patients, professional cooks made them routinely, and sick-dish recipes using barley in one way or another abound in the standard cookbooks of the time.

Though barley enjoyed a place among the preferred health-restoring foods of the day, other cereal grains, and especially wheat, were recognized as possessing ideally temperate qualities and nourishing virtues. Not content merely with recommending a wheat porridge, Aldobrandino describes how to make a wheat-bran plaster that will reduce the swelling and relieve the pain of breasts engorged with too much milk – a plaster which is at the same time useful in the treatment of snake bites and the bites of any other venomous animals.⁴

The anonymous Neapolitan recipe collection outlines a sick-dish of barley porridge (Recipe 32) that uses almond milk and chicken broth. For the same reasons as for barley, chicken turns up very frequently in sick-dish recipes. Physicians and cooks resorted almost as a matter of course to chicken as an all-round problem-solver when it came to feeding the sick, sickly or convalescent. 'Among fowl that are acceptable in a healthful diet, some are more temperate or of moderate temperament. . . . These are young hens, young roosters and their pullets, and fat capons that still tend toward some warmth and moistness.'⁵

> You should know that chicks have a flesh that is more temperate, that digests more easily and that engenders better blood, that gives more strength and is more closely suited to human nature than any domestic fowl. For these reasons they are well eaten by those who have wasted, or whose stomach is weak, or who are just recuperating from illness . . . . You should know too that the rooster, just as it crows for the first time, is better than the hen because its flesh is less viscous, rather it is more moist, warmer and more temperate. Hen's flesh [before the hen begins laying] is less moist than that of the chick, digests less rapidly, but when it digests well it nourishes well. . . . .⁶

---

³ *De ordeo. . . . Febres. Aqua eius est infrigidativa humectativa febrium. In calidis quidem pura et in frigidis cum apio et feniculo. Et datur in potu etiam illud quod coctum est cum ficubus permixtum cum mellicrato ad febres flegmaticas.* Book II, Treatise II. The *Canon of Medicine* is recognized as the most famous medical text ever written and was available from the twelfth century on in Latin translation. In European medical schools during the late Middle Ages this very thick manuscript tome was accorded a position of absolute authority.

⁴ *Op. cit.,* p.116. It is really quite remarkable how many remedies in the Middle Ages are specific to animal bites, and particularly to the bites of venomous animals.

⁵ *Inter carnes volatilium laudabilium in regimine sanitatis, quedam sunt temperatiores et temperamento propinquiores. . . . Temperatiores quedem sunt galline juvenes, galinarum pulli et juvenes, pingues capones que tamen ad aliqualem caliditatem et humiditatem declinant.* Magninus Mediolanensis, *Regimen sanitatis,* ch. 17.

⁶ Aldobrandino, *Le régime du corps,* p.128.

Other poultry, such as capons, were often considered to be just as valuable ingredients in sick-dishes, although in the preparing and cooking of them their slightly different natures had to be taken into account.

When the medieval cook or housewife had a sick member of the household on hand to feed, he or she usually reached for a chicken and made up a mash, a broth, a cullis or a distillate of its meat and juices. Its temperate qualities in particular and the substantial nutritive values recognized in it made it a sort of sick-dish staple. Furthermore, in this overwhelming preference for chicken as the basis of a sick-dish, it was surely not at all irrelevant that, of all meats, domestic and wild, chicken was certainly the most universally available and the cheapest.

Partridge as well had a reputation for temperate qualities quite similar to those of lowly, domestic chicken. For the gentry partridge afforded a classy alternative to the much more plebian chicken.

A third sort of ingredient in late-medieval sick-dishes should be mentioned, and that is sugar. Owing in part to the increased availability of this semi-exotic substance and in part to the nature which learned Arabic scholars ascribed to it, sugar became during the fifteenth century one of the most valued and common ingredients in all sick-dishes. To some extent the quasi-universality of sugar in medical prescriptions, from syrups to electuaries to sick-dishes, reflected a growing predilection of the late-medieval aristocratic palate for sweetness generally in the daily fare. By the second half of the fifteenth century Platina is aware enough of this partiality, which he clearly shares, that he can pity his ancestors who knew sugar *only* as a medicine. 'I think the ancients,' he muses, 'used sugar merely for medicinal purposes, and for that reason no mention is made of it among their foods. They were surely missing a great pleasure, for nothing given to us to eat is so flavourless that sugar does not season it. Hence arose that proverb of frequent use: "No kind of food is made more tasteless by adding sugar." '[7]

Contemporary physicians were careful, however, to excuse the sweet tooth of the period, and to justify it with all the rationality anyone could wish: sugar has a nature which is warm in the first degree and moist in the first degree – identical, therefore, to the temperament of the human being. As Aldobrandino of Siena states enthusiastically: 'Sugar is highly suitable for use by the nature of man.'[8] His assessment was echoed by all of the contemporary health handbooks and, naturally enough, turns up, as we just saw, in that great culinary encyclopedist and vulgarizer, Platina, who admits no disadvantage to it at all.

The force of sugar is warm and moist, so that it is of good nourishment. It is good for the stomach and soothes whatever discomforts there are in it. In persons who are choleric [that is, of a warm and *dry*

[7] *De honesta voluptate*, II, 15.
[8] . . . *Si est moult covignable a le nature de l'homme user. Op. cit.*, p.159.

disposition], however, it is easily converted into the dominant humour.[9]

It is clear that in the course of the fifteenth century every householder who could afford to do so began to include this delicious *and* marvellously beneficial foodstuff in many of the dishes that up until then had been prepared quite successfully without it. It is significant that one of the noticeable features of the recipes of edible dishes added to the most recent copy of the *Viandier*, in the fifteenth century, is that almost without exception they all contain sugar.[10]

In earlier, fourteenth-century copies of the *Viandier* it is primarily the sick-dishes, five out of seven of them, that contain sugar. In the ordinary dishes of this large recipe collection, sugar is relatively rare, appearing in only six or seven dishes out of some 160. The recipe for a standard *Fish Cuminade* (Recipe 75) concludes with the sentence: 'And [if this is to be prepared] for sick persons, it must have sugar added to it.' Throughout the Middle Ages, sugar remained the therapeutic substance *par excellence*. Whatever the rationale behind the very durable conviction, even up to our own day we are certain that 'a spoonful of sugar helps the medicine go down'. In the Middle Ages, sugar was an integral and important part of the medicine.

. . . and Sickly

In referring to those who were living through a transient malady and who had to be fed some appropriate food, we have spoken of the sick and sickly. The term 'sickly' is not entirely correct. It is clear in reading medieval recipe collections that there were indeed two general classes of people for whom the sick-dishes were intended. The first were those whom Chiquart called (as we quoted above), '. . . individuals who are suffering from various diseases or sickness'. The second sort of 'sickly' person might better be defined as 'those with delicate or impaired (that is, less-than-wholly-capable) digestive systems'. The dual idea is expressed quite succinctly in the section heading to Part IV of the *Tractatus* or *Treatise for Preparing and Garnishing any Dish*: 'Herewith an account of preparations for refined gentlemen, of a nature to give sustenance and arouse the appetite.'[11] The same author had already prefaced a previous section of his recipe collection with a distinction

---

[9] *De honesta voluptate*, II, 15.

[10] What is interesting is the insistence of the fifteenth-century writer upon the relative sweetness of his dishes: the phrases *qu'il soit doulx de succre* – 'let [the dish] be sweet with sugar,' and *mettés du succre assés largement* – 'put in sugar quite generously' recur in ten of the twenty edible dishes.

[11] *Modo narrandum est de condimentis delicatis dominorum, ad naturam confortandam et appetitum provocandum. Tractatus de preparendi et condiendi omnia cibaria*, ed. Mulon, p.391.

between foods suitable for nobles and those suitable for labourers. 'It is to be noted that some foods are appropriate for nobles and the wealthy who live sedentary lives, such foods as partridge and pheasant, pullets, capons, hares, deer and rabbits, each variously prepared according to its specific nature; and some foods are appropriate for robust, working men, these foods being beef and goat, salt pork, stag, peas, beans, barley and wheat bread; and some foods are appropriate for the sick and weak, such as gruels of rice, oats or barley, and prepared with almond milk, chickpeas, pullet broths; pomegranate wine, tisanes of pike, and figs and imported grapes.'[12] The anonymous author of the Neapolitan Collection provides a recipe for an Almond Broth expressly for an *homo delicato*. This recipe precedes another which is called, without mincing words, 'Porridge for a Sick Person': *Farinata ad homo infermo*. The two sorts of preparation (here Recipes 31 and 32) always remain very closely related.

The class of persons to which the author of the *Tractatus* is referring in his rubric is, quite simply, the upper class, those of noble birth, the aristocracy. Throughout the later Middle Ages the aristocracy, probably with the connivance of the medical profession, fostered the notion that one of the features that distinguished them from the vulgar masses was a more fastidious digestive system. This idea was rooted in a common enough distinction in Greek antiquity, and that was that the hardy peasant, labouring in his fields, could manage to consume food whose toughness and rusticity was commensurate with his own. Rough food was simply appropriate to his station in life and the fact that he laboured for a living. It was quite natural for the peasant to eat coarse grains and cabbage. And furthermore it was entirely natural that the peasant's stomach be able to draw good sustenance from those uncouth foods – nutriments wholly adequate, that is, for his or her uncouth activities and needs.

On the other hand for the noble a more refined food was appropriate. It was not simply that he or she deserved a *better* or less vulgar food, but rather that his or her stomach was simply unable to handle anything less than the most refined of foods. It was as if an aristocat's digestive system was, perhaps just in the natural scheme of creation, aristocratic. To understand this concept we might consider the etymological relationship between the words dignity and dainty. The two words evolve from the same single source, the

---

[12] *Unde primo sciendum est quod sicut et potus et cibaria secundum tempora et regiones et complectiones hominum, merito, non in vanum nec inutiliter sunt ordinanda. Unde notandum est quod quedam cibaria conveniunt et apta sunt nobilibus et divitibus in quiete existentibus, et ut sunt perdices et fasiani, pulli, capones, lepores, caprioli et cuniculi, variis ac diversis modis conditi; quedam vero apta sunt hominibus robustis et in labore existentibus: ut carnes bovine et arietine, porcine salsate, cervine, pisa, fabe, panis ordaceus ac de siligine factus; quedam vero infirmis et debilibus velud gruelus de riso vel avena vel ordeo factus, et lacte amigdalarum conditus, ciceres et pullorum brodium; vinum pomi granati et tisana lutii atque parte ficus et racemi transmarini. Tractatus,* preamble to Part II.

Latin *dignitatem*, whose senses included roughly the ideas of 'honour' and 'pride'. When a sovereign conferred an exalted rank upon a person, both that social status and the fief that sustained it were themselves referred to as a 'dignity'. The aristocratic honour entailed aristocratic pride, both of caste and of person. In time the word 'dignity' became pronounced 'dainty' but, though the word became used more as an epithet rather than strictly as a noun, the senses of honour and of pride remained integral to it. The aristocrat and everything about him or her was said to be 'dainty'.

And so it was thought to be part of the natural order of things that a person of exceptional social status should be offered only dainty food because that was all that he or she could manage to digest. This food did not have to be particularly nourishing, because the aristocrat did not labour for his or her living. But neither could it be of a nature that placed heavy demands upon a dainty digestive system. It had, then, to have a nature that was close to the human temperament – and so we are back to the category of preparations known as sick-dishes. Sick-dishes were a variety of prepared food for the sick and for those of dainty digestion.

Among the dishes that the *Tractatus* describes for delicate stomachs are the more or less standard Whitedish (with sugar), a deep-fried doughnut called *Mistembec* dipped in a syrup of sugar or honey, a pancake called *Forcres* of ground cake or bread, *Arpa* consisting of teased chicken, ginger, rice flour, sugar and egg yolk, cooked as a pancake, spiced chicken broth, pear or apple sauce with egg yolk (alternative 'fruits' here included quince, gourd or cucumber), an onion dish, quartered pullets boiled with spices and egg yolks, a porridge of wheat, oats, rice or millet in milk and egg yolks, egg yolks boiled in watered wine or beer, and cheese slices and egg yolks boiled in water, wine, herbs and spices. There is a little variety here, and some effort to stimulate the noble appetite with recourse to a limited number of spices, quasi-medicines normally forbidden to those who were really sick unless prescribed by their doctor, but generally we recognize those foodstuffs we have already seen in sick-dishes elsewhere: chicken, cereals, almond milk, some fruits, yolks. Again, these are the foods whose humoural complexions were understood to be moderate and temperate. They are nourishing foods that present no dangers to the eater or hardships to his or her stomach.

It is clear that not all of the aristocracy of medieval Europe saw themselves as needing to be fed on these so-called sick-dishes. Otherwise the job of the medieval cook would have been much more rudimentary than it was, and our manuscript collections of recipes very much thinner. What is equally clear, though, is that the medieval cook had to be ready to feed any aristocrat, technically sick or not, in this way. Undoubtedly those who cook for the great and powerful in our own modern society have to have a similar category in their repertory, which they might even call 'sick-dishes', consisting of dishes useful to offer those with ulcers or with gout, or who are prone to migraine headaches, to acid indigestion or in a vague general way to easily 'upset stomachs'. Sensitive digestions exist in every age and society, and stragely they are rarely found among those of the lowest classes. The poor cannot afford to be fussy, about food or anything else.

Prepared Dishes Appropriate for the Sick

A listing of typical sick-dishes may show just how seriously medieval cookery was concerned with providing a good and varied fare for the sick, sickly and convalescent. We might think that cooks would be inclined to give rather short shrift to this aspect of their duties. But in fact, and what is perhaps quite remarkable, is that few of these preparations are really elementary at all. Most were imaginative and demanded some considerable effort on the part of the kitchen staff to make. In particular it is the French, Italian and Latin[13] manuscript sources that give us a good view of the genre of the sick-dish as it existed at the end of the Middle Ages.

In the On Cookery Chiquart included a section of no fewer than seventeen sick-dish recipes, better than 20% of his total. Apart from a most unusual initial dish, to which we shall come back, most of the others may be sorted into four general categories: those that are based on certain cereal grains or legumes, those that are based on almonds, those that are based on fruits, and those that are based on chicken. Among the grain dishes, we have a Wheat Precipitate (Recipe 66), a Semolina Dish (77), an Oatmeal Porridge (75), a Barley Porridge (78) and a Dish of Chick Peas (76); almonds are the essence of the sick-dishes called simply Almond Butter (67) and Almond Puree (69a); fruits are used in Quince Turnovers (70), Anhydride Pears[14] (72) and Applesauce (73); and finally we have a Cullis of Chicken, Poultry or Partridge (71), a Whitedish of Capon (74) and a Whitedish of Partridge (74a). Several sick-dish recipes, here and in other collections, make use of a particular procedure which is intended to extract the essence of the principal ingredient of the dish in all of its purest potency and without adulterating it with any incidental ingredients. Usually the procedure calls for a heating of the ingredient, whether some fowl or fruit, in a sealed container with little or no moisture, so that the fowl or fruit exudes its juice and nothing but this collects in the bottom of the container. The Viandier prescribes the procedure for its Pink Water of a Capon or Hen (Recipe 91), noting at the end of the recipe that 'the water that comes from the capon . . . provides good sustenance [for the invalid] and the whole body is nourished by it'.

Among Chiquart's sick-dishes that lie beyond the bounds of the above categories are a Green Puree of Spinach and Parsley (69), Stuffed Crayfish

---

[13] Recipe collections in Latin seem often to be related to an Italian tradition.

[14] This is neither an elegant nor accurate translation of the Poyres cuytes sans brase ne eaue ('Pears Cooked Without Coals or Water'), but may suggest the nature of the dish.

(68), Beef Marrow Turnovers (70a) and the first recipe of the series, already mentioned. We can come to this first dish now. The *Restaurant* or *Restaurand* (65) is named for its capacity to restore, in a verbal, gerundive sense. The dish-name might be translated 'Restaurative' – a name which could fundamentally have been appropriate for all of the sick-dishes. Yet Chiquart's *Restaurant* is surely unique in that it employs what we might call supernatural forces to effect the convalescence of the sick person. The primary agent in this dish is boiled capon flesh (our old standby, *with* its bones), but which is cooked in a sealed container with a little rose-water liqueur, gold, in the form of coins, pearls, diamonds, rubies, saphires, turquoises, emeralds, coral, amber, jasper, jacinth, chalcedony, onyx, crystal, chalcedony, sardonyx, chrysolite, beryl, topaz, chrysoprase and amethyst – and, as Chiquart puts it, all other potent precious gemstones. It is true that Chiquart's master, Duke Amadeus of Savoy, was particularly given over to beliefs in magic and the occult; but it is also true that a belief in the potency of precious stones enjoyed a very great currency in therapeutics at this time.[15] The medicinal properties of gold were highly esteemed by the physicians of the time. The *Liber de coquina* (Part II, Chapter 31) even goes so far as to suggest that the cook will never go wrong if he puts gold into any dish that is intended for any wealthy client who is suffering from *any* disease whatsoever.[16] We may smile at the qualification 'wealthy', but in such matters the physician had clearly to distinguish between those patients who could afford all of the best ingredients in their medicines and their foods, and those who could not. It is for the not-quite-so-rich that the professional cook's repertoire of sick-dishes had to encompass the Flemish Cawdle found in the *Menagier de Paris*.

Most sick-dishes seem to be general and unspecific in their medical purposes. In a few recipe collections, though, the authors do comment explicitly that such-and-such a sick-dish is indicated for such-and-such a

---

[15] See the study by Jean Gero, 'Les pierres précieuses en thérapeutique,' a medical thesis at the University of Paris in 1933 (No. 449). To Duke Amadeus a famous physician, Guillaume Fabri, dedicated his work on the philosopher's stone and its specifically medicinal properties. And in the 1340s, Giacomo Albini, also at the court of Savoy, dedicated his medical treatise *De sanitatis custodia* to the heir of Amadeus; this work argues for an electuary called *Diamargariton* whose composition includes gold, jacinth, emeralds, amber, coral, and so forth.

[16] The Italian counterpart of this Latin compilation puts the same instruction this way: 'Note that in any seasoning, sauce or broth, if you can include anything precious such as gold or gemstones, select spices or cardamom, odiferous or common herbs or onions, then you should put in as much as you want for [dishes for either] the well or the sick': *Nota, . . . in ciascuna salsa, savore o brodo, si possono ponere cose preziose, cioè oro, petre preziose, spezie elette, ovvero cardamone, erbe odorifere o comuni, cipolle, porri o tuo volere, per li sani e per li 'nfermi. Libro della cocina*, Recipe 132. The onions are somewhat suspect here: other writers advise the cook diligently to avoid them if cooking for the sick.

malady. If the complaint is constipation, then according to both the Tuscan author of the *Libro della cocina* and the anonymous compiler of the Italian work known now as the *Meridionale*, 'A' an appropriate laxative is furnished by a preparation of herbs, perhaps in a bouillon of chicken broth (Recipes 8 and 164 in the first, 84 in the second). As a purgative, says the Neapolitan writer, one may rely upon a Semolina Porridge (Recipe 160). Some writers offer advice on which foodstuffs to avoid when making sick-dishes. For the *Menagier* these include cow's milk and onions (Recipes 99 and 305); compared with its alternative, almond milk, cow's milk may be 'more appetizing, even though it is scarcely as healthy for the sick'.

The responsibilities of the medieval cook clearly extended into the sickroom. It is a sign of his professionalism that the dishes he prepared for the sick and the 'sickly' incorporated at least some of the concern for gastronomic variety and interest as he demonstrated in his regular dishes. The sick-dish formed an integral part of his professional repertoire.

NINE

International Foods and Regional Favourites

Similar or International Foods and Dishes

Probably more than any other element that goes to defines a human culture, food has potentially the ability to cross over the barriers that are erected, or that develop naturally, to divide one society from another. This is so particularly when that food is recognized as more or less exclusive to an exclusive class, and that class in turn conceives of itself as having as many international interests as strictly national ones.

Furthermore, by their nature food recipes tend to evolve very durable traditions. Innovations in food habits and in cookery do occur, of course, but since time immemorial in the bulk of their work cooks depend universally upon recipes that they have inherited. For professional cooks their stock-in-trade, their professional repertoire, is generally that which the social class for whom they work normally consumes. We should therefore not be surprised to observe that the cookery of late-medieval European states possessed a fund of dishes which could be called international, or 'common property'.

Among the contents of late-medieval cookery manuscripts across Europe there is a large degree of similarity. This is not to say that they all share in the same assortment of broths, pies and sauces; over these two hundred years there were a number of currents of change and novelty whose impact on the kitchen and dining board was relatively serious. But what we do see is such a high proportion of agreement between various recipe collections that patently the compilers, and their cooks and patrons, are merely reflecting a broadly accepted common European usage in the matter of prepared dishes.

A fascinating study which modern scholars have undertaken is to disentangle the highly complex interrelationships among early collections. Four early recipe books from northern Italy have a number of characteristics in common. Glancing through them someone might be tempted to begin to think in terms of some common ancestor for them, a sort of proto-cookbook for Italy. Of course, such a search for an ultimate source would be nipped by common sense while it was just a vague thought. It would be more reasonable to remember that cookery was learned by apprenticeship, and that the craft was above all orally transmitted. These books may have here and there similar contents simply because the practical repertoire that each documents had certain elements in common. Even when echoes of one tradition may be heard in another,[1] each book shows some unique features. Versions of a particular assortment of recipes may exist in different books, and indeed in different languages.[2]

A glance through the English collections of the time is enough to identify the large debt this cookery owed to the French, at least insofar as dish-*names* are concerned. While the English and French traditions are far from being identical, there are enough parallels that we may assume a vital influence of the one upon the other at least at the practical level of the actual cookery of each tradition. Rather than being national and creative, aristocratic cookery in the Middle Ages tended to be international in its scope and evolutionary in its development.

The great *Viandier* illustrates this last point. The name of the chief cook of Charles V (1364–80), Taillevent[3] (c.1315–95), is attached to later copies of this important book of recipes, that is, to those that were contemporary with or postdated the reign of the king. However, an early and somewhat simpler (but anonymous) version of the very same book, from the beginning of the fourteenth century, clearly antedates the professional life of the renowned master chef. Taillevent could not have been at the origin of the book for which he has taken the credit ever since; he both adopted this 'original' book and adapted it. The earlier version, copied onto a long narrow roll of parchment which has become soiled with use, is doubly intriguing because its beginning, where we would expect to be able to read its title and any attribution of authorship, has been cut away.

And in much the same way we can trace the way in which a section on wines in a fifteenth-century copy of the *Viandier* has made its way there, in all likelihood from the *Tractatus*. By borrowings and adaptations, successive recipe collections became enriched. And in general we may suggest that the rate at which this enrichment took place was more or less the rate at which,

---

[1] Both of the fourteenth-century Latin collections, the *Liber de coquina* and the *Tractatus*, clearly reflect Italian cookery of the period, but both refer to certain aspects of French usage and may actually have been produced in France or on the Angevin-French territory of Naples.

[2] This is the case, for instance, with the earliest French collection, the *Enseingnemenz qui enseingnent a apareillier toutes manieres de viandes*, and its Latin homologue, the *Doctrine preparationis ciborum*. See Carole Lambert, *Trois réceptaires culinaires médiévaux*, unpublished doctoral thesis, University of Montreal, 1989.

[3] A nickname, actually, for Guillaume Tirel, an individual the basic data of whose biography were published more than a century ago: see Jérôme Pichon and Georges Vicaire, *Le Viandier de Guillaume Tirel dit Taillevent*, Paris (Leclerc & Cormuau), 1892. Summaries of the biography are offered in Liliane Plouvier, 'Taillevent, la première star de la gastronomie', *L'Histoire*, 61 (Nov. 1983), pp.93–94; and in the edition by Scully, p.30.

from generation to generation, each new apprentice cook first absorbed the traditional rudiments of his craft from his master, and then grafted onto them the infrequent innovations that he or his master happened to discover.

Dish-names

The name given to a particular prepared dish is of paramount importance. When the lord, or the household Steward in his place, wished to ensure that a favorite dish was included somewhere in one of the servings of a meal, he had to know by what precise name to identify that dish. It might not be enough for either of them to say: 'We must have some more of that chunky goo that was so good among the dishes of the third service last week.' *Chunky* and *goo* may be descriptive, but, for a cook who is frequently working with dishes that are both chunky and gooey, a more distinctive identification would probably be more helpful. The cook, more than any other person, had always to label his preparations with unequivocal names. When distributing tasks to his many subordinates, he had to be able to refer precisely to a unique finished product; when receiving orders from his superiors, or when discussing possible menus with them, he had to know and say precisely what was meant by each dish-name.

Strangely enough, there were not many ways in which a dish was named normally in the late Middle Ages. Almost every dish-name referred to some particular quality in the dish; it was extremely rare to find a name that evoked, say, a user, or some historic circumstance. This latter method of naming dishes is fairly common today, so that in the Twentieth Century an amateur cook may have to turn to a thick recipe book in order to find out just what the standard composition is of a Sauce à la King, Ambrosia, Bar-le-Duc, Maître d'Hôtel Butter, Weinschaum or Zabaglione. For the medieval cook the usual dish-names either embodied the dish's principal ingredient, evoked its colour, described the method by which it was cooked, identified the genre or type of the dish, or combined several of these stardard dish-naming techniques.

Of these standard types of dish-name, one is perhaps more remarkable than the others, and that is the one that depends upon appearance in order to identify it, specifically upon the colour of the preparation. We have already mentioned how important appearance was to the medieval gastronome. For the medieval cook the colour of the dish he prepared was a primary concern. In many cases this colour had little or nothing to do with any hue the principal ingredient or ingredients may have given the dish in the course of its cooking. Rather, more often than not the colour resulted from a deliberate addition of a specific colourant to the dish's sauce or broth as it was being prepared, for the express purpose of creating that colour in the finished dish. A wide assortment of products were utilized for a wide range of colours: roots, plants, fungi, woods and minerals, alongside various more commonly consumed foodstuffs such as herbs, spices, toast and egg yolks. Each of these sources of colour, alone or in canny combination, was ground and steeped, eventually yielding as rich a range of tints and hues as any painter could wish. Both the medieval cook and his patron delighted in distinct and cheerful colours in the dishes presented to the table.

The dish-names of the time in fact reflected this interest in the dish's colour. To begin with, white and black: *Cibus albus* (*Coquina*, Part II, Recipe 17) and *Schwarz Pfeffer* (*Büchlein*, Recipe 6). To those old stand-bys could be added virtually every colour of the rainbow: for instance a very popular yellow dish is identified, in most countries, solely by a name derived from the plant 'broom': in Latin, *Ginestinum* (Platina, Part VIII, Recipe 8), in Catalan, *Genestada* (Coch, Recipe 224), in French, *Genesté* (*Menagier*, Recipe 114), in Italian, *Genestrata* (*Neapolitan*, Recipe 39). The English *Flaumpeyns* (*Forme of Cury*, Recipes 4 and 116) are simply 'painted flans', a yellow egg yolk colouring each segment of the pie. The German name *Ruzzige K chin*, 'Sooty Cakes', describes their appearance after they have cooked in hot coals (*Buch von guter Spise*, Recipe 52). For his tile-coloured *Brouet tyolli* Chiquart directs the use of an amount of sandalwood powder 'in the amount required for the proper colour', he says.[4]

Of the broad spectrum of hues with which medieval cooks imbued their dishes, yellow undoubtedly enjoyed the place of preference as we saw in an earlier chapter. In the recipe collections egg yolks and saffron are repeatedly called upon to give a large number and variety of dishes a distinct yellow colour. Some, such as the various *Genestrata*'s mentioned above, and a family of dishes known by the labels *Jane, Janetum, Jaunette, Giannetto, Ianicto*, incorporated the colour yellow into their name. The prestige that yellow possessed in the Middle Ages as a symbol of nobility was clearly well recognized in aristocratic kitchens and, in turn, by those who named the products of their kitchens' output.

The name given to any prepared dish should always meet one important criterion, and that is that it should be unambiguous. For the medieval diner, steward or chef, a descriptive name, evoking the colour, the texture or the overall appearance of the dish, was very much preferred. As a result, early collections are full of recipes called 'Yellow Pottage', 'Pink Dish', 'Black Poree', 'Russet Rice', 'Orange Broth', 'Green Sauce'; or 'Cullis' (that is, strained), '*Grané*' or 'Gravy' (that is, with unground chunks of meat in a sauce), 'Cretonnee' (that is, containing crisply grilled pieces); or certain *entremets* or entertaining dishes such as 'Pilgrim Capons', 'Hodge-Podge', 'Helmeted Cocks'.

---

[4] *. . . Selon la quantité du bouillon pour luy donner couleur, et de celle* [the powder] *y mectés tant qu'il hait la couleur qu'il doibt avoir. On Cookery*, Recipe 15.

Durable Dish-names

Our dinner today may resemble the medieval dinner in certain very general aspects: we may, for instance, begin with an aperitif drink and a dish of fresh fruit, and we may finish with cheese and nuts and perhaps a tasty mint candy. But as was observed earlier, we know more or less what to expect in the course of our modern meal, we can anticipate what sort of choices we shall be having to make in the course of the meal. The dishes that constitute our modern dinner may themselves hold some surprises – pleasant surprises, one always hopes. But then the average diner will usually recognize that what, at first glance, looks (or at first savour, tastes) a little strange is really just a variant of a dish with which he or she is already familiar. Even a dish identified by an unusual or exotic name usually turns out to bear a close relationship to some preparation that is more or less known to us, if not entirely commonplace in our diet. In modern cookery much more often than not, both artistry and delight spring merely from new variations upon some already known theme.

The same we find to be true when we get down to examining the fundamentals of medieval dishes. Leafing through any early recipe collection we may be intimidated by the strangeness of the dish-names we read, and because of these names we may anticipate a certain alien quality in the dishes themselves. Of course, it doesn't help that we may not be entirely fluent in early southern German dialects of the fifteenth century, or in medieval Catalan or Portuguese. Even in the English of the fourteenth century, dishes such as the one called *Garbage of Capons* may tend to be a little off-putting. Once we get beyond the name, though, once we identify the ingredients and begin to combine them, and to prepare the various foodstuffs as the recipe directs, then we learn that some dish-names have little value other than as identification.[5]

There are only so many foodstuffs in current usage in any society; there are only so many combinations of these foodstuffs that are possible, or at least that are sensed to be gastronomically tolerable, in any given society at any one time. As we have seen, in our traditional 'western' (i.e., Western European and North American) society the vast bulk of foodstuffs has been known and used as such for a long time. Most have been cooked in similar ways for many generations, and combined into dishes, whatever their names, with similar textures and flavours during four or five centuries.

Galentine, Dodine, Gingerbread, Lasagne, Ravioli, Miroston. These medieval dishes are still with us, still bear some form of their original names

---

[5] The Bibliography at the end of this book has a section listing a few cookbooks of 'modernized' medieval recipes. Experienced cooks should be encouraged to by-pass these adapted recipes and rather to let their imagination and inspiration be guided by the original versions of the recipes or translations of them.

and, as far as their essential natures is concerned, they have changed relatively little over the years. The medieval gourmet would recognize them on a modern restaurant menu and would feel right at home if they were served to him or her today.

Similar Dish, Variable Names

Of course what is apt to change over time is the name by which today we know a particular dish. Pies, for instance, may may be known to their contemporaries by a variety of names, depending in large measure upon their contents. But a pie is a pie, or at least it has been one since the Middle Ages: pastry dough, whether in a baking pan or not, holds a mixture of ingredients while both dough and filling are cooked. If the pasty is fairly small, so that no pan is necessary to support the dough, then generically we have what may properly be called a turnover, with a similar sort of filling contained in the pastry while both are cooked. Known by such names as *tarts* or *tortes*, *tartlettes* or *tourteletes*, these dishes are merely pies in which either the main ingredient or a condiment predominates sufficiently to give the pie a character, a personality, and ultimately a name. Distinct from other pies because of some characteristic of their filling or the colour of their pastry, each of these pies was endowed with a distinct name.

In a similar way, various names evolve for porridges (*puls, paniccia, paniça*), custards (*crustad, custane, dariol, erbolat, letelorye*) and pancakes (*forcres, basteln, cryspis, froyse, rorkoken, struven*). Doughnuts (essentially a deep-fried batter) were various called *Bingnetz, Otras, Mistembec, Samartard, Krapfen* and *Krepfelin* depending upon the locality where one happened to be and minor variations in the preparation itself. And the same rich variety of names is found across Europe and from age to age designating what are really quite similar dishes.

This parade of names should reassure us that we ought not to be overly intimidated by the strange names written at the head of recipes in these old cookery books. Often these quasi-barbaric names merely represent some preparation that is really quite familiar to us today. Our own favorite names for quite common dishes such as Ambrosia, Pandowdy, Chutney, Baked Alaska, Finnan Haddie, Brown Betty, Divinity Fudge, Welsh Rabbit, Cobbler, Charlotte Russe, Deviled Eggs, and so forth, might look weird to our forebears of five and six centuries ago. The names, then, may bewilder but the actual dishes they represent would likely surprise only by delighting the modern palate.

A good number of dishes, by whatever name they are identified today, remain dishes that our forebears in Europe were commonly eating over 500 years ago. However, when you leaf through a recipe collection from the fourteenth or fifteenth century what is clear is that, while the foodstuffs named may be familiar, most of the final dishes that these recipes aim to prepare may not at first glance be recognizable. While we may say, 'Yes, garlic (or hake), we handle that quite commonly,' recipes that direct us on how to make *Aquapatys* (or *Gyngaudre*, respectively in the *Forme of Cury*, Recipe 77 and *An Ordinance of Pottage*, Recipe 13) might discourage our most willing intentions. It may even be a relief to learn that *Balloc Broth* (of the *Forme of Cury*, Recipe 112) is a delicious fish stew!

'International Cuisine' in the Middle Ages

Despite the quite natural variations in food habits and cookery that we find across Europe toward the end of the Middle Ages, there existed, as we just saw, a surprising number of dishes that were being similarly prepared in kitchens far distant from one another. While some of these dishes may not turn up identical in every national cuisine, the evidence of the recipe books shows that they enjoyed a certain degree of international celebrity. Such preparations seem to have transcended merely regional use and custom. For a variety of reasons they had been incorporated solidly into the repertoires of chefs the bulk of whose regular work reflected more or less traditional local taste.

Why could some dishes be accounted more 'cosmopolitan' than others? For many of the same reasons that might explain why an international traveller today can reasonably expect a *roux* sauce, a *shish kebab* or a *knish* to be at least recognizable as such whether they are prepared in Paris, in Ankara or in Tel Aviv. In the Middle Ages, as today, there was a lot of snobbery attached to food. Because food is one of the most transparent tests of class, the aristocracy had ulterior reasons in determining the selection of their foods. On the one hand it was always to their advantage if members of the aristocracy could demonstrate and justify their membership in their class. The medieval aristocracy tended to be international by blood and by outlook: in very few corners of Europe was the local aristocracy entirely in-bred; in very few corners of Europe did the local aristocracy have the military strength to be totally indifferent to the ambitions of their neighbours. The feudal code recognized interdependence and mutual support as fundamental principles, albeit ones that tended to suffer somewhat at the hands of intractable, rapacious outlaws – the terrorists of the Middle Ages. Belonging to the large, international aristocratic family ensured a certain security.

Of course it would be too much to say that, imitation being the sincerest form of flattery, Count X in country Y imitated the cuisine of Duke A in country B in order to flatter him and win his favour. But what undoubtedly happened was that there was a great deal of emulation of court by court across Europe as the nobility strove to show in the first instance their exceptional worth, and in the second instance their homogeneity. At any rate food became of prime importance in the affirmation of status. And probably as a consequence of that, some dishes became truly international.

A second explanation of international quality of some of the cooks' preparations can be traced to the manner of education of the cooks themselves.[6] Cooks were trained and learned their craft by apprenticeship. They learned the standard procedures under a Master Cook, and absorbed the repertoire of their master by practising it. As neophytes they learned to reproduce the dishes that were most favoured in the household their master's master, the traditional ones; then, as the years of their apprenticeship were fulfilled, they moved on to seek a position elsewhere, perhaps abroad, on their own initially as a journeyman assistant and ultimately as a master in their own kitchen. The employment that the trained chef found could potentially be anywhere in Europe. Though they would have to learn to handle a body of preparations traditional in the household of their new patron, they also brought with them their own learned repertoire and it was natural that elements of this might over time come to be accepted in the new locale.

A third explanation of common usage in prepared dishes is related to the way in which the Church universal marked special days or times in the ecclesiastical calendar.[7] Though some ecclesiastical regions may have resisted the enforcement of certain doctrines, popular practices that were related to significant moments in the calendar tended to to be observed more or less universally.

Feastdays in the late autumn and at the end of the year tended traditionally to see the serving of the meats of domestic animals and fowl that were difficult or costly to maintain over the winter months. Pork and goose became associated with Advent and Christmas meals. Wild pigs could be captured right across Europe and the Christmastide boar's head marked both the end of the hunting season and the time of courageous renewal in the Christian year. Easter fell just after the lambing season, so that it became customary throughout Christian Europe – as the sacrificial practice was long traditional in Jewish Passover use – to celebrate the Easter feast with lamb roast. A practical symbolic substitute might also be marzipan or a cake in the shape of a lamb.

St Nicolas, the patron saint of children, was always perceived as a figure of generosity: for example, so that all girls might have an appropriate dowry to bring to a marriage, he used to distribute purses of gold coins to the homes of the poor. On (and about) December 6 households would serve up all the fresh fruits of the season, both local and exotic, along with the candies, nuts, sweetmeats, spiced cakes and other

---

[6] On the training, situation and status of the medieval cook see the following chapter.
[7] Regarding what follows here see in particular William I. Kaufman, *The Catholic Cook Book. Traditional Feast and Fast Day Recipes*, New York (Citadel Press), 1965.

delicacies that St Nicolas was supposed to have brought. Marzipan and various gingerbreads hence became widely connected with the Christmas season.

The prevalence of fruits at this time and the predilection they enjoyed lead to the incorporation of the sweeter varieties, especially figs, dates and raisins, into a mixture with sugar, spices and bland meats. This 'mincemeat' was merely a appetizing variety of dish whose basis was the ubiquitous ground-meat paste, but it, too, came to mark the Christmas season. Plum pudding was likewise a dish that became firmly established in the food habits of this time of the year. Some cakes had a rich variety of fresh chopped fruits worked into their batter.

A major fast of the year, that preceding Christmas Day, was usually marked by a preparation of the more valued sea-foods: whitefish, sturgeon, eel and oysters. Even today finely sliced salmon and oysters remain favorite foods of this season. The feastday of St John the Evangelist (December 27) was associated with wine because a legend held that by blessing a glass of wine that saint rendered the poison in it harmless.

Since the Feast of the Epiphany (January 6) commemorated the visit of the Wise Men or Magi (kings) to the Christ child, it became universally customary to prepare a cake in the shape of a royal crown for this celebration. Originally in antique times a mere wreath to symbolize power and victory, the crown had come as well to symbolize purity and consecration. As a food, the many versions of the 'King's Cake' testify to the broad popularity of this cake at this time in the ecclesiastical calendar. Certain traditions, involving the hiding of small articles in this cake, grew with its use: if a person eating it found a pea or bean in his piece, he was declared the 'king' or ruler, *pro tem*, over the Epiphany festivities; finding a ring presaged marriage in the coming year for the finder; finding a coin, wealth.

As the forty lean days of Lent approached, in order to clear all perishable foodstuffs from the larder it became usual to consume them in an orgiastic repast or two. It was the time to bid farewell, fondly but blithely, to the pleasures of meat-days until after Easter: in Latin the salute is expressed as *Carne, vale*. Today we might think of it as an excuse for a modest binge. Across Europe Carnival was most frequently marked by the eating of sweetened batter foods, doughnuts, pancakes, crêpes, and simnel cakes.[8] These were invariably served sprinkled with ground sugar (perhaps with sugar and spices mixed together), with chopped nuts or candied fruits. Hot Cross Buns continue to show the sign, in sugar, with which they were originally blessed by a priest. Candied fruits also might be mixed into these breads.

[8] A simnel cake was merely any cake made of very fine flour. The name derives from *simila* or *semolina*.

Immediately following Easter the most commonly eaten foods on normal meat-days return with a vengeance. In particular the humble chicken egg is glorified by being decorated very ornately and by being prepared for eating in a wide variety of ways.

On All Souls' Day, following Hallows' Eve (Hallowe'en), it was customary to share one's meal with one's ancestors by taking some of it to the cemetery. Dishes prepared from peas, beans and lentils – the original 'soul food' as a wag once remarked – were commonly served at that time.

Foodstuffs

Any attempt to characterize late-medieval European cookery by its preference for particular ingredients is bound to be difficult. An accurate assessment of all of those foodstuffs that entered kitchens during two hundred years right across Europe would filter out all but a very short list. If there were foodstuffs that might be considered both 'universal' and 'perennial' in aristocratic cookery these would be spices, almonds, eggs and the domestic meats chicken and pork. There is nothing surprising here, other than the very banality of these food elements perhaps. Yet these ingredients may well be considered to be characteristic of late-medieval food habits.

To an extent that varied primarily with the degree that the wealthier classes in society declared their preeminence, spices were always used in cookery throughout late-medieval Europe. Pepper, cinnamon and ginger flavour dishes universally, either individually or in differing mixtures, and to these cooks everywhere often added salt and occasionally sugar. Over time during these last two centuries of the Middle Ages, beginning in France and then in Italy, pepper tends to lose favour, perhaps being considered an element that defined an old, outmoded taste. At the same time as pepper lost favour in aristocratic cookery this cookery gradually gained the flavour of grains of paradise. Saffron is used ubiquitously.

Despite the fact that the cultivation of almonds was native to the more southern climates of Europe, cooks in every corner of Europe seem to have depended upon a good supply of this nut in their kitchens. Still in their shell, almonds travelled well, they lasted well. Their oil content, their distinct and delicate flavour and their property of making a very practical milk when they were ground made almonds a valuable universal ingredient.

The eternal barnyard cycle of chickens and eggs provided medieval cuisine with its prime ingredients. Their popularity was undoubtedly related in the first instance to their universal availability and secondly to the fact that they lend themselves to so many different ways of preparation. Pork, cooked and eaten normally everywhere, owed its popularity particularly to the relative inexpensiveness of pig-raising: as in the *Très riches heures* illumination for

November, the swineherd could fatten his pigs on the nuts of the local forest.

Several other foodstuffs, such as cheese, the legumes peas and beans, onions and mustard, are almost common enough in the cookery of the time to be qualified as universal. Fish, too, generically, might be so categorized were it not for the natural way in which the favoured species of fish differed in various geographical locations across Europe. If there is a particular fish that was well known to European cooks during this period, it might be the eel or the salmon, both the fresh-water salmon and the sea fish.

Though not exclusively ingredients, two other very usual foodstuffs should be mentioned here: bread and wine. Each is of course normally present on the dining board to be eaten or drunk as is; there are in fact no more common foods *per se* in the Middle Ages. However both bread (and breadcrumbs and toast) and wine (along with all of the other grape products, fermented and unfermented) were available in large quantities in the kitchen, and the cook drew upon both of them constantly in the elaboration of his dishes.

Dishes

There is a tendency to assume that, because travel was relatively difficult and perilous in the Middle Ages, people did not travel. However, some people did indeed travel, both far and often. Individuals, groups, and armies made their respective journeys back and forth between the territories of medieval Europe, slowly and with considerable toil, it is true, but occasionally covering remarkable distances.[9] Their purposes varied as much as the reasons why modern people travel: on pilgrimage, for business, on diplomatic mission, as tourists, for family reunions, for employment. Cooks often accompanied their masters, we may even say that the cooks of potentates regularly travelled with their masters. For whatever reasons, we find a Catalan cook at an English court; a Savoyard cook following a peripatetic Duke who was to become Pope; a German cook in the service of an actual Pope; recipes written in Italian with a marked Catalan accent. What the cooks saw and tasted in foreign parts, and what of their own culinary traditions they brought and implanted in those foreign courts, probably helped to create a certain homogeneous element among the dishes that were prepared throughout Europe at this time.

What follows is a brief survey of the most common common preparations.

[9] On the subject of travel in the Middle Ages, see for instance the works of Arthur Percival Newton, *Travel and Travellers of the Middle Ages*, London (Routledge & Kegan Paul), 1926; J.J. Jusserand, *English Wayfaring Life in the Middle Ages*, tr. Lucy Toulmin Smith, London (Methuen) and New York (Barnes & Noble), 1961; and Linda Kay Davidson and Maryjane Dunn-Wood, *Pilgrimage in the Middle Ages*, New York (Garland), 1992.

White dish

The history of the dish known today in English as 'blancmange' is very long. Anyone might guess that the name is originally French, and that it comes from the time when it consisted of two distinct words, *blanc* – meaning 'white', and *mengier*, a noun – referring to a 'dish' or 'food'.

This so-called 'white dish' was at its origin rather different from the opaque jelly made from gelatin or cornflour and milk, and identified today as 'blancmange'. In what seems to be the earliest known version for Whitedish, a recipe for a *blanc mengier* in the *Enseignements* of 1290 or 1300, the ingredients are elementary and include white chicken meat, rice, sugar and, optionally, almond milk. Throughout the fourteenth and fifthteenth centuries recipes for other Whitedishes abound, being copied in one form or another in virtually every cookery book across all of western Europe.[10]

In French there are at least a dozen versions, in English, roughly the same number called variously *Blank maunger*, *Blomanger* and *Blamang* (Austin, Collection I, Recipe 82, p. 21), in Catalan, *Manjar blanch*, in Portuguese, *Manjar braquo*, in Italian, *Blanmangieri*, *Bramangere* and *Bianco mangiare*, in Flemish, *Blanc mengier*, in Dutch, *Een blanc mengier van capoenen*, in German, *Blamensir*, and in Latin, *Albus cibus* or *Esus albabus*. All of these variants of *blanc mengier* offer a surprisingly consistent list of ingredients: chicken, rice, and almonds ground into almond milk – functioning here in part as a thickener. If there was a truly international dish in the late Middle Ages, it was undoubtedly this Whitedish.

However, a curious problem arises with the name of the Whitedish. It is clear that the literal meaning of the name 'white dish' was adopted right across Europe with very little modification except in language, and that the name was retained, again with little modification, over a good number of generations. The problem lies partly with the actual name of the dish and partly, in fact ultimately, with the meaning or function of the dish itself. An investigation of this dish should begin with the French version of its name, *blanc mengier*, a name which on the face of it appears so simple and self-explanatory: this must be quite literally a *White Dish*. The qualification here, *blanc*, is entirely understandable in the name of a culinary preparation. A reference to the colour of a prepared dish was in fact quite common in the names given to medieval dishes. Among the dishes that were identifiable by their particular colour were also those that had to be white. The *White Leek Sauce*, for example, explicitly specifies the use of the white part alone of the leek; and *White Crêpes* call for only the whites of eggs in their batter. But it is here in some of these so-called 'white' preparations that we encounter a sticky problem: in several French dishes that bear the word *blanc* in their name some of the ingredients are definitely *not* white. A dish called *Blanc*

---

[10] See the pages by C. Anne Wilson devoted to *Blancmange* in 'The French Connection: Part II', *Petits Propos Culinaires*, 4 (1980), pp.17–19.

douchet[11] contains egg yolks. With the basic pieces of fried chicken in another, the *Blanc brouet de gelines*[12], the cook is instructed to stir in a variety of non-white spices including ground cloves, cinnamon, pepper, galingale and saffron. In both of these cases the resultant mixture cannot possibly be anything but some shade of *non*-white.[13]

The *Whitedish* of medieval cookery, one of the most universally known preparations of the day, likewise seems subject to this anomaly of a not entirely appropriate name. Several versions of the ubiquitous *Blanc mengier* call for ingredients that would leave the final dish with a decidedly off-white cast.[14] Eventually the ingredients list of so-called 'Whitedishes' described at various times and in various places across Europe incorporate doses of saffron (producing a reddish yellow hue), and herbs (for a green colour), and sandalwood (yielding a rich russet). Surely it must have become rather difficult toward the end of the Middle Ages even to justify the use of the name Whitedish to designate such a chromatic confection. So the question has to be put: was the *Blanc mengier* really a 'White Dish'?

The agglutinated form of the French name *blamangier* offers a clue to help understand what may have been the nature and origin of this most common preparation. Because the consonant at the end of the French word *blanc* fell – was not pronounced – before the consonant of the following word, *mengier*, we should not assume that the original form of this qualifier was indeed *blanc*, 'white'. What I should like to propose for your consideration is that what was pronounced *blã* and became written as *b-l-a-n-c* was originally the French word *blã* written *b-l-a-n-t*. Both of these words, *blanc* and *blant*, did in fact exist at one time, in the twelfth and thirteenth centuries. However, with the progress of nasalization in French both of them became pronounced merely *blã*. This homophony led inevitably to the decease of the word which was less commonly used: the word *b-l-a-n-t* simply fell out of the language.

The sense of the French word *blant* is well attested in the early Middle Ages. It derives from the Latin *blandus* and expresses the ideas of 'gentle', 'mild', 'mellow'. In time the value of the word shifted semantically from 'soft' to 'pleasing', and then to 'caressing' and even 'flattering'. An Old

---

[11] *Enseignements*, ed. Grégoire Lozinski, in his edition of the *Bataille de Caresme et de Charnage*, Paris (Champion), 1933, p.183, line 97.

[12] *Ibid.*, p.184, line 105.

[13] It might be pointed out that the same curiously inappropriate designation of 'white' is incorporated into the name of a recipe in the Dutch 'Harpestraeng' collection: *Hwit moos* is a compound of milk, wheat bread, a beaten egg and saffron. Rudolf Grewe, 'An Early XIII Century Northern-European Cookbook', *Current Research in Culinary History: Sources, Topics and Methods*, Boston (Culinary Historians of Boston), 1986, 27–45; Recipe 16.

[14] For some of the vast variety in the minor ingredients in this dish see Jean-Louis Flandrin, 'Internationalisme, nationalisme et régionalisme dans la cuisine des XIVe et XVe siècles: le témoignage des livres de cuisine', *Manger et boire au Moyen Age*, 2 vols., Paris (Les Belles Lettres), 1984, pp.75–91.

French verb, *blandir* exists in the sole sense of 'flatter, cajole'. With such semantic instability it is little wonder that *blant* could not retain its sense of 'bland'. (As a footnote we should observe that modern Italian, modern Spanish and modern Roumanian continue to keep the word *blando* alive in the sense of 'bland', 'soft', 'mild', 'gentle'.)

My proposal is that name *blanc mengier* was originally *blant mengier*, and that the original sense of the dish was not that it was a 'white dish' but that it was a 'bland dish'.

The grounds for this proposal are several. Firstly the phonetic developments in medieval French made the confusion possible, and particularly in a profession that was almost entirely oral in its tradition. Secondly, the common reference to colour in the names of culinary preparations made the substitution of *blanc* for *blant* quite compelling. Cooks and the patrons for whom they cooked both *expected* the colours white, yellow, yellow-green, green, orange, red, brown and black to be used in dish names.

Thirdly, in the earliest French recipe collections, *Blanc mengier* is copied into the section in which recipes for the sick and sickly are grouped.[15] This is the case for instance in the *Enseignements*, the early cook book that I mentioned, where *Blanc mengier* is inserted at the very end of the regular meat dishes and just ahead of the fish preparations; it follows a dish called *Soutil brouet d'Engleterre*[16] and another bearing the very interesting name of *Blanc douchet*.[17] Though this section of the manuscript is untitled, it is clearly understood to contain dishes suitable for the sick. In the *Viandier* of Taillevent, itself fundamentally a renaming and enlargement of the *Enseignements*, the chapter of sick-dishes is named and the *Blanc mengier* is one of the six dishes outlined there as proper preparations for the sick.[18]

In his very large collection of recipes useful in a bourgeois household, the *Menagier de Paris* (Recipe 107) gives to his version of the Whitedish the name *Blanc mengier de chapons pour malades*. Similarly, in the fifteenth century in the cookbook compiled for the Duke of Savoy by his head chef Chiquart, two versions of the *Blanc mengier*, one for capons and one for partridge, are placed in the section on 'dishes which are good and refreshing for the sick' or

---

[15] A recipe for a *blanc manger* appears in a German *regimen sanitatis* a full generation before its appearance in a German cookbook. This is in Arnold von Bamberg's *Tractatus de regimine sanitatis*, written probably near Avignon in 1317.

[16] The sense of the word *soutil*, or 'subtle', is directly tied to medico-physical doctrines about the fineness of food particles and the digestibility of that food. A 'subtle' food was readily convertible into good chyle and blood, and so constituted highly appropriate nourishment for the sick or the sickly.

[17] It is enormously tempting to see in this name *blanc douchet* and case of medieval tautology: 'bland mildness'.

[18] *Pour malades: The Viandier of Taillevent. An Edition of all Extant Manuscripts*, ed. Terence Scully, Ottawa, 1988, p.166.

for those persons who are 'afflicted with infirmities or illness'.[19] The Latin recipe collection known as the *Tractatus* has among its clearly delineated chapters one, the fourth, which bears the precise rubric, *Modo narrandum est de condimentis delicatis dominorum, ad naturam confortandam et appetitum provocandum*; that is, 'Now we turn to preparations for delicate lords, of a nature to comfort them and give them an appetite.' The very first item in this chapter of twelve paragraphs for those of finicky appetites is our *Blanc mangier*.[20] In sum, then, the dish called *Bland mengier* was designed expressly as food for invalids, and was copied in sections devoted primarily to foods for the sick.

A fourth and final observation should be made, and this has to do with the ingredients used in the so-called Whitedish. Medical theory posited that the science of cookery consisted in making foodstuffs safe for human consumption. By his choice of ingredients, by the way in which he combined them, cooked them and dressed them, the cook ensured that his patron's stable state of health was not disturbed. The cook must always identify foodstuffs that needed 'correction' because their degrees of warmness, coldness, dryness or moistness might detrimentally affect the temperament of the person eating them. When his patron was either actually sick or at the least of a sickly disposition, the onus upon the cook to prepare innocuous, anodyne food was very great. The *Blanc mengier* was one of the dishes to which a cook could turn when he had to feed the sick in his master's household safely. It was, in fact, a very old, very durable, very reliable stand-by for such purposes. And it was reliable because its ingredients were all deemed by the physicians of the time to be moderate in their temperament. Of all the domestic meats, chicken enjoyed a reputation for possessing, with veal, the most moderately moist and moderately warm qualities. Because these qualities of moderately moist and moderately warm most closely approximated those of healthy human beings, such foods were categorized as ideal by the physicians. Similarly, almonds were considered to produce humours that facilitated digestion; their warmth and dryness in the second degree could readily be corrected when, by grinding and mixing with water, they were reduced to that universal medieval ingredient, almond milk. And likewise, though rice was held to be warm and dry in the second degree, if it was prepared by boiling its dangers could be eliminated. The optional ingredient that is specified in a high percentage of versions of the *Blanc mengier* is sugar. Sugar is *the* sick-dish ingredient *par excellence* in late medieval cookery: it turns up in virtually every one of the sick-dish recipes in late-medieval French collections. Its moderately warm and moderately moist

---

[19] *Chiquart's 'On Cookery'. A Fifteenth-Century Savoyard Culinary Treatise*, ed. and tr. Terence Scully, New York, 1986, pp.109–110.

[20] Marianne Mulon, 'Deux traités inédits d'art culinaire médiéval', *Bulletin Philologique et Historique*, 1968, p.391. The name of this recipe is, quite exceptionally, in French in this Latin treatise.

qualities make it very similar to chicken, and so ideally suitable for completely safe human consumption. And finally, a mention of another optional ingredient I have not had occasion to mention, and that is barley. Rarely a recipe for *Blanc mengier* (notably in the *Tractatus* Part IV, Recipe 1) will allow the substitution of barley for the usual rice, but primarily, one supposes, because the Whitedish is intended for serving to the sick. Barley-water, considered 'nutritious and easy to digest',[21] is perhaps the longest-standing food in European use for sick people.

All of this is clearly what might be termed circumstantial evidence. To my knowledge no medieval manuscript contains a recipe for *Blanc mengier* in which the word *blanc* is actually written as *blant*. If this hypothesis is true, however, and if at its origins the name of the dish *did* in fact embody the qualification *blant* rather than simply *blanc*, several inconsistencies connected with this dish would be explained, and we would better understand the theoretical role of foods in maintaining the health of people in the later Middle Ages.

The names by which prepared dishes are known frequently have only an obscure history. Even today the origins, the original meanings, of the names of the English *Mawmenee*[22] and *Sorengue*[23] are largely a matter of speculation. Even greater mystery surrounds the names of certain dishes that were apparently quite common in medieval kitchens and on medieval tables. Among these probably the most common, a prepared dish so universally popular that its name has survived in English to the present day in the form of 'blanc mange' or 'blamange', is the medieval *Whitedish*.

As the secondary details of the list of ingredients for *Whitedish* varied from generation to generation and from place to place, a more or less constant addition was sugar – sugar which partook of human nature by being slightly warm and slightly moist, and so was most highly valued by physicians, almost as a medicine in itself.

Omelets and egg dishes

Just as chicken was the most commonly eaten meat in the late Middle Ages, so chicken eggs in some form constitute a staple. Omelets could be plain or enriched with cheese or with a whole range of herbs. The *Arboulastre* of the *Menagier de Paris* (Recipe 225) contains dittany, rue, wild celery, tansy, mint, sage, marjoram, fennel, parsley, chard, violet leaves, spinach, lettuce and clary, all of them chopped up and ground in a mortar, as well as the beaten

---

[21] *The Four Seasons of the House of Cerruti*, tr. Judith Spencer, New York 1984, p.53.

[22] Maxime Rodinson suggests that there may be some connection between this name (if not, or at least not entirely convincingly, the dish itself) and the Arabic preparation called *ma'muniya*. See 'La ma'muniyyat en orient et en occident', *Etudes d'orientalisme dédiées à la mémoire de Lévi-Provençal*, Paris (Maisonneuve & Larose), 1962.

[23] This name *may* possibly derive from *sor* or *saur*, meaning 'reddish' and *anguilla*, 'eel'.

eggs of course. The recipe for this particular Herb Omelet also calls for ginger and cheese!

But eggs were prepared in numerous other ways: Martino[24] describes *Frictata* (an omelet), *Ova frictellate* (fried eggs), *Ova sperdute* (poached eggs), *Ova sperdute in lacte o vino dolce* (eggs poached in milk or wine), *Ova piene* (stuffed eggs), *Ova sopra la graticula* (an omelet recooked on a grill with fresh eggs, sugar and cinnamon), *Ova nel speto* (whole eggs on a spit), *Ova in patelletta* (the modern *œufs en cocotte*), *Ova in cenere calda* (whole eggs in the coals), *Ova tuffate con la sua cortece* (boiled eggs), *Ova frictellate a la fiorentina* (eggs fried both sides), *Ova spedute in la brascia accesa* (eggs broken on the coals), *Ova frictellate piene* (as the Florentine eggs, but with the yolks replaced by an herb-and-spice mixture), and, finally, *Ova in forma de raffioli* (eggs deep-fried in a thin dough).

Other recipe collections have many variations on an equally wide variety of treatments for eggs.

Brewets and civets

The universal predilection of the late Middle Ages for pottages is undoubtedly traditional. The most economical, and easiest, way to cook almost any foodstuff is by boiling in a pot. Roasting on a grill or on a spit is relatively wasteful of the fuel; ovens were a quite exceptional luxury in all but the most affluent households of the early Middle Ages, so that the regional lord or commune could tap a good source of income by building and maintaining a public oven for whose use a fee could be charged. Just as the ordinary household from time immemorial would normally have an iron cauldron of vegetables simmering over the central hearth on a more or less permanent basis, so the broth and civet remained even in the refined cookery of the later medieval period a standard genre of dish. Occasionally a pottage of cereal grains was boiled, or those semi-ground grains added to a pot of cabbage or leeks. On special occasions, and increasingly in the late Middle Ages, a little meat, especially pork or mutton, might find its way into the commoner's stewing pot.

It would be misleading to use the modern word 'stew' to designate these relatively simple prepared foods, because today with this term we understand a spiced mixture a meat and vegetables. In medieval Europe a broth or brewet normally referred to some sort of pottage in which only some sort of meat or fish was the prime ingredient. Depending upon the presence in it of a binding agent, the brewet could be of relatively high or low viscosity. Across Europe we find a good variety of such dishes: *Brodium Album*, *Bruet of Almayne*, *Huner in Brueth*, *Blanc Brouet de Chappons*, *Brodo del Pesce* and *Brou Ametllat*.

---

[24] Maestro Martino, *Libro de arte coquinaria*, ed. Faccioli, *Arte della cucina*, I, pp.117–204; specifically pp.180–83.

The *civet* is a little less commonplace in the various national traditions. At its origin and still in its essence this dish is a pottage whose basic flavour is determined by the fried onions with which it begins. When a liquid is added to these onions in a pot, along with a choice of spices, and pieces of some sort of meat are thrown in to cook, the resultant dish is a *civet*. From England to Aragon there are recipes for *Tenche in syvee*, *Civé de Connins*, *Civeri di Lepore* and *Sebada cens let*.

For the same reason that the ubiquitous stewing pot explains the prevalence of brewets and civets in the late-medieval diet, a related preparation, the sop (modern 'soup'), was equally traditional. Where the other pottages had to be eaten with a spoon, the sop allowed the diner to do without any utensil at all other than his fingers: a chunk of table bread soaked up the broth. The plain sop tended to be disdained by the more refined recipe collections,[25] although these often offer directions for making a sop in which the bread or toast, in bite-sized pieces, is an integral part: the diner had no need to dunk his bread in the common bowl but had only to pick up a precut portion of the sop, already bathed as it was in its 'sauce' and covered with melted cheese or small chunks of meat. Regularly, after the sauce is mixed, the final sentence of a recipe for sops reads, 'Then take your bread (or toast) and make up your sops.'

Tortes and pies

We have already seen the important role that pastry played in late-medieval cookery. Across Europe pies enclosed a great variety of foodstuffs, but certain of these seem to have enjoyed particular popularity among the upper classes. One well known variety was the Parmesan Pie.

Though the name of this pie perpetuates the Italian city of Parma in which apparently it originated, versions of it were made in England, Germany, France, Italy and Aragon. The particular features of this pie or *torte* are its tall form and its contents. The manner in which its filling of fowl and meat is set out in alternating layers is likewise distinctive.

The names vary little from language to language, of course: in Latin this pie is qualified as *parmegiana* (Châlons, Recipe 47), *parmesana* (*Liber de coquina*, Part V, Recipe 6), *parmissana* (*Viaticorum*, Recipes 44 and 46) and *parmisciana* (Anon. 'A', Recipe 1); in Italian, *parmesana* (*Libro della cocina*, Recipe 122 and *Libro per cuoco*, Recipe 112), *parmegiana* (Wellcome, Recipe 131), *parmigiana* (*Buone vivande*, Recipe 1 and *Dilicate vivande*, Recipe 70); in

---

[25] Perhaps slightly more plebian than the average upper-class recipe collection, the *Menagier de Paris* (Recipe 57) groups an interesting series of sop recipes under an intriguing but practical general rubric: *Souppe despourveue*: 'Rush Soup(s)'. In case she should find herself suddenly required to set out a supper for unexpected guests, the bourgeoise could avail herself of one of the recipes in the following seven paragraphs in which the primary ingredients are, respectively: butter-fried parsley, cold beef, fried fish, eggs-and-spices, another eggs-and-spices, egg yolks, bacon-and-mackerel.

French, *parmeysine* (*On Cookery*, Recipes 21 and 40), and *parmeriennes*, *Viandier*, Recipe 197). Chiquart's two versions of the Parmesan Pie are designed one for meat days and the other for lean days. In the latter he mixes tuna and pike with fruit (figs, prunes, dates, pine-nuts), herbs (parsley, marjoram, sage), spices (ginger, grains of paradise, pepper, cloves, saffron and sugar) and almond milk with starch in it; this mixture he lays in the pie shell in layers alternating with slices of cooked and fried eels. The Parmesan Pie was one of the richest creations of medieval cookery.

Mortarolum

This universally known dish derives its name from the mortar through which its basic ingredient, ground meat, must pass. At its simplest the dish is really little more than that, a meat paste, although the choice of spices seems to have been at the discretion of the cook and to have allowed for significant variations. More sophisticated versions of the dish also included eggs, various herbs and sugar.

The Latin and Italian names, *mortarolum*, *mortarello* and *mortarolo*, *morteruolo* tend to be similar (*Liber de coquina*, Recipes 12, 63 and 64, *Libro per cuoco*, Recipe 46 and *passim*); in Catalan, *morterol* (*Sent soví*, Recipes 104–7); in French, *mortereul* (*Menagier*, Recipe 236) and *morteyruel* and *mortoeses* (*On Cookery*, Recipe 56); in English, *mortrellus*, *mortreus* and *mortrewes* (*Diversa servicia*, Recipes 5 and 48), Austin, pp. 70 and 19; and in Dutch, *mortroel* (*Keukenboek*, Recipe 17).

As with the Parmesan Pie this generic dish was popular enough to require a meatless version which could be substituted on lean days: in the Latin *Viaticorum* a recipe for a *Mortayrol caremal* is followed by one for a *Mortayrol carnium* (Recipes 31 and 36); the *Sent soví* (Recipe 108) likewise explicitly gives a *Morterol cens carn* – '. . . without meat' as does the *Noble Boke off Cookry* (Recipe 25): *Mortrus of Fische*.

Galentine and other jellies

Medieval cooks made good use of the gel-forming property possessed by proteins obtained from animal hooves and certain animal and fish skins. Recipe collections often copy what we might call basic recipes for extracting elemental jelly from animal and fish sources: the *Viandier* (Recipe 68), for instance, directs the cook to begin by cooking (in wine, verjuice and vinegar) any fish 'whose skin is covered with *limon* – a natural oil', or any meat, repeatedly straining the bouillon and finally letting it cool until it sets. In his *Treasury for the Poor* the physician Arnaldus of Villanova indicates that this *limon* is found particularly on tench, eel, carp and lamprey, among other fish; it is the oily protein that gives a blue cast to the surface of some fish when they are roasted. The *On Cookery* appends two recipes (Recipes 80 and 81) as a sort of afterthought following its formal conclusion, one each for meat jelly and fish jelly. The meat jelly begins with the boiling of an unspecified number of sheep's hooves; the fish jelly begins with pike, perch or carp.

A recipe for Fish Jelly copied in the *Vivendier* (Recipe 29, folio 158v) is perhaps more interesting than others because it specifies explicitly the quantities of spices to be incorporated in the dish. It is the presence of these spices that reminds us of the fundamental function of jelly as a food preservative in the according to the medieval way of thinking.

> Fish Jelly – for carp, tench, bream, turbot and other good fish. The fish should be well cleaned and cooked in wine and water, then take it out of the bouillon onto a clean cloth to drain; when it is thoroughly cooked, get the spices – ginger, cinnamon, cloves grains of paradise, saffron, spikenard and galingale, distempered with pea puree; set everything to boil together; and if you see that it is too thick, take it off the fire and strain it; then set out your fish in bright shining platters and pour the broth hot over it, then put your platters in a cool place on clean sand. Some people garnish the dish with peeled almonds and little laurel leaves painted either gold or silver, and they serve this as an *entremets*.
>
> To make a quantity of 40 bowls [for roughly eighty guests] of jelly you will need the following:
>
> 10 ounces of grains of paradise
> 6 ounces of mace
> 3 ounces of nutmeg
> 4 ounces of ginger
> 1 ounce of cloves
> 6 ounces of cinnamon
> 3 ounces each of spikenard and galingale

Gelatin was used in a variety of other, generic dishes: *Scabec, Scibeccia Escabeyg* and *Escabeche* (a cold fish dish in Italian and Catalan recipes)[26] *Sulcia, Sols, Soux* and *Sulctz* (a vinegar jelly, in Latin, Catalan, French and German), and especially the universally known *Galentine*.

Sulcia was prepared for either meat or fish, using a jelly derived from either meat or fish sources. The *Tractatus* (Part II, Recipe 17) includes a recipe for *Sulta* for pork:

> *Sulta*, that is, *souet* in French, is made this way: cut up the extremities of pork small, that is the feet, ears and head, cook them well and cool them in enough slightly salted good vinegar that they are submerged in it. Some add in finely chopped sage and parsley; some people grind parsley and sage with pepper and ginger, making like a sauce; some put beef stomach, liver, belly and intestines in the *sulta* in order to preserve them a long time.

[26] About this preparation, see Barbara Santich, 'On Escabeche (and Ceviche)', *Petits Propos Culinaires*, 20 (1985), pp.17–21.

The *Menagier de Paris* (Recipe 277) has a *soux* of piglet. The *Sent sovi* (Recipe 71) describes a dish of partridges in *sols*. And the Southern German manuscript mentions *Gesulctzen Vischen* (Recipe 46). The Latin collection in the manuscript at *Châlons* (Recipe 86) is content to say simply that 'You make Pork *Sulcia* in the same way as is described above in the chapter on gelatins.'

Of all jelly dishes the most common is the one generically called *galentine*. At the same time it is a dish that seemed to allow a wide variety of interpretations, depending for its nature as it did upon the spices that a cook chose to include in it. It was essentially a jelly in which dissolved spices, and perhaps some ground herbs, were held in intimate and long-lasting contact with small pieces of meat or fish. In late-medieval recipes from England to the Iberian peninsula there are copies of no fewer than sixty-five recipes for *galentine* in one manner of preparation or another.

Two standard sauces: Cameline, Jance

The two most universally known sauces in the Middle Ages were those that were based upon the two most commonly used spices, cinnamon and ginger. Each of these staple sauces lent themselves to many variations according to the admixtures of other ingredients (other spices, vinegar, verjuice, different thickeners, and so forth) that were used to make them.

Though Cameline Sauce was named after its tawny camel-hair colour, it was always fundamentally a mixture in which the flavour of cinnamon predominated. This was normally a cold sauce; that is, it was not prepared by boiling and it was served cold. One important variant was common within the genre, and that used garlic.

The ginger-based Jance was a boiled sauce. As with the Garlic Cameline there was also a Garlic Jance. Although again other ingredients could modify the net nature of any particular Jance, this was generally a more simple compound than the Cameline Sauces.

Gratonea

Numerous recipes exist in several collections for a dish whose name is a variation on the Latin *Gratonea*. Just as the names varied from *Gratonata* to *Cretonee*, so the dish itself allowed a fairly broad range of versions. In England (*Forme of Cury*, Recipe 61: *Crytayne*) the dish consists of diced capon meat in milk and ultimately fried with egg yolks. In France (the *Viandier*, Recipe 11, and *On Cookery*, Recipe 62: *Cretonnee* and *Gratunee*, respectively) the dish begins with a base of peas or beans but continues in more or less the standard fashion. In Italy (for instance, in the text of the Wellcome manuscript, folio 89r, or the *Anonimo meridionale*, 'A', Recipe 23) the *Gratinato* is a pottage with basically the same ingredients but for which the chicken is usually initially fried. In the Latin collection, the *Liber de coquina* (Part III, Recipes 1 and 2), the *Gratonea* is still fundamentally a fried dish – even if the writer forgot to mention the fried chicken which eventually is to be basted with the milk-and-egg mixture of the recipe.

Crisps and doughnuts

Every major recipe collection of medieval Europe is absolutely bound to contain, somewhere between its first and last pages, directions for at least a dish or two called either a crisp (or crêpe or crispello) or a doughnut. The procedure involved in making either of these is quite simple. All that is needed is, on the one hand, hot grease in a pan or a pot and, on the other, a dough or a batter to drop into it.

For the most part the ingredients for both dough and batter are, universally, relatively straightforward. Even in the fifteenth century the Harleian manuscript edited by Austin (p. 44, Recipe 51) has Cryspez that require only egg whites, milk, flour and a little yeast, all beaten together. Some versions include honey in the batter, some like the batter to be coloured yellow or brown. Where this preparation tended to be different from treatment to treatment was, perhaps naturally, in the garnish with which it was served. The plainest garnish (as here in the late English recipe) was just a sprinkling of sugar; the Anglo-Norman 'A' Collection (Recipe 2) imaginatively suggests garnishing its Blaunches escrepes with pieces of orange.

The basic doughnut gave rise to a slightly larger range of relatives: Bignets, Otras, Mistembec, Samartard, Krapfen and Krapfellin. These and other names names designated doughnuts across Europe, though in principle the derivation of each of these from the blob of batter or dough dropped into deep grease remains clear.

'Regional' Food Habits

Foodstuffs

Certain regions in medieval Europe tended to prefer certain foodstuffs. The reasons for these preferences most likely lay in the products of local agriculture or the goods handled by regional commerce, although they may be related to some intangible historical custom. However, virtually every observation that can be made about food preferences should be bound around with all sorts of caveats having to do with the very uncertain distance between our written records of recipes and actual day-to-day eating habits. A few generalizations may be suggested quite tentatively.[27] The French, for

[27] See also, with some caution, the limited study of Jean-Louis Flandrin in 'Internationalisme, nationalisme et régionalisme dans la cuisine des XIVe et XVe siècles: le témoignage des livres de cuisine', Manger et boire au moyen âge (Actes du Colloque de Nice, 15–17 octobre 1982), Paris (Les Belles Lettres), 1984, II, pp.75–91.

instance, tend to make somewhat more varied and consistent use of spices than is apparent in the cookery of other regions.

Ginger and cinnamon appear frequently in ingredients lists, and grains of paradise are almost commonplace whereas this 'new' condiment remains exceptional in cookery elsewhere. Italians tend to prefer the use of aromatic herbs: marjoram, rosemary, mint, hyssop, sage, parsley, basil. For their cooking oils Italy, the Hispanic peninsula and France rely upon olive oil, while Flanders and the nothern German states make use of poppy oil. Butter was better known in northern France, Flanders and England[28] than elsewhere.

> Almost all who inhabit the northern and western regions use it [butter] instead of fat or oil in certain dishes because they lack oil, in which the warm and mild regions customarily abound.[29]

In Savoy fresh-water fish prevail over salt-water fish, but in Catalan recipes the reverse is true. Little rice turns up in English recipes whereas in kitchens of the Hispanic peninsula rice is very well known. Onions tend regularly to be fried in French, Italian and Hispanic cookery, whereas in English cookery 'raw' onions occasionally enter the pottage directly.[30] Wine is far from being the common cooking ingredient in England and the German states as it was in more southern lands. On the other hand German and English cooks had at least a modest supply of honey at hand in their kitchens, and used it in their recipes, while elsewhere the local usage had almost completely forgotten its delicate flavour.

In the matter of fruits, it is apparent in the various recipe collections that the citrus fruits and pomegranates exerted their greatest effect upon the cookery of the mediterranean countries.[31] Similarly, though figs and dates were traded in a dry state everywhere in Europe, these fruits had only very limited use in northern cooking.

---

[28] C. Anne Wilson, in *Food and Drink in Britain*, London (Constable), 1973, p.163, says that in England butter was especially reserved for the sick, children and the elderly. Butter does, however, turn up in a good number of general-purpose recipes in English collections.

[29] Platina, *De honesta voluptate*, II, 19 On Butter.

[30] Jean-Louis Flandrin, 'Problèmes, sources et méthodes d'une histoire des pratiques et des goûts régionaux avant le XIXe siècle', *Alimentation & régions* (Actes du Colloque 'Cuisines, régimes alimentaires, espaces régionaux', Nancy, 24–27 September 1987), ed. Jean Peltre and Claude Thouvenot, Nancy (Presses Universitaires de Nancy), 1989, pp.347–61; particularly pp.349–50.

[31] By its particular use of pomegranate juice and lime juice, Carole Lambert is able to relate the Provençal recipe collection, the *Modus viaticorum preparandorum et salsarum*, to more southerly culinary practice in Italy and Catalonia: 'La cuisine française au bas moyen âge: pays d'oil vs pays d'oc', *Alimentation et régions*, pp.375–85.

Dishes

The Neapolitan Collection (Recipe 114) contains a recipe for a sauce which in very modest, homey style it calls a *Salsa cotidiana* or 'Everyday Sauce'. It is made from ginger, pepper and saffron, boiled with vinegar or a bitter wine. It is simple and easily prepared. What is interesting is its name. By naming it an 'Everyday Sauce', the anonymous author of the Collection indicates that the cookery of his place and his time had a certain flavour, perhaps even a certain nature that his contemporary countrymen would recognize as 'their hometown' taste. Though each of these late-medieval recipe collections almost invariably include some recipes whose names claim a place of origin for the dish far distant from the place where the collection was compiled, for each of these recipe collections there nevertheless always existed a local, everyday cuisine and a local, everyday taste.

As we tried to show above, medieval aristocracy was conscious of sharing a status that transcended national and state boundaries. Yet not all aspects of their diet or gastronomical habits were reduced to common universal norms. Much of what is eaten depends upon what is locally available in nature or produced by local agriculture, and regional traditions were as strongly marked in the domain of food habits as in any other aspect of medieval life. Food tastes tend on the whole to be conventional matters determined by strong traditions.

At any rate, when we read the recipe collections of the late Middle Ages we find that each one does seem to be centred on certain types of dishes, on certain foods, or on certain flavours. There is indeed much in common among them, so that we *can* speak of 'medieval cookery'; but there are, too, numerous divergences in taste. In particular, on close examination we can perceive certain national usages. It is these slight differences in national taste that we have tried to suggest in the recipe translations that follow.[32] The particularities may or may not be obvious; the palatableness, however, of all of the dishes is.

The following recipes are merely reproductions, in an approximate modern English translation, of what a medieval reader would have found on opening a particular manuscript recipe collection. In very few cases are there any indications of the quantites to be used or of the 'yield' to be expected

---

[32] It will be apparent to the geographically astute reader that we are in a sense mixing apples and oranges here. Our organization is by language and *not* by geography *nor* by time period. There may be as close a relationship between the French work of Chiquart in fifteenth-century Savoy and fourteenth-century north-Italian cookery as between all of the recipe collections of both centuries from the north, centre and south of Italy that just happen to be written in dialects of a common language. And what of the Latin collections, written as they were by, for instance, a German living in Italy or by an Italian living in France? Or of all that 'English' cookery presented in a language whose Frenchness suggests much more of an influence than is often apparent?

from the recipe. Occasionally a writer may even be rather vague about the precise procedures to be followed, what sort of pot or pan is to be used, how hot the fire should be, for how long a food ought to be cooked. The original author of a recipe – if we can imagine such a shadowy, anonymous, humble person – was undoubtedly a professional, in the sense that he *knew* all that he needed to know about proper quantities, pots, heats and cooking times. He, and the series of scribes who transcribed his recipes and recipe collections, and perhaps who even recombined and recompiled other collections themselves, assumed that their ultimate readers might be journeymen or master cooks, too, who had no need to be taken by the hand like some first-day apprentice.

The modern reader of these recipes who is curious actually to make any dish they represent must be willing to read them with a cook's imagination. He or she should be ready to estimate the relative quantities that would be appropriate for the various ingredients, and to make adjustments in these as the dish is being prepared. The professional cook in the Middle Ages worked primarily from an image that was firmly fixed in his mind by experience – an image we might qualify as being gustatory and tactile as well as visual; everything he did while he was cooking worked towards a realization of that image. Until the modern cook has acquired a little of the practical, lifelong experience that his or her medieval counterpart had with this cookery, a lot will depend upon inspiration and gastronomic common sense.

In the five sections that follow are typical examples of five national groups in medieval Europe. Clearly there can be few more difficult tasks than to try to identify characteristic tastes, in any matter but most particularly as regards food customs. Consequently the choice of recipes in each section below is close to being arbitrary. Very many representative dishes have been omitted, many that have been reproduced as typical of one country's standard fare turn up quite acclimatized in another's. The bibliographic listings, at the foot of the page and at the end of this book, of the most important published sources will at least allow the interested reader to explore these national cuisines a lot further.

English

Surviving recipe collections that were written in English come to us from the late-fourteenth and fifteenth centuries. In all they are quite numerous and show a culinary tradition that undoubtedly had much that was indigenous but also much that was derived from contemporary usage in France.[33] That

---

[33] Constance B. Hieatt and Sharon Butler, *Cury on Inglysch. English Culinary Manuscripts of the Fourteenth Century*, London (Oxford University Press), 1985; this publication contains the *Diversa cibaria* (63 recipes) in Part I, pp.45–61; the *Diversa servicia* (92 recipes), Part II, pp.62–79; the *Utilis coquinario* (37 recipes), Part III, pp.81–91; and the *Forme of Cury* (205 recipes), Part IV, pp.93–145. Thomas Austin, *Two Fifteenth-Century Cookery-Books*, London (Oxford University Press), 1888 (258 and 182 recipes).

the French influence was so marked should not be surprising. Cultural links to the continent, and particularly to France, were long-standing and on-going. English monarchs and princes habitually took some account of French usage in their formal court life. However, while the usual English cookery manuscript will betray the origin of a dish for which the recipe is entitled *Chawdoun* or *Mortreux* or *Rapey* or *Hastelets*, it has to be remembered that even at this end of the Middle Ages the use of French still had something entirely normal about it in England: there is no obvious sign here of snobbery. In fact very often these English recipes with their pseudo-French names really describe quite distinct variations on the equivalent dishes on the continent; and quite a few, once one reads past the name, are entirely unique.

Viaunde de Cypre (Vyaunde Cypre: Forme of Cury, Recipe 100)

Get dates, pick out the pits, grind them up small and put them through a strainer; get mead or wine with sugar in it, and add in the dates, spice powder and salt, and allay it all with rice flour until it is thick. If you wish, on a meat day get boiled chicken and pork, grind them up finely and add them in; and serve.

Mawmenee (Mawmenee: Forme of Cury, Recipe 22)

Get two quarts of Greek wine and two pounds of sugar, clarify the sugar with a quantity of wine and put it through a strainer into an earthenware pot; get rice flour, mix it with some of the wine and add it in together; get pine-nuts and dates, fry them a little in grease or oil, and add them in; get cloves and whole cinnamon and add in; get [and add] powdered ginger, cinnamon, cloves; colour [the mixture] with a little sandalwood if necessary; add salt and let it all boil gently over a low fire; it should not be too thick; get finely shredded capon or pheasant flesh and add in.

Mawmenee (Mammenye Bastarde: Austin, Two Fifteenth-Century Cookery-Books: p.22, Recipe 88)

Get two quarts of clarified honey, a pound each of pine-nuts, currants, sandalwood powder, cinnamon and pepper, and two gallons of wine or ale, and put all this into a pot and skim it [when it boils]; then get three pounds of wheat starch, a gallon of wine and a good gallon of vinegar, and let all this steep together then strain it; when the pot boils, add this prepared mixture [lycoure] to it, and let it be thick; then get powdered

From the second half of the fifteenth century comes A Noble Boke off Cookry ffor a Prynce Houssolde, ed. Robina (Mrs Alexander) Napier, London (Elliot Stock), 1882 (270 recipes). An unusual versified cookbook, Liber cure cocorum, is still available only in the edition of Richard Morris for The Philological Society, Berlin (Asher), 1862 (131 recipes). Constance B. Hieatt, An Ordinance of Pottage, London (Prospect Books), 1988 (189 recipes).

ginger, salt and saffron and season it up, and serve it flat on a dish, quite hot, with powdered ginger sprinkled on top.

Sambocade (*Sambocade*: *Forme of Cury*, Recipe 179)

Make a pastry crust in a pie plate; get curds, wring out the whey and strain the curds and put it in the shell; add in one third of that quantity of sugar and a quantity of egg whites, and shake in elderflower blossoms; bake the pie, add in rose-water and serve it.

Custard (*Custarde*: Austin, *Two Fifteenth-Century Cookery-Books*: p.74)

Get veal and chop it up small, wash it clean, put it into a clean pot with clean water and let it boil; then get parsley, sage, hyssop and savory, wash and chop them up and add them to the pot when it boils; then get powdered pepper, cinnamon, cloves, mace, saffron and salt, and put them in together to boil, along with a good deal of wine. When the meat has boiled, remove it from the broth and let the broth cool; when it is cold, strain yolks and whites of eggs and add them to the broth in order to thicken it sufficiently. Make good pie shells and lay three or four pieces of the meat into them. Then get dates and prunes and cut them up, and add to them powdered ginger and a little verjuice [in turn] add this to the broth with salt. Let the pie and the meat bake a little, then add the broth into the pie and let it all bake until done.

French

It was probably the prestige which the French royal court enjoyed throughout Europe that accounts for the super-celebrity of one medieval cookbook in particular, the *Viandier* of Guillaume Tirel, the so-called Taillevent (or 'Slice-Wind'). Though this collection undoubtedly inherited much of its material from previous generations of cooks and recipes collections, and grew by accretion through several generations of copies during its long lifetime, its subsequent influence can be sensed to a greater or less degree in most of the printed cookbooks of the late- fifteenth and sixteenth centuries. The *Viandier* embodies late-medieval French cookery. Only one major work in French manages to modify this standard French corpus, and that is the *On Cookery* of Master Chiquart where we can see how the court of Savoy, sitting astride the Alps, was able to combine the best of contemporary French, Italian and local cuisines.[34]

[34] The principal French recipe collections of the period constitute a relatively and surprisingly brief list. *Enseingnemenz qui enseingnent a apareiller toutes manieres de viandes*, ed. Grégoire Lozinski as Appendix I in his *La bataille de Caresme et de Charnage*, Paris (Champion), 1933, pp.88–108 (55 recipes). Terence Scully, *The Viandier of Taillevent. An Edition of all Extant Manuscripts*, Ottawa (University of Ottawa Press), 1988 (220 recipes; this edition contains an English translation). Georgine E. Brereton and Janet M. Ferrier, *Le Menagier de Paris*, Oxford (Clarendon), 1981 (380 recipes). Terence Scully, 'Du fait de cuisine par Maistre Chiquart, 1420', *Vallesia*, 40 (1985), pp.101–231; translated by Terence Scully as *Chiquart's 'On*

French cuisine, as it is represented by the recipes that were copied into manuscripts, may be characterized by an apparent preference for various pottages and broths (*brouets*), and the attention it pays to wildfowl and fish.

White Brewet of Capons (*Blanc brouet de chappons*: *Viandier*, Recipe 19)
They are cooked in wine and water, broken apart by members and fried in bacon grease; then grind up almonds, the dark meat from your capons and chicken livers, steep this in your broth and boil it with your meat; then grind ginger, cinnamon, cloves, galingale, long pepper and grains of paradise, and boil everything thoroughly together; and add in well beaten egg yolks. It should be quite thick.

Verjuice Brewet (*Brouet de verjus*: *Viandier*, Recipe 25)
Boil your meat, with bacon fat for taste, in such a mixture of wine, water and verjuice that the taste of the verjuice predominates; then grind ginger, and a little bread moistened in the bouillon, and strain this with a great quantity of raw egg yolks, and boil it; then, when your meat has sauteed, dress it with this.

Frumenty (*Formentee*: *Viandier*, Recipe 63)
Clean grains of wheat in warm water, wrap them in a cloth and beat strongly on this with a pestle until all the chaff has separated, and wash it well and cook it in water; when it has cooked, mash it; bring cow's milk to a boil, put the wheat into this and bring it to a boil again, stirring frequently; remove it from the fire, stirring, and add a great quantity of well beaten egg yolks – and it should not be too hot when they are added. Some people add spices and a little saffron and venison water. It should be yellowish and quite thick.

Fresh Lamprey in a Hot Sauce (*Lamproie fresche a la saulce chaude*: *Viandier*, Recipe 69)
The lamprey should be bled by its mouth, and its tongue removed; you should shove a skewer into it to help bleed it – and keep the blood because that is the grease; and scrape the inside of its mouth with a knife; then scald it as you would an eel and roast it on a very slender spit inserted through it sideways once or twice. Then grind ginger, cinnamon, cloves, grains of paradise, nutmegs and a little burnt toast moistened in the blood together with vinegar and, if you wish, a little wine; infuse all of this together and bring it to a boil, and then put you lamprey whole into

Cookery'. A *Fifteenth-Century Savoyard Culinary Treatise*, New York, Berne, Frankfurt am Main (Lang), 1986 (81 recipes). Carole Lambert, *Le recueil de Riom et la Maniere de henter soutillement. Un livre de cuisine et un réceptaire sur les greffes du XVe siècle*, Montréal (CERES), 1987 (48 recipes). Constance B. Hieatt and Robin F. Jones, 'Two Anglo-Norman Culinary Collections editied from British Library Manuscripts Additional 32085 and Royal 12.C.xii', *Speculum*, 61 (1986), pp.859–882 (29 and 32 recipes).

it. The sauce should not be too dark – that is, when the sauce is thin, but when the sauce is thick, and is called 'mud', it should be dark. Also, it is not necessary for the lamprey to be boiled with the sauce; rather the lamprey is brought dry to the table and the thin sauce or the 'mud' is poured over the lamprey or else is served in bowls, and the lamprey should be cut into pieces lengthwise and sent to the table on plates; nevertheless, some gourmets insist on having it dry with the sauce, made of the drippings and fine salt, served on the same plate on which it is brought.

A Soringue (*Une soringue*: *Viandier*, Recipe 79)
Scald or skin the eel, then slice it across and set it to sautee in oil in a covered pot over a low fire with sliced onions and parsley leaves; take toast, pea puree or boiled water, and wine – with the wine predominating – strain it and put it with the other to boil; then add in ground ginger, cinnamon, cloves, grains of paradise, and saffron for colour, infused in verjuice; boil all of this; season it with vinegar.

Calunafree of Partridge (*Calunafree de perdrix*: *On Cookery*, Recipe 47)
The person who will be making this dish should get his partridge and clean them fully, plump them, lard them well, then mount them on the spit and roast them nicely; when they are roasted, take them down onto good clean wooden tables, then take them one after the other and dismember them in the proper way, leaving the wings whole and cutting up the white meat just as small as if you were carving in front of your lord, and put all that into good silver dishes – and if you do not have enough silver dishes, put it into a good clean pan. Take a lot of Camelin Sauce and spread it on in such a way that everything is bathed in it, and put on only enough mustard to give a slight flavour of it, and only enough verjuice to wash over everything. According to the amount of meat you have, get kidneys, chop them up very small and add them in, with sugar, and season it with salt properly; then set it to boil. Then, when it comes to the dresser, dole it out into fine dishes in a suitable manner.

Parmesan Fish Pies (*Tortres parmeysines de poyssons*: *On Cookery*, Recipe 40)
Now I, Chiquart, should like to instruct the person who is ordered to make the Parmesan Fish Pies that he should get tuna bellies, if he is in a place where he can get sea-fish, otherwise he should get all the more fresh-water fish, that is, big filets of carp, big eels and filets of big pike, and of that fish he should get enough for the quantity of pies he is ordered to make. Get candied raisins, prunes, figs, dates and pine-nuts, all of that in an amount appropriate for the quantity of those pies. Then, for those pies, this fish should be cut up, cleaned and washed, and set to cook properly; when it is fully cooked, take it out onto good clean tables or boards, and have all the bones carefully and completely removed so that not even the

smallest bone is left, and cut it all up into tiny pieces. The raisins mentioned above should be carefully seeded, the pine-nuts carefully cleaned, and the figs, prunes and dates chopped up to the size of small dice; when all this is done, everything but the fish should be fully washed in white wine, drained, and mixed in with the above fish. Besides this, you need, according to the quantity of the pies you have to make, parsley, marjoram and sage, and of each of these herbs an amount depending on its strength, that is, more parsley and less of the others; they should be well cleaned, washed and throughly chopped up, then mixed in with the above fish. This done, get good clear, clean, well clarified oil, and a good big clean pan which is set over a good bright fire, and put all of that into it; you should have a good helper with a good big clean spoon to stir that pan energetically. Get your good thick almond milk and strain it through the cloth, and a lot of starch, depending on the quantity of pies you have, and put it all in to bind it. Then mix your spices in with your fish, stirring constantly and vigorously in every part of the pan: white ginger, grains of paradise, a little pepper, enough saffron to give it colour, whole cloves, a great deal of sugar which has been ground into powder, and a reasonable amount of salt. Have your pastry chef make the shells nicely for the pies; when they are done, take the above-mentioned filling and put the right amount into each one. Then make sure you have a very great quantity of good fine slices of good eels which are perfectly cooked; when they have been cooked, put them to fry in good clean oil, and drain; when fried, remove their bones. Then on each pie put three or four pieces, one this way, the other that way, so they are not all together; then cover the pies and put them in the oven. When they are cooked, set them out in your dishes and go and serve them up.

Italian

Of all of the 'national' collections of food recipes, those written in Italian, and presumably representing the gastronomic and culinary customs of at least some of the Italian states, seem to offer the broadest spectrum of prepared dishes. This apparent variety in early Italian cookery may be due to the availability today of a greater number of medieval recipe collections than elsewhere across Europe. For some reason Italian grandees of the time seem to have wanted to have the culinary practice of their kitchens documented, and to have the resulting manuscript treatises copied and constantly amplified.[35]

---

[35] Five important Italian collections have been published: *Libro de la cocina*, Emilio Faccioli, *Arte della cucina. Libri di ricette, testi sopra lo scalco . . . dal XIV al XIX secolo*, 2 vols., Milan (Il Polifilo), 1966, I, pp.19–57 (183 recipes); *Libro per cuoco*, Faccioli, *op. cit.*, I, pp.59–105 (135 recipes); Maestro Martino, *Libro de arte coquinaria*, ed. Faccioli, *op. cit.*, I, pp.117–204 (268 recipes); and two collections by an *Anonimo meridionale* were published by Ingemar Boström in *Due libri di cucina*, Stockholm (Almqvist &

Whether the richness of late-medieval Italian cookery is real or not, it is true that virtually any dish found in another European collection may be found in an Italian collection, at least in its essence if not identified by the same name, and often earlier. One might be tempted to say that Italian recipes travelled almost as far as Italian merchants and tradesmen.

If there are any peculiar features in Italian cookery they may be related in part to the local availability of certain ingredients, such as citrus fruits, and in part to preferences for certain dishes, such as the *composta*.

Ravioli (*Ravioli*: Neapolitan Collection, Recipe 10)

Get a pound and a half of old cheese and a little fresh creamy cheese, and a pound of bacon[?] or of loin[?] of veal that should be well boiled, then chopped; get ground fragrant herbs, pepper, cloves, ginger and saffron, adding in a well ground breast of chicken; mix all of this well together; make a thin dough and wrap the mixture in it the size of a nut; set these ravioli to cook in the fat broth of a capon or of some other good meat, adding a little saffron, and let them boil for half an hour; then set them out in dishes, garnished with a mixture of grated cheese and good spices.

Garnished Turnips (*Rappe armate*: Neapolitan Collection, Recipe 27)

Cook the turnips under the coals, or else boil them whole, then cut them into big slices the width of a knife blade; get Parmesan cheese or some other good fat cheese, cut into slices as large as the turnip slices but thinner; and get sugar, pepper and mild spices mixed together; lay out these slices in a tort pan in layers – on the bottom the slices of cheese with good fresh butter on top, and then the slices of turnip, and so on from layer to layer always adding the spice mixture everywhere; you will cook it all in this pan, with a good deal of butter, for a quarter of an hour or more in the same way as a tort; this banquet dish is served after the others.

Wiksell), 1985 (146 and 65 recipes). There are, furthermore, several important collections which are not yet available in modern printed editions: *Dilicate vivande*: London, British Library, Ms Additional 18,165, folios 1r–20r (114 recipes); *Neapolitan Collection*, New York, Pierpont Morgan Library, Bühler 19, (219 recipes); *Wellcome Manuscript*, London, Wellcome Institute for the History of Medicine, Ms 211, folios 1r–146r (421 recipes). And, finally, four recipe collections that were written in Latin contain material that is certainly related to Italian practice: the *Tractatus de modo præparandi et condiendi omnia cibaria* and the *Liber de coquina*, ed. Marianne Mulon, 'Deux traités inédits d'art culinaire médiéval', *Bulletin Philologique et Historique (jusqu'à 1610) du Comité de Travaux historiques et scientifiques. Année 1968*, Paris (Bibliothèque Nationale), 1971, pp.280–295 (82 recipes) and 396–420 (172 recipes) respectively; Johannes Buckehen, *Registrum coquine*, ed. Bruno Laurioux, 'Le "Registre de cuisine" de Jean de Bockenheim, cuisinier du pape Martin V', *Mélanges de l'Ecole française de Rome*, 100 (1988), 709–60 (74 recipes); and Bartolomeo Sacchi (*alias* Platina, A.D. 1421–81), *De honesta voluptate*, ed. Mary Ella Milham, New York (Renaissance Society of America), 1995.

White Genestrata (*Genestrata biancha*: Neapolitan Collection, Recipe 39)

Get almonds, peel them and grind them up thoroughly and, when ground, strain them; put them in a pot with enough sugar; then make rice flour and mix it into the almond milk and set it to cook, stirring constantly; when it begins to thicken add in dates and pine-nuts and cook them; when you see it thickening, take it off the fire and set it on some warm cinders; then dish it up, putting sugar, rose-water and cinnamon on top.

Crusty Cheese, Bread, etc. (*Crostata de caso, pane, etc.*: Neapolitan Collection, Recipe 94)

Get bread, remove the crust, slice it thin and toast it on the fire to colour it, then coat the slices with fresh butter and put sugar and cinnamon on top, then slices of creamy cheese, then sugar and cinnamon; then put the slices in a tort pan on the coals with its lid on and coals on top; when the cheese has melted, serve it quickly.

Cameline Sauce (*Sapore gamelino*: Neapolitan Collection, Recipe 105)

Get raisins and grind them up as much as you can; get three or four ounces of almonds and grind them with the raisins, and two or three slices of toast soaked in red wine, and grind them together; then get a little red wine, must and verjuice, making it sweet or tart as you wish; strain all this, adding then a lot of cinnamon, and cloves and nutmegs.

White Tort (*A fare Torta biancha*: Neapolitan Collection, Recipe 125)

Get ten or twelve eggs, as you wish, beat them thoroughly; cut up a pound and a half of new cheese small, then grind it with a half pound of fine sugar, a half ounce of peeled ginger, a half pound of lard or butter, and a a *fogleta* of milk; then mix the milk, eggs, cheese, sugar, ginger and butter thoroughly together – and note that to make it whiter there should be fifteen egg whites; then make thin pastry on the bottom of the pan, put this mixture on it, and cook it slowly on a moderate fire; when it is almost done, give it a little colour on top with a stronger fire; when it looks done, take it out and put rose-water and sugar on top, and serve it.

Tartara Julatica (Neapolitan Collection, Recipe 133)

Get an ounce of good Parmesan cheese and grind it up well; get twenty eggs and beat them thoroughly, half a jug of milk, half an ounce of well ground white ginger, half a pound of good butter and half a pound of fine sugar, and mix everything together; then get a big pan and make the following pastry crust on its bottom: get grated bread, and first grease the pan with butter – if you do not like to put such a mixture as this on bread attached to the bottom of the pan, instead of bread get grated cheese or flour, and see that the pan is greased with good butter; then put in the mixture and cook it slowly; put a lot of sugar on top as if it were a marzipan, and rose-water; have it eaten hot with [?] the Catherina Fasanica.

Stuffed Eggs (*Ova piena*: Neapolitan Collection, Recipe 149)

Boil fresh eggs in water until they are quite hard; shell them carefully and cut them in half, and then lift out the yolk without breaking the white; of the yolks grind a part with a few raisins, a little old and new cheese, parsley, marjoram and finely chopped mint, adding in two egg whites with mild spices depending on the amount you are making; mix all of this together with saffron and fill up the hollows [left by] the yolks and fry it gently in good oil; see that cloves and a lot of cinnamon are in the filling; when fried, serve.

Stuffed Frittered Eggs (*Ova fritellate piene*: Neapolitan Collection, Recipe 157)

Make Frittered Eggs in the Florentine Fashion, as directed above, but not too cooked; then from one side remove and set aside all of the yolks one by one; get grated old cheese, mint, parsley, marjoram, raisins, pepper and four of the egg yolks – and more depending on the quantity you want to make; mix everything together and fill the eggs by the hole, and fry them again until it is likely the filling is cooked; take them out and garnish with verjuice or oranges with a little ginger, and serve.

Offelle (Neapolitan Collection, Recipe 159)

Get good soft cheese with little salt and grate it; get eggs, whole raisins, cinnamon, ginger and saffron, mix all this together and make this filling somewhat stiff; get a thin pastry dough as for lasagne and bind the filling in the dough like lasagne, making them large or small as you wish, yellowing the top; bake in an oven that is not too hot; they should not be overcooked.

Good Calisoni (Neapolitan Collection, Recipe 160)

Make a filling like the one I described for the Marzipan Tort among Lenten Dishes; mix up a dough with sugar and rose-water and spread it out as if you were making ravioli; wrap the mixture in this dough, making [the *Calisoni*] as large or small as you wish.

Papal Tort (*Torta papale*: Neapolitan Collection, Recipe 182)

Get a pound and a half of soft-textured sturgeon or a good pike, well cooked by boiling, and be careful not to leave any bones, then grind it up thoroughly; when ground, take it out of the mortar, get a half pound of almonds and a few pine-nuts and grind them together; then get a half pound of rice well cooked in almond milk and grind it with the above; add in a pound of sugar, half an ounce of ginger, a little cinnamon, salt, saffron and a beaker of pike eggs, and strain everything; make a crust in the pan as I directed above, putting the mixture on top of it.

Lemonee of Capons or Pullasters (*Lumonia di Chapponcielli e di Pollastri: Delicate vivande*, Recipe 26)

For twelve persons, get six little capons or six large pullasters; get two ounces of fine spices and three pounds. of almonds, three ounces of sugar, 25 dates, 12 juicy [bitter] oranges, and half a pound of prunes; take your poultry and set it to boil; when it is cooked, get a pound of rendered, strained lard [*istrutto e cholato*] and sautee the poultry in it; split the oranges in four and set them to sautee with the poultry; when both are sauteed, grind the spices and sugar; wash the almonds in the juice [*ghuscio*], grind them and temper them with the lean, filtered broth from the poultry and set this almond milk to boil in a pot by itself; as it boils, first add in some of the spices, then the prunes, washed, thirdly the dates, split in two and washed, fourthly, moistened saffron; when all this has boiled well, put in the poultry and the oranges; make it be thick and spicy and sweet; the poultry is given to the carvers and the sauce is set out in bowls. It you wish to make more or less of this dish, take more or less of all these ingredients in the same proportions.

Elderflower Dish in a Pot (*Sanbuchata in Pentola: Delicate vivande*, Recipe 81)

To be served in bowls to twelve persons: get a pot of goat or ewe's milk, and get a pound of rice, one and a half pounds of lard, 4 ounces of sugar, and have mature elderflowers; when you have prepared these things, set the strained milk to boil; the rice should be ground and, when the milk boils, put this rice flour into it and the elderflowers, the rendered, strained lard, some sugar and moistened saffron; this dish should be yellow, thick and sweet, and should have a flavour of elderflowers; when you wish to make it, do it thus; garnish the bowls with sugar.

Summer Compote of Pears (*Chomposte da state di pere: Delicate vivande*, Recipe 83)

Get Ruggine pears or some other sort of pears that are hard and good enough, and cook them a little; get carrots and parsley leaves, celery hearts [*chorone d'appio*] and parsnips [*pastricciani*], and if you cannot get all of these, get whatever you can; cook them enough; get dates and prunes – that is, *susine*, whether these are bitter or dry – and cook them a little; when everything is cooked, let it cool; get mustard seed, ground and moistened in good white wine with which is mixed a little vinegar, and add in honey, sugar, anise and beaten fennel, and a little horseradish; then put the pears and everything else you have cooked in the pot or in some other container in which you wish to keep them; and make a layer, then cover it with that mixture you have made, and so, layer by layer, put in everything; then keep it covered and it will turn out good.

Catalan Sops (*Suppa a la catelanesca*: Wellcome Ms., Recipe 260)

Get liver of some variety and set it to boil; when it is well cooked, grind it up; get breadcrumbs and soak them in grease, grind them with the liver and mix in eggs; when everything is mixed together, distemper it with grease and put it through the strainer, and into a pot with saffron, cinnamon, pepper, ginger and cloves, and there should be a good lot of cinnamon; add in a little sugar; set it to boil only when about to eat; then get slices of fine bread soaked in good grease – and do this only when the diners are ready; then set out as much of these soaked bread slices as you think reasonable in small plates, and pour the preparation over the bread – this bread should be quite firm; sprinkle cinnamon on top. These are extremely good sops.

Hispanic

During the late Middle Ages – to be a little more precise during three or four centuries before the year of the 'Reconquest', 1492 – the Iberian Peninsula was shared between several 'Latinate' or 'European' principalities and several Arabic ones. A more accurate distinction between the two peoples might be along religious lines: in the north and along the Atlantic coast the Christian kingdoms managed to reestablish themselves; the centre and south remained Islamic, though with ever-diminishing tenure. Historians have demonstrated that there was considerable contact and exchange along the frontier that ostensibly separated the two cultures, and that in many respects – particularly intellectual – the frontier was largely permeable. Until now, however, few scholars have investigated the food habits of Muslim Spain, and no detailed picture has been drawn of Arab cuisine during the time of their presence in the peninsula. For our purposes little has been done except on a piecemeal basis to demonstrate culinary relations between the Christian and Islamic domains in the former Roman province of Iberia.[36]

---

[36] Maxime Rodinson wrote briefly of 'Les influences de la civilisation musulmane sur la civilisation européenne médiévale dans les domaines de la consommation et de la distraction: l'alimentation', in *Atti del Convegno Internazionale della Accademia Nazionale dei Lincei* (April, 1969), Rome (Accademia Nazionale dei Lincei), 1971, pp.479–99; the same author indicated several instances of similarities in Arab and Romance dish-names. Similarly, C. Anne Wilson, essayed 'The Saracen Connection: Arab Cuisine and the Mediæval West', *Petits Propos Culinaires*, 7 (1981), pp.13–22 and 8 (1981), pp.19–27; she identifies several features of Arab cookery (frying before boiling, the colours white and green, yellow and red, almonds, endoring, citrus fruits, spices, rose-water, and so forth) and in effect suggests that their presence in Western cookery can be explained only by their presence in the other. The article of Toby Peterson, 'The Arab influence on western European cooking', *Journal of Medieval History*, 6 (1980), pp.317–341, tends also to be a little too speculative and generalizing in its conclusions. Other scholarly work, such as that of Charles Perry and Claudia Roden on medieval Arabic cookbooks, and A.J. Arberry, 'A Baghdad Cookery-Book', *Islamic Culture*, 13 (1939), pp.21–47 and 189–214, may imply certain connections with

For the cookery in the Christian territory of the Iberian Peninsula we may consult published works in Catalan and in Portuguese.[37] In part, and in very general terms, what these hispanic recipes show is a large reliance upon chicken, large and small game animals, almonds, onions and (bitter) oranges. The *Libre de sent soví* in particular offers a very broad and rich selection of dishes.

Roast Stuffed Chicken (*Con se ffercexen capons e gualines en ast ab fformatge: Libre de sent soví*, Recipe 8)

If you wish to stuff capons or chickens on a spit with cheese, you do it thus: first you remove the viscera, wash it, parboil it, and chop it up with a little salt pork marbled with fat; when chopped add in spices, saffron and eggs and mix it all together; also mix in a little grated cheese, and when the stuffing is all mixed, add in ground salt; and stuff the capons or chickens between the flesh and the skin, in the belly and between flesh and skin in the legs and wings; bind the fowl with a tough cord, mount them on the spit and roast them. The fowl are served with the sauce for chickens, or for geese, or for capons, or with *Puriola*.

Puriola (*Con se deuen donar gualines en ast ab puriola: Libre de sent soví*, Recipe 72)

If you wish to serve spit-roast chickens with Puriola, you do thus: get thinly sliced and sauteed onions, pepper and cooked liver, grind everything, with a little salt, and moisten with cold water; as the chickens are roasting, have the Puriola in a pan beneath to catch the drippings; when the chickens are done, put the Puriola into bowls and serve it together with them.

Asparagus in a Sauce (*Con se deuen aperellar espàrechs ab salsa: Libre de sent soví*, Recipe 118)

If you wish to prepare asparagus with sauce, you do thus: get the tender part of asparagus and boil it well; when cooked, squeeze out the moisture, chop it up and then sautee it in a pan with a lot of [olive] oil; cut up an onion finely and sautee it; and when it the asparagus and onion are almost done frying together, add in a little wine syrup or honey. The sauce is made thus· get toast that has soaked in vinegar and good spices, and add a little hot water or bouillon; when the asparagus has fried, add in the sauce

European cookery. A thoroughgoing evaluation of any influences, in both directions, is enormously difficult, and still to be undertaken.

[37] Rudolf Grewe, *Libre de sent soví (Receptari de cuina)*, Barcelona (Barcino), 1979 (220 recipes; A.D. 1324); Veronika Leimgruber, *Mestre Robert, Libre del coch. Tractat de cuina medieval*, Barcelona (Curial), 1982 (229 recipes; beginning of the sixteenth century); Elizabeth Thompson Newman, *A Critical Edition of an Early Portuguese Cookbook*, Ph.D. Thesis, University of North Carolina, 1964 (67 recipes; end of the fifteenth century).

and boil it all together; stir constantly until it is off the fire and has stopped boiling.

Mushroom Sauce (Con se fa salsa a bolets: Libre de sent soví, 145)

If you wish to make a Mushroom Sauce, parboil them well, and when parboiled, drain them and fry them in [olive] oil. Then make up this sauce: get onions, parsley and coriander, grind them, and distemper them with spices, vinegar and a little water; slice the mushrooms and when they have fried put them with that sauce. Or else cook mushrooms on hot coals and serve them with salt and oil.

Germanic

German culinary practices during the late Middle Ages have been transmitted to modern times within something in the order of sixty-five manuscript recipe collections. Relative to the extant corpus of recipe collections representing other 'national' usages, what we possess for the German states, from the Lowlands down to the south of modern Germany, is almost an *embarras de richesses*. The problem in quite practical terms is that though this comparatively large quantity in German amounts to roughly one-third of the grand total of all existing medieval collections, these German recipes and medieval German cookery in general have, sadly, received only comparatively slight attention from modern scholars.[38]

It is a little difficult to characterize German cookery of the late Middle Ages. Only five of these collections have been published and studied: *Das Buch von guter Spise*,[39] *Ein Büchlein von guter Speise*,[40] *Das Kochbuch Meister Eberhards*,[41] *Ein mittelniederdeutsches Kochbuch*, the editor's identification of an untitled recipe collection,[42] and the (again, untitled) collection in the manuscript Basel, Universitätsbibliothek, D II:30;[43] a further collection of recipes in German, whose beginning and title are missing in the manuscript, has kindly been transcribed and translated for the author by Dr Melitta

---

[38] One of the very few attempts to study late-medieval German cookery is found, with difficulty, in an unpublished academic thesis: Alix Prentki, *Les traités culinaires du sud de l'Allemagne à la fin du moyen-âge*, Ecole des Hautes Etudes en Sciences Sociales, Paris, 1985. It seems likely that new discoveries of medieval recipe manuscripts remain to be made nowdays only in Germany and in the Hispanic peninsula.

[39] Hans Hajek, *Daz Buoch von guoter Spize. Aus der Würzburg-Münchener Handschrift*, Berlin (Erich Schmidt), 1958; 96 recipes.

[40] Anton Birlinger, 'Ein allemannischen Büchlein von guter Speise', *Sitzungsberichts der königl. bayer. Akademie der Wissenschaften zu München*, II (1865), 171–206; 57 + 25 recipes.

[41] Anita Feyl, 'Das Kochbuch des Eberhard von Landshut (erste Hälfe des 15. Jhs.)', *Ostbairischen Grenzmarken*, 5 (1961), 352–66; 24 recipes.

[42] Hans Wiswe, 'Ein mittelniederdeutsches Kochbuch des 15. Jahrhunderts', *Braunschweigisches Jahrbuch*, 37 (1956), 19–55.

[43] This was edited by Alix Prentki in the thesis referred to above.

Weiss-Adamson.[44] To these might perhaps be added a Dutch *Keukenboek*.[45] What these available German recipes seem to show us is a tradition which shares a good number of dishes with the rest of European cookery, but which nevertheless has a few distinct traits. One of these peculiarities is a fondness for pastry, often deep fried in lard; another is a frequent incorporation of fruits in a dish; a third might be a culinary interest in animal viscera, especially intestines and lungs.

It is strange to see already in the Middle Ages certain signs of prejudice against German food on the part of French writers. The *Menagier de Paris* (178), for instance, writes with some disdain that Germans have the peculiar custom of cooking their carp twice as long as the French. The fourteenth-century French bigot Eustache Deschamps (c.1340–c.1406) consistently decries Germanic food habits that have been inflicted upon him during his travels in the Lowlands and beyond the Rhine. In particular he is thoroughly disgusted with the ubiquitous German use of mustard: *everything*, he protests, is smothered in mustard – any roast, mutton, boar, hare, rabbit, bustard, herring, carp, boiled pike, sole, any fresh-water fish or sea-fish! Furthermore, everywhere Deschamps went in Flanders or Bohemia he was assailed by by the sickening, all-pervasive stench of beer!

Any reader who wishes is free to try a gob of mustard on any of the following:

An Excellent Dish (*Ein Kluge Spise: Buch von guter Spise*, Recipe 6)
Take brains and flour and apples and eggs and mix that together with spices and put it on a spit and grill it evenly and serve it. This is called Grilled Brains [*Hirne Gebraten*]. You do the same with lung which you boil first.

Morels (*Der Mawrochen will Machen*: Bressanone, folio 232v)
He who wants to make Morels, let him take a calf's lung and boil it well and then chop it small, and sprinkle on it a pinch of flour and break one or more raw eggs on it to moisten it; for this dish make wooden moulds a little bigger than a finger in both width and length, pointed like a cone on each side; fill the mould as well as you can with the [chopped] lung so that it takes the shape of the mould, then [remove from the mould]; put the Morels into hot lard and let them fry until they turn brown, then remove them from the pan and cut them in two; make a filling with good herbs, made yellow, and as many grapes as you want to have, and stuff the Morels until they get full; then stick them on a little spit and place them

[44] The series of forty-four recipes occupies twelve pages in the manuscript Bressanone (Brixen, Italy), Biblioteca del Seminario Maggiore, 125 (J.5), folios 230r–36v.
[45] *Keukenboek uitgegeven naar een Hs. der vijftiende eeuw.* [Gand, Bibliothèque universitaire, MS 1035], ed. Constant Antoine Serrure, Gand (Annoot-Braeckman), 1872. This collection contains 62 recipes in two series.

by the fire when you are ready to serve them; then they are ready, and send them to the table on the spits in a bowl.

Untitled (Bressanone, folio 233v)

Make three sheets [of dough], green, red and white; then get a little of the best venison you can, boil it, [chop it up,] season it, including grapes in the mixture; take the meat and spread it on the pastry to their full width, then roll them up like a rolled-up letter, each sheet of dough separately and sealed like a turnover; and bake it in lard.

Baked Czoten (Czoten Gepachen: Bressanone, folio 234v)

Take a wooden cooking spoon full of milk and four eggs in a lord's bowl as they enjoy it; get flour so that the mixture becomes as thick as a basting dough, then season it well and make it yellow; put lard of the amount of a walnut into a pan, let it melt and pour the batter into the pan and let it cook slowly ['quite cool'] into a cake; turn it in the pan as well as you can; then, when it is well cooked, and not burnt either, take it and dump it onto a board and cut it up into finger-sized pieces in width and length; then deep fry it in lard and bake it as for any other cake; garnish it with sugar if you have any; then it is done.

Baked Apples (Pachen Oppheln: Bressanone, folio 236r)

Get four apples in a lord's bowl and slice them as thinly as you can; then get four regell pears with an apple and chop them up, season this with spices and grapes and so make a good filling, which should be yellow; then get a piece of wood like a spindle with a knob at one end, push one of the slices [of apple] on it as far as the little knob, then coat this with the mixture as thick as the slice itself, and [continue to] push on slices one after the other with filling in between as much as you want to have so that it will fit into a pan afterwards; then make a dough for it, with two eggs and water, as thick as strauben dough, put the stick with the apple slices and filling on it, and wrap the dough around it; put this in a pan with hot lard and let it bake slowly ['quite cool'] until it turns brown, then take it out and pull out the stick by the little knob; then it is ready.

A Good Dish (Ein gut Spise: Buch von guter Spise, Recipe 51)

Roast a chicken barded with bacon, then cut eight slices of Armeritlere [a preparation of battered slices of bread, fried] and fry them not too dry in lard; peel sour apples, slice them thick, remove the seeds, and fry them a little in lard; then make a big flat dough out of eggs so as to cover the bottom of the whole pan, add spice powder; make the first layer of apples, then the Armeritlere, then the chicken cut up in very small pieces, and sprinkle some spice powder on top of each layer; make a sauce of wine and honey, and don't spice it too hot; fold the crust of dough together and put a bowl over it and turn the pan upside down; cut a little window on the top and pour in the sauce, and serve it; these are called Greek Chickens (*Hunre von Kriechen*).

Heathen Peas (*Heidenische Erweiz: Buch von guter Spise*, Recipe 63)
If you want to make Bohemian Peas (*Behemmische Erweiz*), take almonds and pound them quite fine and mix them with honey one third the amount of almonds, and well mixed with good herbs and spices, the best the cook has; the dish is served cold or warm.

A Good Composed Dish (*Ein Gut Fulle: Buch von guter Spise*, Recipe 83)
Conkavelit is made of cherries, the sour cherries that are called *wiseln*; get these and make a good milk out of almonds, boil the cherries well with wine and with their own juice and press them through a sieve cloth and then pour them into the almond milk; boil this until it is done, with rice flour stirred into it and enough lard added, and enough spices, too; garnish with sugar, and don't oversalt.

TEN

Conclusion: the Cook, the Cookery and the Food

The Medieval Cook: his Training, his Place and his Craft

Professional training

In the late Middle Ages the professional knowledge and skills that a cook had to have in order to exercise his craft publicly were acquired by means of the apprenticeship system. As a professional cook he had to belong to the appropriate guild; his progress through the ranks of his profession, from apprentice to journeyman and eventually to Master, as well as his daily work as a cook, had to conform to rules that governed all of the professional activities of the members of his guild.

Among the very broad range of craft and trade guilds that existed in Paris around 1268, the *Livre des métiers* of Etienne Boileau included those statutes that defined the Cooks' Guild.[1] The significant elements of these statutes are summarized here. The first paragraph sets out what a cook properly may do; in a sense it circumscribes the legitimate activities of any member of the build.

§1. Let any person who wishes to open a shop or shop window in order to sell cooked foods know how to dress every sort of meat that is common and useful to people and that is proper for that person to sell.

§2. No one may take on a journeyman [*varlet*] into the craft unless this latter have been apprenticed to the craft for two years, or unless he be the son of a Master and know something of the craft. Should the son of a Master know nothing of handling the craft's business, let him pay the costs of maintaining one of the craft's workers who is an expert in it, until the time that

[1] The work of Boileau, a Provost of Paris, was edited by René de Lespinasse and François Bonnardot, Paris (Imprimerie Nationale), 1879; repr. Geneva (Slatkine), 1980. The rules applying to the craft of Cooks are found in Title LXIX, pp.145–47 of this edition; assimilated with the Cooks in these statutes are Goose-Roasters.

the Master's son develop a suitable ability in the craft as directed by its Masters.

§3. For each apprentice taken on, his Master will pay to the King and the Guild Masters ten *sous*.

§4. Only one apprentice may be taken on at a time.

§§8 & 11. No one may boil or roast geese, veal, lamb, kid or piglets . . . or beef, mutton or pork unless the meat is good and proper for selling and eating, and unless its marrow is good.

§9. Cooked meat may be kept only three days for buying or selling, unless it is adequately salted.

§§10 & 13. Sausages may be made only from pork and only from healthy meat; . . . no one in the craft may sell blood sausage, for it is a dangerous meat.[2]

§12. All meat sold by cooks must be well and properly cooked, salted and prepared; otherwise this meat may be condemned to being burnt.

§14. One third of all fines levied and that are paid to the Masters of the Guild shall be applied to sustaining the indigent elderly members of the craft who have fallen on hard times owing to their work or to old age.[3]

§§15 & 16. Should anyone be in front of a Cook's stall or window in order to bargain or purchase cooked foods, no other Cook shall call to him before he has turned away on his own from the stall or window; no one shall decry another's meat, if it is good.

For every infraction of these statutes, the fines to be levied are specifically stipulated. Even in the case covered by §12, where the offending meat has already been seized and consigned to destruction by fire, the fine of ten *sous* must still be paid, six *sous* to the King and four *sous* to the Sworn Masters (*les jurés*) of the Guild.

In England, according to John Stow, cooks were able to incorporate themselves professionally only in the later years of the fifteenth century.

Without Aldersgate, on the east side of Aldersgate street, is the Cookes hall: which Cookes (or Pastelars) were admitted to be a Company, and to have a Maister & Wardens in the 22 of Edward the 4 [i.e., 1482 or 1483].[4]

Such a late civic recognition of the craft is difficult to explain. In several places Stow indicates that the activities of cooks were indeed well established in fifteenth-century London, where cooks tended as a natural matter of course to associate with butchers.

---

[2] . . . *Car c'est perilleuse viande.*

[3] . . . *Soient pour soustenir les povres vielles gens dudit mestier qui seront decheuz par fait de marchandise ou de viellece.*

[4] *A Survey of London*, ed. C.L. Kingsford, Oxford (Clarendon), 1971; Vol. I, p.309.

> The streete of Eastcheape is so called of the Market there kept . . . .
> This Eastcheape is now a flesh Market of Butchers there dwelling, on
> both sides of the streete, it had sometime also Cookes mixed amongst
> the Butchers, and such other as solde victuals readie dressed of all sorts.
> For of olde time when friends did meet, and were disposed to be merrie,
> they went not to dine and suppe in Taverns, but to the Cookes, where
> they called for meate what them liked, which they alwayes found ready
> dressed at a reasonable rate . . .[5]

And for a while the work of cooks was apparently well appreciated by the
public as a distinct craft: another passage in Stow[6] shows the sixteenth-
century gazetteer lamenting a growing fusion among the food specialists.

> Fitzstephen in the raigne of Henrie the 2 writeth that upon the rivers
> [Walbrooke] side betweene the wine in ships, and the wine to be sold in
> Taverns, was a common cookerie or Cookes row[7] . . .: whereby it
> appeareth that in those dayes (and till of late time) every man lived
> by his professed trade, not any one interrupting another. The cookes
> dressed meate, and sold no wine, and the Taverner sold wine, but
> dressed no meate for sale, &c.

The passage of time did indeed tend to confound the cook's craft with those
of the tavern-keeper, sauce-maker and pastry-cook. It was natural, on the
one hand, that the cook's talents should be more closely engaged by the
hospitality industry, where the provision of prepared food *and* drink seemed
integral with the provision of lodging; and, on the other, that the various
means of preparing all foodstuffs, should include the handling of meats,
sauces and pasties.

Little documentation exists in which the Cooks' Guilds of medieval
Europe, and their vicissitudes or those of their members, are mentioned.
Guilds existed in large measure in order to regulate competition; one may be
justified in suspecting that there was little difficulty in the matter of irregular
competition among professional cooks, at least compared with the on-going
problems that appear to have troubled other trade and craft guilds in
European towns of the fourteenth and fifteenth centuries.

Whether or not women may have exercised the craft of Cook remains as
yet a moot question. Certainly there is much evidence to the effect that
women were successful in trades that would seem to be physically very
demanding.[8] Yet there seems to be no explicit mention anywhere of female

---

[5] *Ibid.*, I, pp.216–17.

[6] *Ibid.*, I, p.238.

[7] The editor, Kingsford (in Vol. II, p.322), notes that the FitzStephen in question, Stow's
source here, wrote the phrase *publica coquina*: 'public cookery' in his *Descriptio
Londoniæ*.

[8] Especially concerning the crafts of Master Butcher, Pancake-Baker and Brewer, Erika
Uitz writes, 'From the end of the thirteenth century to the second half of the fifteenth

professional cook. Women frequently were accepted as members of a guild of which their deceased husbands were members, and were allowed to continue to exercise his trade. But Boileau's statutes from the middle of the thirteenth century do not refer to this possibility for professional Cooks; and, furthermore, §2 recognizes only the *sons*[9] of a Master as being entitled to special privileges upon entering the craft.

What was the status of a professional cook in his society? In a classification by craft the average annual income of Genoese journeymen, between the years 1230 and 1256, shows the wages for a cook to be one of the least well remunerated trades.[10] The work of which a cook was capable seems to have been esteemed by the general public slightly more than that of a wood-lathe operator and marginally less than that of a mule driver. Though the decades for which these figures are available precede the beginning of our period by a century, they do indicate that there was probably no overwhelming incentive for a young lad of ambition to seek to train as a cook and to devote his life to the craft.

The master cook could be self-employed, perhaps roasting meats and selling them to the public at large, he might work for another Master, or he might enter the employ of a wealthy bourgeois or a noble. It was likely only by securing this last employment that the master cook stood any chance at all of enjoying any sort of status.

The Household

The act of eating in public was recognized from time immemorial as a significant event during which both the person offering food and the person at his or her table who was accepting it demonstrated to the world their respective sense of worth and of dignity. The acts of offering and of receiving food demonstrated, in the first place, that the food represented a worthy part of the offerer's considerable estate, and, in the second place, that the recipient was himself or herself worthy of such a flattering offer. Because the event had such relative importance in the life of an aristocrat or an affluent

century independent female activity in the crafts became widely established in a number of western and central European maritime trade and export centres – the large towns of northern France, Flanders, northern Italy, the Rhine, southern and central Germany, Austria, Switzerland, and, to a lesser extent, in Poland and Bohemia'. *Women in the Medieval Town*, London (Barrie & Jenkins), 1988, p.54. See especially pp.57ff.

[9] The word in the document is *filz* rather than *enfanz*.

[10] Steven A. Epstein, *Wage Labour and Guilds in Medieval Europe*, Chapel Hill and London (University of North Carolina Press), 1991, p.148. The income table published by Epstein shows the following annual amounts: Smith, £15.15; Weaver, £15; Metalworker, £11; Apothecary, £10; Cobbler, £5; Muleteer, £3.18; Cook, £3.12; Turner, £3.

bourgeois in the Middle Ages, it was naturally bound round about with all sorts of formal ceremonial. The more an individual could afford to employ persons to be responsible for various ceremonial elements connected with serving, the more complex the procedures became that were regularly observed. At the bottom of the scale of household opulence would be the bourgeois whose cook, male or perhaps female, dished out and served whatever he or she produced, alone or with minimal assistance, in the kitchen. At the upper end of the social hierarchy, a battery of servants – many of them salaried retainers but a good number of whom were themselves noble – performed a multitude of specific duties before, during and after any meal served in the lord's hall.

At its most developed, dining ceremonial in the late Middle Ages affords us a chance to appreciate an aspect of the systematic 'medieval' mind. The methodological problem of transferring the stew or sops from the kitchen pot to the master's mouth was partly a matter of efficiency, partly one of ostentation, but partly, too, one of security. The prince insisted that the diverse phases of his meal be handled dependably and in an orderly way: the setting up of board and bench, clean tablecloths, saltboat, platters and other silverware, salt, cutlery, dishware, table bread and trenchers, the summoning to table, the washing of hands, the actual serving of prepared dishes and wine, wine replenishing, clearing-away away after every 'course' of dishes, and the sweeping of table scraps into the alms baskets intended for the poor.

In wealthy households the organization devoted to the preparing and serving of food was the most complex of any in the entire house. To ensure that everything related to meals was provided as it should be, and happened when it should happen, responsibility was divided among a corps of many individuals, within which corps a hierarchy of authority was firmly established. The person reponsible for the saltboat was not the person who was responsible for the salt, but both were directed by the same individual; the person who was charged with bearing the platters from the kitchen might not be the person who ultimately placed them in front of the prince, but each of their superiors probably answered for *their* obligations to the same supervisor. This scheme of specialized duties and liabilities, operating under a firm chain of authority, was not original to, nor unique in, the Middle Ages. But its logic was eminently clear to everyone who worked at any level for the welfare of a single medieval master, and was absolutely necessary in order to maintain order and limit waste or theft in any large, wealthy medieval household. Each supervisor could guarantee that the responsibilities of each of his underlings did not exceed his competence; each servant could devote himself to delivering the best possible service without fail. The rationality of the system had at its base something that surely sprang from the scholastic mind. Modern business would approve the organizational checks and balances.

As well as upon efficiency, the prince insisted upon elegance when he was served. The word 'courtesy' derives from the French word *courtoisie* and defines the manner of behaviour proper at court. There is perhaps no word across all of the domains of medieval Europe that has a more common acceptation, no matter what form the word took in the various languages and dialects: *courtoisie*, *courtliness*, *cortesia*, *höveschheit*. All of the variations of the word referred to manners and to those qualities that distinguished the uppermost class from the masses of people who definitely were not part of it. In their public activities, aristocrats – of any period but certainly in the Middle Ages – strove to display conspicuously that they *were* indeed superior. As we saw above in Chapter 7 concerning table manners, nobility breeds refinement, and this refinement must necessarily be reflected in the way in which one walks, talks or eats. Graciousness informs the manner of dining and the manner in which the aristocrat should eat. And so the medieval aristocrat insisted that his cook prepare dishes whose very appearance incorporated the spirit of excellence that his master embodied: the pie emblazoned with his master's coat-of-arms, or the entremets of a meat-paste castle displaying a chivalric knight, declared the master's supereminence to the world. Any refinement in the service that was provided him further confirmed the prince's dignity. His class demanded that this service flatter both himself and his class. To elicit the most flattering behaviour from all of his servants, regulations carefully outlined the rights and privileges which were in turn *their* due.

The chief cook in a noble household in the Middle Ages was not the ultimate authority in matters of food, and what went on in his kitchen was by no means determined by him alone. The kitchen was merely one element in the household's operation, and the cook was just another employee, albeit one with specialized knowledge, abilities and, above all, responsibilities.

The household of the late-medieval aristocracy was a complex organization. Primary control of its diverse parts was exercised through a system which required a continual rendering of accounts. In a Financial Office a couple of dozen individuals gathered records on all disbursements, even the most petty, by the various divisions within the household; in turn the Office supplied information on budgets, awarded contracts for supplies periodically, and rendered summaries of monetary income and outgo. Because certain divisions customarily handled quite significant sums, the role of the exchequer in a large household, that of a count or a duke for instance, or of a very wealthy merchant, took on paramount importance not only in ensuring an efficient day-to-day operation of that household but in safeguarding sound financial health over the longer term.

Responsibility for the operation of a ducal household was hierarchical.[11] The prince appointed a Grand Master of the Household. The ambit of the

---

[11] We are very fortunate to possess a detailed outline of the functionaries and their duties

Grand Master's authority was particularly the operation of the Duke's court, but he was entitled as well to sit on the Justice Council (presided over by the Duke's Chancellor) and on the Military Council. While the First Chamberlain, a noble, exercised supreme authority directly under the Duke – rather like his lieutenant or vicar – his was largely a ceremonial position. The Grand Master of the Household, however, was the chief executive officer of the Duke, the working chief. In his work he was assisted by a gamut of subordinates and underlings whose responsibilities were narrowly specialized. His most public functions were, one the one hand, to arrange receptions of visiting dignitaries, and on the other to see that the Duke's food was brought to his table and set out properly before him. With his chief assistant, the First Master of the Household, and four other assistants, called simply Masters of the Household, he managed the policy, the ceremonial and the accounts of the whole house. For this once a day he called a council of all of his assistants, and other persons of lesser responsibility; there they reviewed all expense accounts of the previous day. Though concerned primarily with examining expenditures, this council had as well the task of hearing grievances from any member of the household staff, of investigating charges of improprieties or malfeasance, and of executing summary justice in all affairs within three days. From a judgement of this domestic tribunal there was no appeal. An Accounting Office also operated under the direction of the Grand Master: it consisted of the Master of the Treasury, Comptroller and two office clerks. This Office identified and recorded two sorts of expenses, those having to do with supplies and those related to wages; the Comptroller visited each of the divisions of the household in order to verify, *in situ*, that claimed expenses were real; the clerks seem to have been engaged endlessly in writing up *daily* accounts for each division and individually for the entire personnel of the house. The business of the court was so rigorously bound by auditing checks that virtually everything had to be accounted for, literally: anyone could have a new candle for his or her work, for example, only by turning in the stump of an old one!

Four Butlers (*Sommelliers*) served the Duke in his chamber, and were assisted in this service by 16 Squires. Six physicians were 'on staff', as were four surgeons. Forty Chamber Valets included such crafts and trades as

in a household of the mid-fifteenth century. In his *Mémoires*, Olivier de la Marche sketched what amounts to a medieval organizational chart. As Maître d'Hôtel and Capitaine des Gardes of Charles the Bold, Duke of Burgundy, Olivier de la Marche had first-hand functional knowledge of the whole operation of a particularly grand household. Henri Beaune and J. d'Arbaumont, *Mémoires d'Olivier de la Marche*, 4 vols., Paris (Renouard), 1888. In England, John Russell, Usher and Marshal to Humphrey, Duke of Gloucester, has left us his *Boke of Nurture* (c.1440) in which the respective functions of members of the Duke's household are described: see Frederick J. Furnivall, ed. *Early English Meals and Manners*, London (Oxford University Press), 1868, pp.1–83. On the organization of royal servitors in England, see A.R. Myers, ed., *The Household of Edward IV*, Manchester (Manchester University Press), 1959.

barbers, hosiers, tailors, seamsters, furriers, cordwainers and painters/artists; a Lodging Master (*Fourrier*) had as principal duty the daily shaking out of the Duke's feather mattress and pillow. A Keeper of the Jewels – holding, as one may imagine, the fullest trust of the Duke – looked after all of the Duchy's gold bullion, reserve cash, jewels, gold and silver plate and vessels, costly chapel hangings, ornaments and treasure; in this work the Keeper had an assistant. Two Spicers (with two assistants), dispensed any and all medicines directly to the Duke; they composed the spiced wine known as hipocras, and on ceremonial occasions one or the other of them enjoyed the privilege of tendering the comfit box of spiced candies (*dragées*) to the Duke at table. Though in a real sense the Spicers were pharmacists, they had to maintain a supply of spices adequate in the first instance to the demands of the kitchen; but according to Olivier de la Marche, it was the cook who was responsible for rendering accounts ('in conscience and at his discretion') for all those spices, including sugar, purchased for any household use.

Which brings us a little closer to the kitchen. Yet in the division of food preparation and serving, the kitchen was nominally only one of four Offices dedicated to the service of the 'body' and 'mouth' of the Duke in this respect. These four Offices were the Pantry, the Buttery[12] (or *Eschansonerie*), the Carvery, and the Kitchen proper. In the Burgundian household *each* of the first three Offices had a chief with fifty (!) assistants. As well, under the ægis of the Chief Pantler a wide variety of functionaries served the house; these included the Saucer, eight valet bakers, two Hall Ushers (who functioned almost as Sergeants-at-Arms), a Bread Bearer, a Waferer, a Linen Keeper and a Launderer. The Chief Butler (or 'Cup-Bearer') directed the activities of a Porter (*Sommellier*) affected to his office, two assistants, two Barrelers and a Cellar Porter. The Carver was assisted merely by his fifty Assistant Carvers.

And finally to the Kitchen. Two Kitchen Clerks were responsible for maintaining order in the kitchen, and for all expenses, for the daily provisioning of foodstuffs, and for the periodic granting of contracts for kitchen supplies. Three cooks had immediate charge of the kitchen work of preparing food for the Duke's table, for that of his guests and for his chamber. Of these three, one was Master, the Chief Cook, and Olivier de la Marche evokes his authority in quaint vignette fashion:

> The Cook orders, regulates and is obeyed in his Kitchen; he should have a chair between the buffet and the fireplace to sit on and rest if necessary; the chair should be so placed that he can see and survey everything that is being done in the Kitchen; he should have in his hand a large wooden spoon which has a double function: one, to test

---

[12] The name of this old office, and its chief officer, the Butler, derive from the bottles (of wine, cider or ale) which were their responsibility. The names Pantry and Pantler derive similarly from the other fundamental food, bread or *panem, pain*.

pottages and brouets, and the other, to chase the children out of the Kitchen, to make them work, striking them if necessary.

Everyone whose appointment at court included an acknowledgement that he could eat at the Duke's 'board' (though he might or might not receive a room at the Duke's expense – the physicians, for instance, enjoyed board without room) benefitted directly or indirectly from the labours of these three cooks. Twenty-five specialists worked immediately under the orders of the cooks, along with a small number of department heads. These latter comprised a Roaster (and helper), a Pottager (and helper), and a Larderer (or Keeper of the Foodstuffs: pork or *lard*, salted, was a very common preserved foodstuff, so that the 'larder' came to designate the place where all preserved food was stored). There were also, as one may imagine, a large number of non-professional workers: fire-tenders (called Blowers or *Souffleurs* by Olivier de la Marche), Fuelers who hauled wood, peat and coal, Potters who scrubbed and drew water, door-keepers who guarded the valuable stocks of foodstuffs from pilferage. Perhaps the most important and the most unsung of the kitchen help were the scullions, unpaid apprentices who performed such menial and inglorious tasks as cleaning fish and turning spits. According to Olivier de la Marche they were designated by the delightful term '*galopins*'; this term evokes much of the lively spirit which alone could have allowed these youths to survive the long hours of dismal drudgery remunerated perhaps mainly by the hope of one day beginning to mount the kitchen's professional ladder.

Beyond the Kitchen proper two Saucers, with their assistants, concocted quantities of the standard sauces and managed as well the reserves of verjuice, of vinegar and of salt. (As a condiment, salt was not really a pharmaceutical product, such as sugar and spices, and so under the control of the court's apothecary; but it was still considered to function as a variety of 'sauce' and is so referred to in medical commentaries.) The Saucers delivered their sauces to the Pantler in the Hall, and salt to the saltboat on the dining table. Under their purview lay all silver vessels for the Duke's service and all vessels of any substance used to serve all other persons dining at his board. So-called Cauldron Varlets – specialized scullions – cleaned whatever was dirtied in the Saucery.

In the Fruitery two Fruiters handled all fresh and dried fruits and nuts. Into their realm also fell responsibility for all of the wax candles and tapers used throughout the court – and by extension all of the more common, cheaper but much smellier, suet candles, and all torches. Olivier de la Marche curiously rationalizes this latter obligation by associating wax with bees, bees with flowers, flowers with fruit trees, and so with fruit. In this work the Fruiters enjoyed the services of two porters and six torch valets.

In the household of Charles of Burgundy two major types of food supply usually came, perhaps surprisingly, from outside the house proper: bread and meat. Bakers delivered bread directly to the Pantry, but pastry to the Kitchen.[13] Butchers delivered cut meat and offal to the Kitchen. Both trades, in supplying their products, were under a term contract, negotiated and issued by the Financial Office, on recommendation of the Kitchen Clerks through the Master of the Household.

Such was the organization, at least as far as the Kitchen was concerned, in one of the few really grand courts of late-medieval Europe. Even in the much humbler neighbouring court of the Dukes of Savoy, a large number of individuals exercised special responsibilities within the overall hierarchy of authority. Under two Masters of the Hall were appointed the Household Steward (in reality a Clerk of the Kitchen), three Pantlers, two Butlers, two Wine Stewards, and two Spicers; within the Kitchen, four cooks (of whom the Duke's Chief Cook was Master Chiquart Amiczo, the author of the *On Cookery*), a Roaster, a Larderer (who handled fresh and preserved pork as well as other stored foodstuffs), a Poulterer, two Ovenmen (perhaps bakers), a Meatman (perhaps a butcher), and no fewer than eleven scullions.

From all of this one conclusion is obvious: the preparing and presenting of food was of enormously great importance in aristocratic houses in the Middle Ages. A significant number of the retainers attached to a noble household, as well as a substantial proportion of the financial resources of that household, were devoted to culinary and gastronomic ends. The grandees of medieval Europe seem firmly to have believed that an investment in the kitchen and the dining hall was eminently worthwhile. In the days before radio and television – influence-at-a-distance – it was important for the prince to impress those guests, whether they were sovereigns themselves or their relatives or ambassadors, whom he received at his court. To the deliberate, conspicuous display of luxury and refinement that the dining hall afforded, the cook was a indispensable contributor.

In the organizational outlines of Olivier de la Marche's *Mémoires*, and in the passing references that Chiquart makes to his superiors and his underlings, we can guess at the professional status of the cook in such a household. Though he was subject to severe restrictions[14], especially financial constraints, on the scope of his activities, within the sphere of those activities he could accord full rein to his professional abilities. He was

---

[13] Clearly the practice is by no means universal: many recipe writers, including Chiquart, instruct their readers to have the pastry cooks 'prepare' pie shells of such-and-such a size. It is barely conceivable in such cases that the pastry kitchen may have received its raw material ready-made.

[14] The Ordinance of 1478, regulating officials and servants in the household of King Edward IV, seems particularly concerned with pilfering or withholding of food in the kitchen: '. . . Yf any suche [food] can be founde by th'aumosner after suche tyme as it is served, . . . that at every defaute the said maister coke [cook] to lose a dayes wages, and he that hath hadde the rule of it under him to lose as moche'. *The Household of Edward IV*, pp.217–18.

245

highly respected for these abilities and undoubtedly took a vast amount of pride in the exercise of his position as 'Chief Cook'. Again Olivier de la Marche helps us appreciate how much this respect was clearly due the medieval cook when he explains, and justifies, how the nomination and appointment of a new cook is carried out:

> . . . I shall raise a question here about the Cook's work: firstly, how is the Cook appointed, who grants the Office, and also who serves as Cook if he should be absent? To these questions I reply that, when a Cook is wanted in a Prince's household, the Masters of the Household should send for the Kitchen Clerks and all the people of the Kitchen one after the other; and by solemn selection, and after having received everyone's statement in the matter, the Cook is named; *for it is not a common estate or office, but is a subtle and costly craft, one which is the essence of trustworthiness; and it is fundamental to the benefit of the Prince, and cannot be dispensed with;*[15] it is quite reasonable that the Prince, on the report of his Masters of the Household, and with a selection made on the basis of this, should award the Cook his position. As for who should serve in his absence – when the Cook is away or sick – the Roaster[16] is the chief person in the Kitchen after the Cook, and it seems reasonable that he should serve ahead of all the others; similarly, the Pottager, who is very familiar with the Prince's taste and with the sauces that the Cook orders for the Prince's appetite; but I reply that neither the one nor the other has any inherent right to the Office of Cook but must be selected as is done for the Cook.

This passage is especially significant because it underscores (as I have done) both the enormous trust that any grandee had of necessity to place in his cook, and the enormous responsibility that the cook bore for the health and well being of his master and the whole of his master's household. The cook proved his master's confidence particularly at the moment when his food was served.

One further concern helped determine formal procedure in serving the medieval prince, and that was security. The possibility of food poisoning was a constant worry that was never far from the consciousness of any potentate of the period, or of those who were responsible for his safety. Quite soberly Platina credits the mythology that had grown around this problem and was illustrated by the remarkably long-lived and seemingly unconquerable enemy

---

[15] My italics. *Car ce n'est pas estat ou office commun, c'est mestier subtil et sumptueux, et qui toute seureté sent, et est le prouffit necessaire du prince, et dont on ne se peut passer* . . . . The whole passage is in Beaune and D'Arbaumont, *op. cit.*, Vol. 4, p.51.

[16] It should be remembered that in 1268 Etienne Boileau, whom we saw above, defined the craft of the Cook as if it bore a close relationship with that of the Goose-Roasters *Oyers* of the city of Paris. In its modern origins the Cook's profession seems to have been thought to owe much to an expertise in preparing a meat, roasting it and dressing it.

of Rome, Mithridates the Great: 'Pompey the Great, after he had conquered Mithridates, found a composition in his writing desk written in his own hand in which he maintained that he was safe and secure against all poisonings for the whole day if he took one walnut, two dried figs (the most potent antidote), twenty leaves of rue and a grain of salt, all ground together and eaten on an empty stomach'.[17] Food poisoning could, of course, be entirely accidental – as, for instance, might result from the occurence of mycobacteria on damp grains, particularly rye – and infect anyone quite inexplicably, and mortally. The pathology of such an infection was totally unknown at this time, of course. Certainly better known were the dangers posed by what were generally called 'poisonous animals'. Such venomous creatures seem to have been ubiquitous; rabies was common enough, and recognized, but the deep forests and lonely corners of Europe abounded with animals whose bites were certain to bring about horrendous suffering and death. The learned Aldobrandino of Siena transmits, for instance, helpful hints about the virtues of onion and garlic in this regard. According to him, onions are much better used in therapy for sickness than as a food for the healthy; furthermore, if ground with rue and salt and used as a plaster, onions are very effective against the bite of a mad dog or of any other venomous beast.[18] Garlic, likewise, counts among its many potent qualities the ability to heal the bite of a venomous animal; so widespread are its virtues as an antidote to the harmful nature of other foodstuffs, he tells us, that it is called the *Triacle de vilains*: the Peasant's Treacle (or universal remedy against poison).[19] Toward the end of the Middle Ages still, in Platina alone the attentive reader could find more than a dozen articles of *food* that are efficacious agents against the bites of poisonous or rabid animals.[20]

What complicated any understanding of the problem of poisons and antidotes immeasurably was the influence of an enormous folklore that originated in antiquity, and undoubtedly long before. This complex body of knowledge concerned the innate powers of all natural things including foodstuffs. One could avail oneself of many specific counteractives that old wives or learned physicians had discovered in a wide variety of animal, vegetable and mineral products. The consequent difficulty that became clear, however, was that, by eating, one was apt also to expose oneself to the potentially dangerous action that any particular foodstuff could exert.

[17] Platina, *De honesta voluptate*; Book I, Chapter 23 On Figs.

[18] *. . . Soit mis sor morsure de chien esragié ou d'autre beste envenimeuse, si vaut moult. Le régime du corps de maître Aldebrandin de Sienne*, ed. Louis Landouzy and Roger Pépin, Paris (Champion), 1911, p.162. A native of Tuscany, Aldobrandino seems to have lived most of his mature life in France; he died at Troyes in 1287. It was as court physician for Saint Louis, Louis IX, that he composed, in the vernacular, his wide-ranging health treatise.

[19] *Ibid.*, p.163.

[20] *De honesta voluptate*, I, 13 (salt); I, 21 (cucumbers); II, 19 (butter); and so forth.

Because an understanding of such potency was vitally important – the health and well-being of virtually every individual depended upon a comprehensive understanding of it – this broad and highly detailed lore was faithfully transmitted and constantly amplified by a series of encyclopedists throughout the Middle Ages. Much of what it said belonged naturally within the purview of the professional cook and had to be clearly grasped by him. 'Isider [Isidore of Seville, c.560–636] seith in this manere: Diptannus is a mount in Creta & therof this herbe, *diptannus* [dittany] hath the name. Therof Virgil speketh & seith that an hynde [hind, female of the red deer] ywounded goth about in the laundes & sekith this herbe *diptannus*. The herbe is of so gret vertu that he dryeth and puteth out yren [iron] out of the body. Therfore bestis ysmyten [smitten] with arwes [arrows] eten therof & dryveth the iren out of the body; for this herbe hath a maner might of werre to dryve out arowes & dartes & quarelles, as Ysider seith'.[21]

Or if food poisoning was not entirely 'natural', it could very possibly be deliberate. Many cases of accidental poisoning must certainly have been suspected of being deliberate, and history books offer accounts of enemies having been apprehended, charged and summarily executed following a gastrointestinal infection presumed to be the consequence of some nefarious plot. Whatever the real threat of innocent or machinated poisoning, every aristocrat invariably had in place some sort of means to test the food that he was given to eat. In the noblest courts, the means to ensure the wholesomeness of the prince's food became multiple and very thoroughgoing.

In actual fact a person intent upon poisoning another person in the Middle Ages had a good variety of poisons at hand to draw upon – what we might well consider an '*embarras de choix*'. There was the very common poison obtained from monkshood or wolfsbane; hemlock, the umbelliferous plant (*not*, of course, the variety of spruce), yielded just as potent a poison as in Socrates' day; black hyoscyamus from herb henbane, could be relied upon by any poisoner, as could thorn apple; and those dear old stand-bys, arsenic, mercury and antimony sulfide could be sprinkled or diluted or spread with dependably efficacious results. It was quite understandable if the sundry resources that were available to the potential poisoner might make the object of his plotting somewhat anxious.

---

[21] *On the Properties of Things. John Trevisa's translation of Bartholomæus Anglicus, De Proprietatibus Rerum*, 2 vols., Oxford (Clarendon Press), 1975; Book 17, Chapter 49. A late-medieval monograph on the marvellous virtues of the herb rosemary further illustrates how extensively the various powers of foodstuffs had been analyzed by this time. Its 22 paragraphs (beginning, *Der win der von roszmarin gemachet wirt der machet den mentschen lustig zu essen* . . .) were published by Volker Zimmermann in 'Der Rosmarin als Heilpflanze und Wunderdroge. Ein Beitrag zu den mittelalterlichen Drogenmonographien', *Sudhoffs Archiv: Zeitschrift für Wissenschaftsgeschichte*, 64 (1980), pp.351–70.

Everything that was intended for the prince's mouth became subject normally to two general sorts of tests, called assays: on the one hand, a test by means of a unicorn horn, and on the other, a test by what vulgarly we might today call guinea-pig experimentation.[22] This second sort of test needs no long explanation: it derived from the principle that one should oneself be willing to stand by the salubrity of what one offers to others while making the claim that it is perfectly harmless. This particular test might also be codified as a variant of the old injunction: 'Do unto thyself as thou wouldst do unto others.' Clearly the test assumed that any poison effective enough to do in the prince – merely harming him could very readily prove in short order to be fatal to the poisoner instead! – would become manifest quickly and plainly enough to spare the prince the danger of ingesting it.

The first variety of assay, that which involved the use of a unicorn horn, was more curious, perhaps because the way it operated was somewhat less obvious than the guinea-pig variety of test. The virtue inherent in the shining unicorn's horn sprang from the fabulous qualities of the beast itself, which came to represent purity. Originally thought of as a remarkably slender hippopotamus, the medieval unicorn was described as particularly fleet, even graceful, but ferocious in combat. It seems to have had the approximate size and appearance of a pure white goat. Its single tusk, up to some four feet in length, possessed magical powers, principally those of detecting poisons and of purifying water. From a very early date the horn and its substance became favoured for the manufacture of safe drinking vessels. The Greek physician and imaginative historian, Ctesias of Cnidus, at the end of the fifth century B.C., wrote, concerning a contemporary practice in India, that 'Those who drink from these horns [of unicorn], made into drinking vessels, are not subject, they say, either to convulsions or to the falling sickness [epilepsy]. Indeed, they are immune even to poisons if, either before or after swallowing such, they drink water, wine, or anything else from these beakers.'[23]

Very few people in fourteenth- and fifteenth-century Europe had actually run into a unicorn around their estate or demesne, or even in their foreign travels; but the rareness of the animal in no way invalidated a firmly held faith in the potency of its horn. In fact, quite the opposite. Many stories testified to the mysterious conduct of this substance in the presence of any poison. On a visit to the Holy Land, a priest from Utrecht, called Johannes of Hese, described how, with his very own eyes, he had seen a unicorn purify

[22] A text describing certain of the assay procedures, practised in 1467 during the installation banquet of George Neville as Archbishop of York and Chancellor of England, is printed in Richard Warner, *Antiquitates Culinariæ, or Curious Tracts Relating to the Culinary Affairs of the Old English*, London (Blamire), 1791, pp.101-5. The highly formalized conduct of serving procedures can also be seen on those pages.

[23] Ctesias of Cnidus, Physician to Persian Kings Artaxerxes II and Darius II, *Treatise on India*.

the polluted waters of a stream by dipping its horn into the stream. Other travellers related how they had witnessed knife handles made of unicorn horn exude a sort of sweat, change colour and tremble violently in the presence of poison. Such was the reputation of unicorn horn as a sure and certain touchstone against poisons that every great medieval household simply had to have a piece of the substance for its own free use.

The fact that this revered piece of ivory might really have come from the tusk of an elephant or of a narwhal whale[24] does not seem overly to have worried those responsible for their masters' well-being. Among the aristocracy this touchstone for poisons seems to have been in such demand that the cost of a whole horn, or even of pieces of one, was quite high. Because of its value it made an appropriate, and thoughtful, gift between members of the upper classes.[25]

Regularly assays of both sorts, by contact with the unicorn horn and by the ingesting of test samples, were conducted extensively at several stages before anything edible was set down in front of the prince. Even before the prince came to table, the Linen-Keeper and Hall Porter had to do an assay for poison on the tablecloths by passing the unicorn horn over them. Both the tapestry which the Hall Usher unrolled onto the prince's bench and the cushion on which he was to sit were similarly tested. The most important element awaiting the prince on his table was the salt. Contained in the precious vessel which, over time and with the skill of silversmiths, conventionally took on the shape of an ornate miniature boat, this salt had itself to be subjected to a test for purity. Conducted into the hall by the Hall Usher, the Pantler directed the Hall Porter, who followed him, where to set the large salt dish; there the Pantler removed the lid from the salt dish and with the lid – in order not to contaminate the salt – picked up a sample which he passed to the Porter to taste. If the results of the test were satisfactory – and one can only assume that this meant that the Hall Porter remained hale and hearty – the Pantler took a knife and with it transferred some of the salt from the large salt vessel into the prince's personal salt boat; the Pantler himself made an assay of this salt in the boat, and set it at the

---

[24] Cut up into much smaller pieces, the nine-foot length of a narwhal tusk afforded enterprising merchants a very lucrative business in peddling pieces of 'unicorn horn'. In this regard it is very interesting to observe that medieval miniaturists often depict a unicorn horn with the spiral that is normal in a narwhal tusk.

[25] Still as late as 1530 Pope Clement arranged to have a unicorn horn, for which he had paid the enormous sum of 17,000 ducats, mounted in an impressive setting of pure gold to present to the French king, Francis I. Benvenuto Cellini, artist, sculptor and worker in precious metals, describes the project he submitted to the pope: My gold mounting, he writes, 'was one unicorn's head of a size corresponding to the horn. I had made the finest thing of it imaginable, for I had modelled it half on a horse and half on a stag, and had added a very fine mane and other kinds of adornments'. *Memoirs*, tr. Anne MacDonnell, London (Dent) and New York (Dutton), 1907, p.92.

prince's place, together with other items also borne in by the Porter: silver platters, to be used by the prince and his Carver, another large silver 'boat' destined to be filled with left-overs for alms, and, most importantly, the vital unicorn horn.

The prince washed his hands in a basin of water that was tested in two ways: the Serving Valet took the unicorn horn in its small boat to the Hall Porter at the prince's buffet,[26] located to one side of the hall; the Porter poured a little of the fresh hand-water over the horn and observed any significant changes in it; then, in the prince's presence, he emptied the water from the boat over his own hands. Only then was the hand-water offered for the prince's use. Similarly, the towel for the prince's wet hands had to be proven safe. The day's history of this 'napkin' began when the Hall Usher conducted the Pantler to the Pantry where the Pantry Porter passed a napkin to his chief, after first having kissed it as an assay or demonstration of its purity; the napkin had to be carried draped (not bundled) openly over the Pantler's shoulder, in contact with the bare flesh of his neck, so that it could be seen manifestly to contain or hide nothing noxious. Later, while awaiting the prince's immediate need of it, the napkin was draped over the small dish containing the unicorn horn; then as the noble fingers dripped pure, harmless water, the Pantler passed the napkin to the First Master of the Household, who in turn passed it to the First Chamberlain, who in turn passed it to any more superior person attendant there upon the prince, who then returned it to the First Master of the Household who, at long last, transmitted it – thus proved absolutely safe – to the waiting hands of the prince. Once used, the towel was given back to the Master of the Household and replaced on the Pantler's shoulder.

In the kitchen the Saucer spread the kitchen buffet with a clean cloth on which the prince's serving dishes were set out, filled and covered; there the Pantler uncovered each of these dishes in turn and he, the Master of the Household along with the Cook, tested samples of what was on them. The cook passed assays to the Master of the Household and to the Pantler; the Master of the Household then passed assays to the Cook. In the same way the products of the Saucery had to be assayed, by means of a bread sop, by the Saucer and the Master of the Household. The Pantler then covered over all of the dishes again, and a procession, consisting of Usher, Master, Pantler, the prince's Pages and Serving Valets (all of them bare-headed), formed up to bear the dishes safely into the hall. The Usher cleared the way to the prince's buffet and the high table; the Master of the Household, from his post at the end of the table near the buffet, vigilantly watched that none of the dishes was tampered with. The Pantler himself assayed each dish once

---

[26] In Italy this side-board became known as a *credenza* because it was there that various 'credence' tests for poisons were performed on food before it was served to the main-board.

again, positioned himself beside the Master, and arranged that twelve or thirteen dishes at a time be set before the prince – in each of two servings at dinner, and in a single serving at supper.

Both the fine table bread and the dark bread that was sliced into personal trenchers had likewise to be assayed. Some of this latter bread was itself reserved in order to assay, by means of dipping, any sauces or liquid foods intended for the prince's consumption. Before the prince's goblets were filled, wine and drinking water were necessarily assayed by the use of a piece of unicorn horn which was literally chained to the prince's pot.

And finally, at end of a banquet when candied spices were served, the First Chamberlain handed the dragée box to the Spicer for an assay, and then passed it to the senior person of the Duke's Household present; this person presented the box to the Prince, and then returned it to the First Chamberlain, who in turn replaced it into the hands of the Spicer – always assuming this last person to have survived the earlier assay of his product!

This complex sequence of tests, or some variant of it, was deemed absolutely necessary to ensure the welfare of any noble in the late Middle Ages. Ultimately the principle was one of accountability: those who prepared and served food for their master must be willing to be accountable for its wholesomeness: they must vouch with their lives for their fidelity in the service of their master.

At the supreme point in this chain of demonstrated responsibility was the cook. The cook in a medieval house had, of course, to be professionally competent – and ideally even more than competent: imaginative – but the *sine qua non* of his position was that he be trustworthy. In a sense the cook who held both his master's glory and his health in his hands was the kingpin in the nobleman's household, and the trust invested in him translated into certain privileges that were accorded to only a few of the master's aristocratic servants: the cook could, for instance, himself bear a dish in to the prince, and make the assay of the dish himself there in the prince's presence; he could then go to drink at the prince's buffet. For the late Middle Ages we have in the cook's privileges a relatively rare case of an individual enjoying recognition and some considerable status because of his native abilities rather than because of his birth.

King Charles V of France, both prince and king, and his son, Charles VI, acknowledged their multiple obligations to their chief cook, Guillaume Tirel, by according him not only a salary and pension sufficient to allow him to purchase and maintain a house in Saint-Germain-en-Laye, but by promoting him eventually to Sergeant-at-Arms and Clerk or Squire of the Royal Kitchen – this latter a position normally reserved for an aristocrat; and, an exceptionally rare privilege for a non-aristocrat, he was granted a coat-of-arms. Interestingly, these armorial bearings, in the shape of a knightly shield, embody a row of three cauldrons set off by six roses. The royal cook's massive tombstone, depicting Taillevent, his two wives and his remarkable coat-of-arms, can still be seen in Saint-Germain-en-Laye, imbedded in the stairwell leading up to the Municipal Library.

The Cook's Craft

> About the Cook. One should have a trained cook with skill and long experience, patient in his work and wanting above all to be praised for it. He should be absolutely clean of any filth or dirt and rightly know the strength and nature of meats, fish and vegetables so that he may understand what ought to be roasted, boiled or fried. He should be alert enough to discern by taste what is too salty or too flat. He should be as much as possible like the man from New Como [Martino, author of the *Libro de arte coquinaria*], the leading cook of our age, from whom I have learned the art of cooking food. He should not be gluttonous or greedy (as was Marisius Gallus) so as not to appropriate and devour food intended for his master.[27]

The craft of an estate cook in the Middle Ages was complex and demanding. He had to know his position in the hierarchy of the household in which he enjoyed his appointment. He had to acknowledge his formal responsibilities to his superiors; he had to organize and accept responsibility for those who worked under his authority. He had to ensure that supplies of foodstuffs, fuel, utensils and labour never failed when they were needed. Given the formal functions of dining in the Middle Ages, he must possess a broad professional repertoire of dishes suitable for various occasions, whether circumstantial, seasonal or as determined by religious requirements, and always be skillful in executing the most appropriate preparations to fulfil those functions. Above all, given the extraordinary trust his employer had vested in him, he had to be certain that he never did anything to impair or endanger the health of his employer, his family or his guests.

The medieval cook was a craftsman – perhaps occasionally even an artist – who both excited and then satisfied the taste of his employer. But he was also at the same time a professional who understood the laws of theoretical physics that must govern all that went on his kitchen. With all of these responsibilities, with this knowledge and skill, he was entirely justified in craving the praise that Platina said was his due. Both Platina and he, the cook, knew his worth.

---

[27] *De coquo. Coquum habeat arte et longa experientia doctum patientem laboris et qui laudari in ea re maxime cupiat. Careat is omni squalore ac spurcitia cognoscat apposite carnium piscium holerum vim atque naturam ut quid assum quid elixum quid frictum fieri debeat deprehendat. Caleat gustu decernere quae salita nimis et quae fatua sunt. Novicomensi nostra aetate coquorum principi et a quo obsoniorum conficiendorum rationem accepi sit omnino si fieri potest persimilis. Non sit gulosis et edax ut Marisius Gallus ne quod dominum edere oportet ipse intercipiat et devoret.* Platina (Bartolomeo Sacchi, 1421–81), *De honesta voluptate et valitudine* (c.1460), Book I, Ch. 11, ed. Mary Ella Milham.

Medieval Cookery

Cookery in late-medieval Europe was in every sense just as much a profession as it remains today. The kitchen of every large household integrated many generations of extensive practical experience in the handling of foods.[28] Within its walls foodstuffs underwent transformations and combinations that were at least as varied as those to which our foodstuffs are subject today, and this work was carried on with a conscious deliberation and competence that likewise was not a whit less than that to which we are accustomed today.

Any limitations that the seasons, the physicians or the Church imposed on this cookery the kitchen had long since learned to compensate for by means of a whole battery of ready alteratives. Similarly any restrictions on the durability of foodstuffs – for instance, the deterioration of sea-fish during lengthy transport, or the rapid souring of animal milk – were routinely solved by effective methods of preservation or, again, alternatives. And there had been developed a good understanding of how to go about preparing dishes in ways that ensured for them an extension of their useful 'table' life.

The kitchens of the time were very familiar with every means of cooking that depended upon fire. With wood, peat or coal, with an open flame or an enclosed flame, with glowing embers, a heated plate or a heated chamber, the cook could boil, steam, coddle, roast, grill, sautee, fry, deep-fry or bake. Often enough the cook used a complex of cooking methods in preparing a single dish. A complete gamut of means of cooking was available in a large kitchen, and fully used.

As well, all of the 'standard' techniques of preparing foodstuffs were entirely familiar to this cookery. Skinning, eviscerating, chopping, slicing, rasping, grinding, sieving and filtering; stirring with a holed spoon, blending with the hand; larding, interlarding, basting, skimming, reducing; techniques for removing excess salt, tricks for removing a smoky flavour, tactics for salvaging a burnt pot of broth; helpful signs to tell when fish are done frying or to discern the relative strength of vinegar, shortcuts for making sauces, strategies to keep eggs from setting too soon in a hot mixture or to avoid a garlic flavour where it is not wanted; advice on jelling jelly; how to put live birds into a cooked pie, to serve a cooked peacock in all the glory of its feathers, or make a roast stag stand as if alive: these processes and procedures, some of them arcane, others wholly commonsensical, are what we find in the medieval cookbooks. The recipes copied in the manuscripts,

---

[28] A good survey of both the kitchen and the hall in late-medieval English manorial life is provided in Mark Girouard, *Life in the English Country House. A Social and Architectural History*, New Haven & London (Yale University Press), 1978.

at considerable cost of effort and materials, reflect both the best and the most remarkable in medieval cookery. In them cooks have not merely bequeathed to posterity the directions necessary for reproducing a wide variety of proven daily fare, but they have also passed on all sorts of additional practical information and suggestions designed to help make a fellow cook's work a little easier and perhaps a little better.

The operative word in the cookery of the medieval recipe collections is practical. This cookery is by no means abstract or idealized. In the manuscripts there are no bright colour photographs of impossibly elegant dishes floating in an empyrean that no practising cook ever even dreamed about. The recipes describe dishes that the cooks made day in and day out, that they had to be able to make regularly with competence and efficiency. Medieval cookery was entirely functional because it satisfied every aspect of a patron's demands.

Medieval Food

Broths and *Buknad*, gruel and *Galentine*, fritters and *Faugrenon*, pies and *Poriola*, omelets and *Orengat*, mortrews and *Mirausto*: the range of dishes to indulge bourgeois and aristocratic palates in the late Middle Ages was remarkably broad. The various recipe collections of the day show literally hundreds of different concoctions which belonged to traditions of greater or less venerability, of greater or less widespread acceptance. The scope and variety of late-medieval gastronomy was at the limits of what was then possible.

The same statement that was made about the cookery of the period has also to be made about its food: these dishes are not just occasional prodigies, paragons of perfection to be elaborated with exceptional effort for some extraordinary purpose. Rather, if we can distinguish the few obvious show-pieces, overwhelmingly the remainder are clearly 'ordinary' preparations in the sense that they were in more or less constant demand on the tables of the patrons, masters and princes. All of their recipes are copied into manuscript collections simply because each of the dishes they describe *had* to be in the standard working repertoire of the professional cook.

A careful review of a range of questions concerning food in late-medieval England, has led one modern historian to an unqualified, clear position: '. . . We must conclude that the prevalent miseries of the period before 1350 gave way to a "dietary optimum" in the fifteenth century.'[29] And the French

---

[29] Christopher Dyer, 'English Diet in the Later Middle Ages', in T.H. Aston, P.R. Cross, Christopher Dyer and Joan Thirsk, *Social Relations and Ideas*, Cambridge (Cambridge University Press), 1983, pp.191–216.

social and economic historian Fernand Braudel proposes a similar conclusion.

> Following the catastrophes of the Black Death [of the mid-fourteenth century], living conditions for workers were inevitably good as manpower had become scarce. *Real* salaries have never been as high as they were then . . . . The paradox must be emphasized since it is often thought that hardship increases the farther back towards the middle ages one goes. In fact the opposite is true of the standard of living of the common people – the majority.[30]

If the standard of living of the common people was indeed relatively high at the end of the Middle Ages, then that of the un-common bourgeoisie and aristocracy, those who could afford the services of professional cooks in their own kitchens, must be thought of as close to relative luxury.

The surviving documents having to do with food and cookery afford firm evidence that these upper classes did in fact eat very well.

---

[30] Fernand Braudel, *Civilization and Capitalism 15th–18th Century*, 3 vols., London (Collins), 1981; I, 192. See the whole of this book's third chapter, 'Superfluity and Sufficiency: Food and Drink'.

BIBLIOGRAPHY

Late-Medieval Culinary Recipe Collections

In the text above, the manner of reference to the recipes in the following recipe collections depends upon the current 'best' source of the collection. Usually a modern editor will number the recipes sequentially in his edition, and this recipe number provides the clearest means of identification. In a few publications, however, where the recipes have not been numbered, we must refer to the page number on which any particular recipe is printed. Furthermore, some recipe collections remain as yet unpublished – and so, unfortunately, are still unavailable to the general public; for recipes found in them we can refer only to the folio (or page) number of the manuscript listed below.

Anglo-Norman: Constance B. Hieatt and Robin F. Jones, 'Two Anglo-Norman Culinary Collections Edited from British Library Manuscripts Additional 32085 and Royal 12.C.xii', *Speculum*, 61 (1986), pp.859–882. Collection 'A' is at pp. 862–66 and 'B' is at pp.866–68; an English translation of the two collections is provided in the same article, pp.873–879.

Anonimo meridionale: Ingemar Boström, *Anonimo meridionale, Due libri di cucina*, Stockholm (Almqvist & Wiksell), 1985; 'Libro A' is found at pp.1–31 and 'Libro B' at pp.32–48.

Apicius: M. Gavius Apicius, *De re coquinaria: Decem libri cui dicuntur de re coquinaria et excerpta a Vinidario conscripta edidit Mary Ella Milham*, Leipzig (Teubner), 1969; *De re coquinaria (De la cuisine)*, ed. Jacques André, Paris (Les Belles Lettres), 1965, repr. 1974. This last edition contains a modern French translation; modern English translations of Apicius are available by Joseph Dommers Vehling, *Cookery and Dining in Imperial Rome*, Chicago (Hill), 1936, republ. New York (Dover), 1977; Barbara Flower and Elisabeth Rosenbaum, *The Roman Cookery Book*, London (Harrap), 1958 and London (Peter Nevill), 1958; and John Edwards, *The Roman Cookery of Apicius*, Vancouver (Hartley & Marks), 1984.

Austin: Thomas Austin, *Two Fifteenth-Century Cookery-Books* (Early English Text Society, O.S. 91), London (Oxford University Press), 1888; repr. 1964.

Bockenheim: Bruno Laurioux, 'Le "Registre de cuisine" de Jean de Bockenheim, cuisinier du pape Martin V', *Mélanges de l'Ecole française de Rome*, 100 (1988), pp.709–60.

Bressanone: an unpublished German collection of the fifteenth century in the Biblioteca del Seminario Maggiore, MS 125, Bressanone (Brixen), Italy.

Buch: Hans Hajek, *Daz Buoch von guoter Spize*, Berlin (Erich Schmidt), 1958.

Büchlein: Anton Birlinger, 'Ein alemannisches Büchlein von guter Speise', *Sitzungsberichte der königl. bayer. Akademie der Wissenschaften zu München*, II (1865), pp.171–199.

Châlons: an untitled, unpublished Latin recipe collection of the fifteenth century evidently written by a doctor of Assisi and now held by the Municipal Library of the city of Châlons-sur-Marne, France, MS 319.

Coch: Mestre Robert, *Libre del Coch. Tractat de cuina medieval*, ed. Veronika Leimgruber, Barcelona (Curial Ediciones Catalanes), 1982.

Cocina: Anonimo Toscano, *Libro de la cocina*, ed. Emilio Faccioli, in *Arte della cucina. Libri di ricette, testi sopra lo scalco, il trinciante e i vini*, 2 vols., Milano (Il Polifilo), 1966; I, pp.19–57.

Coquina: *Liber de coquina*, ed. Marianne Mulon in 'Deux traités inédits d'art culinaire médiéval', *Bulletin Philologique et Historique*, Year 1968, 2 vols., Paris (Comité des Travaux Historiques et Scientifiques), 1971; I, pp.396–420.

Cuoco: Anonimo Veneziano, *Libro per cuoco*, ed. Emilio Faccioli, in *Arte della cucina. Libri di ricette, testi sopra lo scalco, il trinciante e i vini*, 2 vols., Milano (Il Polifilo), 1966; I, pp.61–105.

Cure cocorum: Richard Morris, *Liber cure cocorum*, Berlin (A. Asher, for the Philological Society), 1862.

Curye: Constance B. Hieatt and Sharon Butler, *Curye on Inglysch* (Early English Text Society, SS.8), London, New York, Toronto (Oxford University Press), 1985. (Contains: I, *Diversa cibaria*, pp.43–58; II, *Diversa servicia*, pp.59–79; III, *Utilis coquinario*, pp.81–91; IV, *The Forme of Cury*, pp.93–145; V, *Goud Kokery*, pp.147–156.)

Dilicate vivande: an unpublished fifteenth-century Italian recipe collection in the British Library, Addl. 18165, folios 1r–21v, whose title is *Trattato de buone e dilicate vivande*.

Doctrine: Carole Lambert, *Trois réceptaires culinaires médiévaux: Les Enseingnementz, les Doctrine et le Modus. Edition critique et glossaire détaillé*, unpublished Ph.D. thesis, Université de Montréal, 1989; pp.112–133.

Eberhard: Anita Feyl, *Das Kochbuch Meister Eberhards. Ein Beitrag zur altdeutschen Fachliteratur*, Ph.D. thesis Albert-Ludwigs-Universität, Freiburg im Breisgau, 1963; also published in 'Das Kochbuch des Eberhard von Landshut (erste Hälfte des 15. Jhs.)', *Ostbairischen Grenzmarken*, 5 (1961), pp.352–66.

Enseignements: Grégoire Lozinski in *La bataille de Caresme et de Charnage* (Bibliothèque de l'Ecole des Hautes Etudes, fasc. 262), Paris (Champion), 1933; Appendix I, pp.181–190: *Enseingnementz qui enseingnent a apareiller toutes manieres de viandes*. Edited also by Carole Lambert in *Trois réceptaires culinaires médiévaux: Les Enseingnementz, les Doctrine et le Modus. Edition critique et glossaire détaillé*, unpublished Ph.D. thesis, Université de Montréal, 1989; pp.87–111.

Frammento: Olindo Guerrini, *Frammento di un libro di cucina del secolo XIV edito nel di delle nozze Carducci-Gnaccarini*, Bologna (Nicola Zanichelli), 1887.

Icelandic: Henning Larsen, *An Old Icelandic Medical Miscellany.* Ms. *Royal Irish Academy 23 D 43 with supplement from Ms. Trinity College (Dublin) L-2-27,* Oslo (I Kommisjon hos J. Dybwad), 1931; the culinary recipes are at pp.131–5, with an English translation at pp.214–18.

Keukenboek: Constant Antoine Serrure, *Keukenboek uitgegeven naar een Hs. der vijftiende eeuw* (Maatschappij der Vlaamsche Bibliophilen, Werken nr. X), Gand (Annoot-Braeckman), 1872.

Mandelziger: an untitled German collection published by Anton Birlinger in 'Bruchstücke aus einem alemannisches Büchlein von guter Speise. 15. Jhd.', in *Sitzungsberichte der königl. bayer. Akademie deer Wissenschaften zu München,* 2 (1865), pp.199ff.

Martino: Mestre Martino, *Libre de arte coquinaria,* ed. Emilio Faccioli, in *Arte della cucina. Libri di ricette, testi sopra lo scalco, il trinciante e i vini,* 2 vols., Milano (Il Polifilo), 1966; I, pp.117–204.

Menagier: Georgine E. Brereton and Janet M. Ferrier, *Le Menagier de Paris,* Oxford (Clarendon), 1981; the recipe numbers refer to the sequence of paragraph numbers beginning on p.191.

Mestre Robert: Mestre Robert, *Libre del coch. Tractat de cuina medieval,* ed. Veronika Leimgruber, Barcelona (Curial), 1982.

Mittelniederdeutsches: Hans Wiswe, 'Ein mittelniederdeutsches Kochbuch des 15. Jahrhunderts', *Braunschweigisches Jahrbuch,* 37 (1956), 19–55.

Modus: Carole Lambert, *Trois réceptaires culinaires médiévaux:* Les Enseingnementz, *les Doctrine et le Modus. Edition critique et glossaire détaillé,* unpublished Ph.D. thesis, Université de Montréal, 1989; pp.134–157. the full title of this collection is the *Modus viaticorum preparandorum et salsarum;* Lambert's edition is followed by a modern French translation, pp.158–180.

Neapolitan Collection: an untitled, unpublished Italian recipe collection of the fifteenth century now held by the Pierpont Morgan Library of New York, MS Bühler 36.

Nice: Giovanni Rebora, 'La cucina medievale italiana tra oriente ed occidente', *Miscellanea storica ligure,* 19 (1987), pp. 1431–1579.

Noble Boke: Robina Napier, *A Noble Boke off Cookry ffor a Prynce Houssolde or eny other Estately Houssolde,* London (Elliot Stock), 1882.

On Cookery: Chiquart's 'On Cookery'. A Fifteenth-Century Savoyard Culinary Treatise, ed. and trans. Terence Scully, New York, Berne, Frankfurt am Main (Peter Lang), 1986. The original of this English text is found in Terence Scully, 'Du fait de cuisine par Maistre Chiquart 1420', *Vallesia,* 40 (1985), pp.101–231.

Ordinance: Constance B. Hieatt, *An Ordinance of Pottage. An edition of the fifteenth century culinary recipes in Yale University's MS Beinecke 163,* London (Prospect Books), 1988.

Platina: Bartolomeo Sacchi, *De honesta voluptate et valetudine:* see below.

Portuguese Cookbook: Elizabeth Thompson Newman, *A Critical Edition of an Early Portuguese Cookbook,* Ph.D. thesis, University of North Carolina at

Chapel Hill, 1964; published by University Microfilms, Ann Arbor, Michigan.

Recueil de Riom: Carole Lambert, *Le recueil de Riom et la Manière de henter soutillement. Un livre de cuisine et un réceptaire sur les greffes du XVe siècle* (Le Moyen Français, 20), Montréal (CERES), 1987.

Salssen: an untitled recipe collection whose incipit is *Ein gut salssen. Wiltu machen ein gut salssen von weichselen . . .*, edited by Alix Prentki in *Les traités culinaires du sud de l'Allemagne à la fin du Moyen-Age*, Mémoire de D.E.A., école des Hautes études en Sciences Sociales de Paris, 1985.

Sent soví: Rudolf Grewe, *Libre de Sent soví (Receptari de cuina)*, Barcelona (Barcino), 1979.

Stere Hit Well: *Stere Hit Well. A book of medieval refinements, recipes and remedies from a manuscript in Samuel Pepys's library*, ed. A.J. Hodgett, Cambridge (Cornmarket Reprints), 1972.

Tractatus: *Tractatus de modo preparandi et condiendi omnia cibaria*, ed. Marianne Mulon in 'Deux traités inédits d'art culinaire médiéval', *Bulletin Philologique et Historique*, Year 1968, 2 vols., Paris (Comité des Travaux Historiques et Scientifiques), 1971; I, pp.380–95.

Viandier: Terence Scully, *The Viandier of Taillevent. An Edition of all Extant Manuscripts*, Ottawa (University of Ottawa Press), 1988.

Wellcome Manuscript: an untitled, unpublished Italian recipe collection of the fifteenth century now held by the Library of the Wellcome Institute for the History of Medicine, London, MS WMS.211.

Late-Medieval Medical and Scientific Works Referring to Food Properties

Because the nature of food was a serious concern of physicians during the late Middle Ages, a large number of medical compendia and treatises with encyopledic pretensions deal, either incidentally or systematically, with the properties of various foodstuffs. To a considerable degree these works tend to be interrelated, to derive more or less from one another and from a relatively small number of universally recognized 'authorities' such as Galen and Rassis. The following list is merely a sample of the sort of book that the late-medieval physician, and through him the cook, could consult for information about foodstuffs.

Albini, Jacomo, *Il 'De sanitatis custodia' di maestro Giacomo Albini di Moncalieri con altri documenti sulla storia della medicina negli stati sabaudi nei secoli XIV e XV* (Biblioteca della Società Storica Subalpina, 25), ed. Giovanni Carbonelli, Pinerolo (Tipografia Sociale), 1906.

Aldobrandino da Siena, *Le régime du corps de maître Aldebrandin de Sienne*, ed. Louis Landouzy and Roger Pépin, Paris (Champion), 1911.

Alphita, ed. by Salvatore de Renzi in *Collection Salernitana, ossia Documenti inediti e trattati di medicina appartenenti alla scuola medica Salernitana*, Vol. 3, Naples (Filiatre-Sebezio), 1854, pp.271–322.

Antimus, *De Observatio Ciborum*, ed. Shirley Howard Weber, Leiden (E.J. Brill), 1924; the full title of this composition is *Epistula Antimi viri inlustris comitis et legatarii ad gloriosissimum Theudoricum regem francorum de observatione ciborum*.

Arnaldus de Villanova, *Liber de vinis*: H.E. Sigerist, *The Earliest Printed Book on Wine (1478)*, New York (Schuman's), 1943.

Arnold von Bamberg, *Tractatus de regimine sanitatis*, ed. by Karin Figala in *Mainfränkische Zeitgenossen Ortolfs von Baierland: ein Beitrag zum frühesten Gesundheitswesen in den Bistümern Würzburg und Bamberg*, Pharmaceutical Dissertation, Munich, 1969, pp.160–90.

Avicenna, *Canon of Medicine*: the twelfth-century Latin translation of Gerard de Cremona is available in *Liber canonis Avicenne revisus et ab omni errore mendaque purgatus summaque cum diligentia impressus*, Venice, 1507, repr. Hildesheim (Georg Olms), 1964.

Bartholomaeus Anglicus, *De proprietatibus rerum* English translation, *On the Properties of Things. John Trevisa's translation of Bartholomæus Anglicus, De Proprietatibus Rerum*, 2 vols., Oxford (Clarendon Press), 1975. This work is accessible also in the reprint by Jürgen Schäfer of the edition *Batman vppon Bartholome His Booke De Proprietatibus Rerum 1582* (Anglistica & Americana, 161), Hildesheim and New York (Georg Olms), 1976.

Bibbesworth: *Treatise of Walter of Bibbesworth*, ed. Richard Wright in *A Volume of Vocabularies*, 2 vols., Vol. I, [privately printed], 1857, Vol. II, [privately printed], 1873; repr. 1882; the original text can be read in *La treytez ke moun sire Gauter de Bibelsworth fist*, ed. Annie Owen, Dissertation, Université de Paris, 1929.

Boorde, Andrewe, *A Compendyous Regyment or A Dyetary of Helth made in Mountpyllier, compyled by Andrewe Boorde of Physycke Doctour*, ed. F.J. Furnivall, London (Kegan Paul, Trench, Trübner), 1870.

Cato, Marcus Porcius, *De agricultura*, ed. and trans. by William Davis Hoopter, *Marcus Porcius Cato, On Agriculture, Marcus Terentius Varro, On Agriculture*, London and Cambridge, Mass., (Heinemann and Harvard University Press), 1967.

Celsus, Aulus Aurelius Cornelius, *De arte medica*, ed Charles Daremberg, Leipzig (Teubner), 1859; modern French trans. by A. Védrènes, *Traité de médecine de A.C. Celse*, Paris (Masson), 1876.

Columella, Lucius Junius Moderatus, *De re rustica*, ed. and trans. by E. S. Forster and Edward H. Heffner as *On Agriculture and Trees*, 3 vols., London (Heinemann) and Cambridge, Mass., (Harvard), 1955.

Crescentius, Petrus (Pietro de' Crescenzi), *Commodorum ruralium*, Augsburg (Johannes Schussler), 1471; Louvain, c.1474; Mayence, 1493. In Italian: *Trattato dell'agricoltura, traslato nella favella fiorentina rivisto dallo'Nferigno accademico [Bastiano de Rossi] della Crusca*, 2nd edn., Milan (Società tipografinca de' classici italiani), 1805; rev'd edn., Verona (Tipografica Vicentini e Franchini), 1851–52.

Galen: Claudius Galenus, *Opera Omnia*, ed. by Karl Gottlob Kühn, 20 vols., Leipzig (Car. Cnoblochii), 1821–33 (see especially *De alimentorum facultatibus* in Vol. 6, pp.453ff.); *De sanitate tuenda*, trans. by Robert M. Green as *Galen's Hygiene*, Springfield, Ill., (Charles Thomas), 1951.

John of Garland *Dictionarius*, in Richard Wright *A Volume of Vocabularies*; Vol. I, Pt. VIII, pp.120ff.

Governal, *In this Tretyse that is Cleped Governayle of Helthe (1489)* (The English Experience, 192), facsimile repr. of edition of 1489, Amsterdam and New York (Da Capo), 1969.

Grant Kalendrier et Compost des Bergiers, Paris (Siloe), 1981.

Hake von Westerholt, Johannes (fl.1314–1361), *Recepte ad preservandum ab epydemia* and *Recepte contra epidemeam*, ed. by Karl Sudhoff, *Archiv für Geschichte der Medizin*, 5 (1912), pp.36–39.

Haly Abbas (Ali Ibn al-'Abbas), *Liber Pantegni*: Latin trans. by Constantine, publ. as *Costantino l'Africano, L'arte universale della medicina (Pantegni), Parte I, Libro I*, with modern Italian translation by Marco T. Malato and Umberto de Martini, Rome (Instituto di Storia della Medicina dell'Università di Roma), 1961.

Hippocrates, [*Works*] (Loeb Classical Library, 147–150), 4 vols., ed. and trans. by W.H.S. Jones, London (Heinemann) and New York (Putnam), 1923–27 (see especially Vol. 4, the *Regimen*, Books 2 and 3); [*Works*], ed. by Emerson C. Kelly and trans. by Francis Adams (1849) as *The Theory and Practice of Medicine*, New York (Citadel), 1964.

Isidore of Seville (Isidorus Hispalensis, St), *Etymologicon*: *Isidori Hispalensis episcopi Etymologiarum sive originum libri XX. Recognovit brevique adnotatione critica instruxit Wallace Martin Lindsay* (Scriptorum Classicorum Bibliotheca Oxoniensis), 2 vols., Oxford (Clarendon), 1962.

Livre des mestiers de Bruges et ses dérivés: Quatre anciens manuels de conversation, edited by Jean Gessler, 6 vols., Bruges (Gruuthuse, Sainte-Catherine, Desclée-DeBrouwer), 1931.

Magninus Mediolanensis (Maino de' Maineri), *Regimen sanitatis Magnini Mediolanensis medici famosissimi Attrebatensi Episcopo directum*, Louvain (Johannes de Westfalia), 1482.

Magninus Mediolanensis (Maino de' Maineri), *Opusculum de saporibus*, ed. by Lynn Thorndike in 'A Mediæval Sauce-Book', *Speculum*, 9 (1934), pp.183–190.

Musandinus: *Summula Musandini*, edited by Salvatore de Renzi in *Collection Salernitana*, Vol. 5, Naples (Filiatre-Sebezio), 1854, pp.254–368.

Pegolotti, Francesco Balducci, *La Pratica della mercatura*, ed. Allen Evans, Cambridge, Mass., (Mediaeval Academy of America), 1936; properly titled, *Libro di divisamenti di paesi e di misuri di mercatanzie e d'altre cose bisognevoli di sapere a' mercatanti*.

Palladius, *Opus agriculturæ*, edited and translated by E.S. Forster and Edward H. Hefner in *On Agriculture and Trees*, 3 vols., London (Heinemann) and Cambridge, Mass., (Harvard), 1955.

Platina: Bartolomeo Sacchi di Cremona, known as Platina, *De honesta voluptate et valetudine ad amplissimum ac doctissimum D.B. Roverellam S. Clementis Presbiterum Cardinalem*, n.p., n.d. [c.1474]; Rome (Uldericus Gallus), 1475; Venice (Petro Mocenico), 1475; etc. English translation by Elizabeth B. Andrews, *On Honest Indulgence and Good Health*, St Louis (Mallinckrodt

Chemical Works), 1967. Critical edition and English translation in preparation by Mary Ella Milham, Renaissance Society of America.

Pliny the Elder (Gaius Plinius Secundus), *Historia naturalis / Natural History* (Loeb Clasical Library), 11 vols., ed. E.H. Warmington, Cambridge, Mass., (Harvard University Press); also *Natural History* (Penguin Classics), trans. John F. Healy, Harmondsworth (Viking Penguin), 1991.

Provenzalische Diätetik. Auf Grund neuen Materials, ed. Hermann Suchier, Halle a.S. (Max Niemeyer), 1894.

Le régime tresutile et tresproufitable pour conserver et garder la santé du corps humain, ed. Patricia W. Cummins, Chapel Hill (University of North Carolina), 1976.

Regimen of Health of the Medical School of Salerno, trans. by Pascal Partente, New York (Vantage), 1967.

Regimen sanitatis salernitanum: Flos Medicinæ Scholæ Salerni, in Salvatore de Renzi, ed. *Collectio Salernitana*, 5 vols., Naples (Filiatre-Sebezo), 1852-59; Vol. I, pp.417-516.

Russell, John, *Boke of Nurture*, ed. Frederick J. Furnivall in *Early English Meals and Manners* (Early English Text Society, O.S. 32), London (Oxford University Press), 1868; pp.1-112.

Tacuina sanitatis: Luisa Cogliati Arano, *Tacuinum sanitatis*, Milan (Electa), 1975 (in English translation as *The Medieval Health Handbook Tacuinum Sanitatis*, New York (Braziller), 1976); Judith Spencer, *The Four Seasons of the House of Cerruti*, New York/Bicester, England (Facts On File), 1984.

Modern Adaptations of Medieval Recipes

The following are a sampling of recently published books in which recipes from medieval collections are presented in a conventional modern format in order to facilitate their use in a modern kitchen. Experience alone will convince the user whether any particular published interpretation is apt to be faithful to the intentions of the original author; it some cases the reader may be able as well to check an edition of the original manuscript version.

The arrangement of these books is alphabetical by author.

Black, Maggie, *The Medieval Cookbook*, New York (Thames and Hudson), 1992.

Bourin, Jeanne, *Les recettes de Mathilde Brunel. Cuisine médiévale pour table d'aujourd'hui*, Paris (Falmmarion), 1983.

Buxton, Moira, *Medieval Cooking Today*, Waddesdon, Buckinghamshire, (Kylin), 1983.

Cosman, Madeleine Pelner, *Fabulous Feasts. Medieval Cookery and Ceremony*, New York (George Braziller), 1976.

Ehlert, Trude, *Das Kochbuch des Mittelalters. Rezepte aus alter Zeit, eingeleitet, erläutert und ausprobiert*, Zürich & München, 1990.

Hieatt, Constance B., *An Ordinance of Pottage*, London (Prospect Books), 1988; the recipes of this fifteenth-century collection are adapted for modern use at pp.113-218.

Hieatt, Constance B. and Sharon Butler, *Pleyn Delit. Medieval Cookery for Modern Cooks*, Toronto (University of Toronto Press), 1976.

Redon, Odile, Françoise Sabban and Silvano Serventi, *La Gastronomie au Moyen Age. 150 recettes de France et d'Italie*, Paris (Stock/Moyen Age), 1991.

Sass, Lorna J., *To the King's Taste. Richard II's book of feasts and recipes adapted for modern cooking*, New York (Metropolitan Museum of Art), 1975.

Scully, D. Eleanor and Terence Scully, *Early French Cookery. Sources, History, Original Recipes and Modern Adaptations*, Ann Arbor (University of Michigan Press), 1995.

Willan, Anne, *Great Cooks and Their Recipes From Taillevent to Escoffier*, London (Pavilion), 1992.

INDEX

In the following Index, a place-name implies any associated adjectives or nouns: for instance, the entry for 'Flanders' includes references to 'Flemish.'

Lightning Source UK Ltd.
Milton Keynes UK
25 September 2009

144191UK00001B/9/P